The Copyright Law of Spatial Data

This book provides a thorough comparative analysis of copyright protection of spatial data across Australia, the United States of America (USA), and the European Union (EU).

With the emergence of terrestrial scanners, drones, robotics, and artificial intelligence (AI), the acquisition of data has recently reshaped the landscape of the survey industry, highlighting the importance of protecting the intellectual rights of surveyors. This book investigates the distinct approaches taken by each jurisdiction in protecting copyrights in spatial data and explores commonalities and disparities between these jurisdictions, highlighting best practices. The book also explores the alternative means of protecting spatial data and provides final recommendations aimed at policymakers, with the overarching objective of nurturing a balanced copyright system.

This book will be of interest to students and scholars in the fields of copyright law and spatial data.

Kanchana Kariyawasam is an associate professor at Griffith Business School, Griffith University, Australia. She holds a PhD in intellectual property (IP) law (Griffith University), a Master of Laws in IP law (Advanced) (University of Queensland) and a Bachelor of Laws (Hons) (University of Colombo). She specialises in the field of IP law and has widely published in the IP field.

Rangika Palliyaarachchi is a lecturer at the School of Law, Western Sydney University. She completed her Bachelor of Laws (Hons) at the University of Colombo and holds a PhD in law from Monash University. Over the past four years, her research interests have focused mainly on understanding the construction of content and meaning of laws in the area of commercial law, focusing more particularly on corporate law, consumer protection law, and IP law.

Glenn Campbell is an associate professor in surveying and land information at the University of Southern Queensland. He obtained a Bachelor of Science majoring in physics from the University of Queensland in 1988 and a Bachelor of Applied Science (surveying) in 1993. He has been registered as a cadastral surveyor since 1998 and a member of the Surveyors Board of Queensland since 2005. After 15 years in private practice, he commenced work as an academic and he completed his PhD in the remote sensing of water quality at the University of Queensland in 2011.

The Copyright Law of Spatial Data

Kanchana Kariyawasam, Rangika Palliyaarachchi and Glenn Campbell

Routledge
Taylor & Francis Group
LONDON AND NEW YORK

First published 2025
by Routledge
4 Park Square, Milton Park, Abingdon, Oxon OX14 4RN

and by Routledge
605 Third Avenue, New York, NY 10158

Routledge is an imprint of the Taylor & Francis Group, an informa business

British Library Cataloguing-in-Publication Data
A catalogue record for this book is available from the British Library

Library of Congress Cataloging-in-Publication Data
Names: Kariyawasam, Kanchana, author. | Palliyaarachchi, Rangika, author. | Campbell, Glenn (writer of Copyright law of spatial data), author.
Title: The copyright law of spatial data / Kanchana Kariyawasam, Rangika Palliyaarachchi, Glenn Campbell.
Description: Abingdon, Oxon [UK] ; New York, NY : Routledge, 2024. | Includes bibliographical references and index.
Identifiers: LCCN 2024012864 (print) | LCCN 2024012865 (ebook) | ISBN 9781032731773 (hardback) | ISBN 9781032766478 (paperback) | ISBN 9781003479383 (ebook)
Subjects: LCSH: Copyright—Databases—Australia. | Copyright—Databases—United States. | Copyright—Databases—European Union countries. | Geographic information systems—Law and legislation—Australia. | Geographic information systems—Law and legislation—United States. | Geographic information systems—Law and legislation—European Union countries. | Spatial data infrastructures—Australia. | Spatial data infrastructure—United States. | Spatial data infrastructures—European Union countries.
Classification: LCC K1443.D37 K37 2024 (print) | LCC K1443.D37 (ebook) | DDC 346.04/82—dc23/eng/20240325
LC record available at https://lccn.loc.gov/2024012864
LC ebook record available at https://lccn.loc.gov/2024012865

ISBN: 978-1-032-73177-3 (hbk)
ISBN: 978-1-032-76647-8 (pbk)
ISBN: 978-1-003-47938-3 (ebk)

DOI: 10.4324/9781003479383

Typeset in Times New Roman
by Apex CoVantage, LLC

Contents

Acknowledgements

We express our sincere gratitude to The Surveyors Trust Australia for their invaluable support in making this study possible. We also want to thank Bikalpa Rajbhandari, Anubhav Tiwari, and Armin Agha for their research assistance.

Abbreviations

ABS	Australian Bureau of Statistics
ADEPT	Administrative Data Exchange Protocol for Tasmania
AI	Artificial intelligence
ALI	American Law Institute
API	Application programming interface
CAD	Computer-aided design
CAL	*Copyright Agency Ltd v State of New South Wales*
CDR	Consumer Data Right
CJEU	Court of Justice of the European Union
CMI	Copyright Management Information
CMO	Copyright Management Organisation
DAA	Digital Agenda Act
DAC	Data Analytics Centre
DCDB	Digital Cadastral Database
DD	Database Directive
DDF	Danske Dagblades Forening
DMCA	Digital Millennium Copyright Act
DRM	Digital rights management
EO	Earth Observation
ERMI	Electronic Rights Management Information
EU	European Union
FGDC	Federal Geographic Data Committee
GDA	Geospatial Data Act
GDPR	General Data Protection Regulation
GIS	Geographic information systems
HTML	Hypertext markup language
IITF	Information Infrastructure Task Force
InfoSoc Directive	Information Society Directive
INSPIRE	Infrastructure for Spatial Information in the European Community
IP	Intellectual property
MSDS	Material Safety Data Sheets
NGDAs	National Geospatial Data Assets

NII	National Information Infrastructure
NMCAs	National Mapping and Cadastral Agencies
NSW	New South Wales
OECD	Organisation for Economic Co-operation and Development
PSMA	Public Sector Mapping Agency
QLD	Queensland
RAM	Random access memory
SDIs	Spatial data infrastructures
TDM	Text and data mining
TFEU	Treaty on the Functioning of the European Union
TPMs	Technological protection measures
TRIPS	Agreement on Trade-Related Aspects of Intellectual Property Rights
TSD	Trade Secrets Directive
UAVs	Uncrewed aerial vehicles
UK	United Kingdom
USA	United States of America
VIC	Victoria
WIPO	World Intellectual Property Organization
VPLs	Visual Programming Languages

Table of cases

Australia

Acohs Pty Ltd v Ucorp Pty Ltd
Australian Medic-Care Company Ltd v Hamilton Pharmaceutical Pty Limited
Autodesk Inc v Dyason
Coco v A N Clark (Engineers) Ltd
Campaigntrack Pty Ltd v Real Estate Tool Box Pty Ltd
Copyright Agency Ltd. v State of New South Wales
Data Access Corporation v Powerflex Services Pty Ltd
Desktop Marketing Systems Pty Ltd v Telstra Corporation Ltd (*Desktop case*)
EIFY Systems Pty Ltd v 3D Safety Services Pty Ltd
Freistaat Bayern v. Verlag Esterbauer GmbH
Ian Cubitts Classic Home Improvements Pty Ltd v. Granny Flat Projects
IceTV Pty Limited v Nine Network Australia Pty Limited
JR Consulting & Drafting Pty Limited v Cummings
Kabushiki Kaisha Sony Computer Entertainment v Stevens (*Sony v Stevens*)
Pokemon Company International, Inc. v. Redbubble Ltd
Saltman Engineering Co Ltd v Campbell Engineering Co Ltd
Sands & McDougall Pty Ltd v Robinson
Seafolly Pty Limited v. Fewstone Pty Ltd
StatusCard Australia Pty Ltd v Rotondo & Anor
Surveys & Mining Ltd v Morrison
Telstra Corporation Limited v Phone Directories Company
Thales Australia Limited v Madritsch KG & Anor
Weller & Anor v. Smith

USA

Advanced Computer Services of Michigan, Inc. v. MAI Systems
Alfred Bell & Co. v. Catalda Fine Arts, Inc.
Amsterdam v. Triangle Publication, Inc.
Andrews v. Guenther

Barclays Capital, Inc. v. Theflyonthewall.com, Inc.
Bleistein v. Donaldson Lithographing Co.
Burrow-Giles Lithographic Co. v. Sarony
Campbell v. Acuff-Rose Music, Inc.
Cartoon Network LP v. CSC Holdings, Inc.
CCC Information Services, Inc. v. Maclean Hunter Market Reports, Inc.
Chamberlain Group, Inc. v. Skylink Technologies, Inc.
CoStar Group, Inc. v. LoopNet, Inc (CoStar)
C.S. Hammond & Co. v. International College Globe, Inc.
Feist Publications, Inc. v Rural Telephone Service Co. (*Feist*)
Firoozye v. Earthlink Network
Georgia et al v. Public.Resource.Org
Google LLC v. Oracle Am., Inc
Healthcare Advocates, Inc. v. Harding, Earley, Follmer & Frailey
International News Service Inc v Associated Press
Jeweler's Circular Pub. Co. v. Keystone Pub. Co
Key Maps, Inc. v. Pruitt
Key Maps, Inc. v. Pruitt
Matthew Bender & Co. v. West Pub. Co.
Mason v. Montgomery Data, Inc. (Mason)
MAI Systems Corp. v. Peak Computer, Inc.
Perris v. Hexamer
Photographic Illustrator's Corp. v Orgill, Inc.
ProCD, Incorporated v. Matthew Zeidenberg and
Silken Mountain Web Services, Inc.
RealNetworks, Inc. v. Streambox, Inc.
Ticketmaster v. Tickets.com, Inc.
United States v. Hamilton

EU

Apis-Hristovich EOOD v Lakorda AD
British Horseracing Board, The v William Hill Organization
Cofemel – Sociedade de Vestuário SA v G-Star Raw CV
Eva-Maria Painer v Standard Verlags GmbH and Others
Fixtures Marketing Ltd v AB Svenska Spel
Fixtures Marketing Ltd v Organismos Prognostikon Agonon Podosfairou
Football Dataco v Yahoo! UK Ltd and others
Football Dataco Ltd v Yahoo! UK Ltd
Freistaat Bayern v Verlag Esterbauer GmbH
Funke Medien NRW GmbH v Bundesrepublik Deutschland
Infopaq International A/S v Danske Dagblades Forening

Table of statutes and bills

Australia

Copyright Act 1968 (Cth)
Conveyancing Act 1919 (NSW)
Conveyancing National Law (QLD)
Corporations Act 2001 (Cth)
Competition and Consumer Act 2010 (Cth)
Circuit Layouts Act 1989
Data Sharing (Government Sector) Act 2015 (NSW)
Digital Agenda Act (DAA) 2000
Freedom of Information Act 1982 (FOI Act)
Land Title Regulation 2022 (QLD)
Land Title Act 1994 (QLD)
Privacy Act 1988 (Cth)
Public Sector (Data Sharing) Act 2016
Government Information (Public Access) Act 2009 (NSW)
Surveying and Mapping Infrastructure Act 2003 (QLD)
Victorian Data Sharing Act 2017

USA

Copyright Act 1790
Copyright Act 1909
Copyright Act 1976
Digital Millennium Copyright Act of 1998 (DMCA)
Licensing Act 1622
Statute of Anne 1710

EU

Data Governance Act
Data Act
General Data Protection Regulation (EU) 2016/679

1 Introduction

1.1 Introduction

Maps and geographic information have always had commercial, political, and strategic value. As with any valuable commodity, society relies on the law to allow people to identify their property and assert their ownership of it. However, maps and written descriptions of geographic information have long presented challenges for copyright law, particularly because they are perceived as factual compilations.[1] The last few decades have seen extraordinary transformations in the methods and practices of collecting, storing, using, representing, and disseminating what was once called 'geographic information' but is now more broadly termed 'spatial data'.[2]

The motivation for this work was the consideration of the changing nature of cadastral[3] data. In the 2008 case *Copyright Agency Ltd. v State of New South Wales*[4] (CAL case), the Australian High Court determined that surveyors owned the copyright in registered cadastral plans. Changes in technology have encouraged Australian state governments to require survey plans to be lodged in digital formats in a bid to eradicate paper surveys.[5] Australia is moving towards integrating surveys with a digital spatial database to provide better accuracy, reliability, and ease of access – including by introducing spatial data to assist in creating and verifying the survey plans.[6] Beyond cadastral survey plans, significant advances have been made in surveying technologies, particularly the widespread adoption of terrestrial scanners, drones and robotic total stations, and the incipient adoption of artificial intelligence (AI). AI is increasingly being used in survey work to collect data and aerial imagery, and process the data.[7] There have been discussion on a further move to a digital database of survey plans in three-dimensional (3D) – or even 4D – formats and their common standards across the Australian states for better accessibility.[8] Advancements in geospatial data collection, geographic information system (GIS) technology, digital databases, and online mapping services have completely transformed the landscape of spatial product creation.

While information technology and the Internet have made enormous contributions to the dissemination of spatial data, they have also caused a considerable increase in the copying of data, maps, route descriptions, and hiking trails.[9] Hence, the change from paper maps to electronic spatial databases has given rise to new

DOI: 10.4324/9781003479383-1

challenges.[10] This has led to the need for copyright protection systems to protect the rights of surveyors. The questions arise as to the effect changes in data form and creation may have on the reasoning of the High Court in the CAL case and, by extension, to other copyrightable paper maps and designs.

This book reviews the changing legal and technological landscape that has occurred since the High Court of Australia's decision in the CAL case. To provide an introduction to a legal audience, the following section briefly examines the role of surveyors, the nature of survey plans, and the transition from paper to digital survey plans. The latter chapters examine how copyright law was used historically to regulate the authorship and originality of traditional maps and survey plans, and look at how changes in the digital era have affected the application of laws to digital survey plans/maps and spatial data. This book compares the legal frameworks of Australia, the United States of America (USA), and the European Union (EU) because an international review of case outcomes is important in understanding the broader trends in copyright law and decisions. The book analyses the relevant legislation, case law and policies, and examines how copyright law protects cadastral and spatial products in these jurisdictions. Through comparative analysis, this book identifies consistencies and divergences, as well as best practices and potential areas for harmonising copyright protection for spatial products. This comparative study aims to contribute to a broader comprehension of the global spatial landscape by analysing their respective strengths, challenges, and areas for improvement from the experiences of all three jurisdictions.

The findings contribute valuable insights into the ongoing discourse on copyright reforms for spatial data protection in Australia and other jurisdictions, offering recommendations for policymakers, copyright holders, and users. This book provides context aims to potentially foster a balanced copyright regime which promotes innovation, access to information, and the interests of all stakeholders in the digital mapping and spatial database domains.

1.2 The importance of cadastral data

A modern economy needs efficient and reliable land administration to facilitate the trading and commodification of land and land interests. It is estimated that the total value of real property held in title in Australia in June 2023 was $10.0 trillion AUD[11] with $298 billion AUD of new mortgages given for residential property in the preceding year.[12] The land administration system, supported and enabled by cadastral data, allows access to this capital for the Australian economy. Given that the size of the Australian economy is $2.2 trillion AUD per annum (as of June 2023),[13] the value of a cadastral data to the economy is self-evident.

A fully functioning land administration system is obliged to determine three things: who has the property rights (title), what those property rights are (tenure), and what is the spatial extent of those rights (boundaries). The Torrens system of land titling – which originated in Australia and has been exported to many other jurisdictions – relies upon a base of land and improves security by requiring all land transactions to be public and open to scrutiny via a searchable register. It requires that any interest that is created must be defined as to its spatial extent – that its boundaries are reliably described. In Australia, the responsibility for boundary creation and identification is entrusted to registered cadastral surveyors. Cadastral surveyors, acting for their clients, are obliged to lodge boundary survey plans. These plans are used to create a spatial framework for the compilation of all this title and tenure information to form the cadastre – a fundamental dataset for a jurisdiction.

The registering authorities generate income from charging for searches of their register. Because these plans are prepared to meet stringent content and quality standards set by the registering authorities, they were assumed to be the property of the registering authority, to copy and distribute at their will. The CAL case rewrote established assumptions as to the ownership of copyright to registered plans when the Australian High Court determined that, notwithstanding their lodgement with the registering authority, surveyors retained intellectual property (IP) in plans drawn as part of the process of creating and identifying interests in land. The Court found that cadastral survey plans attracted protection as *artistic works*. It concluded that survey plans were pictorial forms fixed on paper with a clearly identifiable author. This judgement clarified the current legal position of the copyright protection afforded to survey plans, even when the State uses survey plans for public purposes. It is a clear confirmation that Australian copyright law envisages a balance between the author's rights and public interest regarding survey plans. At the time of the decision, all jurisdictions in Australia required cadastral plans to be submitted in hard copy form. Changes in technology, and other types of land dealings, have led to the consensus that economic benefits for the State and consumers will flow if boundary and cadastral data are submitted in an electronic form. What is uncertain is whether this benefit will come at the cost of cadastral surveyors' IP.

1.3 Cadastral plans and surveyors

A cadastral survey plan, or a registered plan, provides details of the dimensions and boundaries of a property, any relevant physical features or boundary monuments on the property, and its area.[14] It is a technical and legal document prepared by a registered cadastral surveyor,[15] who is licenced professional. Cadastral surveyors have in-depth knowledge of common law boundary principles and are responsible for accurately defining property boundaries and understanding the laws of land ownership.[16] Surveyors

> have a quasi-judicial role in the determination of the original boundary locations on which to base new surveys and a responsibility to ensure that future surveyors can likewise locate their work by the information on the plan and the monuments left on the ground.[17]

Surveying is a highly skilled process that attracts significant liability and responsibility on the part of the surveyors. It is said that:

> The signature of a surveyor on a survey plan endures until his/her death and surveyors, almost universally, maintain runoff professional indemnity insurance to cover errors that may only come to light many years after the survey is completed. Consequently, the information contained in survey plans is the result of significant skill, judgment and labour and is very valuable to the community and individuals.[18]

Registered surveyors are the only practitioners warranted with direct management of the land boundary system. They interpret the legal aspects of land ownership, providing an understanding of land, water, and air, as well as the surrounding environment, to protect development from impediments and unlock latent value. They often act as agents for developers and help with, or administer, the plan approval and registration process.[19]

1.4 The nature of spatial products

It is relevant to note at the outset that, through survey plans, surveyors represent the physical characteristics of a site, such as its boundaries and the position of various features. This representation has traditionally been on paper, but has increasingly been digitalised using computer software.

Because survey plans are the technical records of land, water bodies, and other specific areas (which are necessary for legal, commercial, and other purposes), they can take various forms, such as cadastral, hydrographic, mining, topographic, environmental planning, and aerial surveys.[20] This book is initially concerned with cadastral surveys, which are 'technical and legal documents prepared by a cadastral surveyor that records the determination or re-determination of the boundaries of parcels of land'[21] (thus, references to survey plans in this book should be understood as meaning cadastral survey plans). These surveys are integral to the legality of land transactions; therefore, they are relevant to the wider public interest.

To appreciate the legal understanding of cadastral surveys, it is pertinent to refer to a list of state legislation that deals with the registration and professional conduct of surveyors. For instance, The Victorian Surveying Act 2004 defines a 'cadastral survey' as a survey made for or in connection with, or for the purpose of making or obtaining, a plan or survey data to be used for or in connection with one of the following dealings or matters.

(a) Relating to the alienation of Crown land.
(b) Relating to or affecting title to any land.
(c) Relating to the determination, re-establishment, identification, or adjustment of the boundaries of any land.
(d) Without limiting paragraphs (a), (b) and (c), under the Land Act 1958, the Land Acquisition and Compensation Act 1986, the Local Government Act 2020, the Property Law Act 1958, the Transfer of Land Act 1958, the Subdivision Act

> 1988, the Survey Coordination Act 1958 or any other Act or enactment relating to the alienation of Crown land or to title to any land.[22]

This definition highlights two essential elements of cadastral survey plans. First, the surveys are the basis for the transfer of land title; and, second, they identify, determine, (re)establish or adjust the boundaries of a land parcel. On this latter point, Queensland's Surveyors Act 2003 is instructive. It defines a cadastral survey as 'a survey to *identify a boundary of a particular area of land*; but . . . does not include the depiction on a plan of the approximate location of a boundary if the plan states the location of the boundary is approximate' (emphasis added).[23] The aspect of 'identifying a boundary' through survey plans is also illustrated by examples within this definition to include:

> a survey carried out to prepare a survey plan, that reinstates a boundary of an area of land, *for lodgement in the land registry*; a survey that works out the location of a boundary of an area of land that does not have, or has incomplete, survey marks and, the placing of a mark to represent the location of a boundary of an area of land [emphasis added].[24]

Hence, from a legal procedural perspective, cadastral surveys are significant because they are the legal basis for identifying the boundaries of a land parcel, which is subject to transfer, alienation, and so on. Considering these definitions, two additional points should be mentioned regarding survey plans to understand their nature. First, the emphasis on the boundaries of a land parcel means its nature is similar to maps. The surveyor organises the measurements into a dataset that can be analysed. They may also take photographs or notes to provide additional context. The surveyor uses mathematical and statistical methods to analyse the data and determine the exact boundaries of the property. The surveyor collects factual inputs and arranges them in a manner that could be used to present the factual situation to the property owner. They can thus potentially be characterised as *compilations*; this is similar to the nature of maps.[25] Second, the presented definition does not explicitly lay out how survey plans have to be *expressed*, or the medium of expression.

1.5 The administration of survey plans

In Australia, each state has its own legislation that supervises the procedure for surveyors submitting survey plans. Section 6 of the Surveying and Mapping Infrastructure Act 2003 (QLD) sets out survey standards for cadastral surveys in Queensland. It mandates the relevant department to administer the cadastral boundary system, which has several functions:

(a) Setting standards for surveying (by the chief executive).
(b) Managing the collection of records of survey (plans and field records), and making this information available to surveyors.
(c) Maintaining a number of state datasets, including the digital cadastral dataset, the survey control dataset, and the administrative boundaries dataset.[26]

Essentially, the department's role is to enter survey plans submitted to the department into the state's datasets so they are publicly available.[27] Submitted plans must comply with Section 16 of the Survey and Mapping Infrastructure Act QLD, which requires surveyors to submit survey plans within 40 business days of placing a survey mark in carrying out a cadastral survey. Cadastral survey plans can also be varied in nature, such as:

(a) Deposited plans (plans submitted for inclusion in the department's system and assessment prior to the original plan being lodged for registration. These can be the first version of the plan, or a subsequent version submitted in response to a requisition, or a subsequent version submitted when something has changed after the previous version of the plan has already been passed by the department).
(b) Identification survey plans (plans submitted by any surveyor for inclusion in the department's systems which are cadastral surveys that are not lodged for registration).
(c) Redundant catalogue plans (plans submitted by any surveyor for inclusion in the department's systems when the original plan is unlikely to be lodged for registration).[28]
(d) Administrative plans (plans that define boundaries or areas of land subject to dealings under an Act of Parliament where a cadastral survey is not required).

Section 165 of the Land Title Act 1994 (QLD) requires a survey plan to be lodged. Section 164 allows the Registrar to determine if it must be on paper or if that requirement can be dispensed with. Section 9.24 of the Cadastral Survey Requirements[29] requires all plans within the definition of the Survey and Mapping Infrastructure Act must be drawn in black ink. There is now the Electronic Conveyancing National Law (QLD) which allows for electronic conveyancing; presently, however section 4 of the Land Title Regulation 2022 (QLD) does not list a survey plan as an instrument that needs to be lodged electronically. Traditionally, survey plans have been drafted on paper; however, this is changing rapidly with the increasing use of computer programs to create and express survey plans digitally.

1.6 The transition from paper to digital survey plans

Almost all states are transitioning to digital survey plans, in a bid to move away from the current 200-year-old system that relies entirely on paper documents, including survey plans and registration processes. According to the NSW Registrar General:

> The transition to digital plans presents a range of opportunities to enhance the user experience in the planning, development and conveyancing process for industry and the public. The existing paper-based plan system is complex, involving lengthy manual processes, exposing the system to inaccuracy and delays. A digital system will streamline many of these inefficiencies, reduce

> the scope for error, and will allow for greater visibility in the status of plans between creation and registration, ultimately allowing people to settle on and move into their new homes sooner.[30]

From both a consumer and administrative perspective, therefore, the digital transition presents unique opportunities to streamline processes and present a more efficient and cost-effective way to verify land parcel details. However, each state is integrating the digital transition of survey plans into its processes in different ways. For instance, the software that surveyors must use for preparing the plans differs in certain states.[31] The procedures to verify or modify plans also have differences among the states. The emphasis for each state is managing the transition in the best interests of all stakeholders, including surveyors.[32] Utilising technology in this manner is another step forward in the quest for an effective and seamless transition to digital surveying. Even in the use of spatial data with surveying, there are variances between states, and as such, differential processes may potentially need to be harmonised in the future.

Satellites collect spatial data via remote sensing technology.[33] In recent years, Earth Observation (EO) satellites have generated large amounts of spatial data that are freely available to researchers and the general public.[34] Spatial data typically involve large sets of spatial data gleaned from diverse sources in varying formats, including information such as census data, satellite imagery, weather data, mobile phone data, drawn images, and social media data.[35] The past two decades have seen the increasing use of mobile devices, such as mobile phones, portable computers, cloud computing, drones, and small spatial satellites to collect data and generate field maps. Especially, drones (uncrewed aerial vehicles, or UAVs) are cutting-edge technologies that have revolutionised the land surveying industry.[36] Drones with surveillance capabilities may take photos, capture film footage, or collect and aggregate data, which can raise copyright concerns.

> Spatial data are very expensive to collect, store and manipulate, and their value lies in their accuracy and their comprehensiveness. That the creator of this data wants to protect his efforts and his investments in these spatial data is self-explanatory.[37]

The Intergovernmental Committee on Surveying and Mapping has released a national strategy for Cadastral Reform and Innovation in Australia, titled the Cadastre 2034.[38] Whereas the 2014 plan focused on the digitisation of two-dimensional (2D) survey plans from paper-based to electronic formats, the 2034 plan focuses on moving to a digital database of survey plans in 3D (or even 4D) formats and their common standards across Australian states and New Zealand for better accessibility. The Cadastre 2034 'is envisaged as a fully automated cadastral infrastructure where surveyed land parcels are registered in real-time directly from the field to the desktop . . . This means a paperless process, void of duplication and with significantly reduced turnaround times'.[39] There has been a massive push towards 3D survey plans and their *digital* register.[40]

With emerging technologies entering the spatial data field, AI will also play a more significant role in analysing and interpreting large sets of data to use in various applications. AI is increasingly being used in survey works to collect data and aerial imagery, and to process the data. The collected data could be processed in many ways, including generating field maps and computer-aided design (CAD) drawings and providing other insights.[41] AI-driven spatial intelligence is of immense importance to sectors such as urban planning, construction and engineering, critical infrastructure, logistics, smart cities and digital twins, and game development.[42]

1.7 The distinction in digital maps

Today, most maps are stored in electronic form and a significant number are delivered to users through computer screens.[43] Digital maps are categorised as either *static* or *dynamic* based on their characteristics.[44] Static maps are fixed; they do not change in response to user input or real-time data. They are pre-rendered as an image file, usually in a common image format such as PNG or JPEG, which can be printed or shared digitally.[45] Static maps are images that show geographic areas – such as street layouts, landmarks, bodies of water, and other features – in a way that can be easily understood at a glance. They can record a fact, event, or observable occurrence in a particular time and location.[46] Static maps are typically created using mapping software or services that allow the user to select the area they want to display, choose the level of detail, and customise the appearance of the map, such as the colour scheme or labels for specific features. Once the user has configured the map, the software or service generates a static image file that the user can save and use in various applications, such as websites, mobile apps, or printed materials.

Dynamic maps often necessitate user involvement. This can encompass modifying the map's scale or visible region by zooming in or out, choosing which components or layers to display or eliminate (such as roads or images), or even initiating or halting a map animation.[47] Dynamic maps are updated in real time. Static maps used to be the most common type found on the Internet, but due to rapid technological advancements and users' need to see temporal geographic data, most maps found online now are interactive and dynamic.[48] Most digital cartography products enable user interactivity by allowing users to manipulate content and visualisation properties, such as changing the scale, extent, information display, and typography.[49] Therefore, because they grant the map user more authority in determining how and what information is portrayed, interactive maps are superseding static maps in popularity.[50]

Computer-generated maps (either static or dynamic), conversely, are created using software and computer algorithms. They are typically created by inputting data into a software program, which then generates a map based on the data input. Computer-generated maps can be used for purposes such as navigation, urban planning visualisation, and analysis. They offer a wide range of customisation options and can be used to analyse large amounts of data.[51] Computer-generated maps are a great choice for researchers, data analysts, and other professionals who need to visualise and analyse complex data.[52] For example, computer-generated maps can be used to visualise data about population demographics and traffic patterns, weather patterns, temperature, wind speed, and precipitation using data from weather sensors.[53] They can also be used in scientific research to visualise geographical information, such as land use, vegetation cover or ocean currents. Mapping and GIS software companies offer computer-generated maps and mapping software for data visualisation and analysis purposes.[54] Waldo Tobler calls computer-generated maps 'analytical cartography', defining them as the mathematical and analytical parts of cartography that remain independent of technology, a term that applies to both real and virtual maps.[55] Applications of analytical cartography include the development and enhancement of spatial data structures, analytical techniques for annotating maps, generalisation and transformation processes (including associated errors), and the numerical representation of maps.[56]

1.8 International law perspectives on survey plans

The Berne Convention,[57] the oldest international copyright treaty to address the norms and concerns of copyright, protects literary and artistic works including every production in the literary, scientific and artistic domains. For example, under Article 2 of the Berne Convention, 'literary and artistic works' protected by copyright include:

> Every production in the literary, scientific and artistic domain, whatever may be the mode or form of its expression, such as books, pamphlets and other writings; lectures, addresses, sermons and other works of the same nature; dramatic or dramatico-musical works; choreographic works and entertainments in dumb show; musical compositions with or without words; cinematographic works to which are assimilated works expressed by a process analogous to cinematography; works of drawing, painting, architecture, sculpture, engraving and lithography; photographic works to which are assimilated works expressed by a process analogous to photography; works of applied art; *illustrations, maps, plans, sketches and three-dimensional works relative to geography, topography*, architecture or science [emphasis added].[58]

According to the Convention, the literary or artistic work and any of its alterations are protected as original works, regardless of their mode or form of expression unless they prejudice the copyright in the original work.[59] Article 2(5) of the Berne Convention provides copyright on authors' literary and artistic collections, 'which by reason of the selection and arrangement of their contents constitutes an intellectual creation'. Though the Berne Convention does not specifically mention survey plans or spatial data, it is legitimate to deduce that if a work containing spatial data – such as maps, plans, or satellite images – is considered to be a literary or artistic work and meets the *originality* requirements set out in the Berne

Convention, then it would be protected by copyright under the Convention. For instance, if an individual creates a map or survey plan or drawing, and it is considered to be an artistic work because of its distinctive design, drawing, or coding backed by its originality, it would be protected by copyright under the Berne Convention and the creator would be entitled to an exclusive right of authorising the reproduction of their work in any manner or form.[60]

In an attempt to fill the inadequacies created by the Berne Convention in addressing the advent of the digital environment (e.g., software, databases, and computer programs), member countries signed the World Intellectual Property Organization (WIPO) Copyright Treaty 1996 (WIPO Copyright Treaty),[61] protocol to the Berne Convention that deals with copyright in the digital age. This treaty has recognised the impact of the advancement and integration of technology in the fields of information and communication, and its impact on the production and use of literary and artistic works.[62] Article 5 of the WIPO Copyright Treaty states that compilations of data or other material, in any form, are protected if they constitute intellectual creations by reason of the selection or arrangement of their contents. A creator can exercise an exclusive right to make the data publicly available by selling or transferring ownership of it,[63] and communicating it to the public by wire or wireless means.[64] This protection does not extend to the data or material itself, however, and is without prejudice to any copyright subsisting in the data or material contained in the compilation'.[65]

Article 9 of the Agreement on Trade-Related Aspects of Intellectual Property Rights (TRIPS) provides that 'copyright protection shall extend to expressions and not to ideas, procedures, methods of operation or mathematical concepts as such'. In addition, Article 10(2) notes that compilations of data or other materials 'by reason of the selection and arrangement' of their contents constitute an intellectual creation. However, TRIPS states clearly that 'the protection does not extend to the data or material itself and is without prejudice to any copyright subsisting in the data or material contained in the compilation'.[66]

Directive 96/9/EC of the European Parliament and the Council guides the protection of databases in Europe, the definition of which includes literary, artistic, and musical works, or other materials such as texts, sound, images, numbers, facts, and data that are organised systematically or methodically and can be accessed individually by electronic means.[67] The Directive extends its protection to the compilation of works, data, and other materials that are arranged, stored, and accessed by electronic, electromagnetic, or electro-optical processes or analogous processes, as well as non-electric databases. To protect the rights of the creator, the Directive obliges a person legally using a database that is accessible to the public in any way to not engage in actions that go against the typical usage of the database or cause unjust harm to the database's rightful owner.[68]

From this discussion, it is clear that copyright protection is extended to expressions that are fixed and material (expressed) but not to mere ideas, procedures, methods of operation, or mathematical concepts.[69] The digitisation of data and its use has posed enormous challenges in protecting the IP of spatial databases; determining the existence and extent of originality required for the protection of spatial databases is always complex.[70]

1.9 A road map of the book

This book takes readers on a voyage of reflection about the variables and parameters adopted by Australia, the USA, and the EU to protect the copyright of spatial products. The book comprises five chapters.

This introductory Chapter 1 presents the rationale for the book and explains its main arguments. This introduction serves as a roadmap, guiding readers through the nature of spatial products, the profession of surveyors, the administration of cadastral survey plans, the transition from paper to digital survey plans, and the international law perspectives on survey plans.

Chapter 2 examines the copyright of survey plans and spatial data in Australia, providing detailed insights into the extent of copyright protection granted for spatial products. This chapter explores the question of whether maps, including digital maps, can be classified as 'artistic' and/or 'literary' works under copyright law. It provides insights into the broader scope of copyright protection to determine if digital maps can be afforded the same level of protection as traditional artistic and literary works. Unlike traditional cadastral plans/maps, digital maps are inherently dynamic, continuously changing and updating in response to various factors such as user input, real-time data, and algorithmic updates. In analysing the aspects of 'material form' in copyright law for digital maps and the 'originality and authorship' of spatial products, this chapter explains that the introduction of advanced surveying technologies has highly influenced how data are organised and presented in spatial products, and how traditional notions of originality and human authorship of copyright in spatial products are challenged, especially in workflows and AI-generated products. This chapter also reviews the changing legal and technological landscape following the 2008 High Court of Australia's decision on copyright ownership of registered cadastral plans. It examines the implications of the 'fair dealing' defence to copyrighted survey plans in Australia. It discusses the implications of data sharing policies and initiatives and technological protection measures (TPMs) in protecting spatial data, and how blockchain and a decentralised ledger can provide a robust infrastructure for storing, verifying and tracking original data, explaining how blockchain and smart contracts have the potential to revolutionise property transactions in Australia.

Chapter 3 examines the copyright of survey plans and spatial data in the USA. It begins with a brief discussion of the historical origins and constitutional foundations of U.S. copyright principles. The chapter then discusses the application of elements of copyright protection in the context of survey products and data. This discussion focuses on traditional aspects, such as subject matter, material form, originality, authorship, ownership, application of fair use defence, and the existence of implied licences as defences for copyright infringement. The chapter discusses in detail the decision in *Feist Publications, Inc. v Rural Telephone Service Co.* (Feist), a case considered as a high water mark in U.S. copyright law. Furthermore, the chapter focuses on emerging issues, such as the use of AI in the survey industry, open data initiatives, use of technological protection measures, trade secrets, and unfair competition law as alternative protection measures. The chapter recognises the potential of blockchain and smart contracts in land management, and discusses the possible copyright implications regarding spatial data used in these processes.

Chapter 4 examines the copyright of survey plans and spatial data in the EU. It begins with a brief discussion of EU copyright law, highlighting the difference between the traditions of common law and civil law in applying copyright principles. The chapter discusses the premise of the EU's copyright principles, this being the basic principle of the author's own intellectual creation, as well as the implications of the absence of permanency as a requirement. The chapter examines the concept of originality in Europe, as well as the compromise reached between the systems of civil law and common law regarding the threshold of originality for copyright protection. The chapter investigates how the EU's emphasis on authors' rights necessarily recognises the importance of human acts and how the copyright principles provide the assumption that a work's author has copyright ownership. The Database Directive of the EU and its application in the context of spatial data and products are also discussed. Furthermore, the chapter examines the European data strategy, the proposed Data Governance Act/Data Act, the General Data Protection Regulation, and the interaction between these measures and copyright principles. In relation to land management in the EU, the chapter discusses unfair competition laws in some EU Member States, technological protection measures, and the use of blockchain and smart contracts.

As the concluding chapter, Chapter 5 summarises this book's main findings, offering recommendations for how copyright law could best offer protection for spatial products and data as they cross new frontiers.

Notes

1 Isabella Alexander & Marlena Jankowska, 'Rights in geospatial information: A shifting legal terrain' (2018) 3 (41) *Melbourne University Law Review* 957.
2 Ibid. Please note 'raw data, information or mere facts are not protectable subject matter under copyright law but its creative presentation and the compilations can be'.
3 "Pertaining to the valuation of landed property as a basis for taxation", 1850, from French *cadastral* and originally from the Late Greek *katastikhos* <www.etymonline.com/word/cadastral>.
4 [2008] HCA 35.
5 The state of Victoria has undertaken a Digital Cadastre Modernisation project since 2019 which seeks to 'capture and adjust survey measurements observed as part of cadastral surveys to improve the accuracy of the digital cadastre throughout the state'. One of the ways it seeks to do it is by using 'Global Navigation Satellite System (GNSS) positioning services, such as GPSnet to correct GNSS observations in real-time or by post-processing'; see Surveyor General Victoria, Melbourne ed 2 July 2021, 5, see also <www.spatialsource.com.au/the-mysterious-art-of-cadastral-land-surveying/>.
6 See for instance, NSW Government, 'Digital survey plans now available to industry' (2020) at <www.spatial.nsw.gov.au/news/digital_survey_plans_now_available_to_industry>.
7 Liping Yang et al., 'Google earth engine and Artificial Intelligence (AI): A comprehensive review' (2022) 14 *Remote Sensing* 3253.
8 Cadastre 2034, 'Cadastral reform and innovation for Australia – A national strategy' at <www.icsm.gov.au/sites/default/files/Cadastre2034_0.pdf>.
9 Katleen Janssen & Jos Dumortier, 'The protection of maps and spatial databases in Europe and the United States by copyright and the Sui Generis Right' (2006) 24 (2) *UIC John Marshall Journal of Information Technology & Privacy Law* 195.

10 Katleen Janssen & Jos Dumortier, 'The protection of maps and spatial databases in Europe and the United States by copyright and the Sui Generis Right' (2006) 24 (2) *UIC John Marshall Journal of Information Technology & Privacy Law* 195.
11 Australian Bureau of Statistics 2023a, Total value of dwellings, viewed 31 October 2023 at <www.abs.gov.au/statistics/economy/price-indexes-and-inflation/total-value-dwellings/latest-release>.
12 Australian Bureau of Statistics 2023b, Lending indicators, viewed 31 October 2023 at <www.abs.gov.au/statistics/economy/finance/lending-indicators/latest-release>.
13 Australian Bureau of Statistics 2023c, Australian national accounts: national income, expenditure and product, viewed 31 October 2023 at <www.abs.gov.au/statistics/economy/national-accounts/australian-national-accounts-national-income-expenditure-and-product/latest-release>.
14 Queensland Government, 'Survey plans' at <www.business.qld.gov.au/industries/building-property-development/surveying/survey-plans>.
15 Queensland Government, 'Survey plans' at <www.business.qld.gov.au/industries/building-property-development/surveying/survey-plans>.
16 Surveyors Board Queensland, 'Cadastral surveyor' at <http://sbq.com.au/about-surveyors/cadastral-surveyor/>.
17 Submission to ALRC Inquiry – Copyright and the Digital Economy (2012) at <www.alrc.gov.au/wp-content/uploads/2019/08/116._org_siba.pdf>.
18 Spatial Industries Business Association, 'Submission to ALRC inquiry – Copyright and the digital economy' (2012) at <www.alrc.gov.au/wpcontent/uploads/2019/08/116._org_siba.pdf>.
19 NSW Government, 'Digital survey plans review' (2019) at <www.registrargeneral.nsw.gov.au/__data/assets/pdf_file/0010/603595/Grosvenor-Digital-Survey-Plans-Review-Final-Report.pdf>.
20 Types of Land Surveys & What they are used for at <www.adcqld.com.au/5-types-of-land-surveys-what-they-are-used-for/>.
21 Submitting survey plans under *the Survey and Mapping Infrastructure Act 2003* at <www.resources.qld.gov.au/?a=109113:policy_registry/submitting-survey-plans-under-smia.pdf&ver=1.00>.
22 Section 3.
23 Schedule 3 read with section 6.
24 Ibid.
25 This is important to compare the evolving jurisprudence in the absence of a comparable jurisprudence on survey plans specifically; see Isabella Alexander & Marlena Jankowska, 'Rights in geospatial information: A shifting legal terrain' (2022) 41 *Melbourne University Law Review* 957.
26 QLD, 'Submitting survey plans under the survey and mapping infrastructure Act 2003 (2021)' at <www.resources.qld.gov.au/?a=109113:policy_registry/submitting-survey-plans-under-smia.pdf&ver=1.00>.
27 QLD Government, 'Submitting survey plans under the survey and mapping infrastructure Act 2003' at <www.resources.qld.gov.au/?a=109113:policy_registry/submitting-survey-plans-under-smia.pdf&ver=1.00>.
28 Ibid.
29 Cadastral Survey Requirements, n.d. at <www.resources.qld.gov.au/?a=109113:policy_registry/cadastral-survey-requirements.pdf&ver=7.10>.
30 NSW Government, 'Discussion paper – Transitioning from paper to digital survey' Plans (2021)' at <www.registrargeneral.nsw.gov.au/__data/assets/pdf_file/0007/1005865/Discussion-paper_Transitioning-from-paper-to-digital-survey-plans.pdf>.
31 See The Surveying and Spatial Sciences Institute (SSSI) at <https://sssi.org.au/>.
32 GIS for Cadastre Management at <www.esri.com/content/dam/esrisites/sitecorearchive/Files/Pdfs/library/brochures/pdfs/gis-for-cad-mgmt.pdf>.

33 Diane Hoaward & Eric Micheal McAdamis (2006) at <https://airandspacelaw.olemiss.edu/pdfs/jsl-32-2.pdf> at 257.
34 Vitor C. F. Gomes, Gilberto T. Queiroz & Karine R. Ferreira, 'An overview of platforms for big earth observation data management and analysis' at <www.mdpi.com/2072–4292/12/8/1253>.
35 What is geospatial data? at <www.ibm.com/au-en/topics/geospatial-data>.
36 Marvel Geospatial at <www.marvelgeospatial.com/how-are-drones-replacing-other-surveying-techniques/>.
37 Katleen Janssen & Jos Dumortier, 'The protection of maps and spatial databases in Europe and the United States by copyright and the Sui Generis Right' (2006) 24 (2) *UIC John Marshall Journal of Information Technology & Privacy Law* 195, 197.
38 Casastre 2034, n.d., A vision for cadastre 2034 <www.icsm.gov.au/sites/default/files/Cadastre2034_0.pdf>.
39 Ibid.
40 See Behnam Atazadeh et al., '3D Cadastre in Australian and New Zealand jurisdictions: similarities and differences' (2021) at <www.gdmc.nl/3DCadastres/workshop2021/programme/j_3D_CAD_2021_paper_14.pdf>.
41 The Constructor, 'Artificial intelligence in surveying' at <https://theconstructor.org/artificial-intelligence/artificial-intelligence-surveying/555010/>.
42 Ravi Mehta, 'Artificial Intelligence translating geospatial data into knowledge' (2021) at <www.spatialsource.com.au/artificial-intelligence-translating-geospatial-data-into-knowledge/>.
43 Terje Midtbø & Elina Larsen, 'Map animations versus static maps – when is one of them better?' at <http://ishm.elte.hu/cet/madrid-2005/midtbo.pdf> at 1.
44 Menno-Jan Kraak & Allan Brown, *Web Cartography: Developments and Prospectus* (Taylor & Francis, London, 2001) at 231.
45 Alexander Code, 'Static maps vs interactive maps: When to use them' (2021) at <www.line-45.com/post/static-maps-vs-interactive-maps-when-use-them>.
46 Marcello Martinelli & Elizabeth de Souza Machado-Hess, 'Static and dynamic maps, developed from analytical or synthesis reasoning, in school geographic atlas: The methodological feasibility' (2014) at <https://seer.ufu.br/index.php/revistabrasileiracartografia/article/view/44746/23760>.
47 Menno-Jan Kraak & Ferjan Ormeling, *Cartography: Visualization of Spatial Data* (Pearson Education Limited, Boca Raton, 2010) at 147.
48 Kristien Ooms, 'Maps, how do users see them? An in-depth investigation of the map users' cognitive processes' at <http://cartogis.ugent.be/kooms/PhD/PhD_kooms.pdf> at 4.
49 Kristien Ooms, 'Maps, how do users see them? An in-depth investigation of the map users' cognitive processes' at <http://cartogis.ugent.be/kooms/PhD/PhD_kooms.pdf> at 4.
50 Martin Dodge & Rob Kitchin, *Mapping Cyberspace* (Routledge, London, 2001).
51 For example, Analytical cartography has played a key role in serving national needs, from defense and intelligence during the Cold War to serving the needs of civilian federal agencies, see Harold Moellering et al., 'Analytical cartography: UCGIS emerging research themes in GIScience' at <http://dusk.geo.orst.edu/ucgis/web/emerging/ac.pdf>.
52 Harold Moellering et al., 'Analytical cartography: UCGIS emerging research themes in GIScience' at <http://dusk.geo.orst.edu/ucgis/web/emerging/ac.pdf>.
53 Gerald Fleming et al., 'Weather on the internet and other new technologies' *World Meteorological Organisation* at <https://library.wmo.int/doc_num.php?explnum_id=9193>.
54 Maptitude Australia Mapping Software at <www.caliper.com/maptitude/gis-software/gis-software-australia.htm>.
55 Waldo Tobler, 'Analytical cartography' (1976) 3 (1) *The American Cartographer* 21–31.
56 Harold Moellering et al., 'Analytical cartography: UCGIS emerging research themes in GIScience' at <http://dusk.geo.orst.edu/ucgis/web/emerging/ac.pdf>.

57 Berne Convention for the Protection of Literary and Artistic Works as amended on September 28, 1979.
58 See World Intellectual Property Organization, 'Berne Convention for the protection of literary and artistic works' at <www.wipo.int/treaties/en/ip/berne/trtdocs-woOO1.html> (September 28, 1979) (including the full text of the convention, which has been revised seven times since then, for the last time in 1971), see also at <https://repository.law.uic.edu/cgi/viewcontent.cgi?article=1034&context=jitpl> at 198.
59 Art 2(3) of Berne Convention.
60 Art 9(1) Berne Convention.
61 WIPO Copyright Treaty, 1996 at <www.wipo.int/edocs/pubdocs/en/wipo_pub_226.pdf>.
62 Preamble, WIPO Copyright Treaty 1996.
63 Art 6, WIPO Copyright Treaty 1996.
64 Art 8, WIPO Copyright Treaty 1996.
65 Article 5. The scope of protection for compilations of data (databases) under Article 5 of this treaty, read with Article 2, is consistent with Article 2 of the Berne Convention and on a par with the relevant provisions of the TRIPS Agreement, see <https://wipolex.wipo.int/en/text/295166>.
66 TRIPS art. 10(2); see also <https://digitalcommons.law.ggu.edu/cgi/viewcontent.cgi?referer=&httpsredir=1&article=1015&context=theses> at 16.
67 Directive 96/9/EC of the European Parliament and of the Council of 11 March 1996 on the legal protection of databases, OJ L 77, 27 March 1996, Preamble, Article 1.
68 Art 8, Directive 96/9/EC.
69 Art 2, WIPO Copyright Treaty 1996and Art 9 of TRIPS.
70 Katleen Janssen & Jos Dumortier, 'The protection of maps and spatial databases in Europe and the United States by copyright and the Sui Generis Right' (2006) 24 (2) *John Marshall Journal of Information Technology & Privacy Law* 195, 199.

References

Alexander, I. and Jankowska, M., 2018. Rights in geospatial information: A shifting legal terrain. *Melbourne University Law Review,* 3 (41), 957.

Artificial intelligence in surveying, n.d. *The Constructor*. Available from: <https://theconstructor.org/artificial-intelligence/artificial-intelligence-surveying/555010/>.

Atazadeh, B., *et al*., 2021. 3D cadastre in Australian and New Zealand jurisdictions: Similarities and differences. Available from: <www.gdmc.nl/3DCadastres/workshop2021/programme/j_3D_CAD_2021_paper_14.pdf>.

Australian Bureau of Statistics, 2014/2021. https://www.abs.gov.au/statistics/detailed-methodology-information

Australian Bureau of Statistics, 2023a. *Total value of dwellings*, viewed 31 October 2023. Available from: <www.abs.gov.au/statistics/economy/price-indexes-and-inflation/total-value-dwellings/latest-release>.

Australian Bureau of Statistics, 2023b. *Lending indicators*, viewed 31 October 2023. Available from: <www.abs.gov.au/statistics/economy/finance/lending-indicators/latest-release>.

Australian Bureau of Statistics, 2023c. *Australian national accounts: National income, expenditure and product*, viewed 31 October 2023. Available from: <www.abs.gov.au/statistics/economy/national-accounts/australian-national-accounts-national-income-expenditure-and-product/latest-release>.

Cadastral Survey Requirements, n.d. Available from: <www.resources.qld.gov.au/?a=109113:policy_registry/cadastral-survey-requirements.pdf&ver=7.10>.

Casastre 2034, n.d.-a. *A vision for cadastre 2034*. Available from: <www.icsm.gov.au/sites/default/files/Cadastre2034_0.pdf>.Code, A., 2021. *Static maps vs interactive maps: When to use them*. Available from: <www.line-45.com/post/static-maps-vs-interactive-maps-when-use-them>.

Cadastre 2034, n.d.-b. *Cadastral reform and innovation for Australia – A national strategy*. Available from: <www.icsm.gov.au/sites/default/files/Cadastre2034_0.pdf>.

Dillman, D.A., Smyth, J.D., and Christian, L.M. 2014. *Internet, phone, mail, and mixed mode surveys: The tailored design method*. Hoboken, NJ: John Wiley & Sons Inc.

Fleming, G., *et al*., n.d. *Weather on the internet and other new technologies*. World Meteorological Organisation. Available from: <https://library.wmo.int/doc_num.php?explnum_id=9193>.

GIS for Cadastre Management, n.d. Available from: <www.esri.com/content/dam/esrisites/sitecore archive/Files/Pdfs/library/brochures/pdfs/gis-for-cad-mgmt.pdf>.

Gomes, V.C.F., Queiroz, G.T., and Ferreira, K.R., 2020. An overview of platforms for big earth observation data management and analysis. Available from: <www.mdpi.com/2072–4292/12/8/1253>.

Hoaward, D. and McAdamis, E.M., 2006. Available from: <https://airandspacelaw.olemiss.edu/pdfs/jsl-32-2.pdf> at 257.

Janssen, K. and Dumortier, J., 2006. The protection of maps and spatial databases in Europe and the United States by copyright and the Sui Generis Right. *UIC John Marshall Journal of Information Technology & Privacy Law,* 24 (2), 195.

Kraak, M.-J. and Ormeling, F., 2010. *Cartography: Visualization of spatial data*. London: Pearson Education Limited, 147.

Maptitude Australia Mapping Software, n.d. Available from: <www.caliper.com/maptitude/gis-software/gis-software-australia.htm>.

Martin, D. and Rob, K., 2001. *Mapping cyberspace*. London: Routledge.

Martinelli, M. and de Souza Machado-Hess, E., 2014. Static and dynamic maps, developed from analytical or synthesis reasoning. *In*: *School geographic atlas: The methodological feasibility*. Available from: <https://seer.ufu.br/index.php/revistabrasileiracartografia/article/view/44746/23760>.

Marvel Geospatial, n.d. How are drones replacing other surveying techniques. Available from: <www.marvelgeospatial.com/how-are-drones-replacing-other-surveying-techniques/>.

Mehta, R., 2021. Artificial intelligence translating geospatial data into knowledge. Available from: <www.spatialsource.com.au/artificial-intelligence-translating- geospatial-data-into- knowledge/>.

Midtbø, T. and Larsen, E., n.d. Map animations versus static maps – When is one of them better? Available from: <http://ishm.elte.hu/cet/madrid-2005/midtbo.pdf> at 1.

Moellering, H., *et al*., n.d. Analytical cartography: UCGIS emerging research themes in GIScience. Available from: <http://dusk.geo.orst.edu/ucgis/web/emerging/ac.pdf>.

NSW Government, 2019. Digital survey plans review. Available from: <www.registrargeneral.nsw.gov.au/__data/assets/pdf_file/0010/603595/Grosvenor-Digital-Survey-Plans-Review-Final-Report.pdf>.

NSW Government, 2020. Digital survey plans now available to industry. Available from: <www.spatial.nsw.gov.au/news/digital_survey_plans_now_available_to_industry>.

NSW Government, 2021. Discussion paper – Transitioning from paper to digital survey plans. Available from: <www.registrargeneral.nsw.gov.au/__data/assets/pdf_file/0007/1005865/Discussion-paper_Transitioning-from-paper-to-digital-survey-plans.pdf>.

Ooms, K., n.d. Maps, how do users see them? An in-depth investigation of the map users' cognitive processes. Available from: <http://cartogis.ugent.be/kooms/PhD/PhD_kooms.pdf> at 4.

QLD, 2021. Submitting survey plans under the Survey and Mapping Infrastructure Act 2003. Available from: <www.resources.qld.gov.au/?a=109113:policy_registry/submitting-survey-plans-under-smia.pdf&ver=1.00>.

Queensland Government, n.d.-a. Glossary of mapping and surveying terms. Availabe from: <www.business.qld.gov.au/running-business/support-assistance/mapping-data-imagery/maps/mapping-glossary>.

Queensland Government, n.d.-b. Survey plans. Available from: <www.business.qld.gov.au/industries/building-property-development/surveying/survey-plans>.

Spatial Industries Business Association, 2012. Submission to ALRC inquiry – Copyright and the digital economy. Available from: <www.alrc.gov.au/wp content/uploads/2019/08/116._org_siba.pdf>.

Surveyors Board Queensland, n.d. Cadastral surveyor. Available from: <http://sbq.com.au/about-surveyors/cadastral-surveyor/>.

The Surveying and Spatial Sciences Institute (SSSI), n.d. Available from: <https://sssi.org.au/>.

Tobler, W., 1976. Analytical cartography. *The American Cartographer,* 3 (1), 21–31.Types of land surveys & what they are used for, n.d. *ADC*. Available from: <www.adcqld.com.au/5-types-of-land-surveys-what-they-are-used-for/>.Victorian Cadastral Surveys, 2021. *Practice directives* (2nd ed.), 5. Available from: <www.spatialsource.com.au/the-mysterious-art-of-cadastral-land-surveying/>.

What is geospatial data?, n.d. Availabe from: <www.ibm.com/au-en/topics/geospatial-data>.

World Intellectual Property Organization, n.d. Berne convention for the protection of literary and artistic works. Available from: <www.wipo.int/treaties/en/ip/berne/trtdocs-woOO1.html>

Yang, L., *et al*., 2022. Google earth engine and artificial intelligence (AI): A comprehensive review. *Remote Sensing,* 14, 3253.

2 Copyright of survey plans and spatial data in Australia

2.1 Introduction

In the 2008 case *Copyright Agency Ltd. v State of New South Wales*,[1] the Australian High Court determined that surveyors owned the copyright in registered cadastral plans. Maps and written descriptions of geographic information have long presented challenges for copyright law, however, particularly because they are perceived as factual compilations.[2] The last few decades have seen extraordinary transformations in the methods and practices of collecting, storing, using, representing, and disseminating what was once called 'geographic information' but is now more broadly termed 'spatial data'.[3] This is in tandem with the government requirement to lodge survey plans in digital formats in a bid to eradicate paper surveys.[4] Australia is moving towards integrating surveys with a digital spatial database to provide better accuracy, reliability, and ease of access – including by introducing spatial data to assist in creating and verifying the survey plans.[5]

In addition, there have been significant advances in surveying measurement technologies, particularly the increased utilisation of terrestrial scanners, drones, and robotic total stations. For example, surveyors are increasingly using mobile platforms such as drones, cars, or even mobile phones to collect data and generate field maps.[6] Artificial intelligence (AI) is also increasingly being used in survey works to collect data and aerial imagery and process the data.[7] There has been discussion on a further move to a digital database of survey plans in 3D – or even 4D – formats and their common standards across the Australian states for better accessibility.[8] Dramatic advancements in geographic information systems (GIS) and computer technologies have resulted in widely available knowledge of GIS digital vector maps, which are easily accessible and downloadable via the Internet.[9] While information technology and the Internet have made enormous contributions to the dissemination of spatial data, they have also caused a considerable increase in the copying of data, maps, route descriptions, and hiking trails.[10] Hence, the change from paper maps to electronic spatial databases has given rise to new challenges.[11] This has led to the need for copyright protection systems to protect the rights of surveyors.

This chapter reviews the changing legal and technological landscape that has occurred since the High Court of Australia's decision in *Copyright Agency Ltd. v.*

DOI: 10.4324/9781003479383-2

State of New South Wales.[12] It examines how copyright law was used historically to regulate the authorship and originality of traditional maps and survey plans, and looks at how changes in the digital era have affected the application of laws to digital survey plans, maps, and spatial data, including AI-generated products. This chapter also reviews the changing legal and technological landscape following the 2008 High Court of Australia's decision on copyright ownership of registered cadastral plans. It examines the implications of the 'fair dealing' defence to copyrighted survey plans in Australia. It discusses the implications of data sharing policies and initiatives, and technological protection measures (TPMs), in protecting spatial data, and how blockchain and a decentralised ledger can provide a robust infrastructure for storing, verifying, and tracking original data, explaining how blockchain and smart contracts have the potential to revolutionise property transactions in Australia.

2.2 Subject matter of copyright

At the outset, it is important to identify the subject matter of survey plans for copyright protection. In *Copyright Agency Ltd v State of New South Wales* (CAL case),[13] the Australian High Court held that survey plans are 'artistic works' protected by section 10(1) of the Copyright Act 1968, and that surveyors are independent creators who would ordinarily be the first owners of the copyright in such artistic work,[14] having an exclusive right to reproduce survey plans in a material form[15] and communicate them in public.[16] Beyond this, the Court did not elaborate on the aspect of subject matter entitled to copyright protection regarding survey plans.

Section 10(1) of the Act defines 'artistic works' as (a) a painting, sculpture, drawing, engraving or photograph, whether the work is of artistic quality or not; (b) a building or a model of a building, whether the building or model is of artistic quality or not; or (c) a work of artistic craftsmanship, whether or not mentioned in paragraph (a) or (b), not including a circuit layout within the meaning of the Circuit Layouts Act 1989.[17] Under section 10 of the Act, a drawing including a diagram, map, chart, or plan is considered to be an 'artistic work', whether or not the work is of artistic quality. Evidently, from a plain reading of this definition, a survey plan produced on paper can be considered to be a 'drawing' and thus an 'artistic work'. According to section 31(1)(b),[18] surveyors enjoy the exclusive right to reproduce survey plans (as artistic works) in a 'material form', to publish the work, and to communicate the work to the public.

The Copyright Act does not define 'literary work' although the Act states that it includes '(a) a table, or compilation, expressed in words, figures or symbols; and (b) a computer program or compilation of computer programs'.[19] Maps, traditionally viewed as 'compilations', are commonly compiled from other or existing maps, or may be produced from original surveys and photogrammetric compilations.[20] Survey works also consist of a series of data and are expressed as tables, datasets, and so on.[21] Survey works also contain boundary information, dimensions, and measurements expressed in tabular form. Hence, survey works can be eligible for copyright protection as literary works under section 10 of the Act.[22] Moreover, maps and plans can also be considered as literary works under section 204, which includes maps, charts, plans, tables, and compilations as literary works.[23]

2.3 Subsistence of artistic/literary work in digital maps

As previously discussed, a digital map is a visual representation of spatial data on an electronic screen.[24] This raises the question of whether visual images (maps) seen 'onscreen' can be copyright protected as artistic works. The first question is whether the subject matter befits any type of work eligible for copyright protection under section 32 of the Act. The object of consideration here is the digital map (the output) itself, not the coding that generates the map, thus the 'artistic work' category is relevant. Section 31(1)(b) of the Act enlists the types of works that can constitute artistic work, such as a painting, sculpture, drawing, building model, or work of artistic craftsmanship.[25] Of them, 'drawing' is relevant to digital maps because it has been specifically elaborated to contain maps. The courts interpret the definition of drawing quite broadly and in terms of the general meaning of the work.[26] Given that the scope of the drawing includes maps, digital maps would thus fit into this category. However, as discussed, it is required to explore whether digital maps (the output), such as Google Maps displayed on an electronic screen, would be encapsulated under this scope of artistic work.

Images displayed on 'electronic screens' can construe artistic work. In *Pokémon Company International, Inc. v Redbubble Ltd*,[27] for example, the Federal Court recognised as an artistic work the Pokémon Pikachu character uploaded to the Internet and displayed on electronic screens via a website. The Federal Court held that in the online environment, 'uploading' met the publication criteria prescribed under section 32(2). In this case, however, the object in question was developed by a 'human author' and the object exists in a 'static manner'. Additional complications arise with digital maps due to two reasons: (1) static versus dynamic display; and (2) separating the output from the computer program.

The courts have looked for 'fixation' in some material form to recognise artistic work (this is discussed in detail in the following section). A key challenge for the copyright protection of works on electronic displays arises from its 'ephemeral' nature.[28] In *StatusCard Australia Pty Ltd v Rotondo & Anor*,[29] the Supreme Court of Queensland rejected the 'subsistence of an artistic work' in the screen display. The Court explained that because screen displays lasted for a short time (in the Court's terms, 'evanescent'), it would be difficult to recognise the displays as artistic work. While the Court's stance may not be problematic for static digital maps, such as standalone graphics including JPGs or PDF files,[30] it raises significant issues of concern for the attribution of artistic work in 'real-time maps', because many digital maps exist as real-time or interactive models. For example, as digital maps such as Google Maps are constantly being updated, there can be a problem in finding fixation in the work. In congruence with the *StatusCard* case, the courts may fail to find artistic work in such digital maps.

The second issue regarding the recognition of artistic work in digital maps relates to the question of whether a digital map, which is the 'output of a computer program', can be separated from the computer program generating the map. This relates to the dilemma of selecting between 'underlying codes' versus the 'output image'.[31] This is an important question because digital maps are based on electronic databases containing geographical coordinates which are needed to generate the map. In *StatusCard* case, the plaintiff argued that the visual depiction of the data produced by its program was original, artistic or literary work as defined by the Act and that the first defendant's program produced a copy of the same visual depiction, thereby infringing its copyright in the work.[32] The issue before the Court was whether the tables appearing on the screen display produced by the plaintiff's computer program were a literary or artistic work (specifically a compilation) as defined in Part III of the Copyright Act.[33] While the defendant reproduced the plaintiff's screen display, a different computer program was used to generate this display. The Court did not attribute copyright protection to the screen display in its findings. In considering the underlying code, the Court found that the defendant had not copied the plaintiff's source code.[34] The Court highlighted two issues: the simplicity of the screen display and the work backed by functionality. If the onscreen output was more complex and guided by aesthetic purpose, it could command protection in the screen display itself, regardless of the source code. The Court held that 'even if the framework were considered a compilation or table, it is not sufficiently original to qualify for protection under section 32 of the Act'.[35] In light of *StatusCard*, the courts are yet to draw distinctions among the underlying spatial data, the computer program, and the output screen display.

Conversely, spatial databases come broadly within the scope of 'compilations', 'databases', and computer programs, which are recognised as 'literary works' in section 10 of the *Copyright Act*; namely, 'a set of statements or instructions to be used directly or indirectly in a computer to bring about a certain result'.[36] Under the Copyright Act, computer programs can be protected as literary works. This is clear from the legislation itself, which defines literary work to include 'a computer program or compilation of computer programs'.[37] In the 2021 case *Campaigntrack Pty Ltd v Real Estate Tool Box Pty Ltd*,[38] the issue at hand was whether Real Estate Tool Box Pty Ltd had infringed on Campaigntrack Pty Ltd's copyright in its computer programs and literary works. Campaigntrack Pty Ltd claimed that Real Estate Tool Box Pty Ltd had copied and reproduced substantial parts of its computer programs and literary works, which included software programs, databases, and written materials such as brochures and manuals. Campaigntrack Pty Ltd argued that this constituted copyright infringement, as it owned the exclusive rights to these works under Australian copyright law. The Federal Court recognised copyright to subsist as a literary work in a software system, as well as subsets of instructions and statements.[39] This decision confirms that when seeking to protect or enforce copyright in computer software when the potential or actual infringer has copied a substantial part of a specific subset of the software (though not the entire system), copyright may subsist in the subset of instructions or statements within that overall system, exposing the infringer to an action for copyright infringement.[40]

This discussion demonstrates that the question of whether a digital map constitutes artistic or literary work is a complex legal issue that can vary depending on the specific facts and circumstances of each case, such as the purpose for which it was created and the features of the map and the extent to which it is original.

2.4 Material form

Copyright law protects the expression of ideas and not the idea itself.[41] The form of expression itself constitutes the material form. The requirement of 'material form' is one of the most fundamental criteria for copyrightability. The Copyright Act states that the work must be created in 'material form' for it to be protected by copyright. Section 10 of the Copyright Act states that material form 'includes any form (whether visible or not) of storage of the work or adaptation, or a substantial part of the work or adaptation, (whether or not the work or adaptation, or a substantial part of the work or adaptation, can be reproduced)'.[42] The material form defines the medium in which a work or adoption is stored. Section 22 of the Act also provides that a work is only considered to be made once it is reduced to writing or some other material form.[43] This notion can be found in recent cases such as *IceTV Pty Limited v Nine Network Australia Pty Limited*,[44] where the High Court highlighted that 'copyright does not subsist in a work unless and until the work takes some material form'.[45] Thus, a work must meet the criteria of material form to be considered copyright eligible under Australian law.

Accordingly, design plans, subdivision plans, reports, letters, opinions, and field notes would ordinarily be protected by copyright law by being drawn on paper or saved as a digital file, or being photographed or filed. Especially, a map that exists in pictorial form and is deemed copyright protected would not lose its protection when the information it portrays is digitised and stored in an electronic database, as the digital fixation would simply constitute a copy of the protected work.[46]

2.4.1 Material form in digital maps

The criteria of material form for digital maps/databases or digital maps generated through AI is complex because there are uncertainties about what constitutes a material form in this context. Mainly, the difference depends on whether digital maps and spatial databases are 'static' or 'dynamic' in nature. From *StatusCard Australia Pty Ltd v. Rotondo & Anor*,[47] it can be inferred that 'static' digital maps and spatial databases will be considered as 'fixed' for the Copyright Act. For digital maps, static works could include any 'standalone' images such as survey plans, location maps, identification surveys, building designs, and blueprints. Spatial databases can include fixed datasets, which usually represent historical data and thus could be considered as being fixed in a 'sufficiently permanent medium' to satisfy the storage criteria for material form. For example, if the Digital Cadastral Database (DCDB) shape file contains original, creative content and is fixed on a DVD, it is eligible for copyright protection.

Nonetheless, it would be challenging to recognise material form in dynamic digital maps and spatial databases, particularly in the context of works that are 'constantly updated' (i.e., *dynamic* in nature).[48] Digital maps, such as weather maps and traffic movements, are updated in real time, making it difficult to ascertain fixation. The same can be said about spatial databases for variable conditions, such as temperature and wind movement, which are constantly being captured and updated in real time.

Section 10(1) of the Copyright Act defines material form as a 'storage for work or adoption'. However, the Australian Copyright Act does not define what constitutes 'storage'. This issue was discussed to some extent in *StatusCard Australia Pty Ltd v Rotondo & Anor*,[49] wherein the Supreme Court of Queensland considered the copyrightability of images displayed on a computer screen.[50] The plaintiff claimed that 'the visual depiction of the data produced by its program is original, artistic or literary work as defined by the Act and that the first defendant's program produces a copy of the same visual depiction thereby infringing its copyright in the work'.[51] A key question, in this case, was 'whether something as evanescent as a "computer screen display" can be a work for the purposes of the Act'. Regarding images generated by computer programs, the Court held that 'as has already been noted, the definition of "material form" in section (1) which is inclusive, not exhaustive, requires a form of storage, and the ephemeral nature of computer-generated screen displays would appear to fail to satisfy this requirement' (emphasis added).[52] Digital maps in 'dynamic form' would be considered as lasting for a short time to be truly perceived. With their short span, the courts may fail to find a fixation on them because they would not meet the 'storage' requirement to be considered material form. It has been said that:

> While some digital maps will likely be considered fixed works, in that they have a permanent, or semipermanent form, others are constantly updated. While map applications like Google Maps are given minor edits on what is probably a daily basis (or similar), with major edits (like redrawing country boundaries) occurring less frequently, others like OSM are subject to constant minor variations by users. Moreover, it is also important to distinguish between the less-frequently-updated base map, and any overlay, such as traffic updates being streamed in real-time. Even if such maps are considered sufficiently stable for 'material form' purpose in copyright law, further issues are raised as to when the map has been sufficiently altered for it to amount to a 'new' work – thereby acquiring a new copyright term of protection.[53]

Copyright Law Review Committee in its report on computer software protection mentioned that:

> Screen displays may be generated either by retrieving data stored in some form of machine memory or generated during a computer program. . . . Which of . . . these two categories a particular screen display falls into will depend on the nature of what is being displayed, and in some cases, the nature of the program being used. Screen displays generated by a computer program can be characterised as part of the program's behaviour. The question which arises in this context is whether this particular form of program behaviour

> should be protected. The issues concerning the protection of these types of screen displays are different to those that apply where the screen display is generated by the retrieval of a work that is *stored in computer memory*. In respect of such displays, the issue of protection is relatively straightforward. Where copyright subsists in the work that is being displayed, the unauthorised copying of the screen display of the work will infringe copyright in the work (paragraph 9.44 of the committee). [emphasis added][54]

In some instances, however, the courts have considered 'reproduction on a temporary medium' as infringing copyright. In *Kabushiki Kaisha Sony Computer Entertainment v Stevens* (*Sony v Stevens*),[55] one of the facts considered in this case was the establishment of reproduction in RAM as being a reproduction in a material form under section 31(1)(a)(1) of the Act,[56] with Sony contending that illicit reproduction occurred in the PlayStation's RAM. In its analysis, the Court considered the reproduction of a 'volatile' and 'temporary' memory such as RAM to be infringing. According to the majority, the definition of 'material form' insists that for a form of storage to be a 'material form', it must be ordinarily possible at the time of storage for the work to be reproduced from that form.[57]

In reaching that decision, Lindgren J deemed it an unrealistic and strained construction to treat the words 'can be reproduced' in the definition of material form as intended to capture the set of circumstances arising in the Sony case.[58] That is, to encompass 'could be reproduced if an additional device, not supplied with the console and not yet available, were to be manufactured and attached to it' and/or 'could be produced if the RAM under consideration formed part of a future modified console'.[59] This was affirmed by the High Court in its majority judgement, finding that:

> As it is impossible to reproduce the storage of the game code from the RAM of the PlayStation console unless the console is modified with additional, reverse-engineered hardware, it is not possible for the code to be reproduced until that modification occurs. Thus, the definition of 'material form' is not satisfied until the conditions that enable the reproduction of the work from storage in RAM prevail.[60]

In his dissenting judgement in the Federal Court decision, Finklestein J identified the question being considered as 'whether downloading a computer program into a console's RAM amounts to reproduction and thus infringes the copyright contained in the computer program'.[61] Finklestein J observed that a work's reproduction in RAM amounting to an infringement of copyright has found support in the USA, and relevantly, that the U.S. legislation was not so dissimilar to render that decision without utility in the Australian context.[62] Of note, Finklestein recognised the following, which is worthy to note, considering that there are now arguments as to whether the copyright regime is equipped to sufficiently protect (and therefore incentivise) digital maps:

> [208] The legislation should also be construed in a way that accommodates scientific changes. In particular, the meaning to be given to 'form . . . of

> storage' must keep abreast with the digital age. Furthermore, the transitory nature of the memory in RAM is more complex than it first appears. On the one hand, the information that is stored can be wiped out in a second. On the other, it is possible that it may remain stored in RAM for the life of the computer. To hold that RAM is not a form of storage would be to thwart the legislature's intention.[63]

Since this decision, the definition of 'material form' has been amended; it no longer requires that the stored work must itself be capable of being reproduced.[64] In light of this legislative amendment, it can be argued that the majority in *Sony v Stevens* may have reached a different conclusion – perhaps one in line with the dissenting judgement of Finklestein J. This is evident in the majority's decision, which stated 'that in order for a form of storage to be a "material form", it must be ordinarily possible at the time of storage for the work to be reproduced from that form'.[65] This aspect of Finklestein J's judgement may thus be used to argue that material form subsists in digital maps and is therefore protectable under copyright law.

For example, Finklestein J recognised that while at face value, storage in a RAM is transient and often fleeting, it is theoretically possible for something to be stored in RAM for the life of the computer. The dissenting judgement of Finkelstein J in the Full Court of Federal Court is an important criticism of applying traditional provisions to modern technological developments with different natures.[66] The information is stored in the form of electrical impulses, which does not lend itself to the traditional conception of material form. Logically extending this reasoning to digital maps such as Google Maps, it can be argued that however fleeting the fixation may be, it is possible for permanent fixation to occur – and therefore, copyright ought to subsist. This thinking is consistent with Finklestein's overall view that 'The legislation should also be construed in a way that accommodates scientific changes'.[67] As previously mentioned, the provisions at issue, in this case, have since been amended to expand the definition of 'material form' to no longer require that the form in which a work is reproduced must itself be capable of further reproduction.[68] The Australia–US Free Trade Agreement 2005[69] through Article 17.4.1 created an obligation for Australia to enact laws giving copyright owners the right to prohibit all types of reproduction, in any manner or form, permanent or temporary.[70]

2.5 Originality and authorship of survey plans

The Copyright Act provides that copyright is attributed to 'the author of a literary, dramatic, musical, or artistic work' when such work is 'original', expressed in a 'material form', and connected to the Australian jurisdiction.[71] Copyright laws require a work to be 'original' to qualify for copyright protection.[72] This requirement is central to the copyright protection of a work under section 32 of the Act. According to sections 32(1)–(2) of the Act, a work must be original, which means that the work has been produced with the 'author's skill and labour', and has not been copied.[73]

The amount of skill and labour necessary for artistic copyright to subsist in a survey plan is a matter of fact and degree. In assessing an artistic work's originality, a distinction is drawn between what is visually significant (i.e., where the skill and labour employed are highly relevant) and what is not visually significant (i.e., where the skill and labour employed are insignificant).[74] Ordinarily, design plans, subdivision plans, reports, letters, opinions, and field notes would be protected by copyright law if they are an author's original creation.[75]

For literary works, conversely, the question is as to whether the survey plans, a compilation of existing facts, or derivative works are eligible for copyright protection that extends to expression rather than ideas or facts.[76] Derivative work means a work that reproduces a substantial part of an original work and/or other pre-existing works protected by copyright, or that is an adaptation of a literary, dramatic, musical, or artistic work.[77] 'Compilations' and 'derivative works' comprise every copyrightable work that employs pre-existing material or data of any kind, such as a translation, musical arrangement, dramatisation, fictionalisation, motion picture adaptation, sound recording, art reproduction, abridgement, condensation, or any other form in which a work may be recast, transformed, or adapted.[78]

The Australian judicial position has been elaborated in *IceTV Pty Limited v Nine Network Australia Pty Limited*,[79] for example, wherein originality would accrue if the author of the work in question has employed nominal skill, labour, and intellectual effort in creating the work, regardless of whether it could present itself as a 'compilation'.[80] According to Justices French, Crennan, and Kiefel, there is a fine line between the 'skill and labour' needed to produce an original work and the requirement of some 'independent intellectual effort' in creating the work.[81] The Copyright Act appears to refer to the latter:

> (a) complex *compilation* or a narrative history will almost certainly require considerable skill and labour, which involve both 'industrious collection' and 'creativity' in the sense of requiring original productive thought to produce the expression, including selection and arrangement, of the material [emphasis added].[82]

It was held in *IceTV* that copyright subsists if there was 'sufficient effort of literary nature'; it is arguable, however, what constitutes 'sufficient'. The High Court held that sufficient effort should extend beyond mere skill and judgement but should consist of some form of 'creative spark' as intellectual input. For this reason, a weekly broadcast schedule was not protected because its creation did not necessitate significant effort or labour.[83] The *IceTV* case involved a respondent who supplied aggregators with a weekly schedule of television programmes to be broadcast on its channel, which consisted of time and title information.[84] It was general practice for aggregators to use this material to produce TV guides, which were published by various media outlets. Since 2005, the appellant operated a subscription-based electronic TV programme guide, which was created using the guides produced by aggregators without a licence.[85] Initially, the respondent brought proceedings for copyright infringement against *IceTV* and was successful before the Full Federal Court. *IceTV* appealed to the High Court of Australia. The Court allowed the appeal, holding that, although Nine Network's weekly schedule involved a collection of information and creative material, the time and title information did not constitute a form of expression requiring significant effort or labour.[86] Indeed, little expression was even possible through such endeavours; the schedules, therefore, lacked the requisite originality to be protected by copyright law.

In *Sands & McDougall Pty Ltd v Robinson*,[87] the Full Court further confirmed that originality requires 'some independent intellectual effort' and said that Robinson (respondent), by:

> taking the common stock of information in Australia and, by applying to it personal, that is, independent, intellectual effort in the exercise of judgment and discrimination, had produced a map that was new in the sense that, in respect of its size and outlines, its content and arrangement and its general appearance, it presented both in its totality and in specific parts distinct differences from other existing maps.[88]

In this case, the Court considered that 'there were similarities of size, of draftsmanship, of style, of printing type, and the geographical selection and general appearance between the two works'.[89] The Court held that the respondent's map was an original literary work within the meaning of section 1(1) of the Copyright Act because it was the product of 'independent and intellectual effort' and was thus entitled to copyright.[90] The appellants, whose map was not a mere copy of the respondent's map in the ordinary sense, but was a reproduction of a substantial part of it, had infringed copyright.[91]

Essentially, both the tests of 'skill and labour' and 'independent intellectual effort' could apply to the criteria, depending on the sort of compilation in question. Such an originality test was further adopted by the Full Court, in its recent decision *JR Consulting & Drafting Pty Limited v Cummings*[92] held that:

> As to the 'correlative' relationship between authorship and originality, the contemporary question is simply this: Has the author deployed personal independent skill, labour, intellectual effort, judgement and discrimination in the production of the particular expression of the work? However, not too much should be made of the kind of skill and labour that must be expended: the requirement is that the work 'originates' with the author from 'some independent intellectual effort'.[93]

In this case, the Federal Court of Australia stated that 'if database information is organised according to particular subject headings, categories or topics, the "selection" and "arrangement" is likely to be the authorial or original contribution'.[94] This entails that the data collected in survey work can be copyright protected if the arrangement is an outcome of some intellectual activity that produces a meaningful result.[95]

The decision of the Full Federal Court in *Desktop Marketing Systems Pty Ltd v Telstra Corporation Ltd* (Desktop case)[96] had considered whether copyright subsisted in Telstra's White Pages and Yellow Pages telephone directories. The Desktop had produced CD versions of directories with a range of additional features, including the ability to conduct searches for names based on postcode, address, or by reversing the phone number.[97] Telstra contended that the compilation process involved several separate stages such as collecting data, transmitting it to the Genesis Computer System, and verifying and organising all listings and advertisements, which ultimately take material form in the published directory.[98] Telstra additionally claimed that the human inputs were crucial enough to justify the factual conclusion that these activities amounted to the compilation of the directories.[99] The labour and expense of Telstra involved in collecting, verifying, recording, and making judgements to create the directories were seen as worthy of copyright protection.[100] The Full Federal Court held that, for the purposes of copyright, originality can flow purely from the 'sweat of the brow'[101] involved in obtaining and compiling factual information, even if there is no creativity involved in its selection or arrangement.[102] Lindgren J stated that a factual compilation would be original if the compiler has exercised 'sufficient labour and expense' in collecting, verifying, recording, and assembling the information.[103] The judges unanimously concluded that under Anglo-Australian authority, the test of originality in relation to compilations of facts does not require elements of creativity in their selection and arrangement.[104] The Attorney-General's Department submitted that:

> The consequence of the decision in Desktop Marketing v Telstra is that raw data, including raw data that may only be represented in one particular way, will be subject to protection under the Copyright Act 1968, at least where substantial independent skill, labour and effort have been used to compile the data. This would cover most, if not all, databases in existence in Australia.[105]

Desktop applied for special leave to appeal the decision to the High Court of Australia, arguing that the Full Federal Court erred in applying the industrious collection test which states that copyright can subsist in a factual compilation based on labour undertaken or expense incurred.[106] Special leave to appeal the decision of the Full Federal Court was, however, refused.[107] It has been argued that the approach adopted by the Federal Court of Australia in *Desktop* and *Channel Nine v Ice TV* appears to strike a reasonable balance between the need to protect factual compilations from reproduction, on the one hand, and the necessity not to restrain authors from using facts contained in other copyright works, on the other hand.[108]

2.5.1 Authorship and originality in digital maps generated using AI

As discussed, copyright law protects only 'original' works created by humans. Yet, technology such as AI, which seeks to emulate 'human-like intelligence',[109] has proven capable of creating its own brand of originality. Copyright in AI-generated works is a contested subject, however, which has been dealt with through mixed approaches across jurisdictions. Many jurisdictions – such as the USA (United States of America), European Union (EU), and Australia – only attribute copyright to work created by a human author.[110] The main reason behind this ambiguity is the lack of human input in AI-generated works.

The issue of the copyrightability of AI-generated survey works is complex for two reasons. The two reasons are whether survey works collected through AI meet the 'human element' and 'creativity and intellectual input' criteria, thus being able to be considered copyrightable work. The Copyright Act distinguishes between Part III works (including original literary, dramatic, musical, and artistic works) and Part IV works (covering products of investment rather than creativity). The former requires a 'human author' who is an Australian citizen or resident,[111] as well as evidence of independent intellectual efforts, while the latter may vest a person or body corporate as the 'maker'.[112] The Copyright Act does not contain any specific provisions addressing the effect of using computerised or digital technologies when creating materials that fall within the scope of protected works and other subject matter described in Parts III and IV of the Act.[113]

In *Data Access Corporation v Powerflex Services Pty Ltd*,[114] for example, the High Court held that 'a compression table in the plaintiff's Dataflex computer program, which had been produced with another computer program written by the plaintiff, was an original literary work protected by copyright'.[115] In this case, the Court emphasised that it is not an abstract idea or algorithm of a mathematical principle that is protected as a computer program but a particular expression of that abstraction.[116] This case demonstrates that the selection, ordering combination, and arrangement of instructions within a computer program is important for copyright for determining the authorship.[117] The question is 'the originality of the algorithmic or logical relationship between the functions desired and the capabilities of the computer'.[118]

However, in *Telstra Corp Ltd v Phone Directories Co Pty Ltd*,[119] for instance, the Court held that the Yellow Pages and White Pages phone directories were not copyrighted works because they were compiled by an automated process using computer software.[120] The Court held that human agents did not exercise 'independent intellectual effort' or 'sufficient effort of a literary nature'.[121] Per Keane CJ and Yates J:

> it was unnecessary to assess the sufficiency of the individuals' contribution in the present case, as the contributions of those individuals did not relate to the selection, arrangement and presentation of the data in the form in which it was published.[122]

Acohs Pty Ltd v Ucorp Pty Ltd,[123] highlights the difficulties in establishing authorship in computer-aided work and computer-generated work. Acohs (the appellant) and Ucorp (the respondent) were entities engaged in producing and supplying electronic material safety data sheets (MSDS). These sheets were automatically generated through Acohs's 'Infosafe system', a computer program written by Acohs in the late 1990s. In other words, it was created automatically using a predetermined schema.[124] The evidence disclosed that Ucorp had reproduced many Acohs-authored Infosafe MSDSs without a licence. Acohs brought proceedings, claiming copyright over each MSDS and the underlying source code in each of the HTML and PDF files for the MSDSs generated by the Infosafe system. The Court held that the fact that Acohs's program, written by its programmers, had been designed to include information tags into the source code of each MSDS when it was compiled did not mean that the programmers therein became the authors of the HTML source code for each MSDS.[125] While the software program was created by human programmers at Acohs, the reports generated by the program were largely the result of computer algorithms. This raises questions about who should be considered the author or creator of the reports – the human programmers who created the software program, or the computer algorithms that generated the reports? It argued that the source code of each MSDS was therefore not an original literary work under section 32 of the Act.

Evan Farr claims that copyright should always be given to programmers, even in when AI is used rather than deterministic schema.[126] He posit this for several reasons: it is the programmer's idea being expressed, they are the only individual who contributes sufficient creative intellectual effort, and vesting ownership in the programmer provides incentive and thus encourages and promotes the continued existence of computer-created works.[127] Critics of the idea, however, note that the AI has a greater contribution to the final output than the programmer, to the point that sometimes the programmer may not even be aware of what the AI produces.[128] The contribution of the programmer is limited to providing the possibility of a creation, not the creation itself. While an AI with low intelligence (that is, one that needs structured input data, akin to a camera or word-processing program) that creates a work may allow attribution to the creator, it may not be agreeable to afford the same rights to the author of an AI with higher intelligence and independence.[129] Creating an AI requires substantial investment, and it is important that the creator is given an opportunity to recoup that investment. In addition, the benefits brought by a high-functioning AI are countless and incentives should be provided for its continued creation.[130] Dickenson et al. state that the way to approach which necessary arrangements should be made is to look at the person who used their skill, labour, and judgement in that arrangement.[131] Logic points to the possibility that 'necessary arrangements' refer to the original undertakings of creating and developing the program.[132] However, regarding more evolved forms of AI programs that can learn and adapt on their own, this interpretation of 'necessary arrangements' may be over-stretching the concept. Because AIs utilise deep learning algorithms, the distance between the creator who initially made the 'necessary arrangements' and the final output is further increased.[133] For computer-generated deterministic outputs, programmers can be attributed the copyright, given the intellectual effort and the certainty as to the outcome – subject to issues as to originality. For AI (machine learning), it may be problematic, given the distance between the intellectual effort and the outcome.

The success of this argument, however, is highly fact-dependent and stands in contrast to the looser approach taken in other jurisdictions. The editors of Halsbury's *The Laws of Australia* have stated:

> There has been some speculation regarding photographs that are 'computer-generated', [i.e.,] their taking is predetermined by a computer or similar process, such as aerial survey photographs or photographs taken by a satellite, that they may not have an author at all. However, that is to overlook the person who set up the process to take the photographs – of what and when – who surely exercises the required level of authorial contribution.[134]

The key question for the courts, therefore, is whether there has been a 'requisite level of independent intellectual effort exercised by human agents in the relevant output', despite the product ultimately being generated via AI.[135] A challenge with AI-generated works is that the surveyor must be able to show that they have employed a certain level of skill, judgement, effort, and/or labour. If data are collected through sensors and processed on digital platforms, it leaves minimal place for the argument that the surveyors had used any skill, judgement, knowledge, or effort. If they had to use their judgement to enter variables such as coordinates or their knowledge to place sensors at a particular location, however, this could be a claim for the surveyors.

While sensors could collect data on their own, the surveyor's skill and judgement may be essential to know where to place the sensors, which variables to select, and which parameters apply. When surveyors choose which cadastral evidence to collect and apply their professional education in deciding the relative weight of the evidence, they are arguably creating original work. While the spatial data for a particular data point could be considered as raw data, the points at which the surveyor chooses to collect data are based on their individual judgement. When a surveyor is creating a cadastral map or survey plan, they are making decisions about which evidence to collect and how to interpret that evidence to create an accurate representation of property boundaries.[136] This process involves the surveyor applying their professional education and expertise in determining the relative weight of different sources of evidence. The surveyor's decisions about which evidence to use and how to interpret that evidence can have a significant impact on the survey's final result. Moreover, the surveyor's judgement regarding the data points could affect the subsequent survey plans. This knowledge should be considered as necessary skill and judgement, and thus warrants copyright protection. Overall, the surveyor's decisions about which cadastral evidence to collect and how to apply their professional education in interpreting that evidence are important parts of the creative process that go into creating a cadastral map or survey, and should be protected by copyright law.

2.5.2 Authorship and originality in spatial workflows

A spatial workflow is a series of processing steps that inform the process of collection and processing of spatial data.[137] The workflow can encapsulate the entire process, including the duties of the operator to load the image, select the relevant data, and select and run the classifier.[138] Spatial workflows can also encapsulate a set of instructions in the form of a computer program that can result in a desired outcome.[139]

One of the main ways spatial workflows can exist is 'visual programming language' or 'block coding'.[140] In a visual programming language, a user (in this case, the surveyor) can create programs by making changes to the program's graphical elements rather than the text. Pil Kwon states:

> VPLs (Visual programming languages) allow making software or a program with a simple workflow chart.[141] To use VPLs, a user does not need to be well-trained in computer science. VPLs simplify much of computer programming language coding steps into drag-and-drop and a few mouse clicks.[142]

In this context, a workflow can constitute instructions that give out the desired outcome upon execution.

Spatial workflows would be considered as computer programs if the expression via the instructions results in the intended outcome. According to section 10(1) of the Copyright Act, a computer program is a set of statements or instructions used directly or indirectly in a computer to bring about a certain result.[143] Although a spatial workflow may exist in the form of a chart, image, or graphical form, in this case, it does have a functional purpose. As previously discussed, the visual programming language enables a user to create programs by manipulating the elements of the program. This enables the user to make changes to the code according to their needs. For example, a user could be using filters or changing parameters to achieve a desired outcome. Although the visual programming language enables a user to derive desired outputs merely by moving symbols and images,[144] these changes are nonetheless instructions for the computer. The spatial workflow, although graphical, consists of instructions; therefore, it is not merely an artistic work but has a functional purpose as required by the Act.

This meets the criteria set in *Data Access Corporation v Powerflex Services Pty Ltd*,[145] where it was held that to be considered as a computer program, a logical algorithmic code must perform a function.[146] This means that instructions with functionality can be considered a computer program. Moreover, it was held that the outcome must be a result of the instructor's intention.[147] Within the context of a spatial workflow, the output generated is directly related to the instructions included in the workflow.

Another important point is that even the images used for providing instructions can be considered as a part of the computer program. In *EIFY Systems Pty Ltd v 3D Safety Services Pty Ltd*,[148] the Court found copyright in images used in the coding process. The Court held that the source, object code to run the program and images and text, are copyright protected.[149] In light of this, it can be argued that the spatial workflow developed by the surveyor directly causes the output in the desired form, and thus receives copyright protection as a computer program provided that the arrangement of the instructions is the key to deriving the desired outcome.

One of the main challenges with the copyright protection of computer programs is the subsistence of sufficient effort.[150] This is because computer-generated works may not have sufficient intellectual input. The visual programming language simplifies the process of coding, thereby reducing the need to be very skilled at coding. This raises the question of whether there is sufficient intellectual effort by the creator. As previously discussed, in *IceTV Pty Ltd v Nine Network Australia Pty Ltd*,[151] however, it was held that the selector needed to be able to control the work's output. This means that the user/author must be able to determine the outcome. Individuals must be able to show that their contribution to the output was not merely limited to selecting the software, but rather determining the parameters such as choosing, customising, or operating.[152] These actions transcend the mere selection of software and need to be enough to enable the individual to control the outcome of the output.

In a spatial workflow, 'intellectual effort' can be seen in the selection and arrangement of instructions in the workflow. Although the visual programming language may simplify the process of arranging the instructions, the surveyors still must use their judgement to select the parameters, which in turn shapes the outcome. Hence, the element of intellectual input can lie in the selection and changes in the spatial workflow or the instructions. Surveyors also use a series of steps and processes to analyse, visualise, and interpret spatial data.

Related to this finding is that copyright subsists in the intellectual effort; that is, the coding or instructions. It is well established that source and object code are protected, as are the texts and images embedded in the code. In *Autodesk Inc v Dyason*,[153] after a close examination of the original product, the High Court held that the defendant Dyason was liable for copyright infringement for developing a similar product.[154] In the context of spatial workflows, this means that copyright would subsist in the arrangement of the instructions (spatial workflow) itself. The spatial workflow (set of instructions) could be thus protected as a computer program. Third parties would be held liable for copyright infringement if they consciously engaged in copying the code or instructions.

2.5.3 Satellite and UAV imagery as photographs

With advancements in digital technology, using a camera mounted on drones or uncrewed aerial vehicles (UAVs), or a satellite camera, to take pictures or videos is becoming more commonplace.[155] For example, commercial drones with high-resolution cameras are easily available and can be used to take photographs and videos from the air.[156] This is different from conventional photography, whereby one has to adjust the camera settings such as shutter speed and aperture to take the desired photo. The underlying question is whether images taken by these technologies can be considered as photographs and whether they can be copyrightable.

The Copyright Act defines a photograph as 'a product of photography or of a process similar to photography, other than an article or thing in which visual images forming part of a cinematograph film have been embodied, and includes a product of xerography, and photographic has a corresponding meaning'.[157] As per this definition, a photograph has three components:

(a) The output must be the outcome of a process, namely photography or something similar. The *Oxford Learner's Dictionary* defines the term 'photography' as 'the art, process or job of taking photographs or filming something'.[158] The inclusion of the phrase 'something similar' indicates the intention of lawmakers to encapsulate actions broader than merely capturing images via the push of a camera button. This means that actions beyond traditional photography, including the use of an analogue camera to generate photographs, can be covered by this definition.[159] Thus, in the context of spatial data, remotely controlled photography to collect images via satellite or drones can be considered to fall within this definition.[160]
(b) The output must be a visual image. In this context, therefore, images generated by satellites and UAVs are visual images.
(c) The material on which the image is fixed is not copyright protected. This includes paper and screen negative reels.

As per the breakdown of this definition, images generated by satellites or UAVs can be considered as photographs. Under the Copyright Act, photographs are protected as artistic works.[161] Thus, if recognisable as photographs, satellite and UAV images will be protected as artistic works. The main issue with regard to smartphone photography is that smartphones make taking photos much simpler compared to analogue cameras. This reduces the amount of intellectual input required on the part of the photographer. In jurisdictions such as New Zealand, where the 'sweat of the brow' standard meets the criteria for copyrightability, photographs taken by smartphones easily qualify as copyrighted works.[162] Even in jurisdictions such as the USA, where the threshold for copyrightability is much higher, photographs with some creativity taken by smartphones are copyrightable.[163] In the Australian context, although the originality requirement is more than mere 'sweat of the brow' standard, photographs are considered copyrightable simply by the fact that they have been taken.[164] The requirement is to show that the photograph originated from an author.[165] In this light, the process (intellectual effort) required to take photographs by smartphones and UAVs or satellites could be considered similar. As such, images taken by them can be considered copyrightable.

A claimant must be able to show that a photograph is the result of their own work. For example, an important fact highlighted in *Weller & Anor v. Smith*[166] was that the claimant of copyright must be able to show that he/she/they took the photograph. This is the requirement of origin/authorship. With photographs, the author is the person who took the photograph.[167] In this context, the author could be the person operating the satellite or UAV, or setting the coordinates, leading to the capture of such a photograph, who will likely be the surveyor.

Another important feature in the context of satellite or UAV imagery is that copyright extends to the digital files in which the photo exists.[168] This involves two components. First, once an image is captured in digital format, the digital format is also copyright protected. As previously discussed, in *Pokemon Company International, Inc. v. Redbubble Ltd*,[169] the Court held that digital form counts as material form, which is eligible for copyright protection. In *Ian Cubitts Classic Home Improvements Pty Ltd v. Granny Flat Projects*,[170] copyright infringement was held when the respondent converted a physical photo into a digital file and made it accessible online. Conversely, in *Seafolly Pty Limited v. Fewstone Pty Ltd*,[171] the Court considered that developing a physical product from a digital photograph could also constitute infringement. Second, separate copyrights may exist in digital and physical files. While a client may have ownership of the physical image, for instance, the photographer will likely have ownership of the digital file.[172] As discussed previously, the author will likely be the photographer, who likely will be the surveyor.

An argument against the protection of satellite or UAV photography could be that these photographs generally cover public land directed at functional use. As such, there may be an absence of an aesthetic appeal, which is required for the protection of artistic work.[173] However, the key point is that although these photos may include images of public places, 'the parameters of the photo are set by the surveyor'. Moreover, the surveyor can envision what is needed and control the outcome, which demonstrates intellectual effort. This ability to control the outcome[174] has been held as important by the courts as an intellectual input.

2.5.4 Lack of clarity in where intellectual effort lies

One of the challenges to the copyrightability of satellite and UAV photographs relates to originality. Moreover, the lack of physical involvement (i.e., the literal push of a button or the use of AI to take photos) would also contest originality. It is well known that photographs are copyright eligible in Australia.[175] However, there is also a lack of explanation about what constitutes photographic originality.[176] There is also a lack of clarity about where the intellectual input lies. Jani McCutcheon points out that intellectual input can be found in three different stages of photography.[177] Relying mainly on U.S. and EU case laws, defines them in the following three stages.

(a) Pre-shoot choices[178]: This is common in traditional photography and includes actions such as selecting a location, objects, wardrobe, and lighting effects. In the context of spatial imagery, this could include selecting the location or boundaries, and consideration of individual privacy.
(b) Rendition originality[179]: This includes creative choices at the time of actual photography, such as camera settings, framing, focusing, and taking the shot. This can be contested in the context of spatial imagery because the surveyor can use a computer program to make the settings instead of being physically involved. When taking spatial imagery, the surveyor's input can be seen as a set of instructions that are analogous to camera settings in typical photography.
(c) Post-production creative choices[180]: This includes editing the original picture, such as cropping, colour, and tone. Surveyors can edit the image using digital

editing technologies to generate a photograph that meets their needs. This could include setting the parameters, applying privacy settings, and layering with other data and images.

In all of these scenarios, arguably, there is an application of creativity and intellectual input on the part of the surveyor. In light of these considerations, satellite and UAV imagery may be protected as photographs. What constitutes 'original' in photographs, however, is yet to be properly decided by the Australian courts.

2.6 Ownership of copyright and survey plans

The ownership of copyright over survey plans has been contentious due to the interlinked interests of authors, users, the State, and the public, which all use survey plans as the legal basis for land transactions. Surveyors have an obvious interest in protecting their copyright as authors of the survey plans; however, their interest may potentially clash with the public's interests to access such plans at a reasonable price given the legal necessity of survey plans. This brings the government into the picture; it has an obligation to streamline and standardise land transactions in the public interest.

For this reason, the government employs extensive land laws and other regulations to standardise the requirements of survey plans.[181] Finally, the users or clients of the surveyors also have an interest as proprietors of the survey plans. This can lead to an absurd situation arising wherein the owner of a piece of land may not be the copyright owner of the survey plan of such land.[182] Admittedly, many of these relationships and clashes are within the domain of contract law, particularly the provisions on the assignment of copyright; however, in the absence of such contracts, what is the position of ownership of copyrights, particularly between the surveyors and the State? This issue was addressed by the Full Bench of the Federal Court in *Copyright Agency Ltd. v State of New South Wales*.[183] Pursuant to direct reference to the Act, the State is the copyright owner of a work made by or under the direction or control of the Crown.[184] Even if the work is created independently, the creator may still lose copyright if the Crown first published it.[185] In this case, the Court did not accept that the State might have ownership over the copyright in survey plans through the operation of Crown copyright under section 176, which relates to copyright ownership 'in an original literary, dramatic, musical or artistic work made by, or under the direction or control of, the Commonwealth or the State'.[186] The State had argued that since the registration process of survey plans and other directives/regulations strictly bound the requirements of survey plans and the obligations of surveyors, the State under section 176 could be the owner, regardless of whether it was the author.[187]

The Court's rationale was based on the independence of the surveyors from the State and their freedom to create survey plans irrespective of the legislative and regulatory framework that regulates survey plans in Australia.[188] When the Crown is directing or controlling the making of a work, it is actively causing the work to be created, but this does not mean that the Crown is dictating how the work should be made if a citizen chooses to create it voluntarily and without any obligation. The Court concluded that survey plans were not considered to be made 'by, or under the direction or control of' the State because they were created by the surveyor or their client voluntarily, rather than being compelled by the State. Therefore, 'direction and control' does not apply to works created voluntarily by the author.[189] This decision was made despite the fact that the State had given specific guidelines on the plans' format for them to be accepted for registration. The Court established that the application of 'work under direction and control' was relative and not absolute. Because this holding was not contested by the State in the appeal to the High Court, this remains the legal position. In interpreting the CAL case, the Australian courts have reached the *purposive approach*.[190] This is gauged from the High Court's interpretation of the statutory licence towards a creator-friendly perspective, which will be discussed in the next section.

2.7 Copyright infringements by the State: does the State enjoy an implied licence or a statutory defence?

This discussion relates to the infringement of the surveyor's copyright in survey plans. As stated earlier, the surveyor has an exclusive right to publish and reproduce the work and communicate it to the public. Thus, if the State does one or more of these acts in relation to survey plans, it could potentially infringe the surveyor's copyright. This issue is particularly relevant, and assumes importance, due to the ongoing digitisation projects of survey plans in various Australian states. It has been said that:

> Survey plans are highly valued copyright works. Registered Land Surveyors have a high level of education and training and must keep abreast of a vast array of ever changing regulations. A survey plan then is the end result of the efforts of a well-skilled individual who brings to the creation of a survey plan a high level of technical expertise with a high level of professional judgement. Similar considerations apply to the creation of other documents, such as environmental plans; design plans and as constructed plans, that are registered or deposited with governments under statutory obligations. The advent of the digital economy has brought with it increased commercialisation of survey plans and other documents. State governments now authorise information brokers to sell survey plans and other documents to the public. Both government and information brokers make a profit from these sales. *It is only fair and equitable that the creator of the content – for example surveyors – should be entitled to a fair payment for this new type of use.* [emphasis added][191]

In the CAL case, the question before the High Court was whether the State could make digital copies of survey plans after their registration and communicate them to the public without infringing the surveyor's copyright.[192] From a legal standpoint, the main issue was the applicability of the statutory defence to infringement relating to the 'use of copyright materials for the services of the Crown' under section 183 and broadly under Part VII Div 2 of the Copyright Act 1968.[193]

Before analysing the legal position, it is important to note that the appellant in this case (CAL) is a 'relevant collecting society' under Part VII, Div 2 of the Copyright Act 1968.[194] Under the Act, collecting societies are responsible for acting as mediators between the government and copyright owners regarding remuneration and terms envisaged under section 183A. Section 183A was brought in through an amendment in 1997 'to streamline the system for owners of copyright in works and other subject matter to be paid when their materials are copied by the Commonwealth, State and Territory governments.'[195] This amendment and the role of collecting societies have played a key role in the High Court's rationale.

Notably, the main argument of CAL and the State revolved around section 183(1) read with section 183(5). The former provision lays down that when acts resulting in copyright-protected work are done as services for the State, the provision acts as a statutory defence to infringement. In other words, the State cannot have infringed the copyright in such cases. This provision is based on a public interest requirement recognising that the State may have to engage in acts that could lead to copyright infringement; however, when these acts are necessary and relate to predetermined 'services for the State', the statute envisages a balance in favour of the wider public.

The Court also noted that section 183(5) seeks to further balance the interests of the author vis-à-vis the public. According to this provision, the statutory defence under section 183(1) is not unfettered because terms must be agreed upon between the State and the copyright owner, or be fixed by the Copyright Tribunal. This section is replaced by provision section 183A (Special arrangements for copying for services of government), however, when a collecting society is in operation. Section 183A (2) states:

> [i]f subsection 183(5) does not apply to government copies made in a particular period for the services of a government, the government must pay the relevant collecting society in relation to those copies (other than excluded copies) *equitable remuneration* worked out for that period using a method:
>
> (a) Agreed on by the collecting society and the government, or
> (b) If there is no agreement – determined by the Tribunal under section 152K.[196]

Section 183A inserts the aspect of 'equitable remuneration', which can be in the form of royalties. When applied to survey plans, it means that the State is obliged to remunerate the surveyors when it engages in certain acts, regardless of the statutory defence envisaged under section 183(1).[197] Thus, the Court proceeded on the basis that these sections were, in fact, a 'foundation of a statutory licence scheme'.

The State contended that when surveyors created survey plans, there was an implied licence to the State, which was 'binding on the owners of copyright in the plans, to do everything that it (the State) is required to do under the statutory and regulatory framework which governs such plans'.[198] This was necessitated as:

> it is an important State function to provide and maintain public records of landholdings, which includes legal obligations to provide copies of registered plans on request to the public. Furthermore, surveyors typically charge their clients for survey plans which they prepare in accordance with statutory and regulatory requirements knowing the use to which survey plans will be put by the State.[199]

Essentially, the State was pleading to reinstate the balance in favour of the wider public against the creators' rights under copyright law. The Full Bench of the Federal Court agreed with the State on this point, stating when a surveyor assents to the submission of a survey plan to be registered, they authorise the State to do acts that may otherwise constitute an infringement of copyright.[200] To this, CAL contended that the Copyright Act already provided a statutory licence scheme (as previously discussed), and thus there was no basis for substituting an implied licence in its place.[201] Moreover, CAL also contended that an implied licence must be envisaged only if there was a necessity to do so, and with the statutory licence provisions in place under Part VII, Div 2 of the Act, this was not the case.[202]

The Court agreed with CAL after examining the legislative history of the statutory licensing scheme under Part VII Div 2 of the Copyright Act 1968, in particular the observations of the Spicer Committee.[203] It also referred to the State's various uses of the survey plans. It observed:

> (o)n the one hand, the State uses the plans in direct response to lodgement of the survey plans by an applicant to effect, if appropriate, registration, and to issue title. This includes making a working copy of the plans. These uses are directly connected with private contracts for reward between surveyors and their clients for the preparation of plans for the specific purposes of lodgement, registration and the issue of title. On the other hand, there are uses of survey plans by the State which flow from registration, and which involve copying the plans for public purposes or communicating them to the public via a digital system.[204]

Finally, regarding the statutory defence scheme, the Court held that this scheme was compulsory and that:

> (t)here is nothing in ss 183(1), 183(5) or 183A, or other provisions relating to the statutory licence scheme, which suggests that governments may make, or take the benefit of, arrangements which would have the effect of circumventing those provisions as they apply to the copying, and the communication to the public, of registered survey plans.[205]

This discussion clarifies the current legal position of copyright protection regarding survey plans even when the State uses them for public purposes. The law upholds the statutory defence to the State from infringement in cases relating to survey plans; however, it also reiterates that the State needs to remunerate the surveyors for making digital copies and for making such copies available to the public.[206] While Australian copyright law does envisage a balance between the author's rights and the public interest regarding survey plans, the Australian High Court's decision has tilted in favour of the author's rights.

On the other hand, various scholars have made calls to reinspect the doctrine of 'implied licence' so that the doctrine could be enriched and formed into a legal metaphor that would consider the public interest and thereby broaden the scope of implied licence. This questions the extent to which the doctrine may be stretched to allow reasonable use of works in the digital environment, especially on the Internet. When determining if an implied licence exists, courts look at whether approving the act in question is vital to give business meaning to the agreement to purchase the copy.[207] Courts also infuse their analysis with the intent of reasonable parties.[208] Therefore, implied licence spreads much further than an examination of the subjective intent of the contracting parties, to a more objective standard of reasonability.[209] Under the traditional view of implied licences, the Court would consider the doctrine in two situations based on:

> (1) terms that parties probably had in mind but did not put into writing – in other words, terms that reflect the parties' subjective intentions and (2) terms that the parties would probably have expressed if the issues had been brought to their attention.[210]

There is also a third category, in which the Court would imply terms in the name of fairness and reasonableness and on policy grounds.[211]

2.8 Open data initiatives

The World Bank's open data initiative involves making government data more accessible and reusable to enable individuals, organisations, and governments themselves to innovate and collaborate in new ways.[212] The benefits of open data range from greater transparency to the improvement of public services while encouraging innovation and the creation of an economic manner in an efficient, accurate manner.[213] The Organisation for Economic Co-operation and Development (OECD) working paper defines open government data as any data and information produced or commissioned by public bodies which can be freely used, reused, and distributed by anyone.[214] The working paper considers such open government data to include geographic information such as address information, aerial photos, buildings, cadastral information, geodetic networks, geology, hydrographical data and topographic information.[215] One of the primary principles recognised by the OECD is the licence-free nature of open government data, i.e., it should not be subject to any copyright, patent, trademark, or trade secret regulation.[216] At the same time, it also recognises the need for countries to establish a legal and policy framework for data transparency and ensuring that copyright vests with the correct owner of government data.[217]

2.8.1 Data sharing policies/initiatives in Australia

In Australia, policy and legislation on a state/territory level is as follows.[218]

(a) New South Wales (NSW): the NSW Government Information (Public Access) Act 2009 facilitates public access to NSW Government information. The Data Sharing (Government Sector) Act 2015 (NSW) established a Data Analytics Centre (DAC) to facilitate data sharing between government entities and with the DAC.[219]
(b) South Australia: The Public Sector (Data Sharing) Act 2016 authorises agencies to provide public sector data that they control to other public sector agencies for a wide range of purposes.[220]
(c) Victoria: The Victorian Data Sharing Act 2017 promotes the sharing of the use of public sector data as a public resource in support of government policy-making through the office of the Chief Data Officer.[221]
(d) Queensland: the Queensland Open Data Policy Statement (September 2017) outlines the commitment to build a trusted data ecosystem that makes important data open for anyone to access, use, and share.[222]
(e) Western Australia: In August 2019, Western Australia (WA) issued a discussion paper on privacy and responsible information sharing for the public sector in that state. Currently, the state operates with a Whole of Government Open Data Policy (April 2015) that aims to improve the management and use of the WA public sector's data assets.[223]
(f) Tasmania: Tasmania has introduced an information-sharing arrangement called the Administrative Data Exchange Protocol for Tasmania (ADEPT). ADEPT is intended to encourage an organisational culture in which information collected and held by the government is valued and managed as an asset.[224]
(g) The Territories are yet to implement any specific legislation on data sharing, although the Australian Capital Territory provides an open data portal that provides data for a variety of specific use cases.

These state/territory level policies primarily concern the protection of health and personal information, i.e., data protection and privacy, and mostly discuss the process by which governmental agencies are required to share data. There is no discussion on the ownership of the data, leading to the conclusion that the open data policies are limited to data under the sovereign ownership of the Crown or the Commonwealth such as public sector information.[225]

At the federal level, an exhaustive discussion on open data policies was first undertaken by the Productivity Commission in 2017.[226] The Productivity Commission Inquiry Report recognises that no one 'owns' data and copyright (if any) can only exist if the data's form or expression is sufficiently 'original' and expressed in 'material form'.[227] The inquiry report relied on the Federal Court decision of *Telstra Corporation Limited v Phone Directories Company*[228] to note that databases are subject to copyright if they are not copied, if they originate from an identifiable human author, or if they result from independent intellectual effort directed to express the work in final form.[229] In the context of datasets, the inquiry report refers to the Australian IP law limitation of protecting copyright only when compiling the information involves sufficient 'authorship' while also recognising the challenges surrounding the uncertainty around copyright status of each individual dataset.[230]

Subsequently, the Australian government released the Australian Data Strategy, which identifies data as a valuable national asset and highlights the need for creating a Digital Atlas of Australia using location or geographical information.[231] Part of the strategy includes hosting data securely by reducing ownership.[232] Therefore, the policy-based issues concerning the ownership of the copyright over 'geographical information' or 'spatial data' persist can be summarised into the following reasons.

(a) At present, the open data policies/initiatives are focused on data protection and privacy and the Australian government's processing of such data (e.g., health records), or on open public sector information whose ownership already vests with the Australian government.
(b) There is no detailed discussion or contingencies for instances when the Australian government requires access to privately owned information (such as copyrighted cadastral maps) but cannot avail of any of the exceptions under the Copyright Act.
(c) There is little scope for any exceptions under the Copyright Act extending to text or data mining, since the entire dataset or database would need to be reproduced for those activities. Thus, the law on the protection of databases would need to be developed, either through legislation or case law, before a more comprehensive answer regarding copyright over geographical or spatial data can be arrived at.

Therefore, there is a duality between the aims and objectives of the data sharing initiatives and/or data strategy of the Australian federal, state, and territory governments and the current intellectual property (IP) regime. Whereas the government may seek to invoke the exceptions available to it under the Copyright Act using the rhetoric of public interest, the protection of copyright owners should be the primary consideration. These issues were highlighted in the *Copyright Agency Ltd. v State of New South Wales*.[233]

2.9 Fair dealing defence under copyright law

Copyright law in Australia recognises a large range of exceptions including 'fair use' (research or study) and 'fair dealing' (criticism, review, parody, satire, reporting news).[234] The Australian Law Reform Commission, in its 2012–2013 inquiry into copyright law in Australia, specifically recommended a copyright framework that promotes innovation and productivity and helps all Australians participate in the digital economy.[235] Therefore, a crucial component of the standard economic theory behind copyright law is balancing the incentives for professional creators to continue their intellectual work versus justifying the fair use exception in light of public interest.

As discussed, section 10 of the Copyright Act categorises such intellectual work as 'artistic' as recognised by the High Court of Australia in the context of survey plans, a computer program compilation of data, or 'literary', including tables, compilations of words, figures, and symbols, as well as computer programs.[236] The general exceptions for such categories of work apply to cases in which the reproduction is done on behalf of the owner/licensee either: (1) incidentally and automatically as part of a larger technical process;[237] (2) to create back-up copies;[238] or (3) to create an adaptation in the form of an interoperable product on behalf of the owner/licensee;[239] or (4) to correct errors;[240] or (5) for security testing.[241] It is also important to note that these exceptions all exist at the discretion of the copyright owner, and cannot be circumvented either through prescribed legal provisions or agreements.[242]

The fair dealing/use exceptions under the Copyright Act (ss 40–43) specifically recognise instances of research, study, educational purposes, criticism, review, parody, satire, news reporting, and for the purpose of judicial proceedings or professional advice.[243] Therefore, a combined reading of the fair dealing and general exceptions, read with the High Court of Australia's findings in the CAL case, clarify the absence of any exceptions allowing the government to merely access survey maps. Although the only acceptable exception would be for security purposes, this precludes the possibility of the government reproducing such maps for profit or even for public communication without due remuneration to the surveyor(s). Therefore, the government would have to balance its public duties under its data initiatives against its legal obligation to respect the rights of copyright holders.

The balancing act would need to be considered not merely in the context of current copyrighted work to which the Australian government may want access, but also any likelihood that unreasonable 'fair use' treatment may reduce incentives for future authors/creators to invest in copyrightable works.[244] It is also noteworthy that the 'fair use' exception is to be applied on a case-by-case basis and considers factors such as whether the purpose and character of the use of the copyrighted work are commercial in nature or are for non-profit educational purposes.[245]

2.9.1 Implications of 'fair dealing' for copyrighted survey plans

As Australia strives to make public data and information more accessible, in keeping with the Australian Data Strategy, legal issues have arisen in relation to data and text mining, i.e., copying existing electronic information and analysing the data they contain for patterns, trends, and other useful information.[246] One issue is the absence of a specific exemption under the Copyright Act for the exploitation of copyright. The 'fair dealing' exception would not be available for data mining of geographical information or spatial data for the following reasons.

(a) The exception is available when the data mining is being done for research and study purposes. As held by the High Court of Australia in the CAL case, the Australian government levies a price on the copies of survey plans that are used for land and real estate development. Further, there is no educational or research component to their usage.
(b) The exception may not be extended to the whole dataset (which is what text mining entails) but only to reasonable portions of the work or their temporary reproduction.[247]

Additionally, the exception results in increased transaction, compliance, and enforcement costs as it is necessarily applied on a case-by-case basis.[248] This would increase the administrative costs on the part of the Australian government seeking the exception, as well as on the surveyor/copyright holder who would be tasked with ensuring their rights are not being unreasonably exploited.[249] Such an onerous process would also disincentivise surveyors from engaging in future projects, thus stunting economic growth.

On the other hand, the absence of a data mining exception may impede access to data for researchers and act as a disincentive to the adoption of innovative data mining technology.[250] It is to be noted that data mining does not operate in a vacuum and overlaps with database protection, and the High Court has held that copyright protection does not extend to the underlying data forming a database, but only to a particular form of expression of that data.[251] In other words, the survey plans created (expressed) by the surveyor contain an artistic element that makes them distinguishable from the geographical landscape that it represents. Therefore, a blanket application of the fair dealing/use or public interest exceptions under copyright law may be incomplete without deliberation on how copyright applies to databases.

It has been proposed that the fair dealing/use exception should be applied in determining whether text and data mining constitutes copyright infringement but should not constitute a blanket exception and instead should consider whether market considerations need to be taken into account.[252] A key consideration would be whether a use is 'transformative' in nature, i.e., whether the new work merely supersedes or supplants the original work or whether it is for a different expressive purpose from that for which the original was created.[253] Other considerations would include the nature of the copyrighted material (whether it is published or unpublished), the amount of substantiality of the part used, the effect of the use on the market, and whether the use is incidental or technical in nature.[254] However, as previously noted, the reach of the fair dealing exception would not extend to text and data mining when the whole dataset needs to be copied but would only extend to 'non-expressive use', i.e., whereby the text or data is being used for a different expression than that of the original author.[255]

Finally, the Australian Law Reform Commission report on copyright and the digital economy also notes that data and text mining should be limited to non-commercial research and study.[256] The Productivity Commission Inquiry Report also mentions that there are no exceptions under the Copyright Act covering data and text mining, and that '[d]ata or text mining processes involving the copying, digitisation or reformatting of copyright material without permission may give rise to copyright infringement' as fair dealing exceptions may not extend to text mining where the whole dataset needs to be copied, thus falling outside the ambit of a 'reasonable portion'.[257]

Overall, finding a balance between fair access to copyright data and spatial data and protecting surveyors' rights can be challenging, but some potential strategies could help achieve this balance. It is necessary to develop clear copyright exemptions to protect surveyors' rights that enable surveyors to maintain control over their data, while still allowing fair access to the data by others. Alternatively, licensing and data sharing agreements can be effectively used to define the terms of access to spatial data and the conditions under which data can be used and shared to protect the rights of surveyors.[258] Surveyors' IP rights in the data they generate and collect need to be protected. This includes not only the raw data but also the value-added data and products derived from the raw data, such as maps, charts, and reports.

2.10 Unfair competition law for the protection of spatial data

Despite being a widely used form of protection for spatial data, IP rights are the most disputed protection regime among all available options.[259] Copyright law protects neither disparate facts and data, nor unoriginal selection and arrangements. For a work to be protected by copyright, it must meet the threshold of originality; typically, it needs to be the result of some creative effort or original thought on the part of the creator.[260] Although the selection and compilation of data can show some intellectual creation and effort, there is a narrow scope for copyright protection because of the previously discussed limitations on the extent of protection that spatial data receives under copyright law.

In such cases, alternative legal mechanisms such as unfair competition law[261] can be used to protect the investment and competitive advantage of third parties in the creation and use of data without seeking permission or paying compensation to the creator. Several jurisdictions have invoked unfair competition laws to stop this free riding approach. Any behaviour in a commercial or industrial setting that goes against fair and ethical practices is considered to be unfair competition.[262] Being able to 'free ride' on inventions and creative works, in which assets are utilised without compensation and bypass market transactions, could lead to inadequate payment for those investing in intellectual and industrial capital, and a misallocation of resources.[263] It has been said that:

> Once compilations of data are electronically disseminated in databases that are made available to the public, second comers can easily and cheaply copy and manipulate the contents of such databases and disseminate the resulting products to large numbers of people. With access to global information networks becoming ubiquitous in developed nations, compliers of publicly

> disseminated databases face diminishing prospects for commercial success unless they obtain the legal or technical means to thwart egregious forms of free riding.[264]

Spatial data is incredibly valuable for a wide range of applications, including urban planning, environmental monitoring, and transportation logistics.[265] This data can be difficult and expensive to collect and process, making it a valuable asset for those who have invested in it. Unfair competition law can be used to protect this investment and prevent others from taking advantage of the hard work and resources that went into creating this data. Overall, unfair competition law can be an important tool for protecting spatial data and ensuring that those who have invested in creating and processing this data are able to reap the benefits of their work.

2.11 Trade secrets (confidential information) protection for spatial data

The CAL case decision makes it clear that survey work can attract copyright protection.[266] This case focused on survey plans that were required under government legislation to be submitted to the NSW government.[267] However, copyright only applies to data that is the result of sufficient human knowledge, effort, and independent intellectual input.[268] As discussed, what constitutes 'sufficient' for intellectual effort is not certain; it depends upon a determination from the Court. Specifically, survey works created using AI fall into a grey area regarding copyright protection, which is a concern for surveyors using AI to generate spatial data.

A critical aspect within the context of protecting spatial data is the technical knowledge of surveying techniques, as well as the economic costs and potential value associated with them.[269] Collecting and maintaining spatial data is a complex and resource-intensive process which requires specialised skills and a significant investment.[270] Gathering this information can involve a range of techniques, including aerial or satellite imagery, ground-based surveys, and data obtained from various sensors. Moreover, there may be errors in terms of data collected through digital devices. This leads to a serious challenge in maintaining data accuracy.[271] Skill and effort are also required after data collection to process and maintain data accuracy.

One method of protecting IP is simply to keep private as much information as possible about the product, process, technique, model, or method being protected.[272] This is known as 'trade secrets'. Confidential information, including trade secrets, falls under Article 39, Protection of Undisclosed Information, in the Agreement on Trade-Related Aspects of Intellectual Property Rights (TRIPS). Article 39(2) states that natural and legal persons shall have the possibility of preventing information lawfully within their control from being disclosed to, acquired, by or used by others without their consent in a manner contrary to honest commercial practices, so long as such information meets the following criteria.

(a) It is secret in the sense that it is not – as a body or in the precise configuration and assembly of its components – generally known among or readily

accessible to persons within the circles who normally deal with the kind of information in question.
(b) It has commercial value because it is secret.
(c) It has been subject to reasonable steps under the circumstances, by the person lawfully in control of the information, to keep it secret.[273]

A potential solution for surveyors regarding spatial data is 'confidential information'. It is worthwhile examining whether surveyors can find a solution through a regime of confidential information protection. The principle of confidentiality requires that the person to whom a confider shares 'confidential information' does not disclose such information to any third party without the consent of the confider.[274] Nyuk Yin Nahan explains that:

> Specifically, a duty of confidence now arises in a person who has confidential information of another with knowledge only that the information is confidential and the duty is owed to the person who can properly deny access to the confidential information. The same policy, of protecting confidential information, applies irrespective of how the information is obtained or if it is a third party who receives or comes into it.[275]

What constitutes a trade secret or confidential information is determined through the courts. Numerous decisions from the Australian courts have helped to map out the scope of confidential information. One of the first essential elements is that the information must have the quality of confidence. This was highlighted in *Saltman Engineering Co Ltd v Campbell Engineering Co Ltd*,[276] in which the Court held that for a breach of confidentiality to arise, the information must be confidential in character. This means that only that specific information will be treated as confidential information and kept secret. Information that is easily available for public access is not confidential. This means that the confider has taken measures to keep the information hidden and not disclose it. The confider has an obligation to take measures to keep the data protected.

The second criterion relates to the need for an agreement between the parties before disclosing the data. The disclosure of information from the confider to the confidant must be accompanied by an agreement that governs the information transfer. Usually, these contracts are equipped with non-disclosure or confidentiality provisions, which may specify the confidential information and obligation to keep such information secret. In *Australian Medic-Care Company Ltd v Hamilton Pharmaceutical Pty Limited*,[277] the Australian Federal Court highlighted that the duty of confidence would be dictated according to the written contractual agreement. Thus, the confider needs to precisely draft the confidentiality provision of the written agreement.

The third criterion requires that the confider imparts the information to the confidant. The information transfer must occur by way of the contractual agreement mentioned in the previous point. This entails the active dissemination and receipt of information between the parties. As was held in *Thales Australia Limited v Madritsch KG & Anor*,[278] the duty of confidence only arises regarding information transferred from the confider to the confidant. A third party who (innocently) discovers any confidential information on their own cannot be liable for breach of confidentiality.

The fourth general criterion is that the 'confidential information' should not be in the public domain. Once any information enters the public domain, it becomes accessible to the general public and thus loses its confidentiality;[279] thus, any question of confidentiality at this point is immaterial. In *Coco v A N Clark (Engineers) Ltd*,[280] the Court held that for information to be confidential, it should *not* be known to the general public. This is one of the main concerns in the context of spatial data because surveyors are required to share certain types of data with government institutions as a legal obligation. Once such information enters the public domain, however, it loses confidentiality.

The question that arises, therefore, is if the spatial data would attract protection under confidentiality in cases when their disclosure is not mandated by the law. As discussed in this research, there is immense value in spatial data[281] and thus an economic justification for protecting such data. This is supported by the fact that even government entities, such as the Public Sector Mapping Agency (PSMA) and the Australia and New Zealand Land Information Council, have relied on the 'cost-recovery' principle to mark the price for spatial databases.[282]

This issue was discussed in *Surveys & Mining Ltd v Morrison*.[283] In this case, the defendant Morrison had acquired confidential geological information during his tenure as a consulting geologist with the plaintiff. He then used the information from this engagement in other engagements, which adversely affected the interests of the plaintiff. The Court held that the defendant had breached confidentiality and used trade secrets without authorisation.[284] As such, the defendant was restrained from using this information. What this means for this context is that spatial information can be protected as confidential data, provided that other conditions of confidentiality are met. If the surveyors can take sufficient measures to maintain the confidentiality of the spatial information, they therefore could be protected by trade secrets and confidentiality principles.

One of the main problems relates to the confidentiality of data subject to mandatory reporting. The Conveyancing Act of New South Wales 1919,[285] for example, requires surveyors to submit their survey plans to the government institution. As can be seen from the CAL case, the state government could make such files accessible to the public. It may also not be possible for surveyors to include a non-disclosure provision when sharing this data, which leaves the surveyors vulnerable. Moreover, given the intention of the Australian government to make public sector data widely available,[286] the government may not be willing to consider non-disclosure agreements. As such, the spatial information may be released to the public domain. Furthermore, the Australian government is also implementing the Consumer Data Right (CDR) as a major initiative to make private sector data more available. If this becomes applicable to spatial data, consumers will be able to demand spatial data from the data holders (in this case, the surveyors). The statutory right of the CDR will supersede any contractual confidentiality provision. This is another issue that surveyors may need to consider.

2.11.1 Alternative methods of protecting confidential information

Two laws, in particular, are relevant in the protection of spatial data without the application of the Privacy Act or laws enabling access through the exercise of the right to information (e.g., Freedom of Information Act 1982 [FOI Act]). Both the Privacy Act and the Freedom of Information Act, it should be noted, restrict the non-consented disclosure of confidential information.[287] Depending upon the context, confidential information could either be protected through the Corporations Act 2001[288] or the Competition and Consumer Act 2010.[289]

The Competition and Consumer Act 2010 (Cth) is a broader vessel when speaking of the protection of confidentiality issues. Section 52ZA of the Act protects confidential information under the heading 'Trade Secrets'.[290] The provision reads as follows: 'Nothing in this Division requires the giving of information the disclosure of which would reveal a trade secret'.[291] This definition is general in nature and does not provide much information, except that information that would reveal a trade secret must not be disclosed. The term 'trade secret' is not defined in the law, however, which means that the scope of the term 'trade secret' is yet to be determined by the courts.[292] There are thus two questions that are important to know as to whether surveyors can find a solution to the confidentiality principle: (1) can spatial data be confidential?: and (2) who owns the confidentiality?

2.12 Blockchain and smart contracts to protect and track original data used in property transactions (challenges and opportunities)

Blockchain is an important technological advancement that could be useful for surveyors when data sharing. Blockchain is a digital technology that combines peer-to-peer network computing and cryptography, enabling a decentralised public ledger.[293] A decentralised public ledger is a public record of all transactions, which is maintained by independent nodes – no single entity controls it.[294] It is important to determine whether the growth of blockchain technology adds to the complexity of copyright law or offers long-term solutions to its problems.

Blockchain technology can be used to create decentralised registries. This helps to authenticate authors' copyright ownership over their works through the process of online registration or tokenisation of copyright.[295] This is important because the title of authorship is central to copyright law. In terms of the former (i.e., registration of copyright), blockchain technology can be used to register copyrightable works. Although registering a work as original is not a requirement for copyright protection in Australia, having proof of originality does help to ascertain ownership. It can be taken as evidence to determine the work's origin and thereby ascertain ownership.[296] The ownership details could include those of the rights holder, ownership percentage, and origin of the work.

Blockchain technology can also be used for the 'tokenisation' of copyright. Tokenisation entails a cryptographic artefact that is evidence for a material that existed at a particular point in time.[297] Tokens also help to ascertain the origin of a work and maintain transparency about the progress of the work. Tokens serve as evidence of authorship and provenance, which can also enable the precise tracking of an author's work.[298]

This feature of blockchain technology is important for spatial work that is copyrightable. Because blockchain technologies are transparent, and each input is recorded in a block that is reported to users in a network, the user (surveyor) can show evidence of their work.[299] Blockchain technologies could make it easier for surveyors to highlight where their intellectual contributions lie, serving in turn as evidence for the surveyors to claim copyright.

2.12.1 Control over spatial data

Blockchain can be used as a copyright governance technology. Unlike production or information and communication technology, blockchain is an institutional technology that provides novel ways of governing copyright rights.[300] With respect to copyright, blockchain technology can explore the development of new institutional possibilities for governing the recording, exchange, and enforcement of copyright rights (and reshaping or displacing existing institutional possibilities such as collecting societies). This includes monitoring unauthorised copying and distribution of copyrighted material (i.e., preventing piracy). Blockchain technology allows the use of a particular copy of a copyrighted work to be tracked by individualising each digital copy of the copyrighted work (including the assignment of separate licence terms to each copy) via time-stamping functionality.[301] So, it can also be called 'governance technology'.[302]

Blockchain technology has great potential to assist digital rights management (DRM) with the help of computer codes.[303] DRM consists of technologies used to secure copyrighted material in digital format. The DRM acts as a lock to prevent unauthorised access to copyrighted material. DRMs are aimed at enabling the holder of digital information to exercise control over such information by regulating the potential distribution, duplication and access to it.[304] Examples of DRM include the keys or codes used by Netflix and Spotify. Moreover, DRM is protected by civil remedies and criminal penalties under the Copyright Act.[305] Blockchain technology can perform the copyright monitoring and enforcement functions of DRM efficiently. Blockchain can be used to control usage rights and adjust copyright protections. This, in turn, allows control functions to be performed like those allowed by the DRM. For example, access permissions could be regulated through token systems in the blockchain. Only those users with a valid token may be eligible to access various online platforms.

In the context of spatial data, using blockchain technologies as DRM is clear for copyright protected spatial data and maps. There is monetary value in spatial data – even public institutions such as the PSMA of Australia charge a certain amount for providing access to certain types of data.[306] In this scenario, copyright holders of spatial data can use blockchain technologies as DRM to control the duplication, distribution, and access of copyrightable data. Moreover, using blockchain technologies as DRM could be beneficial in the context of non-copyrightable spatial data and maps. There are considerable challenges when discussing the copyrightability of spatial data.[307] Non-copyrightable spatial works could be protected via a confidentiality provision. Surveyors are entitled to maintain the confidentiality of their information and cannot be forced to disclose such information (unless as a legislative requirement).[308] In light of this, blockchain-based DRM may be a feasible and efficient tool for surveyors. A benefit is that it may be more economically feasible and secure than conventional proprietary DRM.[309]

2.12.2 Automation of licences or smart contracts

Another opportunity offered by blockchain technologies for surveyors regarding their spatial work is the possibility of automated licences or smart contracts. A smart contract is a self-executing set of instructions in the form of computer programs that execute commands automatically upon the fulfilment of certain conditions set in the instructions.[310] Self-executing contracts can be defined as 'computer code that automatically executes all or parts of an agreement and is stored on a blockchain-based platform'.[311]

Smart contracts can be used to enhance licensing efficiency. They facilitate automatic payments (e.g., using cryptocurrency) and provide fair compensation to authors.[312] They can also secure copyright agreements of works between authors and businesses by using blockchain technology. When applied to copyright laws, smart contracts can enhance licensing efficiency and automate licensing, including royalty payments and other copyright-related transactions, ensuring transparency and accuracy.[313] As such, smart contracts could substantially decrease the transaction costs for both rights owners and users, and protect the latter from concerns about copyright infringement.[314]

Surveyors could benefit from using smart contracts for spatial work.[315] There are many complications related to the licensing of spatial work, including the copyrightability and confidentiality of the subject matter, ownership of the spatial information, mandatory reporting, and public access and control over spatial information. These complications make it complex for surveyors to be certain about where they stand with their work. Smart contracts could address this point of concern. Because smart contracts are predetermined sets of instructions, surveyors could negotiate their position beforehand and have clarity on their expectations. Moreover, if their work is to be licensed to third parties, it can be easier for surveyors to control access and receive payments by the nature of smart contracts.

2.12.3 Spatial data risks associated with blockchain technologies

Despite the potential use of blockchain technologies for spatial data, they are not without some drawbacks. The weaknesses mainly relate to the very issues identified in the previous subsection as advantages.

One of the main flaws of blockchain relates to its decentralised nature. The main problem with a decentralised versus centralised approach is that it lacks clarity regarding who created the work in the first place.[316] The tokens showing the origin of a work may be arranged informally and may not be visible to the general public.[317] There may be a lack of transparency about where the work originated from, hence raising confusion about authorship. This problem could be pervasive in the survey sector because spatial information may be derived from crowdsourced data.

It may therefore be difficult to identify ownership under the current model of storing metadata and digital content.

There may also be challenges related to enforcing the copyright of such works. Because blockchains are decentralised systems, they may be spread across jurisdictions. Many private blockchains may have trust issues. This raises concerns about enforceability if any problems arise. An ordinary surveyor may not be aware of trustable and non-trustable blockchains. As authors such as Wang state, 'blockchain technology has the potential to become a public copyright registry'.[318] This entails a shift in the existing system of institutional copyright registration. If blockchain technologies emerge as a public copyright registry, for example, this could stand in parallel with existing institutions such as the Copyright Management Organisation (CMO) and Copyright Tribunal of Australia.[319] Although the extent of the impact on the former may be more, this shift in institutional structure could undermine the justification of existing institutional structures (i.e., the role of CMOs in levelling the playing field for individual copyright holders).

Another weakness of blockchain applicability relates to the structure of the smart contracts themselves. As previously discussed, smart contracts would help surveyors automate the licensing of spatial work. Smart contracts in blockchain are designed to be enforceable. Smart contracts are self-executing agreements with the terms of the agreement between the parties being directly written into lines of code.[320] Once the terms of the contract are met, the smart contract automatically executes, and the agreed-upon transaction is completed. However, while smart contracts are often self-executing and enforceable by design, there may be instances when the terms of the contract are illegal or otherwise unenforceable.[321] As such, the transactions based on smart contracts may not align with the applicable local law.[322] Hence, even if a smart contract is technically enforceable, there may be practical challenges to its enforcement. Finally, some forms of blockchain use cryptocurrency to facilitate transactions.[323] Unlike national currencies, cryptocurrencies are not institutionalised. This raises severe concerns about their stability and reliability.[324] Cryptocurrencies are subject to severe value fluctuations, even tending to crash in some scenarios. Therefore, relying on transactions using cryptocurrencies may be a big risk for surveyors.

Blockchain technologies and smart contracts have the potential to revolutionise how property transactions are conducted in Australia by providing a secure and efficient way to protect and track original data. Smart contracts can be used to protect spatial data by ensuring that access to that data is only granted to authorised parties and that the data is not manipulated.[325] By using smart contracts, spatial data can be stored securely on a blockchain, where it is protected from unauthorised access.

2.13 Technological protection measures (TPMs) and protection of spatial data

The Australian Copyright Act allows copyright owners to use digital locks to stop their material from being accessed or copied. These digital locks are defined as technological protection measures (TPMs) that are used to prevent unauthorised access or use of copyright works from being copied, distributed, or used in an unauthorised manner, thereby protecting IP rights from infringement such as encrypting software, passwords, and access codes.[326] Article 18 of WPPT[327] and Article 11 of WIPO Copyright Treaty (WCT)[328] put the contracting parties with the obligation to provide adequate legal protection and effective legal remedies against the circumvention of effective technological measures. Australia has fulfilled its responsibilities under the WIPO Treaty regarding technological protection measures (TPMs) by favouring the use of copyrighted works which has been achieved through amendments to the Copyright Act 1968, as part of the Digital Agenda Act (DAA) 2000.[329] The focus of DAA is on preventing the online availability of circumvention devices that would harm the copyright owner.[330]

Under section 10 of the Copyright Act, a TPM is currently defined as:

> a device, product, technology or component (including a computer program) that is used in Australia or a qualifying country, by, with the permission of, or on behalf of the owner of the exclusive licensee of the copyright in a work or other subject-matter, and connection with the exercise of the copyright, and in the normal course of its operation, controls access to the work or other subject-matter.[331]

TPMs can take several different forms and are generally characterised within two broad categories: 'access control measures' and 'copy control measures'.[332] The former can include measures like passwords, paywalls, IP-based restrictions and incompatibility controls (i.e., software only playable/readable on a certain device). Copy control measures can include preventing printing, copying, or downloading of material (i.e., read only information), and digital watermarks, for example.

It is envisioned that the owners or controllers of spatial data could utilise a variety of these measures to ensure the protection of their valuable data, however, it is worth noting the concern of the High Court in *Stevens v Sony*[333] in construing an 'overbroad' construction of what may constitute a technological protection measure. The majority noted that an overbroad construction may 'extend the copyright monopoly rather than match it'.[334] It has been recognised in the Australian jurisdiction that 'copy control measures are more closely allied with copyright and the infringement of copyright, than access control measures'.[335] This recognition from the House of Representatives Standing Committee is similar in nature to that sentiment echoed by the High Court in *Sony v Stevens*.

It has been identified that cloud computing services have enabled organisations that may lack hardware or scale to outsource management of their data to service providers. It is also noted, however, that there is a danger that both the chosen service provider and/or untrusted parties could sell data to competitors or otherwise infringe on the rights held by the data owner.[336] Yiu *et al*. use the example of a real estate company that owns a large database with property descriptions and their corresponding locations.[337] The company allows paying customers to search for properties located within specific geographic locations, and outsources management of the dataset to a service provider. Issues arise in that the service provider may not be fully trustworthy and could potentially sell the data they have been entrusted with, or further, an attacker could compromise the service provider and steal the valuable data.

In order to circumvent these dangers, Yiu *et al.* present several methods in which data can be protected, ensuring that only authorised can access the content and the service provider only 'blindly' evaluates queries without actually seeing the data.[338] This is referred to as 'transformation', whereby 'the data owner first encrypts the dataset according to a secret transformation and then uploads the encrypted data to the SP. Only authorised users who know the transformation are able' to access and utilise the data.[339] It is important to note that the findings demonstrated that different transformation methods result in varying levels of data privacy, and that generally, increased data privacy may come at the compromise of query efficiency.[340] This is a consideration that will need to be contemplated by spatial data owners, in that the degree of protection afforded may affect useability and efficiency at the consumer level.

These 'transformation' methods are discussed by Zope-Chaudhari and Venkatachalam, who identify specifically that due to the voluminous nature of spatial data, which is ultimately stored on multiple servers, that 'geospatial data needs to be outsourced on trusted servers by applying some modification/transformations'.[341] They propose a specific protection framework for spatial data at both the internal (i.e., storage) layer and the outer (i.e., distribution) layer. They propose also that outsourced data be transformed to trusted servers and, at the outer layer, digital watermarking, identity-based encryption, authentication, and the use of digital signatures to ensure that there is more robust protection against illegal copying and theft of the data.[342]

As identified by de Guise, data exfiltration is a serious concern, in that IP held within data being transferred without authorisation can 'dull competitive edge, cause significant embarrassment to the business, result in litigation, or a variety of other issues'.[343] Consequently, it is of little surprise that spatial data owners would be keen to utilise technological protection measures to safeguard themselves from such issues. De Guise identifies a number of methods within which data can be protected, including through access controls such as 'multi-tenancy', whereby the service owner has completed administrative control over the data while each tenant – in isolation from other tenants – has control over the section they are using.[344] According to de Guise, this prevents data leakage and theft.[345]

Jerome John offers a further avenue through which content like spatial data can be made identifiable and traceable back to the copyright owner.[346] Electronic rights management information ("ERMI") can be utilised to achieve the following.

(a) Identify the material and its author or copyright owner.
(b) Identify all or some of the conditions under which the material may be used.
(c) Specify that its use is subject to terms and conditions.[347]

Jerome Johnson notes that ERMI 'is a way for copyright owners to control their material online,' ensuring that it remains identifiable and safeguards the owner from their work becoming 'orphaned'.[348] He notes that generally, action can be taken against those who strip ERMI from a work. Therefore, ERMI can be seen to offer additional grounds to take action in light of any potential infringement.[349]

2.14 *Sui generis* law for spatial protection

Many jurisdictions,[350] including Australia, have recognised that it is not easy for the creators of spatial data to determine whether they are offered protection under their jurisdiction's copyright regimes.[351] This is problematic because 'collecting, storing and manipulating' spatial data is both complex and expensive.[352] Naturally, the authors and/or owners of spatial data want to protect their efforts and investments.[353] The difficulty in ascertaining whether spatial data has copyright protection demonstrates the importance of introducing a *sui generis* law for spatial data in Australia.

Janssen and Dumortier recognise that 'spatial databases are prime candidates for protection by the *sui generis* database right, which protects the investment in a database, and not creativity'.[354] The United Kingdom (UK) and Member States of the EU have adopted the legislative protection of databases; Australia, however, has not followed suit. In 1996, Directive 96/9/EC of the European Parliament and the Council directed that EU Member States:

> shall provide for a right for the maker of a database which shows that there has been qualitatively and/or quantitatively a substantial investment in either the obtaining, verification or presentation of the contents to prevent extraction and/or re-utilization of the whole or of a substantial part, evaluated qualitatively and/or quantitatively, of the contents of that database.[355]

Importantly, the *sui generis* right offers protection that goes beyond what is granted by copyright law by ensuring that content will still be afforded protection, even if it is not an original creation.[356] This was the result of claims from database operations, which 'require[d] legislative protection to protect their investment in the creation and marketing of databases from free-riders who can quickly and easily reproduce the databases created and maintained by others'.[357] While pre-dating the release of the Directive, the '*sui generis* right' has been summarised as follows:

> This *sui generis* right will be granted to the maker of a database to ensure protection of any substantial investment in obtaining, verifying or presenting the contents of a database, irrespective of whether the database is in itself innovative. Moreover, this sui generis right is important as it will restrict, for a period of 15 years, unauthorised extraction and re-utilisation of the entirety or a substantial part of the database.[358]

The argument for the *sui generis* protection of spatial information relates to the cost associated with collecting and maintaining data. Producing, processing, and managing data can be very expensive.[359] Costs include setting up infrastructure, managing inventory and payroll, and producing high-quality data.[360] Although automation and smart technologies may have reduced the investment required for data collection in terms of human effort, there are still economic costs associated with collecting and sharing data. One example is processing or cleaning the data to maintain accuracy.[361] Another is associated with categorising data into relevant groups for indexing.[362] Data holders are also required to make substantial investments in infrastructure to store their data. The value of spatial data – and the investment and growth that the industry has and will continue to attract – highlights the importance of it having specific protection.

Both general incentive theory and investment protection theory are relevant in this context.[363] Data holders should be able to own or control access to their data to recover their investments. The main foundation for this argument lies in the utilitarian justification for asserting IP rights. Underpinning incentive theory[364] is the principle that any commercial activity will only be meaningful in the presence of a monetary incentive.[365] According to this principle, individuals will not pursue a commercially creative activity if it is not financially viable. This means that, if the data holders do not receive financial benefits from collecting or processing spatial data, they will not engage in this activity.[366] Investment protection theory is more relevant in the context of AI-generated work[367] because it differentiates between the AI tools used and subsequent output.

Because the collection and management of spatial information require a significant amount of capital, this will be unsustainable if private entities are unable to recover their initial costs. The approach adopted by the Australian government corroborates this idea. Government agencies such as the Productivity Commission and Spatial Information Council (ANZLIC) have incorporated the principle of cost recovery when deciding whether to make spatial data public.[368] This considers the need to recover costs sustained in maintaining such data.

The relevant legislation in this regard is the Database Directive of the EU,[369] which is aimed at protecting databases in Member States.[370] In this directive, 'database' has been defined as 'a collection of independent works, data or other materials arranged in a systematic or methodical way and individually accessible by electronic or other means'.[371] One of the most important elements of the Database Directive is the requirement of 'substantial investment'.[372] As per this requirement, a database becomes eligible for protection under this directive only if substantial investment has been made to obtain, verify, or present such a database.[373] The introduction of the Database Directive was thus clearly linked with protecting the investments of data holders.[374] The European Parliament has also actively recognised the investment made in collecting or processing such data. In *Freistaat Bayern v. Verlag Esterbauer GmbH*,[375] the Court of Justice of the European Union interpreted a topographic map as a valid database because it met the requirements pursuant to Article 1(2) of the Database Directive. This approach could be useful in the context of Australian spatial data. A common point between the two jurisdictions is the need to protect the investment made in collecting and managing spatial data.

2.15 Conclusion

This research has shown that advancements in digital technologies have affected the field of survey work. There are three key factors in the protection of digital spatial products. The first is technological advancement, which has enabled the collection and analysis of large volumes of information.[376] This has increased the value of spatial products for both the private and public sectors. The second is that, despite the growing value of spatial data, the regulations governing control and access to it are largely scattered.[377] These complexities can be attributed to the myriad ways in which spatial information is collected or processed, and the complexities regarding their form and the applicability of different IP laws.[378] New technologies provide easy ways to facilitate the copying and distribution of digital content, including spatial data and digital maps,[379] thereby making it difficult for creators/surveyors to maintain the rights to their work. This creates uncertainty about the legal status and applicable laws for the protection of spatial information. The third relates to changing the policies and legislations that focus on building the Australian digital economy.[380]

It cannot be denied that creating spatial data is a challenging task. To create survey plans, surveyors must have a strong understanding of drafting and design software, as well as the ability to interpret and analyse complex datasets. Surveying is a highly specialised and intellectually demanding field, which requires a range of skills and expertise. Surveyors use their expertise and knowledge to make informed decisions about how to collect and analyse data, and to interpret the results meaningfully. This involves a high degree of critical thinking, problem-solving and creativity, as well as the ability to communicate complex technical information to clients and relevant stakeholders. By combining technical knowledge with critical thinking and creativity, surveyors produce accurate and reliable survey plans, which have many applications in the fields of land use and development.

The regulation of spatial data in Australia should be explored within the context of broader economic goals. This goal focuses on enhancing the availability and use of data as spatial data has been identified as a key dataset.[381] However, legal mechanisms such as IP laws and information privacy laws could need to be considered adversely.[382] The complexities identified in the previous sections may therefore pose a challenge to the broader economic objectives of Australia's surveyors.

Notes

1 *Copyright Agency Ltd. v State of New South Wales* [2008] HCA 35.
2 Isabella Alexander & Marlena Jankowska, 'Rights in geospatial information: A shifting legal terrain' (2018) 3 (41) *Melbourne University Law Review* 957.
3 Ibid.
4 The state of Victoria has undertaken a Digital Cadastre Modernisation project since 2019 which seeks to 'capture and adjust survey measurements observed as part of cadastral surveys to improve the accuracy of the digital cadastre throughout the state'. One of the ways it seeks to do it is by using 'Global Navigation Satellite System (GNSS) positioning services, such as GPSnet to correct GNSS observations in real-time or by post-processing';

see Surveyor General Victoria, 'Victorian cadastral surveys practice directives' (2021); see also <www.spatialsource.com.au/the-mysterious-art-of-cadastral-land-surveying/.

5 See for instance <www.spatial.nsw.gov.au/news/digital_survey_plans_now_available_to_industry>.

6 Elevation Data at <www.land.vic.gov.au/maps-and-spatial/imagery/elevation-data>.

7 Liping Yang et al., 'Google earth engine and Artificial Intelligence (AI): A comprehensive review' (2022) 14 *Remote Sensing* 3253.

8 Cadastre 2034, 'Cadastral reform and innovation for Australia – A national strategy' at <www.icsm.gov.au/sites/default/files/Cadastre2034_0.pdf>.

9 Abubahia Ahmed & Cocea Mihaela, 'Advancements in GIS map copyright protection schemes – A critical review' (2017) 76 *Multimedia Tools and Applications* 12205–12231.

10 Katleen Janssen & Jos Dumortier, 'The protection of maps and spatial databases in Europe and the United States by copyright and the Sui Generis Right' (2006) 24 (2) *UIC John Marshall Journal of Information Technology & Privacy Law* 195.

11 Ibid.

12 [2008] HCA 35.

13 Ibid.

14 Section 35(2) of the *Copyright Act 1968 (Cth)*.

15 Section 31(1)(b)(i) of the *Copyright Act 1968 (Cth)*.

16 Section 31(1)(b)(iii) of *Copyright Act 1968 (Cth)*.

17 Section 10(1) of the *Copyright Act 1968 (Cth)*.

18 The right of reproduction is the fundamental right of a copyright owner to reproduce or make copies of the work (ss 31(1)(a)(i), 31(1)(b)(i), 85–88 of the *Copyright Act 1968 (Cth)*.

19 Section 10(1) of the *Copyright Act 1968 (Cth)*.

20 Britannica, 'Compilation' at <www.britannica.com/science/map/Map-projections>.

21 Literary work includes (a) a table, or compilation, expressed in words, figures or symbols; and (b) a computer program or compilation of computer programs.

22 Section 32 of the *Copyright Act 1968 (Cth)*. A compilation is protected by copyright as an original literary work if the author has produced it by the application of 'independent intellectual effort'.

23 Section 204 of the *Copyright Act 1968 (Cth)* states that literary work includes a map, chart, plan, table and compilation.

24 Rights in geospatial information, 1992 at 978.

25 Section 31(1)(b) of *Copyright Act 1968 (Cth)*.

26 John Mackay & James McLachlan, 'Are computer screen displays capable of attracting copyright protection?' (1992) 3 *AIPJ* 203, 207.

27 *Pokemon Company International, Inc. v Redbubble Ltd* [2017] FCA 1541 (19 December 2017).

28 Are computer screen displays capable of attracting copyright protection? (1992) at 204.

29 *StatusCard Australia Pty Ltd v. Rotondo & Anor* [2008] QSC 181 (19 August 2008).

30 They are typically non-interactive and serve as useful guides with visual and textual Information.

31 Regarding underlying code, copyright protection generally applies to the specific expression of the code, rather than the ideas or functionality embodied in it. This means that if someone else independently creates a similar code with a different expression, they would not infringe on the original code owner's copyright. On the other hand, as for output images, survey plans, and spatial data, copyright law may also protect these works if they meet the criteria of originality and creative expression.

32 *Statuscard Australia Pty Ltd v Rotondo* [2008] QSC 181 [77].

33 Ibid.

34 Section 10(1) of the *Copyright Act 1968 (Cth)* defines 'computer program' as a set of statements or instructions to be used directly or indirectly in a computer in order to bring about certain results. This definition includes source code, object code, and firmware,

which are all types of computer programs. Computer programs, including their source code and object code, are considered literary works for the purposes of copyright law in Australia.

35 *Statuscard Australia Pty Ltd v Rotondo* [2008] QSC 181 [77].
36 Section 10 of the Act defines 'computer program' to include any literary work that is (a) incorporated in, or associated with, a computer program; and (b) essential to the effective operation of a function of that computer program, see Isabella Alexander & Marlena Jankowska, 'Rights in geospatial information: A shifting legal terrain' (2018) 3 (41) *Melbourne University Law Review* 957, 979.
37 See the definition of literary work under section 10 (1) of the *Copyright Act 1968 (Cth)*.
38 *Campaigntrack Pty Ltd v Real Estate Tool Box Pty Ltd [2021] FCA 809*.
39 Tim Golder and Stefan Ladd, 'Copyright in software – the latest word from the Federal Court' (2021) <www.allens.com.au/insights-news/insights/2021/09/copyright-in-software-the-latest-word-from-the-federal-court/>.
40 Avoid a hard landing for bundled software at <https://oreillystevens.com/2022/08/01/avoid-a-hard-landing-for-bundled-software/>.
41 Section 31 (1) of *Copyright Act 1968 (Cth)*.
42 Section 10 of the Copyright Act.
43 Section 22 of the *Copyright Act (Cth)*.
44 *IceTV Pty Limited v Nine Network Australia Pty Limited* [2009] HCA 14.
45 *IceTV Pty Ltd v Nine Network Australia Pty Ltd* [2009] HCA 14.
46 Denise S. Karjala, 'Copyright in electronic maps' (1995) 35 (4) *Jurimetrics* 395–415.
47 *StatusCard Australia Pty Ltd v. Rotondo & Anor* [2008] QSC 181.
48 Isabella Alexander & Marlena Jankowska, 'Rights in geospatial information: A shifting legal terrain' (2018) 3 (41) *Melbourne University Law Review* 957, 980.
49 *StatusCard Australia Pty Ltd v. Rotondo & Anor* [2008] QSC 181.
50 Ibid.
51 *StatusCard Australia Pty Ltd v. Rotondo & Anor* [2008] QSC 82.
52 *StatusCard Australia Pty Ltd v. Rotondo & Anor* [2008] QSC 181.
53 Isabella Alexander & Marlena Jankowska, 'Rights in geospatial information: A shifting legal terrain' (2018) 3 (41) *Melbourne University Law Review* 957.
54 *StatusCard Australia Pty Ltd v Rotondo* [2008] QSC 18 at <www.queenslandjudgments.com.au/caselaw/qsc/2008/181>.
55 *Kabushiki Kaisha Sony Computer Entertainment v Stevens* [2003] FCAFC 157 (30 July 2003).
56 Section 31(1)(a)(1) of *Copyright Act (Cth)* states that 'nature of copyright in original works for the purposes of this Act, unless the contrary intention appears, copyright, in relation to a work, is the exclusive right: (a) in the case of a literary, dramatic, or musical work, to do all or any of the following acts: (i) to reproduce the work in a material form'.
57 *Kabushiki Kaisha Sony Computer Entertainment v Stevens* (2003) 200 ALR 96, at [vi].
58 Ibid.
59 Ibid., at [170].
60 *Stevens v Kabushiki Kaisha Sony Computer Entertainment* [2005] HCA 58 at [148].
61 *Kabushiki Kaisha Sony Computer Entertainment v Stevens* (2003) 200 ALR 96 at [196].
62 Ibid., at [208].
63 Ibid.
64 Australia-US Free Trade Agreement, Australian Treaty Series [2005] ATS 1.
65 *Kabushiki Kaisha Sony Computer Entertainment v Stevens* (2003) 200 *ALR* 96, at [vi].
66 WIPO, Australia AU053-j Stevens v Kabushiki Kaisha Sony Computer Entertainment [2005] HCA 58 at <www.wipo.int/wipolex/en/text/580968>.
67 Ibid., at [208].
68 By the *US Free Trade Agreement Implementation Act 2004* (Cth), Schedule 9, which commenced operation on 1 January 2005, see at <https://dcc.com/news-and-insights/high-court-of-australia-rules-on-chipping-of-game-consoles/>.

69 Australia-US Free Trade Agreement, Australian Treaty Series [2005] ATS 1.
70 Ibid, Article 17.4.1.
71 Sections 35 and 22 (Para 1) of *Copyright Act 1968 (Cth).*
72 Section 32 of the *Copyright Act 1968 (Cth).*
73 Sections 32(1)–(2) of the Act.
74 P. Mann & J. Denoncourt, 'Copyright issues on the protection of architectural works and designs' In 25th annual conference of association of researchers in construction management (ARCOM), September 2009 at <https://centaur.reading.ac.uk/4621/1/Mann-Denoncourt.pdf> at 708.
75 Section 32(1)(a) of the *Copyright Act (Cth)* states that copyright protection is available for original works of authorship, including 'plans, drawings, and diagrams made for the purposes of construction or manufacture'. This suggests that design plans and subdivision plans would be eligible for copyright protection if they are the original creations of their authors.
76 Copyright at <www.artslaw.com.au/information-sheet/copyright/>.
77 Other subject matter or neighbouring rights called 'derivative productions'.
78 Section 10(1) of *Copyright Act 1968 (Cth):*
79 *IceTV Pty Limited v Nine Network Australia Pty Limited* [2009] HCA 14.
80 Para 54.
81 *IceTV Pty Limited v Nine Network Australia Pty Limited* [2009] HCA 14.
82 Ibid.
83 See [41] & [44].
84 *IceTV Pty Limited v Nine Network Australia Pty Limited* [2009] HCA 14.
85 Ibid.
86 Ibid.
87 *Sands & McDougall Pty Ltd v Robinson* (1917) 23 CLR 49.
88 Ibid, 52.
89 *Sands & McDougall Pty Ltd v Robinson* (1917) 23 CLR 49, 52–53, see Isabella Alexander & Marlena Jankowska, 'Rights in geospatial information: A shifting legal terrain' (2018) 3 (41) *Melbourne University Law Review* 957, 973.
90 *Sands & McDougall Pty Ltd v Robinson* (1917) 23 CLR 49, 52.
91 Ibid.
92 *JR Consulting & Drafting Pty Ltd v Cummings* (2016) 329 ALR 625, 672 [264].
93 Ibid.
94 Ibid.
95 The pre-decided arrangement would be subject to technical constraints, which will affect the originality.
96 (2002) 55 IPR 1.
97 Ibid; see also Brian Fitzgerald and Cheranne Bartlett, Database Protection under Australian Copyright Law: Desktop Marketing Systems Pty Ltd v Telstra Corporation [2002] FCAFC 112 at <http://138.25.65.110/au/journals/SCULawRw/2003/8.pdf> at 309.
98 (2002) 55 IPR 1.
99 Ibid.
100 Brian Fitzgerald & Cheranne Bartlett, 'Database protection under Australian copyright law: desktop marketing systems Pvt Ltd v Telstra corporation [2002] FCAFC 112' at <http://138.25.65.110/au/journals/SCULawRw/2003/8.pdf> at 309.
101 In a traditional English idiom, the sweat of one's brow refers to the effort expended in labour, and the value created thereby.
102 *Desktop Marketing Systems Pty Ltd v Telstra Corporation Ltd* (2002) 192 ALR 433; see also James Lahore, *Copyright and Designs: Looseleaf Service* (Butterworths, Sydney, 1996), [10,065], [10,115]; see also The Australian Law Reform Commission at <www.alrc.gov.au/publication/genes-and- ingenuity-gene-patenting-and-human-health-alrc-report-99/28-copyright-and-databases/genetic-databases/#_ftn43>.

103 *Desktop Marketing Systems Pty Ltd v Telstra Corporation Ltd* (2002) 192 ALR 433, 474; see also, The Australian Law Reform Commission at <www.alrc.gov.au/publication/genes-and-ingenuity-gene-patenting-and-human-health-alrc-report-99/28-copyright-and-databases/genetic-databases/#_ftn43>.
104 Ibid.
105 Attorney-General's Department, Submission P61, 11 November 2003; see also The Australian Law Reform Commission at <www.alrc.gov.au/publication/genes-and-ingenuity-gene-patenting-and-human-health-alrc-report-99/28-copyright-and-databases/genetic-databases/#_ftn43>.
106 *Desktop Marketing Systems Pty Ltd v Telstra Corporation Ltd* (2002) 192 ALR 433, see also Brian Fitzgerald & Cheranne Bartlett, 'Database protection under Australian copyright law: desktop marketing systems Pvt Ltd v Telstra corporation [2002] FCAFC 112' (2002) at <http://138.25.65.110/au/journals/SCULawRw/2003/8.pdf>
107 Brian Fitzgerald & Cheranne Bartlett, 'Database protection under Australian copyright law: desktop marketing systems Pvt Ltd v Telstra corporation [2002] FCAFC 112' at <http://138.25.65.110/au/journals/SCULawRw/2003/8.pdf> 321–322.
108 Copyright Protection of Databases Under Australian Law – *Nine Network Australia Pty Ltd v IceTV Pty Ltd* [2007] FCA 1172 at <http://classic.austlii.edu.au/au/journals/ANZCompuLawJl/2007/13.pdf>.
109 AI, 'Invention and authorship expanding intellectual property rights to non-human outputs – (2021)' 23(7) INTLB 119, p 119.
110 Andres Guadamuz, 'Artificial intelligence and copyright' *WIPO Magazine* (2017) at <www.wipo.int/wipo_magazine/en/2017/05/article_0003.html>; see *Acohs Pty Ltd v Ucorp Pty Ltd*.
111 Section 32 of the *Copyright Act 1968 (Cth)*.
112 Section 84 of the *Copyright Act 1968 (Cth)*.
113 Anne Fitzgerald & Tim Seidenspinner, 'Copyright and computer-generated materials – is it time to reboot the discussion about authorship?' (2013) 3 (1) *Victoria University Law and Justice Journal* 37, 42.
114 [1999] HCA 49.
115 Ibid, see also Anne Fitzgerald & Tim Seidenspinner, 'Copyright and computer-generated materials – is it time to reboot the discussion about authorship?' (2013) 3 (1) *Victoria University Law and Justice Journal* 37, 43.
116 [1999] HCA 49.
117 See Jani McCutcheon, 'The vanishing author in computer-generated works: A critical analysis of recent Australian case law' (2013) 36 *Melbourne University Law Review* 915–969.
118 [1999] HCA 49.
119 (2010) 194 FCR 142.
120 Ibid.
121 Ibid.
122 See headnote.
123 (2021) 201 FCR 173.
124 Ibid.
125 Ibid.
126 Evan H. Farr, 'Copyrightability of computer-generated works' (1989) 15 *The Rutgers Computer and Technology Law Journal* 63–74.
127 Ibid; see also Tuomas Sorjama, 'I, author – authorship and copyright in the age of artificial intelligence' (2016) at <https://helda.helsinki.fi/bitstream/handle/10138/166456/sorjamaa.pdf?sequence=3&isAllowed=y26> 47.
128 Emily Dorotheou, 'Reap the benefits and avoid the legal uncertainty: Who owns the creations of artificial intelligence?' (2015) 21(4) *Computer and Telecommunications Law Review* 85, 91; note Typically, the output is protected, but in the case of computer

programs, the code serves as the output. Therefore, it's feasible for the programmer to be unaware of what the AI will generate.

129 Tuomas Sorjama, 'I, author – Authorship and copyright in the age of artificial intelligence' (2016) at 47 at<https://helda.helsinki.fi/bitstream/handle/10138/166456/sorjamaa.pdf?sequence=3&isAllowed=y26>.

130 Evan H. Farr, 'Copyrightability of computer-generated works' (1989) 15 *Rutgers Computer and Technology Law Journal* 63, 65.

131 Julia Dickenson, Alex Morgan & Birgit Clark, 'Creative machines: Ownership of copyright in content created by Artificial Intelligence applications' (2017) 39 (8) *European Intellectual Property Review* 458, 459.

132 A. Michel, 'AI-generated creations: Challenging the traditional concept of copyright, a research into the question of works that are created by an artificial intelligence program have copyright protection in the Netherlands and the European Union' at <http://arno.uvt.nl/show.cgi?fid=148002>.

133 Ibid.

134 Westlaw AU, The Laws of Australia (online at 16 December 2020) 23 Intellectual Property, 23.1 'Copyright' [23.1.6390 n 2] ('The Laws of Australia').

135 See Mccullough Robertson, 'The legal 500 country comparative guides: Artificial intelligence in Australia' at <www.mccullough.com.au/2023/12/08/the-legal-500-country-comparative-guides-artificial-intelligence-in-australia/>.

136 See Survey and Mapping Infrastructure Act 2003 (Qld).

137 A. Dasgupta, 'Geospatial technology enabling workflows' (n.d.) at <www.geospatialworld.net/article/geospatial-technology-enabling-workflows/>.

138 Dimitrios Georgakopoulos & Mark Hornick, 'An overview of workflow management: From process modelling to workflow automation infrastructure' (1995) 3 *Distributed and Parallel Databases* 119–153; Dasgupta, A., n.d. *Geospatial technology enabling workflows*. Available from: <www.geospatialworld.net/article/geospatial-technology-enabling-workflows/>.

139 Dimitrios Georgakopoulos & Mark Hornick, 'An overview of workflow management: From process modelling to workflow automation infrastructure' (1995) 3 *Distributed and Parallel Databases* 119–153; Arup Dasgupta, 'Geospatial technology enabling workflows' at <www.geospatialworld.net/article/geospatial-technology-enabling-workflows/>.

140 Pil Kwon, 'Spatial data process using python script and visual programming language in ArcGIS' (2013) 4 *Computer Technology and Application* 275–283; Zdena Dobesova, 'Visual programming language in geographic information systems' at <www.researchgate.net/profile/ZdenaDobesova/publication/236586776_V_isual_programming_for_novice_programmers_in_geoinformatics/links/0deec52c812d2b90f3000000/V-isual-programming-for-novice-programmers-in-geoinformatics.pdf>.

141 Pil Kwon, 'Spatial data process using python script and visual programming language in ArcGIS' (2013) 4 *Computer Technology and Application* 275–283.

142 Ibid.

143 Section 10(1) *Copyright Act 1989*– definitions.

144 Pil Kwon, 'Spatial Spatial data process using python script and visual programming language in ArcGIS' (2013) 4 *Computer Technology and Application* 275–283.

145 Ashley Porter, 'Data access corporation v powerflex services Pvt Ltd' (1996) *ANZ-CompuLawJl* at <http://classic.austlii.edu.au/au/journals/ANZCompuLawJl/1996/32.html>.

146 Ibid.

147 Ibid.: 'something is not a "computer program" . . . unless it intends to express, either directly or indirectly, an algorithmic or logical relationship between the function desired to be performed and the physical capabilities of the [computer]'.

148 *EIFY Systems Pty Ltd v 3D Safety Services Pty Ltd* [2017] NSWSC 1310 (EIFY v 3D).

149 Hwlebswort Lawyers, 'Copyright in computer programs' (2018) at <https://hwlebsworth.com.au/copyright-in-computer-programs/; *EIFY Systems Pty Ltd v 3D Safety Services Pty Ltd* [2017] NSWSC 1310 (EIFY v 3D).
150 Jani McCutcheon, 'The vanishing author in computer-generated works' (2013) 36 *Melbourne University Law Review* 915.
151 *IceTV Pty Ltd v Nine Network Australia Pty Ltd* – [2009] HCA 14.
152 Jani McCutcheon, 'The vanishing author in computer-generated works' (2013) 36 *Melbourne University Law Review* 915.
153 *Autodesk Inc v Dyason* (AutoCAD case) [1992] HCA 2; (1992) 173 CLR 330 (12 February 1992).
154 Ibid.
155 Aerial Photography at <https://encyclopedia.pub/entry/37289>; see also Yuncheng Lu et al., 'A survey on vision-based UAV navigation' (2018) 21 (1) *Geo-Spatial Information Science* 21–32.
156 L. L. Bella, *Drones and Entertainment* (Rosen Publishing, New York, 2017).
157 Section 10(1) of the *Copyright Act (Cth)*.
158 Oxford Dictionary.
159 See Jani McCutcheon, 'Point and shoot: originality, authorship, and the identification of the copyright work in modern photography' (2021) 43(2) *Sydney Law Review* 163.
160 See Isabella Alexander & Marlena Jankowska, 'Rights in geospatial information: A shifting legal terrain' (2018) 3 (41) *Melbourne University Law Review* 957, 979.
161 Artistic work means a painting, sculpture, drawing, engraving, or photograph, whether the work is of artistic quality or not.
162 Section 2 of the *New Zealand Copyright Act 1994*. [A]rtistic work – (a) means – (i) a graphic work, photograph, sculpture, collage, or model, irrespective of artistic quality; or (ii) a work of architecture, being a building or a model for a building; or (iii) a work of artistic craftsmanship, not falling within subparagraph (i) or subparagraph (ii); but (b) does not include a layout design or an integrated circuit within the meaning of section 2 of the Layout Designs Act 1994.
163 C. Cronin, 'Symposium: possession is 99% of the law: 3D printing, public domain cultural artefacts and copyright' (2016) 17 (2) *Minnesota Journal of Law, Science & Technology* 709.
164 Digital Platforms Inquiry Final Report p. 258–259; *Sands & McDougall Pty Ltd v Robinson* (1917) 23 CLR 49.
165 *Weller & Anor v Smith* [2016] FCCA 2822 (4 November 2016).
166 Ibid.
167 Section 10(1) *Copyright Act 1968* (Cth) – Author, in relation to a photograph, means the person who took the photograph.
168 Australian Copyright Council, *Photograph and Copyright* at 6.
169 *Pokemon Company International, Inc. v Redbubble Ltd* [2017] FCA 1541 (19 December 2017).
170 *Ian Cubitts Classic Home Improvements Pty Ltd v Granny Flat Projects* [2015] FCCA 2630 (30 September 2015).
171 *Seafolly Pty Limited v Fewstone Pty Ltd* [2014] FCA 321 (1 April 2014).
172 Australian Copyright Council, *Photograph and copyright*.
173 Justine Pila, 'Works of artistic craftsmanship in the high court of Australia: The exception as paradigm copyright work' (2008) 36 (3) *Federal Law Review* 363; *Burge v Swarbrick* [2007] HCA 17; (2007) 234 ALR 204; 81 ALJR 950 (26 April 2007).
174 *IceTV Pty Ltd v Nine Network Australia Pty Ltd* – [2009] HCA 14.
175 Section 10(1) of the *Copyright Act 1968 (Cth); Grant Matthews v ACP Publishing Pty Ltd* (includes corrigendum dated 18 December 1998) [1998] FCA 1122 (10 September 1998); *Corby v Allen & Unwin Pty Limited* [2013] FCA 370 (24 April 2013); *Verrocchi v Direct Chemist Outlet Pty Ltd* [2015] FCA 234 (17 March 2015).

176 Jani McCutcheon, 'Point and shoot: Originality, authorship, and the identification of the copyright work in modern photography' (2021) 43(2) *Sydney Law Review* 163.
177 Ibid.
178 *Burrow – Giles Lithographic Co v Sarony*, 111 US 53 (1884) (US).
179 *Mannion v Coors Brewing*, 377 F Supp 2d 444 (SDNY, 2005) (US).
180 *Painer v Standard VerlagsGmbH* (Court of Justice of the European Union, C-145/10, ECLI:EU:C:2011:798, 1 December 2011) (EU).
181 Cadastral Survey Requirements (n.d.) at <www.resources.qld.gov.au/?a=109113:policy_registry/cadastral-survey-requirements.pdf&ver=7.10>.
182 Heiko Richter, 'Copyright protection of government-related material before the courts of the United States and Canada: Considerations for future reforms' (2021) 52 *IIC-International Review of Intellectual Property and Competition Law* 6–33.
183 [2007] FCAFC 80.
184 Section 176(2) of the *Copyright Act 1968* (Cth).
185 Section 177 of the *Copyright Act 1968* (Cth)
186 See also Anne Fitzgerald, 'Crown copyright' (2011) at <https://ses.library.usyd.edu.au/bitstream/handle/2123/7326/FitzgeraldA_9781920899714_TEXT.pdf?sequence=1&isAllowed=y>.
187 Id, para 6.
188 Paras 121–131.
189 *Copyright Agency v New South Wales* [2008] HCA 35; 233 CLR 279; 78 IPR 1.
190 In the context of legislation, the 'purpose approach' is a method of interpreting and applying a law by looking at the *underlying purpose or objective of the law*.
191 Digital Land Surveys, 'Copyright and the digital economy: Submission in respect of question 34' at <www.alrc.gov.au/wp-content/uploads/2019/08/27.__org__digital-landsurveys.pdf>.
192 [2008] HCA 35.
193 Australian Law Reform Commission, 'Crown use of copyright material' at <www.alrc.gov.au/publication/copyright-and-the-digital-economy-ip-42/crown-use-of-copyright-material/>.
194 See especially section 182C.
195 Para 16.
196 Section 183A (2) of the *Copyright Act 1968 (Cth)* [Emphasis added].
197 See Brian Fitzgerald & Benedict Atkinson, 'Third-party copyright and public information infrastructure/registries: How much copyright tax must the public pay?' In M. Perry & B. Fitzgerald (eds), *Knowledge Policy for the 21st Century: A Legal Perspective* (Irwin Law Inc., Toronto, 2011) Canada at 225–268.
198 Para 44.
199 Para 45.
200 [2007] FCAFC 80, para 155.
201 Para 43.
202 Ibid.
203 Paras 48–60.
204 Paras 46–47.
205 Para 70.
206 See Brian Fitzgerald & Atkinson Benedict, 'Third-party copyright and public information infrastructure/registries: How much copyright tax must the public pay?' In M. Perry & B. Fitzgerald (eds), *Knowledge Policy for the 21st Century: A Legal Perspective* (Irwin Law Inc., 2011) Canada at 225–268.
207 The Australian decision of *Achos Pty Ltd v. R.A. Bashford Pty Ltd* (1997) 37 I.P.R. 542, 562.
208 17 U.S.C. § 204(a).
209 Boryana Zeitz, 'How high is up: Interstitial dilemmas in nonexclusive copyright licensing cases in the ninth circuit' (2004) 11 *The UCLA Entertainment Law Review* 429.

210 John S. Sieman, 'Using the implied license to inject common sense into digital copyright' (2007) 85 *The North Carolina Law Review* 885.
211 Michael J. Swope, 'Recent developments in patent law: Implied license – An emerging threat to contributory infringement protection' (1995) 68 *Temple Law Review* 287 at 305.
212 WIPO, 'Starting an open data initiative | Data' (13 May 2021) at <https://opendatatoolkit.worldbank.org/en/data/opendatatoolkit/starting>.
213 Ibid.
214 *Open Government Data: Towards Empirical Analysis of Open Government Data Initiatives*, (OECD Working Papers on Public Governance No 22, 27 May 2013) 6 at <www.oecd- ilibrary.org/governance/open-government-data_5k46bj4f03s7-en> ('*Open Government Data*').
215 Ibid.
216 Ibid., 8.
217 Ibid., 30.
218 Deloitte, 'Open by default: Revisiting open data in government' at <https://www2.deloitte.com/content/dam/Deloitte/au/Documents/public-sector/deloitte-au-ps-revisiting-open-data-government-300120.pdf>.
219 Data Sharing (Government Sector) Act 2015 No 60 at <https://legislation.nsw.gov.au/view/whole/html/inforce/current/act-2015-060>.
220 See South Australia Public Sector (Data Sharing) Act 2016 at <www.legislation.sa.gov.au/__legislation/lz/v/a/2016/public%20sector%20(data%20sharing)%20act%202016_61/2016.61.un.pdf>.
221 See Victorian Data Sharing Act 2017 at <www.legislation.vic.gov.au/in-force/acts/victorian-data-sharing-act-2017/002>; also see Victorian Public Sector Data Sharing Policy at <www.data.vic.gov.au/victorian-public-sector-data-sharing-policy>.
222 See Queensland Government Open Data Policy Statement at Queensland Government Open Data Policy Statement at <www.data.qld.gov.au/_resources/documents/qld-data-policy-statement.pdf>.
223 See Open Data Policy at <https://data.wa.gov.au/sites/default/files/Open%20Data%20Policy%20v2%202022.pdf>
224 See Administrative Data Exchange Protocol for Tasmania at <www.dpac.tas.gov.au/divisions/digital_strategy_and_services/policies/digital_data_privacy/adept>.
225 See generally, Professor John McMillan, Open Public Sector Information – from Principles to Practice (Office of the Australian Information Commissioner, 2013).
226 Productivity Commission, 'Data availability and use' (Productivity Commission Inquiry Report No 82, 31 March 2017) (*Productivity Commission Inquiry Report*).
227 Ibid., 65.
228 [2010] FCAFC 149.
229 Productivity Commission Inquiry Report.
230 Ibid., 139.
231 Australian Data Strategy: The Australian Government's Whole-of-Economy Vision for Data at <www.finance.gov.au/sites/default/files/2022-10/australian-data-strategy.pdf>.
232 Ibid., 30.
233 [2008] HCA 35.
234 PricewaterhouseCoopers, 'Understanding the costs and benefits of introducing a 'fair use' exception' (February 2016), Executive Summary at <www.screenrights.org/wp-content/uploads/2017/10/PwC_Fair_Dealing_CBA_Final.pdf> ('*PwC – 'fair use' exception*').
235 Ibid.
236 Section 10 of the Act.
237 Section 47B of the *Copyright Act 1968 (Cth)*.
238 Ibid., s 47C.

239 Ibid., s 47D.
240 Ibid., s 47E.
241 Ibid., s 47F.
242 Ibid., sections 47G, 47H.
243 Sections 40–43 of the *Copyright Act 1968 (Cth)*.
244 Ibid.
245 Australian Law Reform Commission, 'What is fair use' (2013) 2 December at <www.alrc.gov.au/publication/copyright-and-the-digital-economy-alrc-report-122/4-the-case-for-fair-use/what-is-fair-use-2/>.
246 Australian Law Reform Commission, 'Data and text mining' (2012) 16 August at <www.alrc.gov.au/publication/copyright-and-the-digital-economy-ip-42/data-and-text-mining/>; Australian Law Reform Commission, 'Text and data mining' (2013) 4 June at <www.alrc.gov.au/publication/copyright-and-the-digital-economy-dp-79/8-non- consumptive-use/text-and-data-mining/>.
247 Ibid.
248 PricewaterhouseCoopers, 'Understanding the costs and benefits of introducing a "fair use" exception' (February 2016), Executive Summary at <www.screenrights.org/wp-content/uploads/2017/10/PwC_Fair_Dealing_CBA_Final.pdf> ('*PwC – 'fair use' exception*').
249 See Copyright Law Review Committee Reports at <https://www8.austlii.edu.au/cgi-bin/viewdoc/au/other/lawreform/CLRC/1998/13.html>.
250 Australian Law Reform Commission, 'Data and Text Mining' (16 August 2012) at <www.alrc.gov.au/publication/copyright-and-the-digital-economy-ip-42/data-and-text-mining/>.
251 *Ice Tv Pty Ltd v Nine Network Australia Pty Ltd* (2009) 239 CLR 458.
252 Australian Law Reform Commission, 'Copyright and the digital economy' (30 November 2013) at <www.alrc.gov.au/wp-content/uploads/2019/08/final_report_alrc_122_2nd_december_2013_.pdf>, at 38, 255.
253 Ibid., 256.
254 Ibid., 257–259.
255 Ibid., 260–263.
256 Australian Law Reform Commission, 'Data and text mining' at <www.alrc.gov.au/publication/copyright-and-the-digital-economy-alrc-report-122/11-incidental-or-technical-use-and-data-and-text-mining/data-and-text-mining-2/>.
257 Productivity Commission, *Data Availability and Use* (Productivity Commission Inquiry Report No 82, 31 March 2017) (*Productivity Commission Inquiry Report*) at 485.
258 See Anne Fitzgerald, Kylie Pappalardo & Anthony Austin, *Understanding the Legal Implications of Data Sharing, Access and Reuse in the Australian Research Landscape* (Sydney University Press, Sydney, 2008).
259 Katleen Janssen & Jos Dumortier, 'The protection of maps and spatial databases in Europe and the United States by copyright and the Sui Generis Right' (2006) 24 (2) *UIC John Marshall Journal of Information Technology & Privacy Law* 196.
260 Section 31 of *Copyright Act 1968 (Cth)*.
261 Status Report on the Protection Against Unfair Competition in WIPO Member States available at <www.wipo.int/export/sites/www/sct/en/meetings/pdf/wipo-strad-inf-8-prov.pdf> at 180.
262 Paris Convention for the Protection of Industrial Property, 10bis (2).
263 Competition Policy and Intellectual Property Rights 1997, OECD at 73.
264 See J. H. Reichman & Pamela Samuelson, 'Intellectual Property Rights in Data' at <https://scholarship.law.duke.edu/cgi/viewcontent.cgi?article=1402&context=faculty_scholarship> at 67.

265 The Value of Spatial Information: The impact of modern spatial information technologies on the Australian economy (2008) at <www.crcsi.com.au/assets/Resources/7d60411d-0ab9-45be-8d48-ef8dab5abd4a.pdf>.
266 *Copyright Agency Limited v State of New South Wales* [2008] HCA 35.
267 *Conveyancing Act* 1919 (NSW) s 195c.
268 *Telstra Corp Ltd v Phone Directories Co Pty Ltd.*
269 See United Nations Committee of Experts on Global Geospatial Information Management, 'Future trends in geospatial information management: The five to ten year vision' at <https://ggim.un.org/meetings/GGIM-committee/10th-Session/documents/Future_Trends_Report_THIRD_EDITION_digital_accessible.pdf>.
270 GIS for environmental impact Assessment at <www.gispeople.com.au/gis-for-environmental-impact-assessment/>.
271 Productivity Commission, *Data Availability and Use* 2017 p. 113.
272 Roger A. Longhorn, Victoria Henson-Apollonio & Jeffrey W. White, 'Legal issues in the use of geospatial data and tools for agriculture and natural resource management: A primer' at <https://repository.cimmyt.org/bitstream/handle/10883/905/447972.pdf?sequence=4&isAllowed=y>.
273 World Intellectual Property Organization, Agreement on Trade-Related Aspects of Intellectual Property Rights, Article 39 (2).
274 Nyuk Yin Nahan, 'The duty of confidence revisited: The protection of confidential information' (2015) 39 (2) *University of Western Australia Law Review* 270–293.
275 Ibid.
276 *Saltman Engineering Co Ltd v Campbell Engineering Co Ltd* (1948) 65 RPC 203.
277 *Australian Medic-Care Company Ltd v Hamilton Pharmaceutical Pty Limited* (ACN 008 204 635) [2009] FCA 1220 (30 October 2009).
278 *Thales Australia Limited v Madritsch KG & Anor* [2022] QCA 205 (21 October 2022).
279 *Commonwealth v John Fairfax & Sons Ltd* (1980) 147 CLR 39.
280 *Coco v A N Clark (Engineers) Ltd* [1969] RPC 41.
281 Isabella Alexander & Marlena Jankowska, 'Rights in geospatial information: A shifting legal terrain' (2018) 3 (41) *Melbourne University Law Review* 957.
282 Wiersma Mulder & Bastiaan van Loenen, 'Status of national open spatial data infrastructures: A comparison across continents' (2020) 15 *International Journal of Spatial Data Infrastructures Research* 56–87.
283 *Surveys & Mining Ltd v Morrison* [1969] Qd R 470.
284 Ibid.
285 Section 195c of the *Conveyancing Act of New South Wales 1919*.
286 Wiersma Mulder & Loenen, 'Status of national open spatial data infrastructures: A comparison across continents' (2020) *International Journal of Spatial Data Infrastructures Research*; Productivity Commission, *Data Availability and Use*.
287 An overview and update on the protection of trade secrets in Australia, Bird and Bird.
288 *Corporations Act 2001 (Cth).*
289 *Competition and Consumer Act 2010 (Cth).*
290 Section 52ZA *of the Competition and Consumer Act 2010(Cth).*
291 Ibid.
292 An overview and update on the protection of trade secrets in Australia, Bird and Bird at <www.twobirds.com/-/media/pdfs/in-focus/trade-secrets/trade-secrets-points-to-note-article-series–australia–september-2020.pdf>.
293 S. Davidson, P. de Filippi & J. Potts, 'Blockchains and the economic institutions of capitalism' 2018 14 (4) *Journal of Institutional Economics* 639.
294 Mohd Javaid et al., 'A review of blockchain technology applications for financial services' (2022) 2 (3) *BenchCouncil Transactions on Benchmarks, Standards and Evaluations* 100073.

295 Aaron M. Lane & Christina Platz, 'The other side of the ledger: Blockchain makes a new entry in the historical record of copyright law and technology' (2021) 43 (2) *European Intellectual Property Review* 83–97; Annabel Tresise, Jake Goldenfein & Dan Hunter, 'What blockchain can and can't do for copyright' (2018) 28 *Australian Intellectual Property Journal* 144.
296 Annabel Tresise, Jake Goldenfein & Dan Hunter, 'What blockchain can and can't do for copyright' (2018) 28 *Australian Intellectual Property Journal* 144.
297 Ibid.
298 Michele Finck & Valentina Moscon, 'Copyright law on blockchains: Between new forms of rights administration and digital rights management 2.0' (2019) 50 *International Review of Intellectual Property and Competition Law* 77–108.
299 Annabel Tresise, Jake Goldenfein & Dan Hunter, 'What blockchain can and can't do for copyright' (2018) 28 *Australian Intellectual Property Journal* 144.
300 Ibid.
301 Jessie Willms, 'Is blockchain-powered copyright protection possible?' *Bitcoin Magazine* (9 August 2016) at <https://perma.cc/9V88-K8ES>; Alexander Savelyev, 'Copyright in the blockchain era: Promises and challenges' (2018) 34 (3) *Computer Law & Security Review* 550–561.
302 Sinclair Davidson, Primavera de Filippi & Jason Potts, 'Blockchains and the economi institutions of capitalism' (2018) 14(4) *Journal of Institutional Economics* 639.
303 Michele Finck & Valentina Moscon, 'Copyright law on blockchains: Between new forms of rights administration and digital rights management 2.0' (2019) 50 *International Review of Intellectual Property and Competition Law* 77–108.
304 Denise Rosemary Nicholson, 'Digital rights management and access to information: A developing country's perspective' (2009) 19 (1) *Library and Information Science Research Electronic Journal* 1–17; Eric A. Robinson, 'Digital rights management, fair use, and privacy: Problems for copyright enforcement through technology' (2009) at <https://soar.usa.edu/cgi/viewcontent.cgi?article=1012&context=other>; Brian Fitzgerald et al., *Copyright Law, Digital Content and the Internet in the Asia-Pacific* (Sydney University Press, Sydney, 2008) at 260–261.
305 Sections 116A, 116B, 116C, 116AQ(1)(c), 132APC, D, E of the *Australian Copyright Act 1968 (Cth)*.
306 A. E. Mulder, M. G. Wiersma & L. B. van, 'Status of national open spatial data infrastructures: A comparison across continents' (2020) 15 *International Journal of Spatial Data Infrastructures Research* 68.
307 Isabella Alexander & Marlena Jankowska, 'Rights in geospatial information: A shifting legal terrain' (2018) *Melbourne Law Review* 957–998.
308 Section 52ZA *of the Competition and Consumer Act 2010 (Cth)*.
309 Annabel Tresise, Jake Goldenfein & Dan Hunter, 'What blockchain can and can't do for copyright' (2018) 28 *Australian Intellectual Property Journal* 144.
310 Brydon Wang, 'Blockchain and the law' (2016) 19 (1) *Internet Law Bulletin* 250–254, see also B. Bodó, D. Gervais & J. P. Quintais, 'Blockchain and smart contracts: The missing link in copyright licensing?' (2018) 26 (4) *International Journal of Law and Information Technology* 311–336.
311 An Introduction to Smart Contracts and Their Potential and Inherent Limitations (2018) at <https://corpgov.law.harvard.edu/2018/05/26/an-introduction-to-smart-contracts-and-their- potential-and-inherent-limitations/.
312 Alexander Savelyev, 'Copyright in the blockchain era: Promises and challenges' (2018) 34 (3) *Computer Law & Security Review* 550–561.
313 same as 310.
314 Alexander Savelyev, 'Copyright in the blockchain era: Promises and challenges' (2018) 34 (3) *Computer Law & Security Review* 550–561.
315 B. Daho, 'Crypto-spatial: An open standards smart contracts library for building geospatially enabled decentralized applications on the Ethereum blockchain' (2020)

International Archives of the Photogrammetry, Remote Sensing and Spatial Information Sciences 421–426; Pengxiang Zhao et al., 'Towards geospatial blockchain: A review of research on blockchain technology applied to geospatial data' (2022) at <https://agile giss.copernicus.org/articles/3/71/2022/agile-giss-3-71-2022.pdf>.

316 Alexander Savelyev, 'Copyright in the blockchain era: Promises and challenges' (2018) 34 (3) *Computer Law & Security Review* 550–561.

317 Ibid.

318 Wang Zimu, 'Blockchain technology: Opportunities and challenges in copyright industry' (2021) *18th International Computer Conference on Wavelet Active Media Technology and Information Processing (ICCWAMTIP)*.

319 Aaron M. Lane & Christina Platz, 'The other side of the ledger: Blockchain makes a new entry in the historical record of copyright law and technology' (2021) 43 (2) *European Intellectual Property Review* 83–97.

320 Anna Duke, 'What does the CISG have to say about smart contracts? A legal analysis' (2019) *Chicago Journal of International Law* 141–177.

321 Kevin Werbach & Nicolas Cornell, 'Contracts Ex Machina' (2017) 67 *Duke Law Journal* 313; Tatiana Cutts, 'Smart contracts and consumers' (2019) 122 (2) *Western Virginia Law Review* 389; Spencer Williams, 'Edge contracts' (2023) 25 (3) *University of Pennsylvania Journal of Business Law* 839.

322 Wang Zimu, 'Blockchain technology: Opportunities and challenges in copyright industry' (2021) *18th International Computer Conference on Wavelet Active Media Technology and Information Processing (ICCWAMTIP)* at 119.

323 Annabel Tresise, Jake Goldenfein & Dan Hunter, 'What blockchain can and can't do for copyright' (2018) 28 *Australian Intellectual Property Journal* 144.

324 Seungju Lee, Jaewook Lee & Yunyoung Lee, 'Dissecting the terra-LUNA crash: Evidence from the spillover effect and information flow' (2023) 53 *Finance Research Letters*; Forbes Magazine, 'What really happened to LUNA crypto?' <www.forbes.com/sites/qai/2022/09/20/what-really-happened-to-luna-crypto/>; Stylianos Kampakis, 'Auditing tokenomics: A case study and lessons from auditing a stablecoin project' (2022) 5 (2) *The JBBA* 1–7.

325 See the Future of Geospatial Data Collection Blockchain and Distributed Ledger Technology (2023) at <https://utilitiesone.com/the-future-of-geospatial-data-collection-blockchain-and-distributed-ledger-technology>.

326 House of Representatives Standing Committee on Legal and Constitutional Affairs, Review of technological protection measures exceptions, February 2006 Canberra, The Parliament of the Commonwealth of Australia, ISBN 0 642 78764 6, p. 7.

327 Article 18, WIPO Performance and phonogram treaty:

> contracting parties shall provide adequate and effective legal remedies against any person knowingly performing any of the following acts knowing, or with respect to civil remedies having reasonable grounds to know, that it will induce, enable, facilitate or conceal an infringement of any right covered.

328 Article 11, WIPO Copyright treaty:

> contracting parties shall provide adequate legal protection and effective legal remedies against the circumvention of effective technological measures that are used by authors in connection with the exercise of their rights under this treaty or the Berne convention and that restricts acts, in respect of their works, which are not authorized by authors concerned or permitted by law.

329 *Copyright Amendment (Digital Agenda) Act 2000 (Cth)*.

330 Section 116A(1)(b)(vi).

331 Section 10 of the Act.

332 House of Representatives Committees, 'Review of technological protection measures exceptions' at <www.aph.gov.au/Parliamentary_Business/Committees/House_of_Representatives_Committees.aspx?url=laca/protection/chapter2.htm>.
333 *Stevens v Kabushiki Kaisha Sony Computer Entertainment* [2005] HCA 58 at [47].
334 Ibid.
335 House of Representatives Standing Committee on Legal and Constitutional Affairs, Advisory Report on the Copyright Amendment (Digital Agenda) Bill 1999, November 1999, p. 60.
336 Man Yiu et al., 'Enabling search services on outsourced private spatial data' (2010) 19 *The International Journal on Very Large Databases* 363.
337 Ibid.
338 Ibid., at 382.
339 Ibid., at 363.
340 Ibid., at 364.
341 Sangita Zope-Chaudhari & P. Venkatachalam, 'Conceptual framework for geospatial data security' 2013 5(5) *International Journal of Database Management Systems* 29, 35.
342 Ibid.
343 Preston de Guise, *Data Protection: Ensuring Data Availability* (Aurebach Publishers, New York, 2020), Chapter 9 'Security, privacy, ethical and legal considerations' at 92.
344 Ibid.
345 Ibid., at 94.
346 Jerome Johnson, *Copyright and Online Technologies* (Australian Copyright Council, Strawberry Hills, NSW, 2013) at 27.
347 Ibid.
348 Ibid.
349 Ibid., at 28–9.
350 See Katleen Janssen & Jos Dumortier, 'The protection of maps and spatial databases in Europe and the United States by copyright and the Sui Generis right' (2006) 24 (2) *UIC John Marshall Journal of Information Technology & Privacy Law* 195–225.
351 Katleen Janssen & Jos Dumortier, 'The protection of maps and spatial databases in Europe and the United states by copyright and the Sui Generis right' (2006) 24 (2) *UIC John Marshall Journal of Information Technology & Privacy Law* at 197.
352 Ibid.
353 Ibid.
354 Ibid., at 214.
355 Article 7 of the Directive.
356 Data Protection at <https://europa.eu/youreurope/business/running-business/intellectual-property/database-protection/index_en.htm>.
357 M. Davison, 'Sui generis or too generous: legislative protection of databases, its implications for Australia and some suggestions for reform' (1998) 21 (3) *UNSW Law Journal* 729–730.
358 G. Cho, 'Legal dilemmas in geographic information: Property, ownership and patents' (1995) 6 (2) *Journal of Law, Information and Science* 193.
359 João Bachiega Jr., Maristela Holanda & Aleteia P. F. Araujo, 'A proposal to minimize the cost of processing big geospatial data in public cloud providers' (2021) 25 (3) *Transactions in GIS* at <https://doi.org/10.1111/tgis.12754>; Isabella Alexander and Marlena Jankowska, 'Rights in geospatial information: A shifting legal terrain' (2018) *Melbourne University Law Review* 962.
360 Carlos López, 'Watermarking of digital geospatial datasets: A review of technical, legal and copyright issues' (2002) 16 (6) *International Journal of Geographical Information Science* 589–607.
361 Productivity Commission, 'Data availability and use' (2017) at 113.

362 João Bachiega Jr., Maristela Holanda & Aleteia P. F, Araujo, 'A proposal to minimize the cost of processing big geospatial data in public cloud providers' (2021) 25 (3) *Transactions in GIS* at <https://doi.org/10.1111/tgis.12754>.

363 Reto M. Hilty, Jörg Hoffmann & Stefan Scheuerer, *Intellectual Property Justification for Artificial Intelligence* (2021) In book: *Artificial Intelligence and Intellectual Property* 50–72.

364 Ibid.

365 William D. Nordhaus, *Invention, Growth, and Welfare: A Theoretical Treatment of Technological Change* (M.I.T. Press, Cambridge, 1969); Andreas Von Gunten, *Intellectual Property Is Common Property: Arguments for the Abolition of Private Intellectual Property Rights* (Buch & Netz, Zürich, 2015).

366 Reto M. Hilty, Jörg Hoffmann & Stefan Scheuerer, *Intellectual Property Justification for Artificial Intelligence* (2021) In book: Artificial Intelligence and Intellectual Property (pp. 50–72).

367 Ibid.

368 Australian Government Cost Recovery Guidelines (RMG 304), Data Availability and Use at<www.crcsi.com.au/assets/Resources/ANZLIC-Economic-Study-Stage-1-Report.pdf> at 49; also see at <www.pc.gov.au/inquiries/completed/cost-recovery/submissions/australian_surveying_and_land_information_group/subdr131.pdf>.

369 Directive 96/9/EC of the European Parliament and of the Council of 11 March 1996 at <https://eur-lex.europa.eu/legal-content/EN/TXT/PDF/?uri=CELEX:31996L0009&from=EN>.

370 Directive 96/9/EC Article 1.

371 Directive 96/9/EC Article 1.

372 Directive 96/9/EC Article 7.

373 Sandra Gosnell, 'Database protection down under: Would a "sweaty" Australia be better off with a Northerly change?' (2003) 26(3) *UNSW Law Journal* 639.

374 Mark Schneider, 'The European union database directive' (1998) 13 *The Berkeley Technology Law Journal* 551.

375 *Freistaat Bayern v Verlag Esterbauer GmbH* Case C-490/14; Fieldfisher, *The CJEU confirms a topographic map is a database*, 2015 at <www.fieldfisher.com/en/services/intellectual-property/intellectual-property-blog/the-cjeu-confirms-a-topographic-map-is-a-database>; Gilles Bessero, 'Copyright case law: A map is a database' (2016) *International Hydrographic Review* 37–38.

376 Isabella Alexander & Marlena Jankowska, 'Rights in geospatial information: A shifting legal terrain' (2018) *Melbourne University Law Review*; Sandra Gosnell, 'Database protection down under: would a 'sweaty' Australia be better off with a Northerly change?' (2003) *University of New South Wales Law Journal* 639.

377 Productivity Commission, *Data Availability and Use*, 2017.

378 Alexander & Jankowska; Romana Matanovac Vučković, Ivana Kanceljak and Marko Jurić, *Is It Time for New Data Governance*, MIPRO 2021, 27 September – 1 October 2021, Opatija, Croatia.

379 Pengxiang Zhao et al., 'Towards geospatial blockchain: A review of research on blockchain technology applied to geospatial data' (2022) *AGILE: GIScience Series* 3, 71, at <https://agile- giss.copernicus.org/articles/3/71/2022/agile-giss-3-71-2022.pdf>.

380 Commonwealth of Australia, *Data and the Digital Economy* (2021) <https://digital-economy.pmc.gov.au/sites/default/files/2022-03/factsheet-data-and-digital-economy-0322–2.pdf>.

381 Productivity Commission, *Data Availability and Use* (2017) at 71.

382 Romana Matanovac Vučković, Ivana Kanceljak & Marko Jurić, 'Is It Time for New Data Governance', *2021 44th International Convention on Information, Communication and Electronic Technology (MIPRO)*.

References

Achos Pty Ltd v. R.A. Bashford Pty Ltd, 1997, 37 I.P.R. 542, 562.

Acohs Pty Ltd v Ucorp Pty Ltd.

Ahmed, A. and Mihaela, C., 2017. Advancements in GIS map copyright protection schemes – A critical review. *Multimedia Tools and Applications,* 76, 12205–12231.

Alexander, I. and Jankowska, M., 2018. Rights in geospatial information: A shifting legal terrain. *Melbourne University Law Review,* 3 (41), 957–979.

Arts+Law, n.d. Copyright. Available from: <www.artslaw.com.au/information-sheet/copyright/>.

Attorney-General's Department, 2023. Submission P61, 11 November.

Australia–US Free Trade Agreement, Australian Treaty Series [2005] ATS 1.

Australian Competition and Consumer Act 2010 (Cth).

Australian Competition and Consumer Commission, 2019. Digital platforms inquiry final report. Available from: <www.accc.gov.au/about-us/publications/digital-platforms-inquiry-final-report>.

Australian Copyright Act 1968 (Cth).

Australian Copyright Council, n.d. *Photograph and copyright*. Available from: https://www.copyright.org.au/browse/book/Frances-Coyne-Photographers-&-Copyright-9781920778439

Australian Government, n.d.-a. Australian data strategy: The Australian government's whole-of-economy vision for data. Available from: <www.finance.gov.au/sites/default/files/2022-10/australian-data-strategy.pdf>.

Australian Government, n.d.-b. Cost Recovery Guidelines (RMG 304): Data availability and use. Available from: <www.crcsi.com.au/assets/Resources/ANZLIC-Economic-Study-Stage-1-Report.pdf> at 49.

Australian Law Reform Commission, 2012. Data and text mining, 16 August. Available from: <www.alrc.gov.au/publication/copyright-and-the-digital-economy-ip-42/data-and-text-mining/>.

Australian Law Reform Commission, 2013a. Copyright and the digital economy, 30 November. Available from: <www.alrc.gov.au/wp-content/uploads/2019/08/final_report_alrc_122_2nd_december_2013_.pdf>.

Australian Law Reform Commission, 2013b. Text and data mining, 4 June. Available from: <www.alrc.gov.au/publication/copyright-and-the-digital-economy-dp-79/8-non- consumptive-use/text-and-data-mining/>.

Australian Law Reform Commission, 2013c. What is fair use, 2 December. Available from: <www.alrc.gov.au/publication/copyright-and-the-digital-economy-alrc-report-122/4-the-case-for-fair-use/what-is-fair-use-2/>.

Australian Law Reform Commission, n.d. Genetic databases. Available from: <www.alrc.gov.au/publication/genes-and-ingenuity-gene-patenting-and-human-health-alrc-report-99/28-copyright-and-databases/genetic-databases/#_ftn43>.

Australian Medic-Care Company Ltd v Hamilton Pharmaceutical Pty Limited (ACN 008 204 635) [2009] FCA 1220, 30 October.

Autodesk Inc v Dyason (AutoCAD case) [1992] HCA 2; (1992) 173 CLR 330, 12 February.

Bachiega, J., Jr., Holanda, M., and Araujo, A.P.F., 2021. A proposal to minimize the cost of processing big geospatial data in public cloud providers. *Transactions in GIS,* 25 (3). <https://doi.org/10.1111/tgis.12754>

Bella, L.L., 2017. *Drones and entertainment*. New York: Rosen Publishing.

Bessero, G., 2016. Copyright case law: A map is a database. *International Hydrographic Review*, 37–38.

Bird and Bird, n.d. Trade secrets: An overview and update on the protection of trade secrets in Australia. Available from: <www.twobirds.com/-/media/pdfs/in-focus/trade-secrets/trade-secrets-points-to-note-article-series-australia-september-2020.pdf>.

Bodó, B., Gervais, D., and Quintais, J.P., 2018. Blockchain and smart contracts: The missing link in copyright licensing? *International Journal of Law and Information Technology,* 26 (4), 311–336.

Britannica, n.d. Compilation. Avilable from: <www.britannica.com/science/map/Map-projections>.

Burge v Swarbrick [2007] HCA 17; (2007) 234 ALR 204; 81 ALJR 950 (26 April 2007).

Burrow – Giles Lithographic Co v Sarony, 111 US 53 (1884) (US).

Cadastre 2034, n.d. *Cadastral reform and innovation for Australia – A national strategy*. Available from: <www.icsm.gov.au/sites/default/files/Cadastre2034_0.pdf>.

Campaigntrack Pty Ltd v Real Estate Tool Box Pty Ltd [2021] FCA 809.

Cho, G., 1995. Legal dilemmas in geographic information: Property, ownership and patents. *Journal of Law, Information and Science*, 6 (2), 193.

Coco v A N Clark (Engineers) Ltd [1969] RPC 41.

Commonwealth of Australia, 2021. Data and the digital economy. Available from: <https://digitaleconomy.pmc.gov.au/sites/default/files/2022-03/factsheet-data-and-digital-economy-0322–2.pdf>.

Commonwealth v John Fairfax & Sons Ltd (1980) 147 CLR 39.

Competition and Consumer Act 2010 (Cth).

Conveyancing Act 1919 (NSW) s 195c.

Copyright Agency Limited v State of New South Wales [2008] HCA 35.

Copyright Amendment (Digital Agenda) Act 2000 (Cth).

Corby v Allen & Unwin Pty Limited [2013] FCA 370, 24 April.

Corporations Act 2001 (Cth).

Cronin, C., 2016. Symposium: Possession is 99% of the law: 3D printing, public domain cultural artefacts and copyright. *Minnesota Journal of Law, Science & Technology,* 17 (2), 709.

Cutts, T., 2019. Smart contracts and consumers. *Western Virginia Law Review,* 122 (2), 389.

Daho, B., 2020. Crypto-spatial: An open standards smart contracts library for building geo-spatially enabled decentralized applications on the Ethereum blockchain. *International Archives of the Photogrammetry, Remote Sensing and Spatial Information Sciences*, 421–426.

Dasgupta, A., n.d. Geospatial technology enabling workflows. Available from: <www.geo-spatialworld.net/article/geospatial-technology-enabling-workflows/>.

Davidson, S., de Filippi, P., and Potts, J., 2018. Blockchains and the economic institutions of capitalism. *Journal of Institutional Economics*, 14 (4), 639.

Davies Collison Save, n.d. High court of Australia rules on chipping of game consoles. Available from: <https://dcc.com/news-and-insights/high-court-%20of-australia-rules-on-chipping-of-game-consoles/>.

Davison, M., 1998. Sui generis or too generous: Legislative protection of databases, its implications for Australia and some suggestions for reform. *UNSW Law Journal*, 21 (3) 729–730.

de Guise, P., 2020. *Data protection: Ensuring data availability*. New York: Aurebach Publishers.

Deloitte, n.d. Open by default: Revisiting open data in government. Available from: <https://www2.deloitte.com/content/dam/Deloitte/au/Documents/public-sector/deloitte-au-ps-revisiting-open-data-government-300120.pdf>.

Desktop Marketing Systems Pty Ltd v Telstra Corporation [2002] FCAFC 112.

Desktop Marketing Systems Pty Ltd v Telstra Corporation Ltd (2002) 192 ALR 433.

Dickenson, J., Morgan, A., and Clark, B., 2017. Creative machines: Ownership of copyright in content created by artificial intelligence applications. *European Intellectual Property Review,* 39 (8), 458-459.

Digital Land Surveys, n.d. Copyright and the digital economy: Submission in respect of question 34. Available from: <www.alrc.gov.au/wp-content/uploads/2019/08/27.__org__digitallandsurveys.pdf>.

Directive 96/9/EC of the European Parliament and of the Council of 11 March 1996. Available from: <https://eur-lex.europa.eu/legal-content/EN/TXT/PDF/?uri=CELEX:31996L0009&from=EN>.

Dobesova, Z., n.d. Visual programming language in geographic information systems. <www.researchgate.net/profile/Zdena Dobesova/publication/236586776_V_isual_programming_for_novice_programmers_in_geoinformatics/links/0deec52c812d2b90f3000000/V-isual-programming-for-novice-programmers-in-geoinformatics.pdf>.

Dorotheou, E., 2015. Reap the benefits and avoid the legal uncertainty: Who owns the creations of artificial intelligence? *Computer and Telecommunications Law Review,* 21 (4), 85–91.

EIFY Systems Pty Ltd v 3D Safety Services Pty Ltd [2017] NSWSC 1310 (EIFY v 3D).

Farr, E.H., 1989. Copyrightability of computer-generated works. *The Rutgers Computer and Technology Law Journal,* 15, 63–74.

Fieldfisher, 2015. The CJEU confirms a topographic map is a database. Available from: <www.fieldfisher.com/en/services/intellectual- property/intellectual-property-blog/the-cjeu-confirms-a-topographic-map-is-a-database>.

Finck, M. and Moscon, V., 2019. Copyright law on blockchains: Between new forms of rights administration and digital rights management 2.0. *International Review of Intellectual Property and Competition Law,* 50, 77–108.

Fitzgerald, A., 2011. Crown copyright. Available from: <https://ses.library.usyd.edu.au/bitstream/handle/2123/7326/FitzgeraldA_9781920899714_TEXT.pdf?sequence=1&isAllowed=y>.

Fitzgerald, A., Pappalardo, K., and Austin, A., 2008. *Understanding the legal implications of data sharing, access and reuse in the Australian research landscape*. Sydney: Sydney University Press.

Fitzgerald, A. and Seidenspinner, T., 2013. Copyright and computer-generated materials – Is it time to reboot the discussion about authorship? *Victoria University Law and Justice Journal,* 3 (1), 37–42.

Fitzgerald, B. and Bartlett, C., 2002. Database protection under Australian copyright law: Desktop marketing systems Pty Ltd v Telstra Corporation [2002] FCAFC 112. Available from: <http://138.25.65.110/au/journals/SCULawRw/2003/8.pdf>

Fitzgerald, B., *et al.*, 2008. *Copyright law, digital content and the internet in the Asia-Pacific*. Sydney: Sydney University Press, 260–261.

Freistaat Bayern v Verlag Esterbauer GmbH Case C-490/14.

Gandi, A. and Olsen, M., 2021. AI, invention and authorship expanding intellectual property rights to non-human outputs. *INTLB,* 23 (7), 119.

Georgakopoulos, D. and Hornick, M., 1995. An overview of workflow management: From process modelling to workflow automation infrastructure. *Distributed and Parallel Databases,* 3, 119–153.

Golder, T. and Ladd, S., 2021. Copyright in software – The latest word from the Federal Court. Available from: <www.allens.com.au/insights-news/insights/2021/09/copyright-in-software-the-latest-word-from-the-federal-court/>.

Gosnell, S., 2003. Database protection down under: Would a 'sweaty' Australia be better off with a Northerly change? *University of New South Wales Law Journal,* 639.

Grant Matthews v ACP Publishing Pty Ltd (includes corrigendum dated 18 December 1998) [1998] FCA 1122 (10 September 1998).

Guadamuz, A., 2017. Artificial intelligence and copyright. *WIPO Magazine*. Available from: <www.wipo.int/wipo_magazine/en/2017/05/article_0003.html>.

Hilty, R.M., Hoffmann, J., and Scheuerer, S., 2021. Intellectual property justification for artificial intelligence. *Artificial Intelligence and Intellectual Property,* 50–72.

Honig, A., 2007. Copyright protection of databases under Australian law – Nine network Australia Pty Ltd v IceTV Pty Ltd' [2007] FCA 1172. Available from: <http://classic.austlii.edu.au/au/journals/ANZCompuLawJl/2007/13.pdf>.

House of Representatives Standing Committee on Legal and Constitutional Affairs, 1999 November. *Advisory report on the copyright amendment (digital agenda) bill 1999.*

House of Representatives Standing Committee on Legal and Constitutional Affairs, n.d. *Review of technological protection measures exceptions, February 2006 Canberra, The Parliament of the Commonwealth of Australia.*

HWL Ebsworth Lawyers, 2018. Copyright in computer programs. Available from: <https://hwlebsworth.com.au/copyright-in-computer-programs/>.

Ian Cubitts Classic Home Improvements Pty Ltd v Granny Flat Projects [2015] FCCA 2630 (30 September 2015).

Ice TV Pty Ltd v Nine Network Australia Pty Ltd (2009) 239 CLR 458.

IceTV Pty Limited v Nine Network Australia Pty Limited [2009] HCA 14.

Janssen, K. and Dumortier, J., 2006. The protection of maps and spatial databases in Europe and the United States by copyright and the Sui Generis Right. *UIC John Marshall Journal of Information Technology & Privacy Law,* 24 (2), 195–225.

Javaid, M., *et al*., 2022. A review of blockchain technology applications for financial services. *BenchCouncil Transactions on Benchmarks, Standards and Evaluations,* 2 (3), 100073.

Johnson, J., 2013. Copyright and online technologies. *Australian Copyright Council,* 27.

JR Consulting and Drafting Pty Ltd v Cummings (2016) 329 ALR 625, 672 [264].

Kabushiki Kaisha Sony Computer Entertainment v Stevens (2003) 200 ALR 96.

Kabushiki Kaisha Sony Computer Entertainment v Stevens [2003] FCAFC 157 (30 July 2003).

Kampakis, S., 2022. Auditing tokenomics: A case study and lessons from auditing a stablecoin project. *The Journal of the British Blockchain Association,* 5 (2), 1–7.

Karjala, D.S., 1995. Copyright in electronic maps. *Jurimetrics,* 35 (4), 395–415.

Kwon, P., 2013. Spatial data process using python script and visual programming language in ArcGIS. *Computer Technology and Application,* 4, 275–283.

Lahore, J., 1996. *Copyright and designs: Looseleaf service*. Sydney: Butterworths, 10,065, 10,115.

Lane, A.M. and Platz, C., 2021. The other side of the ledger: Blockchain makes a new entry in the historical record of copyright law and technology. *European Intellectual Property Review,* 43 (2), 83–97.

Lee, S., Lee, J., and Lee, Y., 2023. Dissecting the Terra-LUNA crash: Evidence from the spillover effect and information flow. *Finance Research Letters,* 53.

Levi, S.D. and Lipton, A.B., 2018. An introduction to smart contracts and their potential and inherent limitations. Available from: <https://corpgov.law.harvard.edu/2018/05/26/an-introduction-to-smart-contracts-and-their-%20potential-and-inherent-limitations/>.

Longhorn, R.A., Henson-Apollonio, V., and White, J.W., 2002. Legal issues in the use of geospatial data and tools for agriculture and natural resource management. International Maize and Wheat Improvement Center (CIMMYT), Mexico. Available from: <https://repository.cimmyt.org/bitstream/handle/10883/905/447972.pdf?sequence=4&isAllowed=y>.

López, C., 2002. Watermarking of digital geospatial datasets: A review of technical, legal and copyright issues. *International Journal of Geographical Information Science,* 16 (6), 589–607.

Mackay, J. and McLachlan, J., 1992. Are computer screen displays capable of attracting copyright protection? *Australia Indonesia Partnership for Justice,* 3, 203–207.

Mann, P. and Denoncourt, J., 2009 September. Copyright issues on the protection of architectural works and design. *25th Annual Conference of Association of Researchers in Construction Management (ARCOM)*. Available from: <https://centaur.reading.ac.uk/4621/1/Mann-Denoncourt.pdf at 708>.

Mannion v Coors Brewing, 377 F Supp 2d 444 (SDNY, 2005) (US).

McCutcheon, J., 2013. The vanishing author in computer-generated works. *Melbourne University Law Review,* 36, 915.

McCutcheon, J., 2021. Point and shoot: Originality, authorship, and the identification of the copyright work in modern photography. *Sydney Law Review,* 43 (2), 163–179.

McMillan, J., 2013. *Open public sector information – From principles to practice*. Office of the Australian Information Commissioner.

Michel, A., n.d. AI-generated creations: Challenging the traditional concept of copyright, a research into the question of works that are created by an artificial intelligence program have copyright protection in the Netherlands and the European Union. Available from: <http://arno.uvt.nl/show.cgi?fid=148002>.

Mulder, A.E., Wiersma, M.G., and van Loenen, B., 2020. Status of national open spatial data infrastructures: A comparison across continents. *International Journal of Spatial Data Infrastructures Research,* 15, 68.

Nahan, N.Y., 2015. The duty of confidence revisited: The protection of confidential Information. *University of Western Australia Law Review,* 39 (2), 270–293.

New Zealand Copyright Act 1994.

New Zealand Layout Designs Act 1994.

Nicholson, D.R., 2009. Digital rights management and access to information: A developing country's perspective. *Library and Information Science Research Electronic Journal,* 19 (1), 1–17.

Nordhaus, W.D., 1969. *Invention, growth, and welfare: A theoretical treatment of technological change*. Cambridge: MIT Press.

NSW Government, 2020. Digital survey plans now available to industry. Available from: <www.spatial.nsw.gov.au/news/digital_survey_plans_now_available_to_industry>.

OECD, 1997. *Competition policy and intellectual property rights*, 73.

O'Reilly Stevens Lawyers, Avoid a hard landing for bundled software. Available from: <https://oreillystevens.com/2022/08/01/avoid-a-hard-landing-for-bundled-software/>.

Painer v Standard VerlagsGmbH (Court of Justice of the European Union, C-145/10, ECLI:EU:C:2011:798, 1 December 2011) (EU).

Paris Convention for the Protection of Industrial Property, Article 10*bis* (2). Available from: <https://www.wipo.int/wipolex/en/text/288514>.

Pila, J., 2008. Works of artistic craftsmanship in the high court of Australia: The exception as paradigm copyright work. *Federal Law Review,* 36 (3), 363.

Pokemon Company International, Inc. v Redbubble Ltd [2017] FCA 1541 (19 December 2017).

Porter, A., 1996. Data access corporation v powerflex services Pty Ltd. *Australian and New Zealand Societies for Computers and the Law*. Available from: <http://classic.austlii.edu.au/au/journals/ANZCompuLawJl/1996/32.html>.

PricewaterhouseCoopers, 2016 February. *Understanding the costs and benefits of introducing a 'fair use' exception*. Executive Summary. Available from: <www.screenrights.org/wp-content/uploads/2017/10/PwC_Fair_Dealing_CBA_Final.pdf> ('*PwC – 'fair use' exception*').

Productivity Commission, 2017, March 31. *Data availability and use (productivity commission inquiry Report No. 82)*. Available from: <www.pc.gov.au/inquiries/completed/data-access/report/data-access.pdf>.

Productivity Commission, n.d. *Productivity commission review of cost recovery: Comment on draft report*. Available from: <www.pc.gov.au/inquiries/completed/cost-recovery/submissions/australian_surveying_and_land_information_group/subdr131.pdf>.

Q.ai., 2022. What really happened to LUNA crypto? *Forbes Magazine*, 20 September. Available from: <www.forbes.com/sites/qai/2022/09/20/what-really-happened-to-luna-crypto/>.

Reichman, J.H. and Samuelson, P., n.d. Intellectual property rights in data. Available from: <https://scholarship.law.duke.edu/cgi/viewcontent.cgi?article=1402&context=faculty_scholarship>.

Richter, H., 2021. Copyright protection of government-related material before the courts of the United States and Canada: Considerations for future reforms. *IIC-International Review of Intellectual Property and Competition Law,* 52, 6–33.

Robinson, E.A., 2009. Digital rights management, fair use, and privacy: Problems for copyright enforcement through technology. <https://soar.usa.edu/cgi/viewcontent.cgi?article=1012&context=other>.

Saltman Engineering Co Ltd v Campbell Engineering Co Ltd (1948) 65 RPC 203.

Sands and McDougall Pty Ltd v Robinson (1917) 23 CLR 49.

Savelyev, A., 2018. Copyright in the blockchain era: Promises and challenges. *Computer Law & Security Review,* 34 (3), 550–561.

Schneider, M., 1998. The European Union database directive. *The Berkeley Technology Law Journal,* 13, 551.

Seafolly Pty Limited v Fewstone Pty Ltd [2014] FCA 321 (1 April 2014).

Senftleben, M., Status report on the protection against unfair competition in WIPO member states. Available from: <www.wipo.int/export/sites/www/sct/en/meetings/pdf/wipo-strad-inf-8-prov.pdf>.

Sieman, J.S., 2007. Using the implied license to inject common sense into digital copyright. *The North Carolina Law Review,* 85, 885.

Sorjama, T., 2016. I, Author – Authorship and copyright in the age of artificial intelligence. Available from: <https://helda.helsinki.fi/bitstream/handle/10138/166456/sorjamaa.pdf?sequence=3&isAllowed=y26> 47.

Spatial Information Systems, 2008. The value of spatial information: The impact of modern spatial information technologies on the Australian economy. Available from: <www.crcsi.com.au/assets/Resources/7d60411d-0ab9-45be-8d48-ef8dab5abd4a.pdf>.

Spatial Source, 2018. The mysterious art of cadastral land surveying. Available from: <www.spatialsource.com.au/the-mysterious-art-of-cadastral-land-surveying/>.

StatusCard Australia Pty Ltd v. Rotondo & Anor [2008] QSC 181 (19 August 2008).

Stevens v Kabushiki Kaisha Sony Computer Entertainment [2005] HCA 58.

Surveys & Mining Ltd v Morrison [1969] Qd R 470.

Swope, M.J., 1995. Recent developments in patent law: Implied license – An emerging threat to contributory infringement protection. *Temple Law Review,* 68, 287–305.

Telstra Corporation Limited v Phone Directories Company Pty Ltd [2010] FCAFC 149.

Thales Australia Limited v Madritsch KG & Anor [2022] QCA 205 (21 October 2022).

Tresise, A., Goldenfein, J., and Hunter, D., 2018. What blockchain can and can't do for copyright. *Australian Intellectual Property Journal,* 28, 144.

Ubaldi, B., 2013. *Open government data: Towards empirical analysis of open government data initiatives*. OECD Working Papers on Public Governance No 22, 27 May, 6. Available from: <www.oecd- ilibrary.org/governance/open-government-data_5k46bj4f03s7-en>.

US Free Trade Agreement Implementation Act, 2004 (Cth).

Verrocchi v Direct Chemist Outlet Pty Ltd [2015] FCA 234 (17 March 2015).

Victoria State Government, Elevation data. Available from: <www.land.vic.gov.au/maps-and-spatial/imagery/elevation-data>.

Victorian Cadastral Surveys, 2021. *Practice directives* (2nd ed.), 5. Available from: <www.spatialsource.com.au/the-mysterious-art-of-cadastral-land-surveying/>.

Von Gunten, A., 2015. *Intellectual property is common property: Arguments for the abolition of private intellectual property rights*. Zürich: Buch & Netz.

Vučković, R.M., Kanceljak, I., and Jurić, M., Is it time for new data governance. *2021 44th International Convention on Information, Communication and Electronic Technology (MIPRO)*. IEEE.

Wang, B., 2016. Blockchain and the law. *Internet Law Bulletin,* 19 (1), 250–254.

Weller and Anor v Smith [2016] FCCA 2822 (4 November 2016).

Werbach, K. and Cornell, N., 2017. Contracts ex machina. *Duke Law Journal,* 67, 313.

Williams, S., 2023. Edge contracts. *University of Pennsylvania Journal of Business Law,* 25 (3), 839.

Willms, J., 2016. Is blockchain-powered copyright protection possible? *Bitcoin Magazine*, 9 August. Available from: <https://perma.cc/9V88-K8ES>.

World Bank, 2021. Starting an open data initiative | data, 13 May. Available from: <https://opendatatoolkit.worldbank.org/en/data/opendatatoolkit/starting>.

World Intellectual Property Organization, n.d. Agreement on Trade-Related Aspects of Intellectual Property Rights.

World Intellectual Property Organization, n.d. Copyright treaty. Available from: <https://www.wipo.int/treaties/en/ip/wct/summary_wct.html>.

World Intellectual Property Organization, n.d. Performance and phonogram treaty. Available from: <https://www.wipo.int/treaties/en/ip/wppt/summary_wppt.html>.

Yang, L., *et al.*, 2022. Google earth engine and artificial intelligence (AI): A comprehensive review. *Remote Sensing,* 14, 3253.

Yiu, M., *et al.*, 2010. Enabling search services on outsourced private spatial data. *The International Journal on Very Large Databases,* 19, 363.

Your Europe, n.d. Data protection. Available from: <https://europa.eu/youreurope/business/running-business/intellectual-property/database-protection/index_en.htm>.

Zeitz, B., 2004. How high is up: Interstitial dilemmas in nonexclusive copyright licensing cases in the ninth circuit. *The UCLA Entertainment Law Review,* 11, 429.

Zhao, P., *et al.*, 2022. Towards geospatial blockchain: A review of research on blockchain technology applied to geospatial data. *AGILE: GIScience Series,* 3, 71. Available from: <https://agile-giss.copernicus.org/articles/3/71/2022/agile-giss-3-71-2022.pdf>.

Zimu, W., 2021. Blockchain technology: Opportunities and challenges in copyright industry. *Paper presented at the18th International Computer Conference on Wavelet Active Media Technology and Information Processing (ICCWAMTIP),* 17–19 December 2021, The Institute of Electrical and Electronics Engineers, Inc., Chengdu. Available from<https://www.proceedings.com/content/062/062218webtoc.pdf>.

Zope-Chaudhari, S. and Venkatachalam, P., 2013. Conceptual framework for geospatial data security. *International Journal of Database Management Systems,* 5 (5), 29, 35.

3 Copyright of survey plans and spatial data in the USA

3.1 Introduction

The protection for copyright in the United States of America (USA) can be traced back to the colonial period, when the invention of the printing press and the resulting publication of books necessitated a legal regime to regulate book publishing. Though British copyright law was never considered part of the law constituting the law of the American colonies, the Licensing Act of 1622 and Statute of Anne in 1710 can be identified as influential sources of U.S. copyright law, together with various colonial and state practices.[1] In order to provide a brief background as to the sources of copyright law in the USA and the manner in which state and federal law interact and operate in that nation, the next section will discuss the statutory framework for the protection of U.S. copyright law, followed by a detailed discussion of the application of the elements of copyright protection to survey products and data.

3.2 Statutory framework for the protection of copyright in the USA

Until 1790 (when the first federal statute on copyright was enacted), the developments in copyright protection occurred at the state level through individual legislative grants and general copyright statutes of states enacted in the 1780s, except in the state of Delaware.[2]

While the era of state copyright law was brief due to the national legislative developments that occurred with the federation of the USA, state copyright law constitutes an important aspect of the current copyright regime. These statutes provided the broader framework for the development of the federal statute and introduced the concepts of 'authors' of copyright and its two main rationales – natural rights and public utility.[3] State copyright laws also provided the natural template for federal copyright legislation that stemmed from the express constitutional recognition provided to intellectual property (IP) by Article I, Section 8, Clause 8 of the U.S. Constitution (the 'Intellectual Property Clause').[4] The express powers given to Congress to legislate on patents and copyright demonstrated the increasing difficulties of local protections that were insufficient for the technological and innovative advancements witnessed in the emerging national markets.[5] The inclusion of

DOI: 10.4324/9781003479383-3

IP rights – and, by extension, copyright protection in the U.S. Constitution – has significant ramifications in developing the broader IP legal doctrine in the USA. The clause's formulation has also been used as a justification for the political and public debate on the expansion and/or restriction of IP rights, including copyright, at different periods.[6]

The Copyright Act 1790[7] was enacted during the first session of the first federal Congress, and the Act was applied to 'Maps, Charts, and Books'. The protection under the Act was provided to authors and their assignees for published works, as well as unpublished and future works. The rights afforded under the Act consisted of 'the sole right and liberty of printing, reprinting, publishing and vending' for a term of 14 years, with the possibility of renewing for another term of 14 years.[8] The Copyright Act 1790 not only established a general system of universal rights regarding copyright, but it also, for the first time, recognised the centrality of authors, as opposed to publishers or printers.[9] It must be noted, however, that authors' use of copyright protection was a slow process during which the publishers and printers continued to dominate the registered works during the early days of the Act.

Driven by the extensive lobbying efforts of Noah Webster, the first major statutory reform was made in 1831, whereby the existing subject matter categories were consolidated alongside the extension of the copyright period and limitation period with a simplified notice form. The early copyright jurisprudence of the USA, while coloured greatly by British developments, was a 'hybrid between the new regime of authors' rights and the previous system of publishers' trade privileges'.[10] The fourth decade of the 19th century and the beginning of the 20th century witnessed changes in American copyright law,[11] where individual authorship took prominence over publishers' privileges. The institutional apparatus was created through first the Library of Congress and then the Copyright Office, which led to a more formalised and systematic application of copyright law in the USA. The Copyright Act 1909 was a clear indication that the selective and incremental development of the subject matter of copyright had given its way to protecting creative works of authorship.[12] The next major development in U.S. copyright law came with the revision effected in 1976. The integration of international copyright law practices and the need to address issues related to copyright in view of technological innovations and advancement necessitated the 1976 revisions, which constitute current copyright law in the USA.

3.3 Sources of copyright law in the USA

There are four authoritative sources for U.S. copyright law: the U.S. Constitution, statutory provisions, court decisions, and regulations.[13] While the origins of U.S. copyright law date back to colonial times, the ratification of the U.S. Constitution provided the opportunity to include copyright protection in the Constitution itself. Article 1, Section 8, Clause 8 of the U.S. Constitution contains the 'Copyright Clause', which states that 'the Congress shall have Power . . . to promote the Progress of Science and useful Arts, by securing for limited times to Authors and Inventors the exclusive Right to their respective Writings and Discoveries'.

This power had been granted to Congress to ensure the promotion of the progress of science, which was identified as the basis for enacting a copyright regime.[14] It is important to note this purpose when analysing the protection granted to spatial data and products because any interpretative exercise will have to be taken within this general framework of promotion of the progress of science. Such purpose has been elaborated in judicial decisions to mean that copyright law should promote 'both the creation and dissemination of creative works'[15] because copyright law has been identified as the 'engine of free expression'[16] that provides 'a marketable right to the use of one's expression',[17] thereby supplying the 'economic incentive to create and disseminate ideas'.[18] While there have been several other reiterations of the exercise of this power by Congress, the current Copyright Act (the Act) was enacted in 1976 and has been amended several times since then. Regulations have been made under the Copyright Act 1976, and together with copyright jurisprudence established by the federal courts, they are the sources of copyright law in the USA. While there are laws passed by the states, it must be noted that the Act pre-empts[19] state law as long as the protections provided by state law are equivalent to those provided in the Act.

3.4 Subject matter of copyright

The subject matter of copyright is defined in section 102 of the Act as 'original works of authorship fixed in any tangible medium of expression, now known or later developed, from which they can be perceived, reproduced or otherwise communicated, either directly or with the aid of a machine or device'. The three main concepts of copyright law in the USA are based on fixation, originality, and expression.[20] In terms of the requirement of 'originality', this has been interpreted to include the need for an 'independent creation by the author' and a 'modest quantum of creativity'.[21]

The statute recognises eight categories of works of authorship. These include: (1) literary works; (2) musical works, including any accompanying words; (3) dramatic works, including any accompanying music; (4) pantomimes and choreographic works; (5) pictorial, graphic, and sculptural works; (6) motion pictures and other audiovisual works; (7) sound recordings; and (8) architectural works. Section 103 of the Act recognises that the subject matter of copyright could also include 'compilations' and 'derivative works', as long as the pre-existing materials have been used lawfully. Compilations cover two types of work: 'collective work' and 'databases'.[22] In relation to compilations and derivate works, copyright protection is granted only to the material contributed by the author of such work that could be distinguished from the pre-existing materials that are employed in the works.

According to section 105, copyright protection is generally not available for any work of the U.S. government.[23] However, the government is not precluded from receiving and holding copyright transferred to it by assignment, bequest, or otherwise. In addition, a number of institutions are identified in the statute as 'covered institutions'.[24] While the civilian members of the faculty of a covered institution generally own the copyright to any literary works produced by an author in the course of employment at a covered institution for publication by a scholarly press or journal, it is possible for the Secretary of Defense to direct such an author to provide the federal government with an irrevocable, royalty-free, worldwide, non-exclusive licence to reproduce, distribute, perform, or display such covered work for the purposes of the USA.

One important aspect concerning the statutory provisions related to copyright protection in the USA is the distinction between ideas and expressions. The copyright protection for an original work of authorship does not extend to 'any idea, procedure, process, system, method of operation, concept, principle, or discovery, regardless of the form in which it is described, explained, illustrated, or embodied in such work'.[25]

3.4.1 Spatial data and products

In view of these discussed general principles, it is important to consider the category/categories under which 'raw spatial data, processed spatial data and spatial products' could be protected in the USA. This discussion is guided by the basic categorisation made in the first case study about the focus areas of this research. Therefore, this section will look into the traditional depiction of maps on paper as pictorial representations and the digitalisation of cadastral survey plans and the map-making process. Moreover, this discussion will consider the impact of copyright principles on the subject matter in relation to geographic electronic information systems (databases) that have been created with raw spatial data gathered through different sources.

3.4.2. Survey plans as pictorial representations

It must be noted that the first copyright statute in the USA provided protection specifically for three types of works, which included 'maps'. The classification of maps in 17 USC § 5(f) reflected a *sui generis* status for maps distinct from books, works of art, drawings, or plastic works of scientific or technical nature.[26] Given that it was a requirement to register maps under section 5(f) of the Copyright Act 1909, attempts have been made to define this particular category under the Copyright Office Regulations.[27]

Given the focus of this section on survey plans, it must be noted at the outset that the discussion of maps as a broader category has a determinative effect on how survey plans – a specific type of map – may be protected under U.S. copyright law. Therefore, the copyright protection granted to maps in the USA would provide the necessary guidelines for understanding the protection given to survey plans in the USA.

A survey plan containing a map and textual material combined into a single work could be protected as a literary work[28] for the textual portion, while the map is protected as a graphic work.[29] Therefore, traditionally, surveyors' maps were considered as 'pictorial representations of geographic and demographic facts organised to allow the user to readily understand and easily extract the factual information portrayed'.[30] Thus, one would assume that selecting the relevant subject matter is a straightforward exercise, given the express recognition of maps within the category of 'pictorial, graphic and sculptural works'. However, this categorisation must be read in line with the limitations previously discussed as to the inability to copyright ideas, systems, etc., together with the limits specified in the definition of 'pictorial, graphic and sculptural works' itself. The definition prescribes explicitly that the protection does not extend to works of artistic craftsmanship that cannot be 'identified separately from' and are incapable of 'existing independently of' the utilitarian aspects of useful articles.

Therefore, the facts depicted on maps, such as the boundary lines and locations of landmarks, and the organising principles of how the information is presented (i.e., selection of particular signs and keys), may not be copyrightable.[31] As illustrated in the case of *Perris v. Hexamer*,[32] the Court denied copyright protection for the arbitrary colouring and signs used on a series of maps of New York City to indicate the general characteristics of the buildings. The colourings and signs were explained by reference or key, and the owners of the map claimed that the map maker from Philadelphia had breached copyright because the latter initially adopted the same system of colouring and signs. The Court, in this case, held that the publisher of a map did not receive the exclusive right to the signs and keys used in the map's delineation. Similarly, in the case of *Andrews v. Guenther*,[33] the Court held that the mere use of three different kinds of types and symbols to indicate the population of the cities selected was not sufficient to be considered as warranting copyrightability. Furthermore, similar principles were said to be applied regarding the names of lakes, creeks, streams, and other geographic loci which the copyright holder had invented and later became common usage by the residents of and visitors to the area.[34] Therefore, even if a map is considered as falling within the category of 'pictorial, graphic and sculptural works', there could be some elements within the map that would not receive copyright protection and, therefore, were possible to be copied and used by subsequent cartographers.

In terms of the work involved with creating and producing maps, such a position could unfairly affect the cartographers who have invested significant time and effort in this process. Therefore, the protection for survey plans has been also considered under the category of 'compilations'.

3.4.3 Compilations and survey plans

This recognition of compilations as a possible category is imperative in the current context, as survey plans have moved beyond the traditional model of paper-based pictorial depictions to digitalised materials produced by making use of comprehensive geographic electronic information systems containing both spatial and non-spatial data.[35] Therefore, it is important to consider the protection granted to different types of survey plans/maps (outcomes that could be presented as 'static or dynamic and tangible or virtual') that could be created within such geographic electronic information systems. While the answers to such questions will have to be considered within the broader context of copyrightability, which includes the elements of 'originality' and 'material form' (fixation), this discussion will focus on the law as applicable in the USA about the possibility of identifying survey plans in general as compilations.[36] It is recognised under U.S. copyright law that a 'compilation' could be registered with the U.S. Copyright Office,[37] provided that it constitutes copyrightable subject matter.[38] Therefore, compilations under U.S. law are to be considered a subset of the eight subject matter categories previously mentioned, rather than considered the same as a distinct category of work. Because the category of 'pictorial, graphic and sculptural works' includes maps, it can be concluded that this requirement could be satisfied with the different types of survey plans that could be produced as a result of such compilation.

Regarding identifying the relevant category of subject matter for geographic electronic information systems and the data contained within such systems, it is important to consider databases and the treatment of data under U.S. copyright law. Databases are specifically recognised in the 1976 House Judicial Committee report as falling within the category of literary works.[39] Furthermore, the databases are considered to fall within the broader category of compilations. The definition of 'compilation' recognises that it involves the collection and assembling of pre-existing materials or data in a way that the 'resulting work as a whole constitutes an original work of authorship'; thus, copyright protection is granted only to the material contributed by the author of such work that could be distinguished from the pre-existing materials employed in the works.[40] For example, the protection is awarded to a compilation or the resulting original work of authorship by 'selecting, coordinating or arranging the data'. However, as in Australia, the ideas, facts, or data that are not protected under copyright law would be considered as falling within the limitations highlighted in section 102(b) of the Act. As noted in *Feist Publications, Inc. v. Rural Telephone Service Co., Inc.* (*Feist*),[41] 'No one may claim originality as to facts . . . because facts do not owe their origin to an act of authorship'.[42] Therefore, copyright protection only applies to the 'creative elements' of a compilation and not to the underlying data that would be considered facts.

In the context of raw spatial data and databases containing the same, it could be noted that while the raw spatial data would not be considered the subject matter for copyright purposes, 'the databases containing these raw spatial data could be considered as copyrightable subject matter.' One important aspect in this regard is the possibility of using survey plans and data in derivative works. Therefore, anyone who creates a derivative work containing pre-existing data/survey plans would be able to claim copyright protection for the new materials that the author contributed to that work as long as there has been a 'process of recasting, transforming, or adapting one or more pre-existing works'.[43]

3.5 Material form (fixation)

As per section 102 of the Act, a work of authorship must be 'fixed in any tangible medium of expression, now known or later developed, from which they can be perceived, reproduced, or otherwise communicated, either directly or with the aid of a machine or device'. This definition identifies essential elements that a work must satisfy to obtain copyrightability in terms of fixation.

Given that the work of authorship must be 'fixed in tangible form', section 101 defines the term 'fixed' as an embodiment in a copy or phonorecord, by or under the authority of the author, that is sufficiently permanent or stable to permit it to be perceived, reproduced, or otherwise communicated for a period of more than transitory duration. A work consisting of sounds or images, or both, that are being transmitted is considered 'fixed' for purposes of the Act if a fixation of the work is being made simultaneously with its transmission.

The need for tangibility has been traced back to the constitutional requirements of 'writing',[44] which have also been identified as adding another layer of complexity.[45] According to the constitutional provision, unless a work is reduced to tangible form, it cannot be regarded as 'writing', and thereby, it would fall outside the legislative authority of Congress to legislate in this regard. According to the statutory provisions, the tangible medium of expression or the material object consists of either 'copies'[46] or 'phonorecords'.[47] This differs from the 'original work of authorship' as mentioned in the Act. The distinction lies in the fact that 'copies' and 'phonorecords' represent all the materials and objects that can be used for the purposes of fixing copyrightable work.[48] The historical interpretation given to what constitutes a 'copy' as a work 'in a form which others can see and read'[49] was rejected in the Copyright Act 1976. The Act defines 'copy' as a material object whereby the fixation could 'be perceived, reproduced, or otherwise communicated, either directly or with the aid of a machine or device'. It is important to recognise the difference between 'original work', which is the product of 'authorship', and the multitude of material objects in which it can be embodied.

In defining what constitutes a 'copy' under U.S. copyright law, the Court in *Matthew Bender & Co. v. West Pub. Co.*[50] rejected the argument that the plaintiffs' CD-ROM discs were a 'copy' because West's copyrighted arrangement was 'fixed' on the disc in a way that can be 'perceived . . . with the aid of a machine or device.' In this case, the plaintiffs encoded West's printed compilations of federal and state judicial opinions in CD-ROM discs that adopted a chronological order, which was different from the order West used. However, it was possible for a user to manipulate the content to obtain the order in which West arranged the content. Thus, the argument raised by West was that the CD-ROM was a 'copy' because West's copyrighted arrangement was 'fixed' on the disc in a way that could be 'perceived . . . with the aid of a machine or device'. The Court rejected this argument and held that it is possible for a CD-ROM disc to infringe a copyrighted arrangement when a machine or device that reads it perceives the embedded material in the copyrighted arrangement or a substantially similar arrangement. However, if a machine could perceive the arrangement only after another person uses the machine to rearrange the material into the copyright holder's arrangement, then such a CD-ROM disc would not result in an infringement of the copyright holder's rights.

While these definitions appear to provide a straightforward application of the fixation element under U.S. law, it is not always a simple determination as to whether the subject matter of copyrightable authorship is recorded or not. While it is possible to discern the purpose of fixation as a possible limitation or restriction of the purview of copyright,[51] it is also important to note the administrative and evidentiary functions of the fixation requirement, which make it possible to give effect to the basic tenant of copyright that while ideas are not copyrightable, it is possible for an expression of an idea to be granted copyright protection. Therefore, while it is not possible to obtain copyright protection for an 'idea, procedure, process', etc., it is still possible for a person to obtain copyright in a tangible expression of such an 'idea, procedure, process', etc., fixed in a tangible medium of expression.

In view of these discussion, spatial products – whether expressed by making use of paper or digital files – will satisfy the fixation requirement under U.S. copyright law. Especially, spatial products, whether in physical or digital form, meet this requirement, as they are typically produced with the intent of being reproduced or communicated to others.

3.5.1 Material form in digital maps

In view of the increased use of digital maps created through spatial data, further investigation is needed as to the application of the previously described principles within the context of digital maps ('static' and 'dynamic') and the spatial data used for such purposes. This is imperative in view of the requirement of 'perceivability' in the statutory definition based on duration and stability. The legislative history of the Act identified that it was not possible to provide copyright protection for 'purely evanescent or transient reproductions such as those projected briefly on a screen, shown electronically on a television or other cathode ray tube, or captured momentarily in the "memory" of a computer'.[52] However, the case law in this area has not been consistent in its application of this legislative intent when 'pixels . . . updated every 1/70th of a second'[53] and 'pop-up advertisements'[54] were not identified as sufficiently 'fixed' while 'volatile RAM copies'[55] and 'transitory work (software program loaded into RAM)'[56] were held as able to satisfy the fixation requirement.

In terms of computer programs, it has been held that both computer programs that can be 'deciphered by humans, as well as programs which can only be read by machines, are within the scope of copyright'.[57] Therefore, the program's source code, object code, firmware, and software are all considered as copyrightable works.[58] While programs written on discs pose a limited issue as to the fixation,[59] a program embedded on ROM chips would also be considered fixed in a tangible medium of expression.[60] Furthermore, courts have also recognised that in relation to electronic video games, whereby the player's participation may cause the audio-visual presentation to change in some respects from one game to the next, these games nevertheless meet the fixation requirement of the Copyright Act.[61]

In *MAI Systems Corp. v. Peak Computer, Inc.*,[62] a leading case on the issue of fixation, the Court held that the representations created in RAM had been identified as capable of being fixed because they provide sufficiently permanent and stable expression.[63] In this case, MAI tried to prevent third parties from performing maintenance on their computers and operating systems by claiming that switching on the computers and loading MAI's software into the memory to view the systems' error log to diagnose and service MAI computers constituted 'copying' by the third-party service provider. The Court's decision that 'the representation created in the RAM' is 'sufficiently permanent to be perceived, reproduced, or otherwise communicated for a period of more than transitory duration' failed to explain the reasons behind the 'non-transitory' nature attributed to the representations created in RAM other than the possibility to be displayed.[64] In *Advanced Computer Services of Michigan, Inc. v. MAI Systems*,[65] the Court confirmed the decision of the MAI case and held that 'useful representations of the program's information or intelligence can be displayed . . . virtually instantaneously' and that the information stored in RAM was thus ' "stable" enough under the statute'.[66]

In the case of *Cartoon Network LP v. CSC Holdings, Inc.*,[67] however, the Court held that the decision of *MAI Sys. Corp. v. Peak Computer, Inc.*[68] should not be read as 'loading a program into a form of RAM always results in copying'.[69] While recognising the possibility of creating a copy by 'temporary buffering of bits of data from the live feed into a remote server (at the request of a customer wishing to record a program) at a rate of 1.2 seconds before automatically being erased', the Court emphasised the need to consider the durational aspect of fixation. In determining what duration may constitute a 'transitory' presence in memory, the Court held that the duration of 1.2 seconds was not sufficient to be considered as an embodiment for more than transitory duration. While 1.2 seconds was not intended by the Court as a benchmark in determining the 'transitory duration', it provides valuable guidance as to the duration aspect in the embodiment analysis.

In the context of 'dynamic' cadastral plans, digital maps, and geospatial data – including weather maps, traffic movements, and maps depicting temperature and wind movement captured and updated in real time – the question is whether such maps could be considered fixed for a period of more than a transitory duration. The answer to this question will depend on how much transitory duration is acceptable for copyrightability.[70] In *CoStar Group, Inc. v. LoopNet, Inc* (*CoStar*),[71] the Court provided guidance about the transitory duration as follows:

> transitory duration had both a qualitative and quantitative characteristic that needed to be considered: It is quantitative insofar as it describes the period during which the function occurs, and it is qualitative in the sense that it describes the status of transition.[72]

The *CoStar* case involved LoopNet Inc. (LoopNet), an internet service provider (ISP) and CoStar Group, Inc. (CoStar), a real estate listing service provider. CoStar brought a copyright infringement action against LoopNet, in which CoStar alleged that by allowing LoopNet subscribers to post photographs of commercial real estate owned by CoStar, LoopNet infringed the copyright owned by CoStar. In discussing the fixation element, the Court identified the role of an ISP as a conduit of information and data that connects users over the Internet. According to the decision in the *CoStar* case, whenever transmission occurs based on user requests, the ISP operates only as a conduit and does not engage in making 'copies' – even though that information and data are downloaded into the ISP's RAM or another component as part of the transmission function.

The judicial approach towards fixation has been characterised by some scholars as not in 'accord with a correct understanding of the purpose and character of computer memory, and, when applied to the facts both within and outside of the field of computing, it produces arbitrary and capricious results in a contravention of the statute'.[73] However, the Information Infrastructure Task Force (IITF), a committee established to define the U.S. government's vision for the National Information Infrastructure (NII), in its 'Report of the Working Group on Intellectual Property Rights' (White Paper) issued in 1995, adopted the reasoning given in *MAI* and subsequent cases as having determined the issue sufficiently.[74]

In view of this discussion, it is clear that even when survey plans are of dynamic nature, it is possible for digital maps to be considered as 'fixed' – as long as the embodiment and duration elements are satisfied as per the stated requirements. Compared to the Australian context, whereby digital maps and geospatial data in 'dynamic form' would be considered as lasting for a short time to be truly perceived, the U.S. approach provides an opportunity for such maps to be considered as 'fixed' as long as the display is for a non-transitory duration. While it is not possible to predict the transitory duration deemed acceptable by the courts to be considered in the context of digital maps, the positive reception towards *MAI* indicates that the courts would be more willing to find a fixation in such a context. It must also be noted that the 'displays which are depicted on a computer screen may be separately protectable as audiovisual works distinct from the copyrightability of the program's underlying code'.[75]

3.6 Originality

As noted previously, copyright protection in the USA is granted only for 'original works of authorship'. While the Act does not define the term 'original', however, the legislative materials indicate that the legislature intended to incorporate the standard of originality established under the Copyright Act 1909 into the current statutory regime.[76] Thus, it is required to look into the case law under the 1909 statute to understand the generally established standard for originality, as well as originality in the context of pictorial, graphic, and sculptural work and compilations. Such an examination is important, given the possibility of positioning maps under the subject matter category of pictorial, graphic, and sculptural work, as well as compilations.

Originality in the copyright context means that the work owns its origin to the author who creates such work independently without copying from other works.[77] Therefore, the originality requirement under copyright could be satisfied by independent creation and sufficient creativity. Independent creation merely requires that the work be created by the author without copying from another. In terms of independent creation, the work has to be only new to the author and not to the whole world. Thus, it is not necessary for the work to be novel as in patents. In terms of the requirement for creativity, it has been noted that the quantum of creativity needed[78] is minimal. In order to determine the required level of creativity, the courts have adopted the 'distinguishable variation' test, in which the determinative criteria are whether there is a variation and if such variation is the product of the author's independent efforts and is more than merely trivial.[79] For example, in the case of *Alfred Bell & Co. v. Catalda Fine Arts, Inc.*,[80] the Court held that originality for copyright purposes amounts to 'little more than a prohibition of actual copying. No matter how poor the "author's" addition, it is enough if it is his own'.[81] In this case, the copyright originality was related to mezzotint engravings of paintings of old masters. Alfred Bell & Co., an art publisher in London, brought an infringement action against Catalda Fine Arts, Inc. for reproducing the same by a lithographic process. The Court held that mezzotints were sufficiently distinguishable from the paintings that they allegedly reproduced to warrant the granting of copyright. In the case of *Bleistein v. Donaldson Lithographing Co.*,[82] the Supreme Court agreed to such an extremely modest standard of originality[83] and recognised the 'aesthetic non-discrimination principle'.[84] In an attempt to review the previous judicial pronouncements regarding originality requirement in U.S. copyright law, the leading case of *Feist Publications, Inc. v. Rural Telephone Service Co.* (*Feist*)[85] concluded that as a constitutional matter, the term 'original' in the copyright context means only that the work was independently created by the author (as opposed to copied from other works), and that it possesses at least some minimal degree of creativity.[86] Thus, under the current copyright principles, the originality requirement in the USA could be satisfied by the establishment of independent creation and creativity.

In the context of spatial products, the establishment of independent creation and creativity should be discussed in relation to the 'three main doctrines' that have shaped the originality of spatial products, including maps and survey plans. These three concepts are the 'direct observation rule', the selection of items in the public domain, and the 'sweat of the brow' doctrine.

Though the originality requirement applicable to maps as pictorial, graphic, and sculptural work is similar to the general requirements of originality, some earlier cases have attempted to introduce a higher standard by requiring the maps to comply with the 'direct observation rule'. This rule was first expressed in the case of *Amsterdam v. Triangle Publication, Inc.*[87] In this case, a publisher of maps alleged that a newspaper infringed its copyright by using a map of Delaware County (Pennsylvania) in connection with a historical article relating to the county in the newspaper. The defendant accepted the copying of the maps but argued that the maps, as published by the plaintiff, were not entitled to copyright. The Court acknowledged that the plaintiff studied every map of Delaware County that he could find to make his maps. However, neither the plaintiff nor anyone on his behalf was involved in actual surveys or investigations of any of the elements included in the maps because this information was gathered from maps that had been created by the plaintiff previously or that were publicly available through the township and municipal authorities. The Court denied copyright protection to the plaintiff's map, created merely by copying the information on other maps without engaging in an independent survey. This resulted in the addition of a requirement of 'direct observation' of the geographic features in order to satisfy the originality requirement for maps. However, it was stated in *United States v. Hamilton*[88] that:

> [E]xpression in cartography is not so different from other artistic forms seeking to touch upon external realities that unique rules are needed to judge whether the authorship is original. Recording by direct observation is only one measure of a cartographer's skill and talent, and originality should not be made synonymous with a requirement that features of a copyrighted map be observed and recorded directly before they will be entitled to copyright protection.[89]

The decision in *United States v. Hamilton* by the U.S. Court of Appeals, Ninth Circuit does not have a binding precedent on decisions of any other federal circuit or district court outside of its jurisdiction. However, given that the decision was made more than 20 years after *Amsterdam* and the subsequent rejection of the 'sweat of the brow' doctrine by the Supreme Court, in which the roots of *Amsterdam* lie, would mean that the direct observation rule no longer represents good law under U.S. copyright principles.

Another way in which the Court has attempted to introduce extra requirements in relation to the originality of maps is in the area of 'selection and arrangement of materials in the public domain'. Generally, case law recognises that the selection and arrangement of materials available in the public domain had been generally considered sufficient to satisfy the originality requirement.[90] In terms of cadastral survey plans/map-making, however, it has been held in several decisions that if the selection is 'obvious' and 'requires no subjectivity,' then such work would lack originality.[91] While this may hold cartographers to a higher standard, cases such as *C.S. Hammond & Co. v. International College Globe, Inc.*,[92] have upheld the originality of maps as long as the cartographer independently selects the items – even if such items are commonly known. While both the 'direct observation rule' and the 'selection of items in the public domain' have historically imposed limitations on the originality of the spatial products in the USA, these principles do not presently have a limiting impact on the originality of the spatial products. However, it should be noted here that any limitations would hinder the development of truly innovative and unique spatial products and lead to a homogenisation of spatial data.

The next concept that has been vital to the originality of cadastral survey plans/maps was the 'sweat of the brow' or 'industrious collection' doctrine.[93] The relevance of this doctrine to the survey plans lies in the fact that maps are viewed mostly as a compilation of facts. The underlying notion was that copyright was a reward for the hard work that went into compiling facts. Such recognition is clearly based on the historical context of map-making in the USA. Maps were seen as a tool for population and economic growth in the mid-20th century, and the government had a monopoly on map-making through the U.S. Geological Survey.[94] The government placed its imprimatur on maps and confirmed the centrality of their factual elements.[95] Piracy claims discouraged any form of variation in the form or style of the map because it may conceal piracy of the factual materials as depicted in the maps.[96] Thus, maps as a presentation of objectively verifiable reality would have limited ability to be protected based on artistic expression; rather, the effort exerted to get the raw data needed for the map was considered to provide the possible copyright protection.

As noted in the discussion as to the subject matter of copyright, a compilation provides the creator with copyrightability as to the original contribution and not to the pre-existing work contained in the compilation. However, there has been a line of cases that have been developed in the USA based on the rationale that no one should be able to freely benefit from the industry, effort, and investment of time in reporting and researching facts or other public domain materials.[97] A classical formulation of this rule was provided in the case of *Jeweler's Circular Pub. Co. v. Keystone Pub. Co.*[98] It was stated in this case that:

> [T]he right to copyright a book upon which one has expended labor in its preparation does not depend upon whether the materials which he has collected consist or not of matters which are publici juris, or whether such materials show literary skill or originality, either in thought or in language, or anything more than industrious collection. The man who goes through the streets of a town and puts down the names of each of the inhabitants, with their occupations and their street number, acquires material of which he is the author. He produces by his labor a meritorious composition, in which he may obtain copyright, and thus obtain the exclusive right of multiplying copies of his work.[99]

However, this position was rejected in the case of *Feist Publications, Inc. v. Rural Telephone Service Co.* (*Feist*),[100] the leading authority in this regard. This case arose due to a dispute between Rural Telephone Services Company Inc. (Rural Telephone Services), which was a local telephone company that published telephone directories, and Feist Publications Inc. (Feist Publications), another telephone directory publishing company with much wider coverage. Rural Telephone Services obtained information from its subscribers to publish the telephone directories. Upon refusal by Rural Telephone Services to grant a licence to Feist Publications to use its information, Feist Publications extracted the listing information required to publish White Pages directories without the consent of Rural Telephone Services. While many listings were altered by Feist Publications when publishing its White Pages, many listings were identical to those of Rural Telephone Services. Rural Telephone Services sued Feist Publications for copyright violation in relation to the White Pages directory it published, a compilation that contained the data extracted from Rural Telephone Services' telephone directories.

In *Feist*, the Supreme Court unanimously rejected the 'sweat of the brow' doctrine and held that copyright protection was to be granted for originality rather than industry. Furthermore, the Supreme Court recognised the possibility of establishing originality in factual compilations due to choices about the selection and arrangement independently made with a minimum degree of creativity. The Supreme Court further held that to be considered as satisfying the originality requirement, a compilation must be 'selected, coordinated, or arranged in such a way that the resulting work as a whole constitutes an original work of authorship'.[101]

In determining whether the author's compilation is sufficiently original, the U.S. Copyright Office may consider the following factors:

(a) What type of material or data did the author compile?
(b) How is the material or data presented?
(c) Was the selection, coordination, and/or arrangement made from a large or diverse pool of material or data?
(d) Was the coordination or arrangement standard?
(e) Is the selection exhaustive (e.g., a parts catalogue containing standard information for all the parts sold by a particular company)?
(f) Is the coordination or arrangement obvious (e.g., is the information listed in alphabetical, numerical, or chronological order)?[102]

Mason v. Montgomery Data, Inc. (*Mason*),[103] the first major court case related to maps after *Feist*, dealt with an alleged infringement of copyrights in land ownership maps. Mason was the creator and publisher of about 233 original and revised real estate ownership maps of the whole of Montgomery County (Texas). The maps pictorially portrayed the location, size, and shape of surveys, land grants, tracts, and various topographical features within the county. In addition, the numbers and words on the maps identified deeds, abstract numbers, acreage, and the owners of the various tracts. In order to prepare his maps, Mason used a variety of sources and he used substantial judgement and discretion in the process to address the inconsistencies found among different sources.[104] In this case, the Court held that:

> [M]aps prepared by taking government topographical maps and superimposing data regarding land ownership possessed *sufficient originality to be copyrightable*; maps were creative in selection, coordination and arrangement of facts they depicted and in the pictorial graphic nature of the way they did so. [emphasis added][105]

Thus, the decision in this case, while accepting the *Feist* requirements for compilations, decided the matter by categorising the maps in dispute as a pictorial representation instead of compilations to address the limitations imposed by *Feist*. However, the danger of such a categorisation lies in the inherent nature of cadastral survey plans/maps because the 'transformation of factual data to a map will still be no more than a graphical representation of that data, of which the most important value still lies in the accuracy and exactness'.[106] The selection and arrangement of elements to be included in a cadastral survey plan/map and the choices made in that regard are all important aspects of the map-making process, which entails the level of creativity required by the *Feist* case. However, such creativity will be in the process rather than the final product. Thus, the *Feist* requirement of 'expressive creativity in the end product, independent of the manner or methodology by which the product was created'[107] would render such a creative selection process as unqualified for the originality requirement.

There has been some effort since the *Feist* decision was issued to add 'database' protection to U.S. law.[108] Given that the USA does not have a federal law protecting data, however, the originality and resulting protection continued to be based on the elements of 'selection and arrangement'. In 2015, the American Law Institute (ALI) launched a project to create a 'Restatement of the Law, Copyright'. The 2020 draft Restatement's presentation of U.S. copyright law's threshold requirement for protection, while recognising the *Feist* case as the applicable authority in terms of originality, provided a detailed explanation in Clause 7 as to the minimum creativity requirement.[109] Clause 7 adopted a doctrine similar to the 'sweat of the brow'[110] doctrine and emphasised the 'author's "choices," not the actual expression that results from those choices'.[111] While the Restatement has followed the *Feist* case's references to the formulation of creativity, there has been very little attempt to define the level of creativity required. However, Clause 7 sheds some light as to what creativity is and is not.[112]

To address this issue of the data not being protected when compiled into a database, there have been some attempts to address this concern by using contract law as a measure. Using licensing schemes, it is possible to prohibit the end user from extracting data for uses that are not envisaged by the creators of the database. As noted previously, the statutory pre-emption provided in section 301 of the Act prohibits individual states from enacting contradictory laws. Because contract law is governed under state laws, some have argued that these contracting protections are subject to statutory pre-emption. However, recent decisions have taken the opposite direction and have enforced such contracts, given that a breach of a contract claim is not equivalent to any exclusive rights provided under the Act and is therefore not pre-empted. In *ProCD, Incorporated v. Matthew Zeidenberg and Silken Mountain Web Services, Inc.*,[113] it was held that the end user of the CD-ROM phone database breached the contract by way of a 'shrinkwrap' licence.[114] It is important to note that the Court only decided the matter as to the shrinkwrap licences, not that there could never be a time the contract would be pre-empted.

Assessing the impact of *Feist* after 25 years, some commentators have opined that the impact has not been detrimental as expected, given that many databases seem to be able to meet the 'minimal degree of creativity' required by *Feist* and that contract law has been used to ensure sufficient protection is provided to the databases.[115] However, it must not be forgotten that the originality requirement in relation to compilations after the *Feist* case has the potential to deny spatial databases copyright protection, regardless of the importance of such work for the promotion of the progress of science and overall benefit to society.[116] The discussed contractual measures, while providing some protection, may fail to attain the overall objectives of the copyright law, given the limited access it would provide to a limited number of individuals/entities.

The lack of incentives and opportunities for creators to recoup their investments will result in a limited amount of investment and creation in these databases.[117] Furthermore, this will open up the possibility for costly economically and socially valuable products such as spatial databases to be misappropriated. The tension between the need to grant protection to products and the principles of originality, as depicted in *Feist* for compilations, has led some of the subsequent courts to revive the 'sweat of the brow' principle under another name: 'sweat of the brain'. 'Sweat of the brain' has been defined as the 'finding of intellectual creative activity in the process of creating the work'.[118] Therefore, in such a situation, even if there is no evidence of creativity in the final product, copyright protection should be granted based on the creativity in the process.

In *Mason v. Montgomery Data, Inc.*[119] the Court referred to the expert evidence given by licenced surveyors and experienced mapmakers that 'the differences between Mason's maps and those of his competitors are the natural result of each mapmaker's selection of sources, interpretation of those sources, discretion in reconciling inconsistencies among the sources, and skill and judgment in depicting the information'.[120]

The case of *CCC Information Services, Inc. v. Maclean Hunter Market Reports, Inc.*[121] has also been identified as an attempt to revive the 'sweat of the brow' doctrine in the USA. In discussing the application of originality requirements in the context of a computer database containing valuations of used vehicles, the Court held that the vehicle values included in the database were sufficiently 'original' as to warrant copyright protection as such values were not 'discovered' from pre-existing facts. The Court emphasised the professional judgement and expertise required in making predictions of future prices and the fact that 'the compilation was not merely a list of pre-existing facts but rather a selective exercise requiring independent judgment'.

Applying this principle to the creation of spatial databases, it can be argued that the intellectual creativity involved in the selection of data from different sources – resolving inconsistencies, coordinating, arranging, or even drawing the information differently would be sufficient to prove the creativity needed for copyright protection. In the context of U.S. copyright law, it has been suggested that the best protection for spatial databases may be attained either through a legislative amendment to the definition of term compilation to accommodate lower authorship works or by the introduction of a *sui generis* protection for databases, as has been done in Europe.[122]

3.7 Authorship

In terms of authorship requirement, the copyright *Compendium* specifically provides that the U.S. Copyright Office will register an original work only if it was created by a human being.[123] An author was defined in *Burrow-Giles Lithographic Co. v. Sarony*,[124] as 'he to whom anything owes its origin; originator; maker; one who completes a work of science or literature'.[125] The Court referred to 'authors' as human in this case. The *Compendium* clarifies this position by stating that 'copyright law only protects 'the fruits of intellectual labor' that are 'founded in the creative powers of the mind'.[126] Because copyright law is limited to 'original intellectual conceptions of the author',[127] the U.S. Copyright Office will not register works produced by nature, animals, or plants. Likewise, the Office cannot register a work purportedly created by divine or supernatural beings, although the Office may register a work when the application or the deposit copy(ies) state that the work was inspired by a divine spirit.[128]

Regarding works produced by a machine or mere mechanical process that operates randomly or automatically without any creative input or intervention from a human author, the same principles have been applied in the USA. The test used in this situation had been formulated in the *Compendium* as to whether the 'work' is one of human authorship, with the computer [or other device] merely being an assisting instrument, or whether the traditional elements of authorship in the work (literary, artistic, or musical expression or elements of selection, arrangement, etc.) were conceived and executed not by a human but by a machine.[129]

This issue was raised recently when Steven Thaler[130] filed an application to register a copyright claim of a 2D artwork, whereby the author was identified as 'Creativity Machine' with Thaler listed as the claimant, alongside a transfer statement.[131] In his application, Thaler claimed that the artwork 'was autonomously created by a computer algorithm running on a machine' and he was 'seeking to register this computer-generated work as a work-for-hire to the owner of the Creativity Machine'.[132] In his second request, Thaler argued for authorship to be granted to computer-generated works because non-human entities are capable of obtaining such authorship under the 'work made for hire' doctrine.[133] While this matter is yet to be decided by the court of law, the Board concluded that Office policy and practice make human authorship a prerequisite for copyright protection.[134]

In view of this discussion, it is important to consider the authorship of spatial products created through automation and artificial intelligence (AI). Spatial products created through automation could be considered as satisfying the human authorship requirement as the procedure is applied 'using human-derived rules and workflow'. In such a situation, the human creative effort is applied at the time when the spatial product is created, and 'the choices and decisions' made by the cartographer would qualify the work to be considered conceived and executed by a human author. Given that 'the automation process is deterministic', resulting in the same output for the same input, the specific output could be predicted by the creators, and this would qualify as another tool that creators use. As long as the automation process is merely an instrument that assists the cartographer in the creation of spatial products, such a process would not hinder the copyrightability of spatial products created in this manner.

In determining the answer to the question of whether the authorship of spatial products and data should be traced and protected through the process of data aggregation and compilation of derivative products, the answer can be found in section 103(b). As per the guidance provided in the *Compendium*, 'the author of a derivative work may claim copyright in a work that recasts, transforms, or adapts a pre-existing work, provided that the pre-existing material has been used in a lawful manner'.[135] Therefore, while the pre-existing spatial products and data will be protected through the process of data aggregation and compilation of derivative work under section 103(a), a reference must be made to this discussion about the limited protection granted to data that would prevent pre-existing materials having copyright protection to begin with.

In terms of digital maps generated using AI, it is clear from this discussion that authorship in such maps will not be recognised by the U.S. Copyright Office if there is no creative input or intervention from a human author. In determining the copyrightability of *Zarya of the Dawn*,[136] the U.S. Copyright Office on 21 February 2023 determined that while the human author could be considered as the author of the text of the graphic novel as well as the selection, coordination, and arrangement of the novel's written and visual elements, they were not entitled to obtain copyright protection for the individual images within the novel, as they are not a product of human authorship.[137] The process explained by the applicant illustrates the basic functioning of most AI software, and the U.S. Copyright Office, in this instance, decided that there was a:

> [S]ignificant distance between what a user may direct Midjourney to create and the visual material Midjourney actually produces, Midjourney users lack sufficient control over generated images to be treated as the 'master mind' behind them.[138]

In its decision, the U.S. Copyright Office recognises the possibility that 'other AI offerings that can generate expressive material operate differently than Midjourney does'[139] and, therefore, that it may be able to grant authorship to the creator of the work. This is further evidenced by the fact that the U.S. Copyright Office was willing to recognise the authorship of the works that Kashtanova made substantive edits to form an intermediate image generated by Midjourney.

While courts have not specified what may constitute human intervention or creative input in the context of digital maps, the decisions of the U.S. Copyright Office clearly indicate that the distance between the human input and the output, the level of control over the visual output, and the manner in which such control is exercised would constitute an integral part in the determination of the authorship of AI-generated survey plans.

3.8 Ownership of copyright

The ownership of copyright in the USA is provided under section 201(a) of the Act, which states that the initial ownership of a work is vested with the author or authors of the work.[140] The authors of a joint work are considered co-owners of the copyright in the work.[141] Section 201(b) recognises works made for hire, and prescribes that the employer or other persons for whom the work was prepared is considered the author (unless the parties have expressly agreed otherwise in a written instrument signed by them) and owns all the rights comprised in the copyright. A work is considered as made for hire in two circumstances: first, when prepared by an employee within the scope of their employment; or second, when prepared by an independent contractor (where the parties expressly agree in writing that the work is made for hire) and falls within one of the categories of specially ordered or commissioned works specified in the definition provided in the statute. Note that the common law agency doctrine applies when determining whether a person is an 'employee' within the meaning of the statute.[142] Section 202 recognises the distinction between the ownership of copyright and ownership of any material object in which the work is embodied. The ownership of any material object does not convey any rights in the copyrighted work embodied in the object.

Generally, a surveyor is considered to be an independent contractor unless they are employed as an in-house professional. A surveyor who produces a spatial product as an independent contractor would retain the ownership of that product. However, it is possible for a surveyor acting as an independent contractor to lose the ownership of a spatial product if the work is ordered or commissioned based on an agreement between the parties whereby the parties agree in writing the work to be one made for hire. Thus, U.S. surveyors should be mindful of the contractual terms upon which the spatial products are created, because a written signed agreement may have terms that would make their work a work made for hire, even if they are hired as independent contractors, and they would thus lose the ownership of the spatial product.

When determining whether a surveyor is an independent contractor or an employee, the Restatement (Second) of the Agency[143] guidelines are valuable. How parties identify their relationship is only one aspect that the Court will consider when determining whether a person is an employee or independent contractor; surveyors, therefore, must pay special attention to the factors identified in the Restatement to avoid accidentally being qualified as an employee. To avoid such a situation, surveyors must ensure that they exercise control over the details of the work; engage in a distinct occupation or business; perform work without direction or supervision; employ the specific skillset of a surveyor; use their own supplies, instruments, tools, and place of work; and be specific about the length of time and method of payment in the contract.

A person who engages a surveyor may be able to claim joint ownership of a work if there is an actual contribution to the development. In this situation, they will become the co-author of a joint work. In the context of survey products, however, a client's ability to make such directions will be limited. Even if the client provides ideas, comments/feedback, and suggestions for changes, such interactions will not result in joint ownership.[144]

In terms of section 202, making a distinction between the ownership of copyright and ownership of any material object in which the work is embodied would enable a surveyor to reproduce the survey products and retain copyright over those products, regardless of whether they were commissioned by another party. Thus, a client receiving the survey product would only be able to claim ownership for such product if it is a map, plan, or model; they would not receive any right as to the copyright of the survey product.

In terms of defining who is qualified as an author, the courts have held that the 'author is the party who actually creates the work, that is, the person who translates an idea into fixed, tangible expression entitled to copyright protection'.[145] Compilations include collective works, the ownership of which are specified in section 201(c). The ownership of a collective work as a whole and each separate contribution to a collective work have been distinguished in the Act.[146] While the author of a contribution to a collective work would have separate copyright for the contribution made, the copyright owner in the collective work would (unless otherwise agreed upon by the parties) have the privilege of reproducing and distributing their contribution as part of that particular collective work.[147] Under section 104(a), an unpublished work is protected under the Act regardless of the nationality or domicile of the author while it is unpublished and not in the public domain. Regarding published works, section 104(b) provides that foreign authors may be eligible for protection in the USA as long as they can be qualified within one of the categories mentioned in the statute. According to section 104(b)(1), foreign works could be protected if, upon the work's first publication, one or more author(s) of the work is: (1) a national or domiciliary of the USA; (2) a national, domiciliary, or sovereign authority of a treaty party; or (3) a stateless person wherever that person is domiciled.

The relationship between U.S. government work and the copyright attached to it is also important. As a general principle, there is no copyright protection for any U.S. government work. In deciding whether the annotations of the Georgia State Code commissioned by a private publisher (LexisNexis) could be protected by copyright, the Supreme Court in *Georgia et al v. Public.Resource.Org*[148] reverted to the 'government edicts doctrine', holding that annotations are ineligible for copyright protection. The 'work of the United States Government' is defined in the statute as 'a work prepared by an officer or employee of the United States Government as part of that person's official duties'.[149] However, the U.S. government is not precluded from receiving and holding copyrights transferred to it by assignment, bequest or otherwise. The Act identifies specific copyright requirements in relation to certain government institutions. Literary work produced by a civilian member of the faculty of a covered institution (covered worker)[150] would own the copyright of such work, unless the Secretary of Defense directs the covered worker to provide the federal government with an irrevocable, royalty-free, worldwide, nonexclusive licence to reproduce, distribute, perform, or display such work for the purposes of the U.S. government.[151] Under U.S. copyright principles, works created by independent contractors commissioned by the U.S. government would not fall within the definition of works of the U.S. government, and would therefore be eligible for copyright protection.[152] The above limitations to copyright are applicable only to the federal government; state governments can generally apply for copyright to works of authorship prepared by the employees of state governments.

In light of these basic principles, the ownership of survey products in the USA should be considered. Unlike Australia, the United Kingdom (UK), and Canada, the USA does not have the concept of Crown copyright at the federal level. While political, historical, and constitutional differences have contributed to this distinction, government works in the USA are considered to be prepared for and on behalf of the people, enabling people to have free access to such information.[153] Placing the survey products with a government office does not result in transferring the copyright that the surveyor owns.[154] As per section 101, a 'public performance or display of a work does not of itself constitute publication'. Therefore, placing copies of a work in a government office, where it is available for inspection by the public, will not impair the surveyor's right to control the making of copies of the deposited materials.[155] While such use may be subject to the fair use principle, the absence of a Crown copyright concept would enable surveyors to keep the copyright in the work – even if copies are placed in public files.

3.9 Copyright infringements by the State: Does the State enjoy an implied licence or a statutory defence?

Unlike in Australia, the U.S. copyright regime does not recognise government use as a statutory defence within the statute. Given the absence of the concept of Crown copyright in the federal copyright statute, it is no surprise that this concept is not recognised in the Act. The general statutory provisions for copyright infringement are provided in section 501 of the Act, which states that 'anyone' who violates any of the exclusive rights of the copyright owner or author, or who imports copies or phonorecords into the USA in violation of these rights, infringes the rights of copyright holders. The copyright protection granted to works extends to infringement by 'the United States, by a corporation owned or controlled by the United States, or by a contractor, subcontractor, or any person, firm, or corporation acting for the government and with the authorisation or consent of the government'.[156] The copyright owner can bring a claim against the USA in the Court of Federal Claims for the recovery of reasonable and entire compensation as damages for such infringement, including the minimum statutory damages.[157]

In relation to state governments, there is a specific reference to states in the Act where the term 'anyone' is defined to include:

> any State, any instrumentality of a State, and any officer or employee of a State or instrumentality of a State acting in his or her official capacity. Any State, and any such instrumentality, officer, or employee, shall be subject to the provisions of this title in the same manner and to the same extent as any nongovernmental entity.

Section 511(a) provides for the liability of the states, instrumentalities of states and state officials for copyright infringement, and abrogates state immunity under the Eleventh Amendment to the U.S. Constitution. The statutory provision states that the same remedies that apply to any other copyright infringement would be available in a violation of copyright by states, instrumentalities of states, and state officials (including remedies both at law and in equity).[158]

One concept that requires some reference in this context is the 'eminent domain' over copyright property that the federal and state governments may be able to exercise. Eminent domain has been defined as 'the inherent ability of federal and state sovereigns to take private property for public use without obtaining the property owner's consent'.[159] The Fifth Amendment to the U.S. Constitution, however, qualifies the federal government's eminent domain power by necessitating that private property can only be taken for public use and that just compensation must be paid in such circumstances. These requirements are also applicable to state governments.[160] While there have been no recorded instances when the government has affirmatively exercised this power in relation to copyright, there have been some in which the copyright holders have claimed the exercise of eminent domain by the government without just compensation.[161]

In view of these statutory provisions, both federal and state governments could be held responsible for the infringement of works subject to copyright, including maps and survey plans. While the statute does not provide for an identical statutory defence, as in some Commonwealth countries, including the UK and Australia, the U.S. government could rely on other defences including the fair use defence[162] as provided in the statute. An important aspect to consider in this regard is whether an implied licence could be claimed under U.S. copyright law.

Section 204(a) of the Act provides that:

> [A] transfer of copyright ownership, other than by operation of law, is not valid unless an instrument of conveyance, or a note or memorandum of the transfer, is in writing and signed by the owner of the rights conveyed or such owner's duly authorised agent.

The term 'transfer of copyright ownership' has been identified in section 101 to include:

> an assignment, mortgage, exclusive license, or any other conveyance, alienation, or hypothecation of a copyright or of any of the exclusive rights comprised in a copyright, whether or not it is limited in time or place of effect, but not including a nonexclusive license.

The statute, therefore, recognises the written element in relation to instruments of transfer, and the possibility of an implied nonexclusive licence has been accepted by the U.S. courts, as there is no reference as to this aspect in the statute. The potential availability of an implied nonexclusive licence was recognised in cases that could demonstrate that the parties intended the work to be used for a specific purpose.[163] The existence of a licence could be claimed as an affirmative defence, and the existence of an implied licence would be determined based on the totality of the parties' conduct,[164] as well as the objectively manifested intention.[165] The Court has identified several elements over the years when determining the existence of an implied licence.[166] While these elements are not exhaustive, the Court would look into 'objective evidence permitting a reasonable person to conclude that the parties had reached an agreement'.[167]

It could be argued that a person who commissions a survey plan may have an implied, nonexclusive licence if the requirements of request, delivery, and intent are satisfied. In the case of *Key Maps, Inc. v. Pruitt*,[168] Key Maps, Inc. – the copyright holder in the map of Houston, Harris County, Texas, known as the 'Major Thoroughfare Map' – claimed that the fire marshal of Harris County and Harris County had infringed their copyright after an unsuccessful agreement to produce a map resulted in the fire marshal's unlawful reproduction of 300 copies of the map. The initial oral agreement was for Key Maps to use its maps as a base, then the County Engineer's Office would draw the county fire zones and Key Maps would print the resulting composite fire zone map. The parties were informed that these maps were only to be used for the official business of the fire marshal's protection programme in the unincorporated areas of Harris County. The maps were never meant for public dissemination. Because Key Maps failed to produce the maps as agreed even after six weeks, the fire marshal made a reproduction of the composite map. Later, this map was found to be too small for the intended purpose, and a different map was produced without using Key Map's composite fire zone map. In deciding whether there was an implied licence to use the maps in the manner that the fire marshal did, the Court held that Key Maps gave an implied licence to reproduce the 'Major Thoroughfare Map'. This permission was given for the limited purpose of using it as a base upon which to create a fire zone map for distribution to county agencies. Because Key Maps sold its maps knowing the purpose for which they were to be used and had given specific instructions to the fire marshal to prepare the composite fire zone map, it was reasonable for the fire marshal to believe that he had permission to order a reproduction of the resulting composite map from someone other than Key Maps.

From this judicial decision, it can be concluded that a map buyer would be able to make copies of the work and use it for the original transaction. Whether an implied licence could be argued for subsequent transactions involved with the same survey plan would depend on what the parties had agreed about the use and purpose of the work. In 2020, the Court identified the possibility of implied sublicensing in copyright law in the case of *Photographic Illustrator's Corp. v Orgill, Inc.*,[169] whereby a licensee had a nonexclusive licence that allowed for unrestricted sublicensing.[170] In this case, the Court assessed the licensee's right to impliedly sublicense photographs of lightbulbs to its distributor. Given that the licensor had permitted unrestricted sublicensing in the nonexclusive licence, the Court held that an express sublicense was not required. The intention between the parties was the determining factor in establishing an implied sublicence. This decision has important implications in the context of survey products, for which the licensing agreements between the surveyors and clients may contain clauses about sublicensing. The sublicensing clauses would have to be closely scrutinised, because they could lead to the possibility of an implied sublicence between the licensee and sublicensee, which may prevent the copyright owner from taking action against the use of copyrighted materials by third parties. The focus made on the intention – not on the request and delivery aspects – may lead to situations in which the interactions of licensees (who is not the owner of the copyright and has no motivation to protect the value of the copyright) with third parties would easily establish an implied sublicense.

3.10 Open data initiatives and data sharing policies/initiatives in the USA

While access to government information has long been an area of focus in the USA, the developments witnessed during the administration of former U.S. President Barack Obama (from 2009–2017) set a new phase in open data initiatives.[171] President Obama's 2013 'Memorandum on Transparency and Open Government' and Executive Order on 'Making Open and Machine Readable the New Default for Government Information' resulted in a renewed commitment to collaborations among government agencies, entrepreneurs, developers, and the general public, which came together to create data-driven products and services.[172] The Open Data Policy of 2013 was approved by the U.S. Congress and therefore has the force of law in the USA.[173] The website Data.gov[174] was set up as a requirement under the statute to enable 'federal agencies to publish the information online as open data using standardised, machine-readable data formats with their metadata included in the data.gov catalogue'.[175] The website offers the opportunity to search more than 335,000 datasets. In addition, the Geospatial Data Act of 2018 (GDA)[176] has resulted in establishing the Geospatial Platform (GeoPlatform),[177] which aims to make federal geospatial data assets more 'Findable, Accessible, Interoperable, and Reusable with special emphasis as the authorised source for all the official National Geospatial Data Assets (NGDAs) across 18 data themes as guided by the U.S. Federal Geographic Data Committee (FGDC)'.[178] The website's data policy statement explicitly recognises the copyright-free status of the data and content created by government employees within their employment.[179] However, the policy statement recognises that any non-federal data available through the website may have different licensing requirements.[180] While the data.gov website provides the general public with access to federal data without any restrictions, access to copyright-protected data is provided within the website, subject to restrictions.

These open data initiatives provide an important source of information for surveyors when searching for cadastral information. The geospatial data and related survey products that are available through open data initiatives provide a useful source when gathering relevant information. However, extreme care is suggested when making use of plans that need to be registered or have undergone prior examination. Issues such as missing information, incorrect data, and mosaic effect as to confidentiality, privacy, and consent issues may limit the value of the open data initiatives to surveyors. Furthermore, the licensing requirements associated with some of the datasets would require the surveyors to abide by the licensing agreements and be aware of the terms of use for such datasets. The incorporation of open data in the production of survey plans and other products would not result in copyrightable work as long as the selection, arrangement, and organisation of such data is not an original expression. Therefore, while open data would provide ready access to the required information, products that result from using such data would have limited protection.

3.11 Fair use defence under copyright law

Section 107 of the Act provides for fair use defence in the USA. The statutory provision provides that:

> Notwithstanding the provisions of sections 106 and 16A, the fair use of a copyrighted work, including such use by reproduction in copies or phonorecords or by any other means specified by that section, for purposes such as

> criticism, comment, news reporting, teaching (including multiple copies for classroom use), scholarship, or research, is not an infringement of copyright. In determining whether the use made of a work in any particular case is a fair use the factors to be considered shall include[:]
>
> (1) the purpose and character of the use, including whether such use is of a commercial nature or is for non-profit educational purposes;
> (2) the nature of the copyrighted work;
> (3) the amount and substantiality of the portion used in relation to the copyrighted work as a whole; and
> (4) the effect of the use upon the potential market for or value of the copyrighted work.
>
> The fact that a work is unpublished shall not itself bar a finding of fair use if such a finding is made upon consideration of all the above factors.

Under U.S. law, fair use is an affirmative defence and is determined on a case-by-case basis. The listed factors are not exhaustive, and each factor should be examined to make a determination.[181] In determining the use's purpose and character, 'transformative use' has been held as central to a proper analysis of fair use.[182] The Court has identified the value generated by the second use and resulting transformation as justification for a finding of fair use. In discussing the element of the nature of a copyrighted work, the Supreme Court has identified that the use is less likely to be fair when the copyrighted work is a creative product.[183] Furthermore, fair use is more likely to be found in factual than fictional work.[184] There is also a higher likelihood of finding fair use in relation to published rather than unpublished work.[185] The Court has identified the quantity of material used in the original work and the value of that material as important factors in determining fair use. It has been noted that 'as the amount of the copyrighted material that is used increases, the likelihood that the use will constitute a "fair use" decreases'.[186] The fourth factor, the effect on the market for the copyrighted work, has been considered as the single most important factor in earlier cases.[187]

The case of *Campbell v. Acuff-Rose Music, Inc.*[188] emphasised that all four factors 'are to be explored, and the results weighed together, in light of the purposes of copyright'.[189] The case of *Key Maps, Inc. v. Pruitt*[190] tested the application of the fair use defence in the context of maps. In this case, the Court held that the fire marshal's use of the composite map was for a 'legitimate, fair and reasonable purpose'. Because the use was not of a commercial nature, it did not diminish or prejudice the potential sales of Key Map's copyrighted maps. Further, the fire marshal's use of the maps was done fairly and in good faith. The Court also referred to the public interest in disseminating fire zone maps to various fire departments for fire-prevention purposes. Because there was no express consent from Key Maps about the use of the maps, the Court said that it was reasonable for the fire marshal to believe that he had permission to commission a reproduction because of the significant delay experienced in performing the original agreement.

In a landmark decision in *Google LLC v. Oracle Am., Inc.*,[191] the Supreme Court discussed the four factors in detail regarding the fair use of the software. In this case, Oracle America, Inc., a copyright owner in Java Platform, Standard Edition (Java SE), argued that Google's copying of roughly 11,500 lines of code from the Java SE program was not a fair use of the work and Google should therefore be liable for copyright infringement. The copied lines were part of a tool called an application programming interface (API), a portion of the platform enabling a programmer to call up prewritten code that – together with the computer's hardware – would carry out a large number of specific tasks. On the four factors of section 107, the Court held that regarding the nature of copyrighted work, the code was inextricably bound with a non-copyrightable general system of dividing computing tasks and with copyrightable implementing code, which Google had not copied. The use of API (which had been created for use in desktop and laptop computers) in smartphone programs was considered as using the copyrighted work for a transformative purpose. Google used a substantial portion of the code by copying approximately 11,500 lines (the total set of API computer code amounted to 2.86 million lines); the Court held that the code was copied because programmers had already learned to work with the API's system, and it would have been difficult – perhaps prohibitively so – to attract programmers to build the company's smartphone system without the copied code. Regarding market effects, the Court held that the ability of Oracle America's API to compete in the smartphone marketplace was uncertain because it had been created for desktop and laptop computers. The Court concluded that because of the costs and difficulties of producing alternative APIs with similar appeals to programmers, the public would be harmed by copyright enforcement that limited the future creation of new programs.

The case of *Google LLC v. Oracle Am., Inc.*[192] has further developed public interest as a factor in the fair use analysis. Therefore, when copyright holders attempt to exert control outside their copyright's rightful scope and engage in anti-competitive conduct, the Court has been willing to identify fair use. Regarding survey plans and spatial data, the fair use defence would permit any person to use them, as long as such use is within the four factors identified in section 107.

3.12 Unfair competition law for the protection of geospatial data

The structural limitations and infirmities embedded in the U.S. copyright system about the protection afforded to data and databases mean that alternative ways in which the rights of copyright holders may be protected should be considered. Furthermore, it has been noted that the 'rapid proliferation of utilitarian works for which copyright protection is sought in the "information age" has placed copyright law under increasing strain with respect to the protection of these works'.[193] This is an important consideration because of the importance of investment due to the inherent value of spatial data and databases to society. As discussed in the previous sections, there is a lack of protection for spatial data under copyright law; spatial databases have limited protection due to the standards of originality required to be considered as a compilation. Thus, even though spatial data and products are valuable to society and may contain a significant amount of labour and investment, they would be open for competitors to appropriate without compensation for the creators. This would result in the removal of the economic incentive to create desirable products and the ability of creators to control the publication and dissemination of their work.[194]

There is a possibility of using principles of misappropriation under the common law (at the State level) when protecting computer databases. In limited circumstances when the database lacks a minimal amount of creativity, the common law misappropriation can be used as long as copyright laws do not pre-empt it. To bring an action for misappropriation, it must be shown that the '(1) plaintiff has made a substantial investment of time, money, or intellectual effort in creating the database; (2) defendant has appropriated the product of plaintiff's investment; and (3) defendant's appropriation has injured plaintiff'.[195] The common law misappropriation recognises the 'sweat of the brow' of the database creator, enabling a protection mechanism to secure the creator's investment and effort.

The principles of pre-emption as applicable to copyright issues are important when determining the applicability of the unfair competition law in protecting geospatial data in the U.S. context. In this discussion, not only should the subject matter of the pre-emption be investigated, but also the interplay between federal and state laws. In terms of the latter, the Act contains express pre-emption in section 301(a), as follows.

> all legal or equitable rights that are equivalent to any of the exclusive rights within the general scope of copyright as specified by section 106 in works of authorship that are fixed in a tangible medium of expression and come within the subject matter of copyright as specified by sections 102 and 103, whether created before or after that date and whether published or unpublished, are governed exclusively by this title. Thereafter, no person is entitled to any such right or equivalent right in any such work under the common law or statutes of any State.[196]

Any state law dealing with works that fall within the subject matter of copyright and rights equivalent to those protected by the Act would be pre-empted under section 301(a).[197] When determining whether a matter deals with rights that are equivalent to those protected by the Act, the 'courts examine whether the plaintiff's state law claim contains an "extra element" that "changes the nature of the action" so that it is "qualitatively different" from a copyright infringement claim'.[198] Generally, if the unfair competition claims are based on issues such as fiduciary duties, misrepresentation, passing off, and conversion, it would not be pre-empted under section 301(a).[199] If the unfair competition claims concern the unauthorised copying and use of the plaintiff's product, however, then such claims would be pre-empted because they concern rights protected by the Copyright Act.[200]

In the context of geospatial data, the determining factor would be whether it falls within the subject matter of copyright, with works listed in sections 102 and 103 of the Act. When copyright protection is not granted, the data has been generally identified as falling within section 102. In *Firoozye v. Earthlink Network*,[201] it was stated that 'the work at issue "does not necessarily have to be protected by a specific copyright or even itself copyrightable; it just has to be "within the subject matter" of the Act'. Any unfair competition claim regarding geospatial data would be pre-empted, as long as the claim deals with equivalent rights to those protected by the Act. The rights protected under the Act are reproduction of the copyrighted work, preparation of derivative works, distribution of the work, and public performance and display of the work. Therefore, if the rights claimed are different from these, such unfair competition claims would not be pre-empted.

An example of unfair competition principles offering protection against 'free-riders' was seen in the USA in 1918, in the case of *International News Service Inc v Associated Press*.[202] In that case, the Supreme Court found that Associated Press was unable to recoup its investment in news gathering if third parties could appropriate the findings without compensation or permission.[203] Injunctive relief was ultimately provided for by the Supreme Court, resulting in International News Service being unable to appropriate the news gathered by Associated Press until it 'lost its value as fresh news'.[204] The principles, in relation to the particular set of facts in that case, were explained as follows by the Court:

> But one who gathers news at pains and expense, for the purpose of lucrative publication, may be said to have a quasi-property in the results of his enterprise as against a rival in the same business, and the appropriation of those results at the expense and to the damage of the one and for the profit of the other is unfair competition against which equity will afford relief.

The majority of the Court recognised that unfair competition could be contemplated as follows:

> If that which the complainant has acquired fairly at substantial cost may be sold fairly at substantial profit, a competitor who is misappropriating it for the purpose of disposing of it to his own profit and to the disadvantage of the complainant cannot be heard to say that it is too fugitive or evanescent to be regarded as property. It has all the attributes of property necessary for determining that a misappropriation of it by a competitor is unfair competition because contrary to good conscience.[205]

This decision led to the recognition of the common law tort of 'hot-news' misappropriation based on unfair competition. This doctrine resulted in recognising a property right in 'time-sensitive information'.[206] In the case of *Barclays Capital, Inc. v. Theflyonthewall.com, Inc.*,[207] financial services firms brought an action against an Internet-based subscription news service, alleging 'hot-news' misappropriation and copyright infringement about securities recommendations. The financial services firms had invested a significant amount of time and money preparing financial recommendations, which were copied and posted on Theflyonthewall.com minutes after their release. While the facts of the case did not warrant the application of the doctrine,[208] the Court recognised the viability of the doctrine in situations when the action was not pre-empted by the Copyright Act.

3.13 Trade secrets (confidential information) protection for geospatial data

In determining the availability of trade secrets protection for spatial data, the principles regarding pre-emption are significant. The trade secrets law protects facts, ideas, and information that have commercial value because of their secrecy[209] and are currently governed by state[210] and federal[211] statutes. Because actions for the disclosure and exploitation of trade secrets require a status of secrecy not required for copyright, generally, such claims are not pre-empted in the USA. A party could thus use the trade secrets provisions to protect spatial data. If the claim is simply against an action of misappropriation via reproduction, however, in cases when there is no secrecy element involved, then such a claim would be pre-empted under the Act.[212]

The application of trade secrets protection to spatial data must be considered within the context that such data is used. The use of spatial data in producing spatial products and the registration of those products with the Copyright Office would result in the loss of trade secrets protection for such products. Given that copyright registration is optional in the USA, and that the copyright holder is not required to make copyrighted work public, it is theoretically possible to retain trade secrets protection for spatial products. However, the advantages of registering copyright and the need for copyright holders to obtain economic benefit from their creative expression are compelling reasons for registering copyright. This would result in the Copyright Office making the work available for public view; this 'availability precludes the showing of the secrecy element required for trade secret protection'.[213] In general, therefore, obtaining copyright registration would result in the loss of trade secrets protection. In the USA, an applicant can file only the identifying portions of the software or other trade secret business information, thereby protecting the trade secrets contained therein.[214] The application of this practice to spatial data is doubtful, however; a spatial product that obtains copyright registration would thus not be able to obtain trade secrets protection under U.S. law.

3.14 Blockchain and smart contracts to protect and track original data used in property transactions

The use of blockchain and smart contracts in land administration has triggered a scholarly discussion on the pros and cons of using a decentralised digital ledger technology to record and verify land transactions.[215] Experiences in Georgia, Sweden, Dubai, Honduras, Ukraine, and Ghana, for example, have raised much interest in the future possibilities of implementing these systems in other countries.[216] Attempts have already been made in the USA to adopt similar strategies.[217] The Cook County Recorder's office in Illinois is often cited as an example of an experiment on using blockchain technology for land record management.[218] Factors to consider in this context include the interaction between the principles of copyright and the decentralised digital ledger technology in general, as well as how spatial data used in property transactions may be tracked and protected using these technologies.

In its simplest form, a blockchain is a 'digital protocol that enables the creation of an unalterable, decentralised distributed ledger across a public or private network'.[219] The individual computers or nodes connect and communicate with other nodes directly without needing to go through a central server. The blocks created by uploading information by individual nodes create a digital fingerprint called a 'hash'. This can then be used to ensure not only the authenticity of the blocks but also the relationship with the previous and subsequent information to each block.[220] Smart contracts are an important tool in this process. Blockchain technology allows for self-executing contracts that are coded into the blockchain and can automatically verify and execute the contract without intermediaries. While this is a simplistic view of how blockchain and smart contracts operate, all blockchain systems are based on four main concepts: immutability, time stamping, accessibility, and smart contracts.[221] The information used to create the blocks will be the main focus of this section, because the spatial data is the main component used to create blocks in a blockchain created for land management purposes.

The use of blockchain for property transactions enables land registration, cadastre, and land governance to be connected, and provides for effective and efficient land governance policies. The ability to have high-quality data and mining of such data the same would enable informed and accurate land governance policies to enhance the transparency, accountability, and efficiency of one of the most important administrative aspects in modern society.[222] A blockchain-based land registry would ensure faster implementation of a pending ownership transaction; enable automated notifications, whether about ownership changes or changes in the land register and cadastre; allow for a higher level transparency of transactions; establish digital archives for documentation, flexibility, and robustness; and enable greater security for land registry actors.[223] ARUP projects that the implementation of title records as smart contracts could be a reality for many as early as 2030–2033.[224]

It has been noted from the perspective of surveyors, a blockchain may be used to do the following in the context of a land management system.

(a) Final field notes and data can be uploaded to the chain sequentially for authentication, safekeeping, and reference.
(b) Legally accepted descriptions and definitions of property can be recorded on the chain and made accessible to others by giving them permissions.
(c) Existing hard copy documents can be digitised and uploaded.
(d) Previous surveys can be posted, and subsequent access given to others.
(e) Current satellite images and GIS data – including lot dimensions, parcel tax identification numbers, and building and utility information – can be stored without danger of tampering.
(f) Digital building information models can be safely stored, exchanged, or networked to support decision-making.[225]

In terms of tracking spatial data, blockchain allows for the creation of tamper-proof evidence regarding the time of recording given information. These hashed and time-stamped records let the original data be tracked. However, having accurate and clean data is vital because once data is placed onto a blockchain, there is no mechanism to correct it or ascertain the reliability of the data.[226] The considerations about using blockchain technology as a standalone copyright protection system have been mainly driven by this ability to trace back to the original information.[227] Being able to time-stamp the information and data, as well as the tamper-proof nature of the records, would enable alternative means of registration when it comes to proof of time of creation. Even for unregistered works, this will provide an opportunity to create a digital identity while protecting the privacy of the authors.[228]

Two aspects are important regarding the copyright protection granted to the information stored on a blockchain: protection for individual information stored on a blockchain and the ownership of the compilation of information. As discussed in this report regarding originality and subject matter,[229] facts cannot be granted copyright protection under U.S. law. If the creation of blocks results from mere recording of facts, it will not be copyrightable. The need to record information in a specific manner dictated by functional considerations also affects the originality. The blockchain's functionality includes its distribution and updating over the network, including transmission between nodes and storage in the medium of individual nodes. Only a copyright holder could enjoin individual nodes from transmitting blocks that contain copyrighted work.[230] Mostly, the individual information stored on a blockchain may not be able to reach the level of originality required under the law. This position is equally applicable to spatial data, which would have limited protection under U.S. copyright law.

A second aspect related to copyright in blockchain is whether the entirety of the information recorded on a blockchain could be protected under U.S. copyright law. As discussed in the *Feist* case, the 'selection' and 'arrangement' of information with a minimum level of creativity is required to obtain protection as a compilation of information. Because selection has been held to be non-original if all available data is recorded, a block may not satisfy the minimum level of creativity – most current blockchain applications involve the storage of all available information, thereby disregarding the need for creative selection.[231] In terms of the 'arrangement' of information, it depends mainly on the technical considerations related to efficiency.[232] Although an original arrangement that increases efficiency may be able to satisfy the originality requirement, the arrangement of information on a blockchain based on the chronological order, as done in most blockchain systems, may exclude the protection granted to such an arrangement.[233]

3.15 Technological protection measures (TPMs)

TPMs can be an important tool in protecting spatial products. There is limited protection available to databases in the USA as compilations; TPMs have been identified as providing an extra layer of protection to spatial products. The Digital

Millennium Copyright Act of 1998 (DMCA)[234] is an important milestone for TPMs because it includes protection against the circumvention of copyright protection systems. Proponents of TPMs have advocated for these statutory provisions to be introduced to ensure the protection of digital materials in the Internet era.[235]

The statutory scheme introduced by the DMCA does not require copyright owners to apply any specific protective measures. TPMs are adopted at the discretion of the copyright holder. The development of TPMs is expected to result from a consultative process between content owners and the makers of computers, consumer electronics, and telecommunications devices. It is further expected that those who are affected by TPMs will be consulted in this process.[236] The aim of Congress has been to protect the interests of copyright owners and encourage owners to make digital works more readily available by making sure that those works could be protected by TPMs.[237]

Three main prohibitions are provided in section 1201 of the DMCA. The *basic provision* bans those who engage in unauthorised circumvention of TPMs, the 'prohibition of trafficking and additional violations'. Section 1201(a)(1)(A) provides that no person shall circumvent a technological measure that effectively controls access to a copyright-protected work. The statutory provisions aim to 'bar one whom technology "locks out" of a copyrighted work from "breaking into" it'.[238] Section 1201(a)(1)(A) applies to both 'those who perform prohibited services and those who manufacture equipment designed for that function'.[239] These measures do not apply to works in the public domain, because statutory provisions apply only to works protected by U.S. copyright law.

Section 1201(a)(3) defines the term 'circumvent a technological measure' to include 'descramble a scrambled work, to decrypt an encrypted work, or otherwise, to avoid, bypass, remove, deactivate, or impair a technological measure, without the authority of the copyright owner'. A technological measure that 'effectively controls access to a work' has been defined as a 'measure, in the ordinary course of its operation, requires the application of information, or a process or a treatment, with the authority of the copyright owner, to gain access to the work'. Thus, these measures include encryption, scrambling, authentication or the use of a 'key' to gain access to a work.

In *Healthcare Advocates, Inc. v. Harding, Earley, Follmer & Frailey*, while recognising that not all robots.txt files (a text file webmasters create to instruct search engine robots how to crawl pages on the websites) would qualify as TPMs, a simple robots.txt file that blocked users from accessing archived screenshots was considered to be a technological measure that effectively controlled access to the work. Known as a 'secret handshake' protocol, it was considered to be a TPM protected under DMCA in the case of *RealNetworks, Inc. v. Streambox, Inc.*[240] In *Chamberlain Group, Inc. v. Skylink Technologies, Inc.*,[241] the Court considered the application of section 1201 in relation to a universal remote transmitter capable of activating certain garage door openers manufactured by Chamberlain Group, which contained a 'rolling code computer program that would prevent the capture and recording of transmitter signals'. This technology had been developed to prevent 'code-grabbing', whereby capturing and recording transmitter signals have been used to obtain illegal access to garages. In this case, the Court held that Skylink did not violate section 1201 of the DMCA because Chamberlain's technology was not being used to protect copyrighted content or materials. The Court also held that there was no unauthorised access to Chamberlain's copyrighted software, and the control introduced by Skylink's remote control only worked if the door owners stored its signal in the opener's memory. TPMs are especially effective in situations in which practices such as deep linking may have the effect of bypassing the contractual agreement (clickwrap or the digital version of the shrinkwrap agreements discussed previously). In the case of *Ticketmaster v. Tickets.com, Inc.*,[242] the Court did not recognise the copyright infringement by Tickets.com when large amounts of data from the Ticketmaster website were downloaded. The Court held that the deep linking done by Tickets.com was not a breach of Ticketmaster's terms, which prohibited the deep linking of its databases. In such a situation, the contractual agreements may not be able to provide sufficient protection, and websites and databases should be set up in ways such that clickwrap licence cannot be avoided and TPMs are employed to protect the works.

The prohibition on trafficking is provided under section 1201(a)(2),[243] while additional protections are provided in 1201(b).[244] While these two provisions appear to be similar in wording, they are attempting to protect two distinct rights. While the former is aimed at TPMs that 'effectively control access to a work protected', the latter is directed towards TPMs that 'effectively protect a right of a copyright owner'. Nimmer explains the difference as follows: section 1201(a)(2) can be compared to 'breaking into another's domain' while section 1201(b) is equivalent to 'upon being permitted entry . . . proceeding to violate the host's "house rules" '.[245] Thus, the definitions of the terms 'circumvent protection afforded by a technological measure'[246] and a TPM that 'effectively protects a right of a copyright owner under this title'[247] regarding section 1201(b) has been changed to prevent TPMs that violate the 'house rules'.

The statutory provisions have tipped the scales in the copyright owners' favour by 'creating liability for "digital trespass" via the basic provision, and for facilitating that circumvention via the trafficking ban, as well as for facilitating infringement under the additional violations'.[248] As per section 1201 of the DCMA, these three aspects of TPMs will be considered protected, and any person who attempts to circumvent these measures would be subject to both civil and criminal penalties under sections 1203 and 1204 of the DMCA.

The statutory provisions provide for exceptions to the anti-circumvention prohibitions, as well as policy safeguards.[249] The exemptions include a 'shopping privilege' for non-profit libraries, archives, and educational institutions; an exemption for law enforcement, intelligence, and other government activities; reverse engineering; encryption research; and security testing.[250] The provisions regarding preventing access to minors and protecting personally identifying information and design equipment aim to promote social welfare.

Apart from the anti-circumvention provisions, Chapter 12 also contains the protection of 'copyright management information (CMI) provisions in section 1202'. This section prohibits the intentional provision, distribution, or import distribution of false CMI with the intent to induce, enable, facilitate, or conceal infringement. Eight categories of CMI are identified in the statute. The first three are information about the work's title, author, and copyright owner. Under these categories, the protection extends to information identifying the work, as well as information set forth on a notice of copyright in relation to the work's title and its copyright owner. The fourth category is the name of a performer whose performance is fixed on a work other than an audiovisual work (excluding the public performance of works by radio or television broadcasting stations). The fifth category is the name of – and other identifying information about – a writer, performer, or director who is credited with an audiovisual work (excluding the public performance of works by radio or television broadcasting stations). The sixth category protects the terms and conditions for the use of the work; the seventh category protects identifying numbers or symbols referring to such information, or links to such information; and the final category provides for the right of the Register of Copyrights to prescribe any other information that may be categorised as CMI.

Regarding spatial products, TPMs could provide an opportunity to protect the access and unauthorised use of spatial products by third parties. The protection is granted only to copyrighted works, however; to obtain the benefit of DMCA provisions, the spatial products must be copyrightable. Therefore, the limitations discussed in the preceding sections about the copyrightability of the spatial data and spatial products would have to be considered.

3.16 *Sui generis* law for database protection

The case of *Feist* was seen as limiting the protection granted to databases, because of the requirement about the minimum level of creativity in the selection, arrangement, and coordination of databases. With databases, what is protected under copyright law is creative compilations. Any data used in the database could be used by someone else to create another database, as long as the arrangement is different from the original database.[251] There is a lack of judicial guidance about the level of creativity required by compilations to satisfy the minimum level of creativity threshold, so the subsequent cases have adopted different yardsticks when determining the matter.[252] For example, a directory of Chinese-American businesses[253] and Maclean Hunter's *Red Book* predicting the value of used cars were considered as sufficiently creative to warrant copyright protection, while horse racing charts containing historical information on winning numbers[254] and a database holding descriptions of yachts for sale[255] were considered as lacking the required level of creativity.[256] Given the lack of consistency in this area, there have been numerous attempts to introduce a *sui generis* law in order to protect databases as it has been done in the European Union (EU). There have been several legislative initiatives have been introduced in the USA based on the principles of misappropriation, unfair competition, and the EU directive on database protection. At the outset, it must be noted that there is no *sui generis* protection for databases in the USA, regardless of early attempts like the Committee on Data for Science and Technology as established by the National Research Council in 1994, when a detailed report was presented as to the legal protection for databases.[257]

The legislative initiatives have recommended numerous ways in which a balance could be achieved about needing to prohibit unauthorised copying while ensuring reasonable access to information. However, none of these legislative initiatives has been successful in the USA. The debate in the USA about the *sui generis* right for databases has been largely influenced by lobbying groups, and the series of draft legislation proposed by the Subcommittee on Courts, Intellectual Property, and the Internet of the Committee on the Judiciary of the U.S. House of Representatives to provide greater protection to database owners has been opposed by the Energy and Commerce Committee, thereby leading to legislative inactivity in this regard. Many commentators have noted that the *sui generis* right is not going to benefit the USA because there has not been a proven impact of the EU directive on the production of databases in the EU.[258] Some commentators have claimed that the USA has long given up the intention to introduce a *sui generis* protection for databases, and that the protection for databases is provided under the fair use principle.[259]

3.17 Conclusion

As discussed in this study, the copyright system in the USA has common roots in the common law principles as discussed in relation to Australia. Similar to the Australian context, it is quite clear from the discussions in this chapter that technological developments have caused significant challenges concerning the protection of spatial products and data in the USA.

The recognition made in earlier cases as to the identification of maps as pictorial representations was insufficient to accommodate the rapid change witnessed in the collection, storing, and analysis of spatial data and the resulting spatial products. The protection of spatial products and data based on principles applicable to compilations, while providing a logical avenue for protection, would have very limited scope since the *Feist* decision. While the U.S. system is also subject to limitations regarding the recognition of the effort, time, and expertise involved in the production of spatial products, as in Australia, it is essential to consider the impact this would have on the copyright protection granted to spatial products and data. While the possibilities of a *sui generis* right of databases containing data created and produced through significant and substantial investment and effort have been considered in the USA numerous times, such recommendations have not been considered favourably in the USA. Given the limited likelihood that such a change will be accepted in the future, one aspect that may be considered in the USA and may also be relevant for Australia is the possibility of introducing a 'sweat of the brain' approach to originality.

While the statutory provisions provide much more clarity as to the element of the materials from the USA, it is essential to note that concerning new technologies, the courts have been adopting a case-by-case approach when determining the requirement of 'perceivability'. While this provides a certain level of flexibility, it would be prudent to set some guidelines in line with the correct understanding of the purpose and character of computer memory and related technology.

The use of AI has been one of the important technological considerations in recent years and is yet to be discussed in detail, either in judicial decisions or legislative instruments, in relation to copyright. It is important to note that there has been some scholarly discussion about moving away from the idea of copyright as necessarily including a human act to include a broader view of authorship in copyright. While no recognition has been made as to the authorship of digital work produced by AI so far, the decisions of the U.S. Copyright Office do not entirely disregard the possibility that it would be possible to recognise AI authorship in future. With the increased use of AI products in the day-to-day life of surveyors, there are significant implications if such recognition is made. Thus, it would be imperative for the surveyors to be aware of the primary considerations involved with the determination of authorship that include – but are not limited to – human input and the output, the level of control over the visual output, and the manner in which such control is exercised.

One of the crucial distinctions between Australia and the USA in relation to ownership copyright is the lack of recognition given to the concept of Crown copyright in the latter. While the historical circumstances certainly explain these differences, it is important to consider the relevance of such a concept in the modern context. As noted in this chapter, both federal and state governments in the USA could be held responsible for the infringement of works subject to copyright, including maps and survey plans. Such recognition is pivotal in the modern context, as the gathering of spatial data has moved beyond the realm of government authority. While there are references to concepts like the 'eminent domain' over copyright that could be raised in the USA, it must be noted that the different approaches to private property have played a significant role in the recognition and protection of copyright in the USA. Another important aspect that may be relevant to Australia is the recent development of licensing and implied sub-licensing, which could affect the copyright ownership of spatial products.

The global open data initiatives have highlighted the need for sharing data more openly and widely among different stakeholders. Several initiatives have been made in this regard in the USA, and this would provide valuable guidance to Australia in terms of how geospatial data may be shared and how it may be made available to the stakeholders.

One last aspect that must be noted in relation to the USA is the relevance of international conventions and trade agreements in data initiatives and how such changes have affected the application of copyright principles for the supply of services by surveyors to overseas markets. The increased importance of the data initiatives in Europe and the application for companies/individuals that provide goods/services to European citizens would have to be mindful of such initiatives and the interaction between data initiatives and the principles of copyright.

Notes

1 O. Bracha, 'United States copyright, 1672–1909'. In I. Alexander & H. Tomás Gómez-Arostegui (eds), *Research Handbook on the History of Copyright Law* (Edward Elgar Publishing, Cheltenham, 2016) at 335.

2 Ibid., 1. The exclusive rights granted to Andrew Law in 1781 to his book *Collection of The Best and Most Approved Tunes and Anthems for the Promotion of Psalmody* and to

John Ledyard in 1783, who participated in Captain James Cook's expedition, could be identified as one of the first attempts at authorship copyright in the USA.

3 Ibid., 342.

4 K. Fenning, 'Origin of the patent and copyright clause of the constitution' (1928) 17 (2) *Georgetown Law Journal* 109.

5 O. Bracha, 'United States copyright, 1672–1909'. In I. Alexander & H. Tomás Gómez-Arostegui (eds), *Research Handbook on the History of Copyright Law* (Edward Elgar Publishing, 2016) at 335–343.

6 K. Fenning, 'Origin of the patent and copyright clause of the constitution' (1928) 17 (2) *Georgetown Law Journal* 116.

7 The full title of the Act is 'An Act for the encouragement of learning, by securing the copies of maps, charts, and books, to the authors and proprietors of such copies, during the times therein mentioned', and one cannot see the similarities between the British counterpart the Statute of Anne, 'An Act for the Encouragement of Learning, by Vesting the Copies of Printed Books in the Authors or Purchasers of such Copies, during the Times therein mentioned.'

8 Oren Bracha, 'United States copyright, 1672–1909'. In Isabella Alexander & H. Tomás Gómez-Arostegui (eds), *Research Handbook on the History of Copyright Law* (Edward Elgar Publishing, 2016) at 335–343.

9 Ibid., 350.

10 Ibid., 357.

11 Ibid., 359.

12 Ibid., 360.

13 U.S. Copyright Office, 2021. *Compendium of U.S. Copyright Office Practices* § 101 (3rd ed.), 102 at <www.copyright.gov/comp3/>.

14 Golan v. Holder 565 U.S. 302, 323–25 (2012).

15 Ibid., at 888–89.

16 Harper & Row Publishers, Inc. v. Nation Enterprises et al. 471 U.S. 539, 558 (1985).

17 Golan v. Holder 565 U.S. 302, 323–325 (2012) at 890.

18 Ibid.

19 Copyright Office, *Compendium of U.S. Copyright Office Practices* § 102.5 (3rd ed. 2021) at <www.copyright.gov/comp3/>. Section 301(a) of the 1976 Act pre-empts all similar protections provided by state law, other than with respect to sound recordings fixed before February 15, 1972, as provided under section 301(c) of the Act.

20 W. S. Strong, *The Copyright Book: A Practical Guide* (6th ed., MIT Press, 2014) at <http://ebookcentral.proquest.com/lib/monash/detail.action?docID=3339814> ('The Copyright Book'). These elements will be discussed in full in the next sections and the concepts will be only introduced in this section.

21 K. Janssen & J. Dumortier, 'The protection of maps and spatial databases in Europe and the United States by copyright and the Sui Generis right' (2006) 24 *UIC John Marshall Journal of Information Technology & Privacy Law* 195–206. The level of creativity necessary and sufficient for 'copyrightability' has been described as 'very slight', 'minimal', and 'modest'. This aspect will be discussed in detail in the subsequent sections.

22 A 'compilation' is defined in section 101 of the Act as a work formed by the collection and assembling of pre-existing materials or data that are selected, coordinated, or arranged in such a way that the resulting work as a whole constitutes an original work of authorship. The term 'compilation' includes collective works.

23 It would be important to consider the implications of this legal position in view of the fact that the government is the major investor/sponsor in remote sensing data gathering operations. Y. Chen & M. Yang, 'Legal issues on public access to remote sensing data in Taiwan'. In *Proceedings of 2005 IEEE International Geoscience and Remote Sensing Symposium, 2005* (2005). *IGARSS '05*. M. T. Rice, 'Intellectual property control for maps and geographic data' (PhD, University of California, Santa Barbara) at <www.proquest.com/docview/305003538/abstract/4B513DD2D2AA45DCPQ/1>.

24 The term 'covered institution' means the following: (1) National Defense University; (2) United States Military Academy; (3) Army War College; (4) United States Army Command and General Staff College; (5) United States Naval Academy; (6) Naval War College; (7) Naval Postgraduate School; (8) Marine Corps University; (9) United States Air Force Academy; (10) Air University; (11) Defense Language Institute; and (12) United States Coast Guard Academy.

25 Section 102(b).

26 D. B. Wolf, 'Is there any copyright protection for maps after feist part I' (1991) 39 (3) *Journal of the Copyright Society of the U.S.A* 224–226.

27 C.F.R. § 202.9 (1959).

28 A literary work is defined in section 101 as

> works, other than audiovisual works, expressed in words, numbers, or other verbal or numerical symbols or indicia, regardless of the nature of the material objects, such as books, periodicals, manuscripts, phonorecords, film, tapes, disks, or cards, in which they are embodied.

29 *Compendium of U.S. Copyright Office Practices* §503.1(3rd ed. 2021). A graphic work has been defined to include:

> Drawings, prints, art reproductions, maps, technical drawings, diagrams, architectural plans, architectural drawings, applied art (i.e., two-dimensional graphic artwork applied to a useful article), works of artistic craftsmanship, online or digital artwork (e.g., computer-aided artwork, digital imaging, pixel art), and similar types of graphic works.

30 Dennis S. Karjala, 'Copyright in electronic maps symposium' (1994) 35(4) *Jurimetrics Journal* 395.

31 Ibid., 396.

32 99 U.S. 674 (1879).

33 60 F.2d 555 (S.D.N.Y. 1932).

34 Hayden v. Chalfant Press, Inc. 281 F.2d 543 (9th Cir. 1960).

35 Ibid.

36 D. B. Wolf, 'Is there any copyright protection for maps after feist part I' (1991) 39 (3) *Journal of the Copyright Society of the U.S.A*. at 224–227. Wolf pointed out:

> This tension has run through the history of court cases on maps: on the one hand, maps are viewed as factual compilations based on objectively verifiable data, which necessarily have antecedents in pre-existing works and yet may have original aspects of selection and organization; on the other, maps are seen as pictorial or graphic works that are works of both art and craft with creative and utilitarian aspects. Courts have generally resolved this tension by demeaning the selective, organizational, and pictorial originality of cartography and by protecting the utilitarian and fact-gathering aspects of the craft.
>
> However, this has changed somewhat after the case of *Feist Publications, Inc. v. Rural Telephone Service Company, Inc*. 113 L.Ed.2d 358, 111 S. Ct. 1282 (1991), which will be discussed in detail in the next section.

37 In the USA, copyright is automatic upon the creation of the work (section 302). It must be noted that no registration is required as per section 408(a). However, registration is a prerequisite to filing an infringement action (not applicable to non-US work). Moreover, registration prior to infringement is necessary in order to obtain attorney fees and statutory damages under section 412. Given the difficulty of proving actual damages, the ability to obtain statutory damages is pivotal in a copyright infringement claim. Furthermore, in most instances, it may very well be that attorney fees often exceed the damages at stake. Therefore, the ability to claim attorney fees is an important consideration to be taken into account in relation to a copyright infringement action.

38 *Compendium of U.S. Copyright Office Practices* §312.1 (3rd ed. 2021). There is a reference to the legislative history in the *Compendium* that explains, '[a] "compilation" results from a process of selecting, bringing together, organizing, and arranging previously existing material of all kinds, regardless of whether the individual items in the material have been or ever could have been subject to copyright'. H.R. REP. NO. 94–1476, at 57, reprinted in 1976 U.S.C.C.A.N. at 5670; S. REP. NO. 94–473, at 55.

39 § 3:69. Electronic databases, 2 Patry on Copyright § 3:69.

40 17 U.S.C. § 103(b).

41 499 U.S. 340 (1991). Discussed in detail under the element of originality.

42 Ibid., 347.

43 *Compendium of U.S. Copyright Office Practices* §507.1 (3rd ed. 2021).

44 The Copyright Clause in the Constitution provides that the Congress is authorised to legislate in relation to 'Writings and Discoveries'. It must be noted that there exists a debate in the USA as to the fact whether fixation is a constitutional requirement given the Copyright Clause in the Constitution refers to 'writings' which have been used by some scholars to argue that the statute in recognising the fixation requirement is merely giving effect to the constitutional requirement. See Stefan Hubanov, 'The multifaceted nature and problematic status of fixation in U.S. Copyright law comment' (2006) 11 (1) *Intellectual Property Law Bulletin* 111, 113.

45 E. Brown, 'Fixed perspectives: the evolving contours of the fixation requirement in copyright law' (2014) 10 (1) *Washington Journal of Law, Technology & Arts* 17. Stefan Hubanov, 'The multifaceted nature and problematic status of fixation in U.S. Copyright law comment' (2006) 11 (1) *Intellectual Property Law Bulletin* 111, 113.

46 17 U.S.C. § 101. 'Copies' are material objects, other than phonorecords, in which a work is fixed by any method now known or later developed, and from which the work can be perceived, reproduced, or otherwise communicated, either directly or with the aid of a machine or device. The term 'copies' includes the material object, other than a phonorecord, in which the work is first fixed.

47 17 U.S.C. § 101. 'Phonorecords' are material objects in which sounds, other than those accompanying a motion picture or other audiovisual work, are fixed by any method now known or later developed, and from which the sounds can be perceived, reproduced, or otherwise communicated, either directly or with the aid of a machine or device. The term 'phonorecords' includes the material object in which the sounds are first fixed.

48 1 Melville B. Nimmer & David Nimmer, *Nimmer on Copyright* §2.03 [C] (Matthew Bender, Rev. Ed.).

49 1 Melville B. Nimmer & David Nimmer, *Nimmer on Copyright* §2.03 [B][1] (Matthew Bender, Rev. Ed.). *White-Smith Publishing Co. v. Apollo Co.* 209 U.S. 1, 28 S. Ct. 319, 52 L. Ed. 655 (1908). The question as to whether piano rolls could be considered as a 'copy' the court answered that given these are merely 'parts of a machine which, when duly applied and properly operated in connection with the mechanism to which they are adapted, produce musical tones in harmonious combination. But we cannot think that they are copies within the meaning of the copyright act'.

50 158 F.3d 693 (2d Cir. 1998), cert. denied, 526 U.S. 1154, 119 S. Ct. 2039, 143 L. Ed. 2d 1048 (1999).

51 It was stated in *Falwell v. Penthouse International, Ltd.*,521 F. Supp. 1204 (W.D. Va 1981) that 'if copyright did encompass unfixed expression, then "every utterance"' would be protected. As a consequence, 'the courts would be inundated' with copyright claims.

52 Stefan Hubanov, 'The multifaceted nature and problematic status of fixation in U.S. Copyright law comment' (2006) 11 (1) *Intellectual Property Law Bulletin* 111, 122.

53 *Wells Fargo & Co. v. WhenU.Com, Inc.* 293 F. Supp. 2d 734, 771 (E.D. Mich. 2003).

54 *1–800 Contacts, Inc. v. WhenU.com, Inc.* 414 F.3d 400 (2d Cir. 2005).

55 *Advanced Computer Services of Michigan, Inc. v. MAI Systems Corp.*, 845 F. Supp. 356, 364 (E.D. Va. 1994).

56 *MAI Systems Corp. v. Peak Computer, Inc.* 991 F.2d 511 (9th Cir. 1993).

57 P. Burshtyn, 'Illuminating the law of copyright: Holographic data storage takes intellectual property to a new dimension' (1998) 9 (1) *Fordham Intellectual Property, Media and Entertainment Law Journal* 384. *Apple Computer, Inc. v. Franklin Computer Corp.*, 714 F.2d 1240, 1247 (3d Cir. 1983).

58 *Apple Computer, Inc. v. Franklin Computer Corp.*, 714 F.2d at 1251–1252.

59 This issue has been discussed in detail in the *Information Infrastructure Task Force, Intellectual Property and the National Information Infrastructure: The Report of the Working Group on Intellectual Property Rights* (September 1995) where it was stated that:

> In digital form, a work is generally recorded (fixed) as a sequence of binary digits (zeros and ones) using media specific encoding. This fits within the House Report's list of permissible manners of fixation. Virtually all works also will be fixed in acceptable material objects – i.e., copies or phonorecords. For instance, floppy disks, compact discs (CDs), CD-ROMs, optical disks, compact discs-interactive (CD-Is), digital tape, and other digital storage devices are all stable forms in which works may be fixed and from which works may be perceived, reproduced or communicated by means of a machine or device.
>
> Lehman Bruce A., *Intellectual Property and the National Information Infrastructure - The Report of the Working Group on Intellectual Property Rights* (September 1995) 26 at <www.eff.org/files/filenode/DMCA/ntia_dmca_white_paper.pdf>.

60 *Tandy Corp v. Personal Microcomputers, Inc.* 524 F. Supp. 171, at 173.

61 *Williams Electronics, 685 F.2d at 874; Atari Games Corp. v. Oman,* 888 F.2d 878, 884n.6 (D.C. Cir. 1989).

62 *MAI Sys. Corp. v. Peak Computer, Inc.* 991 F.2d 511, 518 (9th Cir. 1993).

63 Ibid.

64 Andrew Lloyd, 'Inherently transitory transistors: Legal, factual, and policy issues with "Ram fixation"'. In *Copyright* (Michigan State University College of Law, 2010) at 4 <www.law.msu.edu/king/2009-2010/Lloyd.pdf>.

65 845 F.Supp. 356 (E.D. Vir. 1994).

66 Andrew Lloyd, 'Inherently transitory transistors: Legal, factual, and policy issues with "Ram fixation"'. In *Copyright* (Michigan State University College of Law, 2010) at 4 <www.law.msu.edu/king/2009-2010/Lloyd.pdf>. 5.

67 536 F.3d 121 (2d Cir. 2008).

68 991 F.2d 511 (9th Cir. 1993).

69 M. Carpenter & S. Hetcher, 'Function over form: Bringing the fixation requirement into the modern era' (2013) 82 (5) *Fordham Law Review* 2221–2252.

70 Ibid., 2255.

71 373 F.3d 544 (4th Cir. 2004).

72 Ibid., at 551. The court discussed the process of creating the copies at issue, noting that the larger infrastructure of the internet is designed as a conduit for data and within that automatic system Internet service providers (ISPs) passively store material. The court held that the process of transmission creates a temporary, automatic response and that those electronic copies made during the transmission were not 'fixed' because such copies were used to automatically transmit users' material and they were not 'of more than transitory duration'.

73 I. L. Brandriss, 'Writing in frost on a window pane: E-mail and chatting on RAM and copyright fixation part I' (1995) 43 (3) *Journal of the Copyright Society of the U.S.A* 237; Melissa A. Bogden, 'Fixing fixation: The RAM copy doctrine' (2011) 43 (1) *Arizona State Law Journal* 181; A. Lehman Bruce, 'Intellectual property and the national information infrastructure -the report of the working group on intellectual property rights' (September 1995) 26 at <www.eff.org/files/filenode/DMCA/ntia_dmca_white_paper.

pdf>; M. Carpenter & S. Hetcher, 'Function over form: Bringing the fixation requirement into the modern era' (2013) 82 (5) *Fordham Law Review* 2221–2252.

74 A. Lehman Bruce, 'Intellectual property and the national information infrastructure – the report of the working group on intellectual property rights' (September 1995) 26 at <www.eff.org/files/filenode/DMCA/ntia_dmca_white_paper.pdf>. 27. It was noted that:

> The question of whether interactive works are fixed (given the user's ability to constantly alter the sequence of the "action") has been resolved by the courts in the context of video games and should not present a new issue in the context of the NII. Such works are generally considered sufficiently fixed to qualify for protection.

75 *Computer Assocs. Int'l, Inc. v. Atlai, Inc*. 982 F.2d 693, 703 (2d Cir. 1992). This aspect will be discussed in detail in the subsequent parts of this report.

76 1 Melville B. Nimmer and David Nimmer, *Nimmer on Copyright* § 2.01 [A] (Matthew Bender, Rev. Ed.).

77 1 Melville B. Nimmer and David Nimmer, Nimmer on Copyright § 2.01 [C] (Matthew Bender, Rev. Ed.).

78 The *Compendium of U.S. Copyright Office Practices* § 308.2 (3rd ed. 2021) explains the level of creativity to 'be presented in an innovative or surprising way', but it 'cannot be so mechanical or routine as to require no creativity whatsoever'. It further notes that a work that it is 'entirely typical', 'garden-variety', or 'devoid of even the slightest traces of creativity' does not satisfy the originality Requirement. It has been noted that '[T]here is nothing remotely creative about a work that merely reflects an age-old practice, firmly rooted in tradition and so commonplace that it has come to be expected as a matter of course'. Finally, it has been noted that a work 'does not possess the minimal creative spark required by the Copyright Act if the author's expression is "obvious" or "practically inevitable"'.

79 *Best Medium Publishing Co. v. National Insider, Inc*. 385 F.2d 384 (7th Cir. 1967) (Treatise cited), cert. denied, 390 U.S. 955, 88 S. Ct. 1052, 19 L. Ed. 2d 1150 (1968).

80 191 F.2d 99 (2d Cir. 1951).

81 1 Melville B. Nimmer and David Nimmer, *Nimmer on Copyright* § 2.08[3] [B] (Mathew Bender, Rev. Ed.).

82 188 U.S. 239 (1903). In this case, the alleged infringements consisted of copying in the reduced form of three chromolithographs prepared by employees of the plaintiffs for advertisements of a circus owned by One Wallace.

83 188 U.S. 239 (1903) at 250–251. The court prescribed the relevant test as:

> [E]ven if they had been drawn from the life, that fact would not deprive them of protection. The opposite proposition would mean that a portrait by Velasquez or Whistler was common property because others might try their hand on the same face. Others are free to copy the original. They are not free to copy the copy. The copy is the personal reaction of an individual upon nature. Personality always contains something unique. It expresses its singularity even in handwriting, and a very modest grade of art has in it something irreducible, which is one man's alone. That is something he may copyright unless there is a restriction in the words of the act [E] ven if they had been drawn from the life, that fact would not deprive them of protection. The opposite proposition would mean that a portrait by Velasquez or Whistler was common property because others might try their hand on the same face. Others are free to copy the original. They are not free to copy the copy. The copy is the personal reaction of an individual upon nature. Personality always contains something unique. It expresses its singularity even in handwriting, and a very modest grade of art has in it something irreducible, which is one man's alone. That is something he may copyright unless there is a restriction in the words of the act.

84 The court held (188 U.S. 239 (1903) at 251–52) that:

> It would be a dangerous undertaking for persons trained only to the law to constitute themselves final judges of the worth of pictorial illustrations, outside of the narrowest and most obvious limits. At the one extreme, some works of genius would be sure to miss appreciation. Their very novelty would make them repulsive until the public had learned the new language in which their author spoke. . . . At the other end, copyright would be denied to pictures which appealed to a public less educated than the judge. Yet if they command the interest of any public, they have a commercial value-it would be bold to say that they have not an aesthetic and educational value-and the taste of any public is not to be treated with contempt.

85 499 U.S. 340 (1991).
86 Ibid., 345.
87 93 F. Supp. 79 (E.D. Pa. 1950), aff'd, 189 F.2d 104 (3d Cir. 1951).
88 *United States v. Hamilton*, 583 F.2d 448, 451 (9th Cir. 1978).
89 Ibid.
90 1 Melville B. Nimmer and David Nimmer, *Nimmer on Copyright* § 2.08 [A] (Matthew Bender, Rev. Ed.). See *General Drafting Co. v. Andrews*, 37 F.2d 54 (2d Cir. 1930); *Crocker v. General Drafting Co.,* 50 F. Supp. 634 (S.D.N.Y. 1943); *Rockford Map Pub., Inc. v. Directory Serv. Co., of Colo.,* 768 F.2d 145 (7th Cir. 1985), cert. denied, 474 U.S. 1061, 106 S. Ct. 806, 88 L. Ed. 2d 781 (1986); *Rand McNally & Co. v. Fleet Management Sys., Inc*. 634 F. Supp. 604 (N.D. Ill. 1986).
91 *Andrews v. Guenther Publishing Co.,* 60 F.2d 555 (S.D.N.Y. 1932). See *United States v. Hamilton,* 583 F.2d 448 (9th Cir. 1978); *Chamberlin v. Bekins Van & Storage Co.,* 23 F.2d 541 (S.D. Cal. 1928). 23 F.2d 541 (S.D. Cal. 1928); *Carter v. Hawaii Transp. Co.,* 201 F. Supp. 301 (D. Haw. 1961).
92 210 F. Supp. 206 (S.D.N.Y. 1962).
93 Craig Joyce & Tyler T. Ochoa, 'Reach out and touch someone: Reflections on the 25th anniversary of Feist Publications, Inc. v. Rural Telephone Service Co. Authorship in America (and beyond): Institute for intellectual property & information law symposium: historical essay' (2016) 54 (2) *Houston Law Review* 257, 268.
94 D. B. Wolf, 'Is there any copyright protection for maps after feist part I' (1991) 39 (3) *Journal of the Copyright Society of the U.S.A* 224–226.
95 Ibid.
96 Ibid.
97 1 Melville B. Nimmer and David Nimmer, Nimmer on Copyright § 3.04 (Matthew Bender, Rev. Ed.).
98 281 F. 83 (2d Cir. 1922).
99 281 F. 83, 88 (2d Cir. 1922).
100 499 U.S. 340 (1991).
101 Ibid., at 358.
102 *The Compendium of U.S. Copyright Office Practices* § 312.2 (3rd ed. 2021).
103 967 F.2d 135 (5th Cir. 1992).
104 Ibid., 136–37. The steps adopted in this process were described in the decision as follows:

> Mason initially determined the location and dimensions of each survey in the county, and then drew the corners and lines of the surveys onto topographical maps of the county that were published by the United States Geological Survey (USGS). He then determined the location of the property lines of the real estate tracts within each survey and drew them on the USGS maps. Finally, Mason traced the survey and tract lines onto transparent overlays, enlarged clean USGS maps and the overlays, added names and other information to the overlays, and combined the maps and overlays to print the final maps.

105 Ibid., 135.

106 Katleen Janssen and Jos Dumortier, 'The protection of maps and spatial databases in Europe and the United States by copyright and the Sui Generis Right' (2006) 24 *UIC John Marshall Journal of Information Technology & Privacy Law* 195, 210.

107 Ibid., 211.

108 Numerous Congressional hearings have taken place, the Copyright Office has issued a study on the subject, the House even passed as part of the Digital Millennium Copyright Act a title entitled 'Collections of Information Anti-Piracy Act.'

109 7. Originality: Minimal-Creativity Requirement holds that:

(a) A work meets the minimal-creativity criterion for originality if the work embodies expression that is at least minimally creative.
(b) The requirement that a work embodies expression that is at least minimally creative can be satisfied by an author's creative choices. In the case of a compilation, choices regarding the selection, coordination, or arrangement of elements can satisfy the minimal-creativity requirement even if those elements are not themselves original.
(c) The minimal-creativity requirement is not satisfied by choices that are routine, or by choices that are significantly constrained by external factors (such as the function the work is intended to serve, the tools used to produce the work, or practices or conventions standards to a particular type of work).
(d) The amount of time, labor, skill, or investment employed by the author in creating a work is not relevant to whether the minimal-creativity requirement is satisfied.

110 Dennis S. Karjala, 'Copyright in electronic maps symposium' (1994) 35 (4) *Jurimetrics Journal* 395.

111 Justin Hughes, 'Restating copyright law's originality requirement' (2020) 44(3) *Columbia Journal of Law & the Arts* 383, 390.

112 Ibid., 397–398. The following have been identified as the basic principles illustrated in Clause 7, as follows.
Creativity cannot be:

(a) Author's choices that are 'merely routine' cannot contribute to minimal creativity.
(b) Author's choices that are 'significantly constrained by external factors' cannot contribute to minimal-creativity.
(c) The amount of 'time, labor, or investment employed by the author in creating a work does not constitute or generate the creativity necessary for a work to be original.'

Creativity can be, but need not be:

(a) Author's choices do not need to be 'artistic' or 'aesthetic' to confer minimal creativity.
(b) Author's 'choices [made] among options without being fully aware of those options' can contribute to minimal-creativity.
(c) Author's choices 'that may be characterized as "arbitrary"' (as distinct from random).
(d) Author's choices 'need not have been made rationally'.
(e) Author's choices 'need not have been made . . . with conscious awareness' or 'consciously'.

Creativity must be:

(a) Only author's choices which 'involves expression' are 'relevant' for minimal creativity.
(b) That author's choices that do contribute to minimal creativity 'are those that inhere in making non-obvious choices from more than a few options.'

113 86 F.3D 1447 (7TH CIR. 1996).

114 The 'shrinkwrap license' gets its name from the fact that retail software packages are covered in plastic or cellophane 'shrinkwrap' and some vendors have written licenses that become effective as soon as the customer tears the wrapping from the package. *ProCD, Inc. v. Zeidenberg*, 86 F.3d 1447, 1449 (7th Cir. 1996). In relation to the Internet, the shrinkwrap license is included as one of the first screens. In order to view or download the program, it is necessary to accept the terms of the license by clicking on the acceptance button on the screen.

115 Craig Joyce & Tyler T Ochoa, 'Reach out and touch someone: Reflections on the 25th anniversary of Feist Publications, Inc. v. Rural Telephone Service Co. Authorship in America (and beyond): institute for intellectual property & information law symposium: historical essay' (2016) 54 (2) *Houston Law Review* 257.

116 See *CCC Info. Servs., Inc. v. Maclean Hunter Mkt. Reps., Inc*. 44 F.3d 61 (2d Cir. 1994). It was stated that 'Protection of compilations is consistent with objectives of copyright law to promote the advancement of knowledge and learning by giving authors economic incentives, in the form of exclusive rights to their creations, to labor on creative, knowledge-enriching works'.

117 Dennis S. Karjala, 'Copyright in electronic maps symposium' (1994) 35 (4) *Jurimetrics Journal* 395,397.

118 Ibid., 401.

119 *Mason v. Montgomery Data, Inc*. 967 F.2d 135, 139 (5th Cir. 1992).

120 *Mason v. Montgomery Data, Inc*. 967 F.2d 135, 139 (5th Cir. 1992).

121 *CCC Info. Servs., Inc. v. Maclean Hunter Mkt. Reps., Inc*. 44 F.3d 61 (2d Cir. 1994).

122 Dennis S. Karjala, 'Copyright in electronic maps symposium' (1994) 35 (4) *Jurimetrics Journal* 395, 411.

123 *The Compendium of U.S. Copyright Office Practices* § 306 (3rd ed. 2021).

124 111 U.S. 53, 58 (1884).

125 Ibid., 58.

126 *The Compendium of U.S. Copyright Office Practices* § 306 (3rd ed. 2021).

127 Ibid.

128 *The Compendium of U.S. Copyright Office Practices* § 313.2 (3rd ed. 2021).

129 Ibid.

130 Copyright Review Board, 2022. Second request for reconsideration for refusal to register a recent entrance to paradise (Correspondence ID 1–3ZPC6C3; SR # 1–7100387071) (Case Determination. Copyright Review Board. Retrieved from: <www.copyright.gov/rulings-filings/review-board/docs/a- recent-entrance-to-paradise.pdf>.

131 Ibid; According to Thaler,

> there is no binding authority that prohibits copyright for [computer generated works], . . . that copyright law already allows non-human entities to be authors under the work made for hire doctrine, . . . and ultimately that the Copyright Office is currently relying upon non-binding judicial opinions from the Gilded Age to answer the question of whether [computer-generated works] can be protected.

132 Ibid., 2.

133 Ibid.

134 Ibid., 6.

135 *The Compendium of U.S. Copyright Office Practices* § 507 (3rd ed. 2021).

136 The graphic novel *Zarya of the Dawn* was created by Kristina Kashtanova, who used MidJourney (a form of generative AI) to create the images used alongside the storyline in the graphic novel.

137 United States Copyright Office, *Zarya of the Dawn* (Registration # VAu001480196) (Case Determination No 1–5GB561K, United States Copyright Office, 21 February 2023) at <www.copyright.gov/docs/zarya-of-the-dawn.pdf>.

138 Ibid., 9; the description of the process by the U.S. Copyright Office included:

> First, she entered a text prompt to Midjourney, which she describes as 'the core creative input' for the image . . . (providing an example of a first generated image in response to prompt 'dark skin hands holding an old photograph – . . .'). Next, 'Kashtanova the picked one or more of these output images to further develop.' . . . She then 'tweaked or changed the prompt as well as the other inputs provided to Midjourney' to generate new intermediate images, and ultimately the final image. Ms. Kashtanova does not claim she 'created, developed, refined, and relocated' and as containing elements from intermediate images 'brought together into a cohesive whole.' . . . . To obtain the final image, she describes a process of trial-and-error, in which she provided 'hundreds or thousands of descriptive prompts' to Midjourney until the 'hundreds of iterations [created] as perfect a rendition of her vision as possible.'

139 Ibid., 10.

140 While this is true as to any work created after 1 January 1978, it must be noted that for any work created prior to this date, the protection was provided only upon the publication with notice or in relation to some of the works upon registration as an unpublished work. Therefore, such protection is provided if there had been a transfer of copyright by way of *inter vivos* or testamentary disposition, and if such transferees were considered as the owners of the copyright instead of the original creator.

141 A 'joint work' is defined in section 101 as 'a work prepared by two or more authors with the intention that their contributions be merged into inseparable or interdependent parts of a unitary whole'.

142 *Community for Creative Non-Violence v. Reid*, 490 U.S. 730, 739–740, 109 S. Ct. 2166, 2172–2173 (1989).

143 Restatement (Second) of Agency § 220 (1958).

144 This principle was applied in a similar context in relation to architectural plans and the court in *Aitken, Hazen, Hoffman, Miller, P. C. v. Empire Const. Co.*, 542 F. Supp. 252, 254 (D. Neb. 1982) held that the involvement of the client in the development of the architectural plans would not result in joint ownership with the client.

145 *Community for Creative Non-Violence v. Reid*, 490 U.S. 730, 737, 109 S. Ct. 2166, 104 L. Ed. 2d 811 (1989).

146 Section 201(c).

147 Ibid.

148 140 S. Ct. 1498 (2020).

149 The legislative history provides some guidance in this regard where it had been stated 'that section 105 is to be 'construed in the same way' as the first clause of the definition of 'work made for hire' in section 101' of the Act. H.R. Rep. No. 1476, 94th Cong., 2d Sess. 58 (1976).

150 These include National Defense University, United States Military Academy, Army War College, United States Army Command and General Staff College, United States Naval Academy, Naval War College, Naval Post Graduate School, Marine Corps University, United States Air Force Academy, Air University, Defense Language Institute, and United States Coast Guard Academy.

151 Section 105(c).

152 1 Melville B. Nimmer and David Nimmer, *Nimmer on Copyright* § 5.13 [b][2] (Matthew Bender, Rev. Ed.).

153 Andrew Hubbertz, 'Crown copyright and privatization of government information in Canada, with comparisons to the United States experience' (1990) 17 (2) *Government Publications Review* 159; Heiko Richter, 'Copyright protection of government-related material before the courts of the United States and Canada: Considerations for future reforms' (2021) 52 (1) *IIC – International Review of Intellectual Property and Competition Law* 6.

154 1 Melville B. Nimmer & David Nimmer, *Nimmer on Copyright* §4.10 (Matthew Bender, Rev. Ed.).
155 *John G. Danielson, Inc. v. Winchester-Conant Props., Inc.* 186 F. Supp. 2d 1, 16 & n.2 (D. Mass. 2002).
156 § 19:75. Patent and copyright infringement by government, 7A Fed. Proc., L. Ed. § 19:75.
157 ibid.
158 John T. Cross, 'Suing the states for copyright infringement' (2000) 39 (2) *Brandeis Law Journal* 337.
159 Roberta Rosenthal Kwall, 'Governmental use of copyright property: the Sovereign's prerogative' (1988) 67 (4) *Texas Law Review* 685, 692.
160 *Chicago B. & Q. R.R. v. City of Chicago*, 166 U.S. 226, 227 (1897); *Missouri Pac. Ry. v. Nebraska*, 164 U.S. 403, 417 (1896).
161 Ibid., 694.
162 Discussed in detail below in the section titled 'Fair dealing defense under copyright law.'
163 *Photographic Illustrators Corp. v. Orgill, Inc.* 953 F.3d 56 (1st Cir. 2020).
164 *Geophysical Service Inc. v. TGS-NOPEC*, 784 Fed.Appx. 253, 2019 WL 4410259, at 2 (5th Cir. Sept. 13, 2019).
165 *Reinicke v. Creative Empire, LLC*, 2016 WL 5845734 (9th Cir. Oct. 6, 2016).
166 § 5:131. Implied licenses, 2 Patry on Copyright § 5:131. The instances in which implied licence would be considered to exist are situations when 'putative licensee asks the copyright owner to create the work for it; (2) the copyright owner creates the work and delivers it to the alleged licensee; and (3) the copyright owner intends the licensee to use the work as it does.' Also, 'a failure to object can constitute an implied license if there are other factors about the parties' relationship supporting such a license.' The instances in which courts have found that implied licenses cannot exist are:

> (1) where the work was not created at defendant's request;43 (2) where the nature of the license is contested;44 (3) where the implied license is based on the unilateral expectations of one party;45 or (4) where the implied license is legally impossible as with a sublicense.

167 *Simplexgrinnell LP v. Integrated Systems & Power, Inc.* 2009 WL 857504, at *20 (S.D.N.Y. March 31, 2009).
168 470 F.Supp. 33.
169 No. 19–1452 (1st Cir. 2020).
170 Rohena Rajbhandari, 'License to sublicense: The legal possibility of impliedly sublicensing a copyrighted work annual survey of Federal En Banc and other significant cases: Comments' (2021) 62 *Boston College Law Review E. Supp.* II, 425.
171 Luis F. Luna-Reyes et al., 'The US open data initiative: the road ahead' (2019) 24 (2) *Information Polity: The International Journal of Government & Democracy in the Information Age* 163.
172 Ibid., 163.
173 Title II of the Foundations for Evidence-Based Policymaking Act of 2018 Public Law 115–435.
174 Data.Gov. *Data.gov* (27 July 2021) at <www.data.gov/>
175 'Open Government', *Data.gov* at <www.data.gov/open-gov/>.
176 U.S. Code, Title 43 – Public Lands, Chapter 46: GEOSPATIAL DATA.
177 Federal GeoAgraphic Data Committee (FGDC), 'About | GeoPlatform.Gov' at <www.geoplatform.gov>.
178 Ibid.
179 'Data Policy Statements', *Data.gov* at <www.data.gov/data-policy/>.
180 Ibid.

181 *Mathews Conveyer Co. v. Palmer-Bee Co.*, 135 F.2d 73, 85 (6th Cir. 1943). The court has summarised the process as:

> Fair use is to be determined by a consideration of all of the evidence, and among other elements entering into the determination of the issue, are the extent and relative value of copyrighted material, and the effect upon the distribution of objects of the original work. Whether a particular use of a copyrighted article, without permission of the owner, is a fair use, depends upon the circumstances of the particular case, and the court must look to the nature and objects of the selections made, the quantity and value of material used, and the degree in which the use may prejudice the sale, diminish the profits, or supersede the objects of the original work . . . fair use is to be determined by a consideration of all the evidence in the case.

182 *Campbell v. Acuff-Rose Music, Inc.* 510 U.S. 569, 577, 579,114 S. Ct. 1164, 1170, 127 L. Ed. 2d 500, 22 Media L. Rep. (BNA) 1353, 29 U.S.P.Q.2d 1961 (1994).
183 *Stewart v. Abend*, 495 U.S. 207, 237, 110 S. Ct. 1750, 109 L. Ed. 2d 184, 14 U.S.P.Q.2d 1614 (1990).
184 Ibid.
185 *New Era Publications Intern., ApS v. Carol Pub. Group*, 904 F.2d 152, 157, 17 Media L. Rep. (BNA) 1913, 14 U.S.P.Q.2d 2030 (2d Cir. 1990).
186 *A.V. ex rel. Vanderhye v. iParadigms, LLC*, 562 F.3d 630, 642, 90 U.S.P.Q.2d 1513 (4th Cir. 2009) (quoting Bond, 317 F.3d at 396).
187 *Harper & Row*, 471 U.S. at 566, 105 S.Ct. at 2233.
188 *Campbell v. Acuff-Rose Music, Inc.* 510 U.S. 569, 577, 579,114 S. Ct. 1164, 1170, 127 L. Ed. 2d 500, 22 Media L. Rep. (BNA) 1353, 29 U.S.P.Q.2d 1961 (1994).
189 § 15:16. Defenses to copyright infringement – Fair use, 9 Ariz. Prac., Business Law Deskbook § 15:16 (2022–2023 ed.).
190 470 F.Supp. 33.
191 141 S.Ct. 1183.
192 Ibid.
193 Teresa Scassa, 'Originality and utilitarian works: the uneasy relationship between copyright law and unfair competition' (2003) 1 *University of Ottawa Law & Technology Journal* 51, 53.
194 Dennis S. Karjala, 'Copyright and misappropriation copyright symposium part II – Copyright protection for computer databases, CD-Roms and factual compilations' (1991) 17 (3) *The University of Dayton Law Review* 885, 886.
195 David G. Wille, Dana Jewell & Pamela Ratliff, 'Protection and enforcement of new intellectual property symposium – exploring emerging issues: New intellectual property, information technology, and security in borderless commerce' (2001) 8(3) *Texas Wesleyan Law Review* 467.
196 Section 301(a).
197 *Del Madera Props. v. Rhodes & Gardner, Inc.* 820 F.2d 973, 976 (9th Cir.1987).
198 § 12.09 Preemption of State Unfair Competition and Antitrust Claims by *the Copyright Act of 1978*, 2014 WL 9967500.
199 It was noted in *In re Jackson*, 972 F.3d 25, 44–45 (2d Cir. 2020) that:

> [W]e have upheld § 301 preemption as to a variety of state law claims that included an "extra element" – including claims of unfair competition, unjust enrichment, conversion, tortious interference with contractual relations, and commercial misappropriation – when the extra element was not of such important character as to differentiate the claim substantially from a copyright claim. On the other hand, we have recognized that other state law claims based on uses of works within the 'subject matter of copyright' – including claims alleging breaches of fiduciary duty, 'unfair competition claims based upon breaches of confidential relationships,' and trade secret claims – survive pre-emption when such claims include a sufficiently

significant 'extra element' that 'qualitatively distinguishes such claims from claims for copyright infringement'.

200 *Fractional Villas, Inc. v. Tahoe Clubhouse, No. 08CV1396-IEG-POR*, 2009 U.S. Dist. LEXIS 39522, at 5, 2009 WL 1298532, at 2 (S.D. Cal. May 8, 2009).
201 153 F.Supp.2d 1115, 1124 (N.D.Cal.2001).
202 248 U.S 215 (1918).
203 J. H. Reichman & Pamela Samuelson, 'Intellectual property rights in data' (1997) 50 (1) *Vanderbilt Law Review* 49.
204 Ibid., at 140.
205 *International News Service Inc v Associated Press* 248 U.S 215 (1918) at 241.
206 J. E. Vekstein, 'A hot mess: How hot-news misappropriation bypassed copyright law in barclays v. theflyonthewall.Com and gave originators a property right in facts note' (2011) 61 (1) *Catholic University Law Review* 297–298.
207 650 F.3d 876 (2d Cir. 2011).
208 Given the financial firms' reports culminating with recommendations constitute a type of works covered by copyright law and the financial firms' rights were subject to abridgement by news service's allegedly infringing acts, and news service was collecting, collating, and disseminating factual information. *Barclays Cap. Inc. v. Theflyonthewall.com, Inc*. 650 F.3d 876 (2d Cir. 2011).
209 § 5:41. Overview, Lee, Entertainment and Intellectual Property Law § 5:41.
210 State laws are based on the Uniform Trade Secrets Act (UTSA) articulated by the National Conference of Commissioners on Uniform State Law. According to UTSA, A plaintiff must prove the following to establish trade secret misappropriation under the UTSA:

    (1) That information qualifies as a 'trade secret' – i.e., that it is information, which derives economic value from not being generally known to the public, and that it is the subject of reasonable efforts to maintain its secrecy; and
    (2) That the defendant acquired, used, or disclosed the information through improper means. 'Improper means' includes theft, bribery, misrepresentation, breach, or inducement of a breach of a duty to maintain secrecy or espionage through electronic or other means. The UTSA definition expands on the first Restatement's requirement that the information has value for use in business.

211 Defend Trade Secrets Act of 2016," S. 1890, 104th Congress (2d Session), codified at 18 U.S.C.A. § 1836 et al. (2016).
212 *Computer Associates Intern., Inc. v. Altai, Inc*. 982 F.2d 693.
213 § 18:28. Loss of trade secret protection – Disclosure in patents or copyrights, 20A2 Minn. Prac., Business Law Deskbook § 18:28.
214 Ibid.
215 J. Michael Graglia & Christopher Mellon, 'Blockchain and property in 2018: At the end of the beginning' (2018) 12 (1–2) *Innovations: Technology, Governance, Globalization* 90; Anniina Saari, Seppo Junnila & Jussi Vimpari, 'Blockchain's grand promise for the real estate sector: A systematic review' (2022) 12 (23) *Applied Sciences* 11940; Qiuyun Shang & Allison Price, 'A blockchain-based land titling project in the republic of Georgia: Rebuilding public trust and lessons for future pilot projects' (2019) 12 (3–4) *Innovations: Technology, Governance, Globalization* 72; Abdulaziz Aborujilah, Muhammad Naqib Bin Mohd Yatim & Abdulaleem Al-Othmani, 'Blockchain-based adoption framework for authentic land registry system in Malaysia' (2021) 19 (6) *TELKOMNIKA (Telecommunication Computing Electronics and Control)* 2038; Prince Donkor Ameyaw and Walter Timo de Vries, 'Transparency of land administration and the role of blockchain technology, a four-dimensional framework analysis from the Ghanaian Land perspective' (2020) 9 (12) *Land* 491.
216 Qiuyun Shang & Allison Price, 'A blockchain-based land titling project in the republic of georgia: Rebuilding public trust and lessons for future pilot projects' (2019) 12 (3–4) *Innovations: Technology, Governance, Globalization* 72.

217 However, it must be noted that these attempts are not widespread and it has been predicted that it will be years before blockchain is implemented in a meaningful way connecting all counties in the USA. Matt Koronczok, 'The new chain of title: How blockchain will affect land title research, recordation, and insurance' (2019) 5 (3) *Texas A&M Journal of Property Law* 401.
218 Paul Peterson, 'Problems blockchain doesn't solve' (2019) 107 (2) *Illinois Bar Review* 36.
219 Matt Koronczok, 'The new chain of title: How blockchain will affect land title research, recordation, and insurance' (2019) 5 (3) *Texas A&M Journal of Property Law* 401, 404.
220 Ibid., 405.
221 Nicolas Nogueroles Peiro & Eduardo J. Martinez Garcia, 'Blockchain and land registration systems' (2017) 6 (3) *European Property Law Journal (EPLJ)* 296; Barikisa Owusu Ansah et al., 'A systematic review of the institutional success factors for blockchain-based land administration' (2023) 125 *Land Use Policy* 106473.
222 John Dean Markunas, 'Blockchain for surveyors' (2019) *Land Journal* 10.
223 Hartmut Müller & Markus Seifert, 'Blockchain, a feasible technology for land administration?' at <www.fig.net/resources/proceedings/fig_proceedings/fig2019/papers/ts01i/TS01I_seifert_mueller_10110.pdf>; Anniina Saari, Seppo Junnila & Jussi Vimpari, 'Blockchain's grand promise for the real estate sector: A systematic review' (2022) 12 (23) *Applied Sciences* 11940.
224 Digital at Arup, *Blockchain and the Built Environment* (ARUP, 2019) at <www.arup.com/en/perspectives/publications/research/section/blockchain-and-the-built-environment>.
225 John Dean Markunas, 'Blockchain for surveyors' (2019) *Land Journal* 10.
226 Barikisa Owusu Ansah et al., 'A systematic review of the institutional success factors for blockchain-based land administration' (2023) 125 *Land Use Policy* 106473.
227 Sarah Anderson, 'The missing link between blockchain and copyright: How companies are using new technology to misinform creators and violate federal law' (2018) 19 (4) *North Carolina Journal of Law & Technology* 1; Sebastian Pech, 'Copyright unchained: How blockchain technology can change the administration and distribution of copyright protected works' (2020) 18 (1) *Northwestern Journal of Technology and Intellectual Property* 1.
228 Seda Fabian, 'Blockchain and intellectual property rights comments' (2020) 25 (2) *Intellectual Property and Technology Law Journal* 147–157.
229 Under the section 'Copyright and IP of spatial data and products in the USA'.
230 Sebastian Pech, 'Who owns the blockchain? How copyright law allows rights holders to control blockchains' (2021) 16 (1) *Journal of Business and Technology Law* 59–65.
231 Ibid., 68.
232 Ibid.
233 Ibid.
234 (Pub. L. No. 105–304, 112 Stat. 2860 (1998).
235 J. Boland-Devito, 'Yo ho and a bottle of rum – The DMCA takes on movie pirates' (2006) 15 *Currents: International Trade Law Journal* 70–73. The debate in this regard has been identified by one author as: YiJun Tian. 2005. 'Problems of Anti-Circumvention Rules in the DMCA & More Heterogeneous Solutions'. 15 *The Fordham Intellectual Property, Media and Entertainment Law Journal* 749, 762–63.

> a battle between Hollywood and Silicon Valley. Hollywood and its allies, representing the copyright industries, sought the strongest possible protection for the technological measures they used to protect their copyrighted works, while Silicon Valley and its allies, representing the information technology industries and the public user groups, opposed the expansive protections and argued that overbroad protection would bring deleterious effects 'on their ability to engage in lawful reverse engineering, computer security testing and encryption research.' It seems that Hollywood and its allies won this battle when they successfully persuaded Congress to pass the

broad anti-circumvention rules. These rules are only subject to some very specific exceptions that respond to some of (the) concerns from Silicon Valley.

236 1 Melville B. Nimmer and David Nimmer, Nimmer on Copyright § 12A.03[1][b] (Matthew Bender, Rev. Ed.).
237 *Yout, LLC v. Recording Indus. Ass'n of Am., Inc. No. 3:*20-CV-1602 (SRU), 2022 WL 4599203, at 6 (D. Conn. Sept. 30, 2022).
238 1 Melville B. Nimmer and David Nimmer, Nimmer on Copyright § 12A.03[a][1][a] (Matthew Bender, Rev. Ed.).
239 1 Melville B. Nimmer and David Nimmer, Nimmer on Copyright § 12A.03 (Matthew Bender, Rev. Ed.).
240 *Real Networks, Inc. v. Streambox, Inc. No. 2:99CV02070*, 2000 U.S. Dist. WL 127311 (W.D. Wash. Jan. 18, 2000).
241 *Chamberlain Group, Inc. v. Skylink Tech., Inc.* 292 F. Supp. 2d 1040, 1040 (N.D. Ill. 2003).
242 No. CV 99–7654 HLH (BQRx), 2000 U.S. Dist. LEXIS 4553, at *3–4, 54 USPQ2d 1344, 1345 (C.D. Cal. Mar. 27, 2000).
243 The section reads:

No person shall manufacture, import, offer to the public, provide, or otherwise traffic in any technology, product, service, device, component, or part thereof, that –

(A) is primarily designed or produced for the purpose of circumventing a technological measure that effectively controls access to a work protected under this title;
(B) has only limited commercially significant purpose or use other than to circumvent a technological measure that effectively controls access to a work protected under this title; or
(C) is marketed by that person or another acting in concert with that person with that person's knowledge for use in circumventing a technological measure that effectively controls access to a work protected under this title.

244 The section reads:

No person shall manufacture, import, offer to the public, provide, or otherwise traffic in any technology, product, service, device, component, or part thereof, that –

(A) is primarily designed or produced for the purpose of circumventing protection afforded by a technological measure that effectively protects a right of a copyright owner under this title in a work or a portion thereof;
(B) has only limited commercially significant purpose or use other than to circumvent protection afforded by a technological measure that effectively protects a right of a copyright owner under this title in a work or a portion thereof; or
(C) is marketed by that person or another acting in concert with that person with that person's knowledge for use in circumventing protection afforded by a technological measure that effectively protects a right of a copyright owner under this title in a work or a portion thereof.

245 4 Nimmer on Copyright § 12A.03[C] (2022).
246 Defined as 'avoiding, bypassing, removing, deactivating, or otherwise impairing a technological measure'.
247 Defined as 'if the measure, in the ordinary course of its operation, prevents, restricts, or otherwise limits the exercise of a right of a copyright owner under this title'.
248 Melville B. Nimmer and David Nimmer, Nimmer on Copyright § 12A.03 [D] [3] (Matthew Bender, Rev. Ed.).
249 These are included in section 1201(d)-(j).
250 These are included in section 1201(h), (i) and (j).
251 Katleen Janssen and Jos Dumortier, 'The protection of maps and spatial databases in Europe and the United States by copyright and the Sui Generis Right' (2006) 24 (2) *UIC John Marshall Journal of Information Technology & Privacy Law* 195–221.

252 Key Publications, Inc. v. Chinatown Today Pubig.Enterprises, Inc., 945 F.2d 509 (2d Cir. 1991).

253 CCC Info. Services v. Maclean HunterMkt. Reports, 44 F.3d 61 (2d Cir. 1994).

254 Victor Lalli Enterprises, Inc. v. Big Red Apple, Inc. 936 F.2d. 671 (2d Cir. 1991).

255 Ibid.

256 Katleen Janssen & Jos Dumortier, 'The protection of maps and spatial databases in Europe and the United States by copyright and the Sui Generis right' (2006) 24 (2) *UIC John Marshall Journal of Information Technology & Privacy Law* 195–221.

257 M. Davison, 'Database protection: Lessons from Europe, congress, and WIPO law, technology and the arts symposium: the WIPO copyright treaties: 10 years later' (2006) 57 (4) *Case Western Reserve Law Review* 829–845. It has been noted that '[T]he history of the American legislative proposals for database protection looks a little like the European history run backwards in time. It started where the Europeans finished, with a proposal for an exclusive property right that would have been very similar to the right of extraction and reutilization under the Directive. It seems destined to finish where the Europeans started, namely, with no special legislation on the topic but various approaches to unfair competition within different jurisdictions, in this case, American states, that may provide limited protection to unoriginal databases in some limited circumstances.'

258 M. Davison, 'Database protection: Lessons from Europe, congress, and WIPO law, technology and the arts symposium: The WIPO copyright treaties: 10 years later' (2006) 57 (4) *Case Western Reserve Law Review* 829–845; Marshall Leaffer, 'Database protection in the United States is alive and well: Comments on Davison law, technology and the arts symposium: the WIPO copyright treaties: 10 years later' (2006) 57 (4) *Case Western Reserve Law Review*.

259 M. Davison, 'Databases and copyright protection'. In Tanya Aplin (ed.), *Research Handbook on Intellectual Property and Digital Technologies* (Edward Elgar Publishing Limited, 2020) 75 at <http://ebookcentral.proquest.com/lib/monash/detail.action?docID=6029047>.

References

1–800 Contacts, Inc. v. WhenU.com, Inc. 414 F.3d 400 (2d Cir. 2005).

Aborujilah, A., Yatim, M.N.B.M., and Al-Othmani, A., 2021. Blockchain-based adoption framework for authentic land registry system in Malaysia. *TELKOMNIKA (Telecommunication Computing Electronics and Control)*, 19 (6), 2038.

Advanced Computer Services of Michigan, Inc. v. MAI Systems Corp., 845 F. Supp. 356, 364 (E.D. Va. 1994).

Aitken, Hazen, Hoffman, Miller, P. C. v. Empire Const. Co., 542 F. Supp. 252, 254 (D. Neb. 1982).

Alfred Bell & Co. v. Catalda Fine Arts, Inc. 191 F.2d 99 (2d Cir. 1951).

Ameyaw, P.D. and de Vries, W.T., 2020. Transparency of land administration and the role of blockchain technology, A four-dimensional framework analysis from the Ghanaian land perspective. *Land,* 9 (12), 491.

Amsterdam v. Triangle Publication, Inc. 93 F. Supp. 79 (E.D. Pa. 1950), aff'd, 189 F.2d 104 (3d Cir. 1951).

An Act for Preventing the Frequent Abuses in Printing Seditious Treasonable and Unlicensed Books and Pamphlets and for Regulating of Printing and Printing Presses 1622 (Licensing of the Press Act 1662) (UK).

An Act for the Encouragement of Learning, by Securing Copies of Maps, Charts, and Books, to the Authors and Proprietors of Such Copies, during the Times therein mentioned 1790 (Copyright Act 1790) (USA).

An Act for the Encouragement of Learning, by Vesting the Copies of Printed Books in the Authors or Purchasers of Such Copies, during the Times Therein Mentioned 1710 (Statute of Anne 1710) (UK).

An Act to Amend and Consolidate the Acts Respecting Copyright 1909 (USA).

Anderson, S., 2018. The missing link between blockchain and copyright: How companies are using new technology to misinform creators and violate Federal Law. *North Carolina Journal of Law & Technology*, 19 (4), 1.

Andrews v. Guenther Publishing Co., 60 F.2d 555 (S.D.N.Y. 1932).

Ansah, B.O., *et al.*, 2023. A systematic review of the institutional success factors for blockchain-based land administration. *Land Use Policy*, 125, 106473.

Apple Computer, Inc. v. Franklin Computer Corp., 1240 (3d Cir. 1983).

Arizona Business Law Deskbook, Thomson West, 2022–2023 ed., vol. 9, § 15:16.

A.V. ex rel. Vanderhye v. iParadigms, LLC, 562 F.3d 630, 642, 90 U.S.P.Q.2d 1513 (4th Cir. 2009).

Barclays Capital, Inc. v. Theflyonthewall.com, Inc. 650 F.3d 876 (2d Cir. 2011).

Best Medium Publishing Co. v. National Insider, Inc. 385 F.2d 384 (7th Cir. 1967).

Bleistein v. Donaldson Lithographing Co. 188 U.S. 239 (1903).

Bogden, M.A., 2011. Fixing fixation: The RAM copy doctrine. *Arizona State Law Journal,* 43 (1), 181.

Boland-Devito, J., 2006. Yo ho and a bottle of rum – The DMCA takes on movie pirates. *Currents: International Trade Law Journal,* 15, 70–73.

Bracha, O., 2016. United States copyright, 1672–1909. *In:* I. Alexander and H. Tomás Gómez-Arostegui eds. *Research handbook on the history of copyright law*. Cheltenham: Edward Elgar Publishing, 335–343.

Brandriss, I.L., 1995. Writing in frost on a window pane: E-mail and chatting on RAM and copyright fixation part I. *Journal of the Copyright Society of the U.S.A.*, 43 (3), 237.

Brown, E., 2014. Fixed perspectives: The evolving contours of the fixation requirement in copyright law. *Washington Journal of Law, Technology &* Arts, 10 (1), 17.

Burrow-Giles Lithographic Co. v. Sarony. 111 U.S. 53, 58 (1884).

Burshtyn, P., 1998. Illuminating the law of copyright: Holographic data storage takes intellectual property to a new dimension. *Fordham Intellectual Property, Media and Entertainment Law Journal*, 9 (1), 384.

Campbell v. Acuff-Rose Music, Inc. 510 U.S. 569, 577, 579,114 S. Ct. 1164, 1170, 127 L. Ed. 2d 500, 22 Media L. Rep. (BNA) 1353, 29 U.S.P.Q.2d 1961 (1994).

Carpenter, M. and Hetcher, S., 2013. Function over form: Bringing the fixation requirement into the modern era. *Fordham Law Review*, 82 (5), 2221–2252.

Carter v. Hawaii Transp. Co., 201 F. Supp. 301 (D. Haw. 1961).

Cartoon Network LP v. CSC Holdings, Inc. 536 F.3d 121 (2d Cir. 2008).

CCC Info. Servs., Inc. v. Maclean Hunter Mkt. Reps., Inc. 44 F.3d 61 (2d Cir. 1994).

Chamberlain Group, Inc. v. Skylink Tech., Inc. 292 F. Supp. 2d 1040, 1040 (N.D. Ill. 2003).

Chamberlin v. Bekins Van & Storage Co., 23 F.2d 541 (S.D. Cal. 1928).

Chen, Y. and Yang, M. 2005. Legal issues on public access to remote sensing data in Taiwan. *In: Proceedings of 2005 IEEE international geoscience and remote sensing symposium, 2005. IGARSS '05.*

Chicago B. & Q. R.R. v. City of Chicago, 166 U.S. 226, 227 (1897).

Community for Creative Non-Violence v. Reid, 490 U.S. 730, 739–740, 109 S. Ct. 2166, 2172–2173 (1989).

Computer Assocs. Int'l, Inc. v. Atlai, Inc. 982 F.2d 693, 703 (2d Cir. 1992).

Copyright Office Regulations C.F.R. §202.9 (1959).

Copyright Review Board, 2022. Second request for reconsideration for refusal to register a recent entrance to paradise (Correspondence ID 1–3ZPC6C3; SR # 1–7100387071) (Case Determination). *Copyright Review Board.* Available from: <www.copyright.gov/rulings-filings/review-board/docs/a- recent-entrance-to-paradise.pdf>.

CoStar Group, Inc. v. LoopNet, Inc (CoStar) 373 F.3d 544 (4th Cir. 2004).

Crocker v. General Drafting Co., 50 F. Supp. 634 (S.D.N.Y. 1943).

Cross, J.T., 2000. Suing the states for copyright infringement. *Brandeis Law Journal*, 39 (2), 337.

C.S. Hammond & Co. v. International College Globe, Inc. 210 F. Supp. 206 (S.D.N.Y. 1962).

Data.Gov. Data.gov (27 July 2021). Available from: <www.data.gov/>.

Data Policy Statements, Data.gov. Available from: <www.data.gov/data-policy/>.

Davison, M., 2006. Database protection: Lessons from Europe, Congress, and WIPO law, technology and the arts symposium: The WIPO copyright treaties: 10 Years later. *Case Western Reserve Law Review,* 57 (4), 829–845.

Davison, M., 2020. Databases and copyright protection. *In:* T. Aplin ed. *Research handbook on intellectual property and digital technologies*. Edward Elgar Publishing Limited, 75. Available from: <http://ebookcentral.proquest.com/lib/monash/detail.action?docID=6029047>.

Defend Trade Secrets Act 2016 (Public Law No. 114–153).

Del Madera Props. v. Rhodes & Gardner, Inc. 820 F.2d 973, 976 (9th Cir. 1987).

Digital at Arup, 2019. Blockchain and the built environment. *ARUP*. Available from: <www.arup.com/en/perspectives/publications/research/section/blockchain-and-the-built-environment>.

Digital Millennium Copyright Act 1998. Public Law No. 105–304, 112 Stat. 2860 (1998).

Fabian, S., 2020. Blockchain and intellectual property rights comments. *Intellectual Property and Technology Law Journal*, 25 (2), 147–157.

Falwell v. Penthouse International, Ltd.,521 F. Supp. 1204 (W.D. Va 1981).

Federal GeoAgraphic Data Committee (FGDC)., n.d. About | GeoPlatform.Gov. Available from: <www.geoplatform.gov>.

Federal Procedure, L.Ed, 2023. Thomson Reuters, Lawyers Cooperative Publishing.

Feist Publications, Inc. v. Rural Telephone Service Company, Inc. 113 L.Ed.2d 358, 111 S. Ct. 1282 (1991), 499 U.S. 340 (1991).

Fenning, K., 1928. Origin of the patent and copyright clause of the constitution. *Georgetown Law Journal,* 17 (2), 109.

Firoozye v. Earthlink Network 153 F.Supp. 2d 1115, 1124 (N.D.Cal. 2001).

Foundations for Evidence-Based Policymaking Act 2018 (Public Law No.115–435).

Fractional Villas, Inc. v. Tahoe Clubhouse, No. 08CV1396-IEG-POR, 2009 U.S. Dist. LEXIS 39522, at 5, 2009 WL 1298532, at 2 (S.D. Cal. 8 May 2009).

General Drafting Co. v. Andrews, 37 F.2d 54 (2d Cir. 1930).

Geophysical Service Inc. v. TGS-NOPEC, 784 Fed.Appx. 253, 2019 WL 4410259, at 2 (5th Cir. 13 September 2019).

Georgia et al v. Public.Resource.Org 140 S. Ct. 1498 (2020).

Golan v. Holder 565 U.S. 302, 323–25 (2012).

Google LLC v. Oracle Am., Inc. 141 S.Ct. 1183.

Graglia J.M. and Mellon, C., 2018. Blockchain and property in 2018: At the end of the beginning. *Innovations: Technology, Governance, Globalization*, 12 (1–2), 90.

Harper & Row Publishers, Inc. v. Nation Enterprises et al. 471 U.S. 539, 558 (1985).

Hayden v. Chalfant Press, Inc. 281 F.2d 543 (9th Cir. 1960).

Healthcare Advocates, Inc. v. *Harding, Earley, Follmer & Frailey*, 49 7 F. SUPP. 2D 62 7 (E.D. PA. 2007).

House of Representatives, *Copyright Law Revision* (H.R. Rep. No. 1476, 94th Cong., 2d Sess. 58 (1976).

Hubanov, S., 2006. The multifaceted nature and problematic status of fixation in U.S. copyright law comment. *Intellectual Property Law Bulletin*, 11 (1), 111–113.

Hubbertz, A., 1990. Crown copyright and privatization of government information in Canada, with comparisons to the United States experience. *Government Publications Review*, 17 (2), 159.

Hughes, J., 2020. Restating copyright law's originality requirement. *Columbia Journal of Law & the Arts*, 44 (3), 383–390.

In re Jackson, 972 F.3d 25, 44–45 (2d Cir. 2020).

International News Service Inc. v Associated Press 248 U.S 215 (1918).

Janssen, K. and Dumortier, J., 2006. The protection of maps and spatial databases in Europe and the United States by Copyright and the Sui Generis Right. *UIC John Marshall Journal of Information Technology & Privacy Law*, 24, 195–206.

Jeweler's Circular Pub. Co. v. Keystone Pub. Co. 281 F. 83 (2d Cir. 1922).

John G. Danielson, Inc. v. Winchester-Conant Props., Inc. 186 F. Supp. 2d 1, 16 & n.2 (D. Mass. 2002).

Joyce, C. and Ochoa, T.T., 2016. Reach out and touch someone: Reflections on the 25th anniversary of feist publications, Inc. v. rural telephone service Co. authorship in America (and beyond): Institute for Intellectual Property & Information Law Symposium: Historical essay. *Houston Law Review*, 54 (2), 257–268.

Junnila, A.S.S. and Vimpari, J., 2022. Blockchain's grand promise for the real estate sector: A systematic review. *Applied Sciences*, 12 (23), 11940.

Karjala, D.S., 1991. Copyright and misappropriation copyright symposium part II – Copyright protection for computer databases, CD-ROMs and factual compilations. *The University of Dayton Law Review*, 17 (3), 885–886.

Karjala, D.S., 1994. Copyright in electronic maps symposium. *Jurimetrics Journal*, 35 (4), 395.

Key Maps, Inc. v. Pruitt 470 F. Supp. 33 (S.D. Tex. 1978).

Koronczok, M., 2019. The new chain of title: How blockchain will affect land title research, recordation, and insurance. *Texas A&M Journal of Property Law,* 5 (3), 401.

Kwall, R.R., 1988. Governmental use of copyright property: The sovereign's prerogative. *Texas Law Review*, 67 (4), 685–692.

Leaffer, M., 2006. Database protection in the United States is alive and well: Comments on Davison law, technology and the arts symposium: The WIPO copyright treaties: 10 Years Later. *Case Western Reserve Law Review,* 57 (4), 855.

Lee, M.S., 2023. *Entertainment and intellectual property law*. Thomson Reuters, LegalWorks.

Lehman B.A., September 1995. Intellectual property and the national information infrastructure -The report of the working group on intellectual property rights, 26. Available from: <www.eff.org/files/filenode/DMCA/ntia_dmca_white_paper.pdf>

Lloyd, A., 2010. Inherently transitory transistors: Legal, factual, and policy issues with "Ram fixation. *In*: *Copyright*. Michigan State University College of Law, 4. <www.law.msu.edu/king/2009-2010/Lloyd.pdf>.

Luna-Reyes, L.F., *et al*, 2019. The US open data initiative: The road ahead. *Information Polity: The International Journal of Government & Democracy in the Information Age*, 24 (2), 163.

MAI Systems Corp. v. Peak Computer, Inc. 991 F.2d 511 (9th Cir. 1993).

Markunas, J.D., 2019. Blockchain for surveyors. *Land Journal* 10.

Mason v. Montgomery Data, Inc. (Mason) 967 F.2d 135 (5th Cir. 1992).

Mathews Conveyer Co. v. Palmer-Bee Co., 135 F.2d 73, 85 (6th Cir. 1943).

Matthew Bender & Co. v. West Pub. Co. 158 F.3d 693 (2d Cir. 1998).

Missouri Pac. Ry. v. Nebraska, 164 U.S. 403, 417 (1896).

Müller, H. and Seifert, M., 2019. Blockchain, a feasible technology for land administration?. Available from: <www.fig.net/resources/proceedings/fig_proceedings/fig2019/papers/ts01i/TS01I_seifert_mueller_10110.pdf>.

New Era Publications Intern., ApS v. Carol Pub. Group, 904 F.2d 152, 157, 17 Media L. Rep. (BNA) 1913, 14 U.S.P.Q.2d 2030 (2d Cir. 1990).

Nimmer, M.B. and Nimmer, D., 2023. *Nimmer on copyright* (Matthew Bender, Rev. Ed.).

Open Government, Data.gov. Available from: <www.data.gov/open-gov/>.

Party, W.F., 2023. *Party on copyright*. Thomson West.

Pech, S., 2020. Copyright unchained: How blockchain technology can change the administration and distribution of copyright protected works. *Northwestern Journal of Technology and Intellectual Property*, 18 (1), 1.

Peiro, N.N. and Garcia, E.J.M., 2017. Blockchain and land registration systems. *European Property Law Journal (EPLJ),* 6 (3), 296.

Perris v. Hexamer 99 U.S. 674 (1879).

Peterson, P., 2019. Problems blockchain doesn't solve. *Illinois Bar Review*, 107 (2), 36.

Photographic Illustrators Corp. v. Orgill, Inc. 953 F.3d 56 (1st Cir. 2020).

ProCD, Incorporated v. Matthew Zeidenberg and Silken Mountain Web Services, Inc. 86 F.3D 1447 (7th Cir. 1996).

Rajbhandari, R., 2021. License to sublicense: The legal possibility of impliedly sublicensing a copyrighted work annual survey of Federal En Banc and Other significant cases: Comments. *Boston College Law Review E. Supp*. II, 62, 425.

Rand McNally and Co. v. Fleet Management Sys., Inc. 634 F. Supp. 604 (N.D. Ill. 1986).
Real Networks, Inc. v. Streambox, Inc. No. 2:99CV02070, 2000 U.S. Dist. WL 127311 (W.D. Wash. Jan. 18, 2000).
Reichman, J.H and Samuelson, P., 1997. Intellectual property rights in data. *Vanderbilt Law Review*, 50 (1), 49.
Reinicke v. Creative Empire, LLC, 2016 WL 5845734 (9th Cir. Oct. 6, 2016).
Restatement (Second) of Agency (1958).
Rice, M.T., Intellectual property control for maps and geographic data (Ph.D., University of California, Santa Barbara). Available from: <www.proquest.com/docview/305003538/abstract/4B513DD2D2AA45DCPQ/1>.
Richter, H., 2021. Copyright protection of government-related material before the courts of the United States and Canada: Considerations for future reforms. *IIC – International Review of Intellectual Property and Competition Law*, 52 (1), 6.
Rockford Map Pub., Inc. v. Directory Serv. Co., of Colo., 768 F.2d 145 (7th Cir. 1985).
Scassa, T., (2003). Originality and utilitarian works: The uneasy relationship between copyright law and unfair competition. *University of Ottawa Law & Technology Journal*, 1, 51.
Shang, Q. and Price, A., 2019. A blockchain-based land titling project in the republic of Georgia: Rebuilding public trust and lessons for future pilot projects. *Innovations: Technology, Governance, Globalization,* 12 (3–4), 72.
Simplexgrinnell LP v. Integrated Systems & Power, Inc. 2009 WL 857504 (S.D.N.Y. 31 March 2009).
Stewart v. Abend, 495 U.S. 207, 237, 110 S. Ct. 1750, 109 L. Ed. 2d 184, 14 U.S.P.Q.2d 1614 (1990).
Strong, W.S., 2014. *The copyright book: A practical guide* (6th ed.). MIT Press. Available from: <http://ebookcentral.proquest.com/lib/monash/detail.action?docID=3339814>
Tandy Corp v. Personal Microcomputers, Inc. 524 F. Supp. 171 (N.D. Cal. 1981).
Ticketmaster v. Tickets.com, Inc. No. CV 99–7654 HLH (BQRx), 2000 U.S. Dist. LEXIS 4553.
U.S.C Title 17 - Copyright.
U.S.C Title 43 - Public Lands.
Uniform Trade Secrets Act 1979 (U.T.S.A.) (Uniform Law Commission).
United States Constitution 1789.
United States Copyright Office, 2021. *Compendium of U.S. copyright office practices* (3rd ed.), 102. Available from: <www.copyright.gov/comp3/>.
United States Copyright Office, *Zarya of the Dawn* (Registration # VAu001480196) (Case Determination No 1–5GB561K, United States Copyright Office, 21 February 2023). Available from: <www.copyright.gov/docs/zarya-of-the-dawn.pdf>.
United States v. Hamilton, 583 F.2d 448, 451 (9th Cir. 1978).
Vekstein, J.E., 2011. A hot mess: How hot-news misappropriation bypassed copyright law in barclays v. theflyonthewall.Com and gave originators a property right in facts note. *Catholic University Law Review,* 61 (1), 297–298.
Victor Lalli Enterprises, Inc. v. Big Red Apple, Inc. 936 F.2d. 671 (2d Cir. 1991).
Wells Fargo & Co. v. WhenU.Com, Inc. 293 F. Supp. 2d 734, 771 (E.D. Mich. 2003).
White-Smith Publishing Co. v. Apollo Co. 209 U.S. 1, 28 S. Ct. 319, 52 L. Ed. 655 (1908).
Wille, D.G., Jewell, D., and Ratliff, P., 2001. Protection and enforcement of new intellectual property symposium – Exploring emerging issues: New intellectual property, Information technology, and security in borderless commerce. *Texas Wesleyan Law Review,* 8 (3), 467.
Williams Electronics, 685 F.2d at 874; *Atari Games Corp. v. Oman,* 888 F.2d 878, 884n.6 (D.C. Cir. 1989).
Wolf, D.B., 1991. Is there any copyright protection for maps after feist part I. *Journal of the Copyright Society of the U.S.A.,* 39 (3), 224–226.
Yout, LLC v. Recording Indus. Ass'n of Am., Inc. No. 3:20-CV-1602 (SRU), 2022 WL 4599203, at 6 (D. Conn. 30 September, 2022).

4 Copyright of survey plans and spatial data in the European Union

4.1 Introduction

In this chapter, the copyright regime of the European Union (EU) is examined to compare and contrast the application of copyright principles in the context of survey products and data. Such a study is important as the EU copyright regime has developed based on certain fundamental principles that are a result of the European legal tradition as opposed to Anglo-American copyright principles. This chapter begins with a brief discussion of EU copyright law, highlighting the difference between common law and civil law traditions in applying copyright principles. This discussion is then followed by a brief introduction to the sources of EU copyright law and introduction to the practice of surveyors in the Europe, followed by a detailed discussion on the application of EU copyright elements to survey products and data.

4.2 EU law on copyright

EU copyright law consists of a collection of directives and regulations harmonising basic rights in the Member States.[1] The legislative competence concerning copyright and related rights in the EU is derived from Article 114 of the 2010 Treaty on the Functioning of the European Union (TFEU). Article 114 specifies the general mandate to establish an internal market by harmonising national laws. The principle of non-discrimination requires Member States to offer the same level of protection to all EU citizens and residents. Regardless of the extensive harmonisation effects,[2] however, there is no unitary EU-wide copyright law as in in the cases of EU trademark and EU design rights.[3] The territorial protection of copyright and the need for the free movement of goods and services in a single market has created tensions within the harmonisation process, and have been mainly resolved through findings of the Court of Justice of the European Union (CJEU), where violations of the free movement of goods were recognised with regards to national copyright law.[4]

4.3 Sources of EU law on copyright

The most important sources of EU copyright law are directives, regulations, and the CJEU's decisions. Directives are binding about the result to be achieved, while national authorities have the discretion to determine the form and methods

DOI: 10.4324/9781003479383-4

of the incorporation (transposition) of directives into national laws. Generally, Member States are given two years to ensure the adaptation of directives at a national level. The directives are addressed to the Member States and do not directly bind the citizens of the Member States. Regulations, conversely, are directly applicable in all Member States from their date of entry into force without needing to be transposed into national law. The national courts of Member States are obliged to interpret their national laws in line with the principles of EU law and refer to appropriate cases for preliminary hearings about the meaning and interpretation of EU law. The EU and Member States are also bound by international treaties on copyright law.[5] The harmonisation effects carried out in relation to EU law on copyright have been greatly justified based on the internal market rationale, ensuring the EU's competitiveness against third-party countries and remedying the imbalance in the marketplace for copyright content and related services.[6]

TFEU Article 118 provides a specific competence to establish a unified intellectual property (IP) protection regime throughout the EU. This Article has the potential to be used in the future to introduce a unitary copyright law to replace national copyright laws.

4.4 Surveyors and development as to survey plans/spatial data in the EU

In Europe, the primary activity of land surveyors is to provide accurate and reliable (legal) data about a property. The execution of this activity is influenced mainly by national legal elements.[7] Cadastral surveyors in Europe can operate either as private or public cadastral surveyors, or in both capacities. In Spain and Sweden, for instance, there are no licensed private cadastral surveyors.[8] Cadastral services are provided by surveyors employed by the National Mapping and Cadastral Agencies (NMCAs), by municipalities, or by individuals contracted to perform such services. In countries that have private surveyors, the Chambers of Surveyors or NMCAs generally carry out licensing activities. Surveyors employed by the NMCAs are not required to obtain separate licences. Concerning the licensing (authorisation) requirements for private surveyors, different conditions exist across Europe.[9] In most European countries, the minimum qualifications to perform cadastral activities include obtaining a higher education in geodesy (or related disciplines) and a certain period of professional practice.[10] Two directives, including the 'Free Movement of Professionals' (Directive 2005/36/EC on the Recognition of Professional Qualifications) and 'Services Directive' (Directive 2006/123/EC on Services in the Internal Market), have resulted in the ability of European surveyors to not only have their national qualifications recognised within the EU but also provide services beyond their national boundaries. The most common activities of the European cadastral are to 'take technical measurements, mark parcel corners, advise (landowners), validate (depends on the authority) and acquire approval for cadastral documents from relevant authorities'.[11] Responsibility for the accuracy and reliability of the data provided by surveyors is shared between the State and the cadastral surveyors. While most cadastral surveyors in Europe are fully responsible for any mistakes they make in their work, the mechanisms for third-party compensation are not well developed, resulting in sanctions on their level of qualification.[12] In 2007, most surveyors relied on civil litigation instead of purchasing professional indemnity insurance to deal with matters between surveyors and clients.[13] This has changed over the years, however; the survey's 2018 revision indicated that professional liability insurance has become compulsory for the purposes of operating as a surveyor in most EU Member States.[14]

Several directives have had a direct impact on the activities performed by surveyors in the EU. One of the most important directives in this regard is the 'INSPIRE Directive' (Directive 2007/2/EC Establishing an Infrastructure for Spatial Information in the European Community [INSPIRE]). The INSPIRE Directive is the legal framework set forth to achieve standardisation with geospatial information infrastructure. This Directive aims to ensure that the Member States' spatial data infrastructures (SDIs) are 'compatible and usable in a Community and transboundary context'.[15] The Directive addresses 34 spatial data themes and provides for adopting common implementing rules in several specific areas (metadata, data specifications, network services, data and service sharing, and monitoring and reporting). While the Directive's primary aim has been to establish infrastructure to make use of spatial information concerning environmental policies, the infrastructure's establishment has resulted in extending the use of this infrastructure in public administration matters.[16] Discussion about the implementation of the INSPIRE Directive in the context of Polish SDI (PSDI) has noted that 'Geoportal 2' (the main access point for the PSDI) is increasingly considered by surveyors as 'a resource for information from geodetic and cartographic service centres and from previous field reconnaissance'.[17]

At the EU level, several organisations directly affect the activities that surveyors carry out. These include the EuroGeographics,[18] the European Land Registry Association,[19] the Permanent Committee on Cadastre in the European Union,[20] and the Council of European Geodetic Surveyors.[21] In 2021, the Permanent Committee on Cadastre in the European Union conducted a survey, titled *Status and Adopted Innovations Over the Last Decade in Cadastre and Land Administration in Europe*, which noted that most Member States had digitalised the cadastre with integrated systems to manage land, citizen, and address registries.[22] For example, Estonia has a 100% digital Land Cadastre, which allows the use of digital signatures and fully digital (paper-free) cadastral procedures that enable data exchange between cadastre and land surveyors. Furthermore, the digital topographic database has been used to match boundaries with the topographic database.[23] Future plans for the Estonian digitalisation of cadastre include visualising all kinds of restricted real rights (servitudes, encumbrances) having spatial extent, and developing the Land Cadastre to the environment of land procedures, thereby making its dynamic register.[24] The Netherlands, conversely, has moved to an automated land registration system.[25] Future innovations for the Netherlands include highlighting the integration/connection within the value chain of the land market, in which all stakeholders are connected. Integrating measurement information with the parcel information of the index map and shifting towards 3D registration are also future possibilities. These two examples indicate the level of digitalisation in the EU concerning the cadastre system. These developments significantly affect how surveyors carry out their activities and how the spatial data/products would be protected under copyright and related rights in the EU. This research will therefore commence with one of the most important aspects of EU copyright law concerning the protection of data and databases in the EU.

4.5 The Database Directive

The Directive 96/9/EC of the European Parliament and of the Council of 11th March 1996 on the Legal Protection of Databases (Database Directive, or DD) was introduced with the aim of harmonising the laws within the EU regarding the protection granted to databases and increasing the protection for databases created in the EU while ensuring the harmonisation effects.[26]

Before the DD was introduced, the protection granted to databases in EU Member States differed significantly; some countries opted for using unfair competition law principles in protecting databases, while others relied on the 'sweat of the brow' principle.[27] In this context, the effect of the DD was twofold; first, it harmonised the legal treatment of databases under copyright law as applicable to Member States, and second, it introduced a *sui generis* right for the creators of databases for the content of their databases. The former harmonised the protection granted to the design and structure of databases, while the latter created a new right that protects the contents of databases that may or may not be protected by copyright principles. Of the two initiatives, the *sui generis* right is considered an EU innovation.

The importance of the DD for surveyors in general – and for national mapping, cadastral, and land registration authorities in particular – was highlighted in the EuroGeographics' briefing paper as part of a 2018 review of the DD.[28] EuroGeographics recognised the shift from analogue to digital in the industry, and how standardised database structures and interoperability tools in the design of geospatial databases limited the ability to demonstrate creativity and thereby qualify for copyright protection.[29] Geospatial databases were thus considered as exemplifying the need for protection under the *sui generis* right.

4.5.1 Protection for the structure and design of databases

The first part of the DD is directed towards harmonising the protection granted to databases in Member States. As per the DD, the 'selection or arrangement of contents of a database' (the structure and design of the database) in the EU would be protected as long as such selection and arrangement constitute the 'author's own intellectual creation.' This standard indicates a typical European compromise, in which the standard adopted for protection is higher than the common law standard but lower than the civil law standard.[30] The elements of the DD for the protection of database structure and design will be discussed in detail in this section.

Article 1 of the DD provides legal protection to databases in any form, including analogue and digital databases. This includes paper databases, online databases, and any database stored in CD-ROMs or similar methods. The definition has been kept broad to contain any potential future format.[31] While not explicitly been mentioned in Article 1, in the case *Fixtures Marketing Ltd v Organismos Prognostikon Agonon Podosfairou* (OPAP),[32] the CJEU held that to be protected, a database must be fixed. The term 'database' is defined in Article 1(2) as 'a collection of independent works, data or other materials arranged in a systematic or methodical way and individually accessible by electronic or other means.' While not defined, the element of 'independence' has been subject to judicial interpretation to mean that 'the materials must be separable from one another without their informative, literary, artistic, musical or other value being affected'.[33] To be 'independent', the material must have an autonomous informative value.[34] Using Recital 17 of the DD, it has been argued that to be independent, materials must be able to be assessed or withdrawn without affecting the database as a whole.[35]

The case of *Freistaat Bayern v Verlag Esterbauer GmbH*[36] provides for the clarification and application of Article 1 in the context of maps. This case involved a response to a reference from the Bundesgerichtshof (Germany's highest court of civil and criminal jurisdiction), whereby the dispute was between the Free State of Bavaria and the publishing house Esterbauer. The dispute related to the topographic maps of Bavaria produced by the Land of Bavaria and published in analogue (hard copy) form. Esterbauer scanned these hard copy maps and extracted information to create new maps primarily aimed at cyclists and hikers. The question to be determined was whether the data describing the nature of specific points of the Earth's surface constitute 'independent materials' within the meaning of Article 1(2) of the DD.[37] When deciding on this broad question, the CJEU first held that the analogue nature of the topographic maps, which required them to be scanned using a scanner, did not preclude them from being recognised as a 'database' within the meaning of Article 1(2) of the DD.[38] Concerning the question of whether geographical data extracted from a topographic map retain sufficient informative value after extraction to be held as 'independent materials' of a 'database', Esterbauer observed that first, the relevant material considered in this case was a combination of two pieces of information: the 'geographical coordinates point' (the numbered code corresponding to a certain coordinates point of the 2D grid network) and the 'signature' (the numbered code used by the map producer to designate a unique feature). Thus, Esterbauer observed that, once extracted from the topographic map, the informative value of that information was reduced to almost zero. In this regard, the CJEU held that not only an individual piece of information but also a combination of pieces of information could constitute 'independent material' within the meaning of Article 1(2) of the DD.[39] Further, the CJEU held that while the value of material from a collection, when extracted, would tend to result in a corresponding decline in value, this decline would not affect its classification as an 'independent material' provided that the material retains autonomous informative value.[40] As to the assessment of the autonomous value of the materials, the Court referred to the judgement of *Fixtures Marketing Ltd v Organismos Prognostikon Agonon Podosfairou*,[41] reiterating:

> the autonomous informative value of material which has been extracted from a collection must be assessed in the light of the value of the information not for a typical user of the collection concerned, but for each third party interested by the extracted material.[42]

In assessing the autonomous value of the materials making up topographic maps, the Court noted that topographic maps could be used for various purposes by a typical user.[43] However, the autonomous informative value of the materials making up topographic maps must be determined based on each third party interested in the extracted material; in this case, Esterbauer's customers. Given that the information extracted by Esterbauer from the Land of Bavaria's topographic maps provided Esterbauer's customers with relevant information,[44] the CJEU ruled that geographical information extracted from a topographic map by a third party to produce and market another map retains sufficient informative value following its extraction to be classified as 'independent materials' of a 'database' within the meaning of Article 1(2) of the DD. This decision has addressed any concerns surveyors may have had regarding the application of copyright protection to databases containing spatial data.

The DD does not define the term 'systematic or methodical arrangement' as mentioned in Article 1. Recital 21, however, indicates that database materials are not required to be physically stored in an organised manner. Thus, it could be some technical means (such as electronic, electromagnetic, or electro-optical processes) or other more common means (such as an index, table of contents, or particular plan or method of classification) to allow the retrieval of any independent material contained within the database.[45] As per Article 1(3), the computer programs used in making or operating a database accessible by electronic means would not qualify as a database to be protected under the DD. The protection for computer programs is provided under the Software Directive (SD),[46] and Article 2[47] of the DD avoids any conflicts by providing that the SD prevails if there is any inconsistency between the SD and the DD.

Article 3 of the DD provides for the originality criterion for database protection. Article 3(1) provides that the 'author's own intellectual creation' in the selection or arrangement of materials in a database is the object of protection under the DD. In the case of *Football Dataco v Yahoo! UK Ltd and others*,[48] the CJEU held that the 'criterion of originality is satisfied when, through the selection or arrangement of the data it contains, its author expresses his creative ability in an original manner by making free and creative choices'.[49] The requirement of a 'personal touch'[50] rules out protection for databases that are 'dictated by technical considerations, rules or constraints which leave no room for creative freedom'.[51] The 'author's own intellectual creation' is the only criterion applied in determining the eligibility of a database for protection under the DD; other considerations, including whether the selection or arrangement includes 'adding important significance' to that data or whether the setting up of the database required the significant labour and skill of its author, have been held to be irrelevant when considering questions of originality.[52] In *Football Dataco and others v Yahoo! UK Ltd and others*, the case concerned the fixture lists created by Football Dataco to provide information on scores, penalties, and player substitutions. These lists were made available to the online customers of Football Dataco via their website. Football Dataco claimed that the use of these lists by Yahoo! to compile data for its databases without a licence was an infringement of Article 3 of the DD, given that Yahoo!'s business was largely – if not solely – reliant upon Football Dataco's supply of this data. While the case settled on remand to the Court of Appeal of England and Wales, it must be noted that, as per the CJEU's interpretation, there will be no copyright in the fixtures lists. Article 3(2) of the DD specifically rules out any protection for the content of the databases. National courts mainly determine the originality requirement,[53] and as per Janssen and Dumortier, the case law from the national courts indicates that the threshold for the copyright protection of databases is relatively low.[54] However, they also note that spatial databases using standard structures that need interoperability may limit the possibility of any indication of originality or intellectual creation in the selection and arrangement of the data.[55]

In Article 4 of the DD, the authorship of databases is left for Member States to decide. The authorship could be given to a natural person, group of natural persons, or legal person as per the laws of the Member States. Article 4(2) recognises collective works as applicable in some countries, such as France, and provides that the person holding the copyright shall own the economic right. Because there is no reference to the authorship of databases authored by employees, the national laws would be applicable. One important parallel in this regard would be the SD, which provides for an employer to have exclusive economic rights in a database unless otherwise provided by contract. Recital 29 of the DD states that Member States may also follow the same principle in relation to databases. Therefore, spatial databases created in EU Member States would have national laws determining the applicable laws about the authorship of the databases. Given the guidance provided in the recitals, there would be a very limited opportunity for a surveyor who has created a database within the course of his or her employment to claim authorship of that database.

Article 5 of the DD provides for the rights of a database's author as to the expression of the database for which protection has been granted.[56] Article 6(1) recognises the rights of lawful users to access and use the contents of the database normally. Article 6(2) of the DD provides exceptions to the rights set out in Article 5, which Member States have the discretion to include in their national laws.[57] Article 6(3) recognises the three-step test of interpreting the Article in such a way as to allow its application in a manner that does not unreasonably prejudice the rights holder's legitimate interests or conflicts with the normal exploitation of the database.[58]

Given this discussion, the EU copyright protection granted to the structure and design of databases is similar to Australian standards, because the originality requirement necessitates intellectual creation as a precondition for protection.

Based on the national laws of Member States, the civil law or common law basis of the legal system would determine the applicable standards in each country. The *sui generis* right provided by the DD becomes important in a context in which a spatial database that may or may not be able to satisfy the originality requirement still has the means to protect its contents.

4.6 *Sui generis* right

Article 7, Chapter III of the DD provides for the *sui generis* right to protect the contents of a database. The *sui generis* right is an IP right under EU and national laws; however, it is not part of the copyright in a database. Article 7(1) provides that:

> Member States shall provide for a right for the maker of a database which shows that there has been qualitatively and/or quantitatively a substantial investment in either the obtaining, verification or presentation of the contents to prevent extraction and/or re-utilisation of the whole or of a substantial part, evaluated qualitatively and/or quantitatively, of the contents of that database.[59]

There are several reasons for the introduction of a *sui generis* right. First, there was a lack of protection given to content, which is the main investment in a database under copyright law. Because copyright protects only the structure and design of a database, and not the content, it is necessary to have additional protection to prevent unlawful extraction of content from databases.[60] Second, it was to ensure that Europe's database industry was equipped to compete in the global market, especially in terms of the competition it faced from U.S. companies. Third, the *sui generis* right was thought to be more appropriate than attempting to harmonise the unfair competition laws in Member States that could have been used to protect the contents of a database. Thus, creating a new IP right was far easier than attempting to harmonise unfair competition laws in Member States.[61] As per Recitals 42 and 48, the *sui generis* right is intended to protect the database maker and their investment against acts by unlawful users, and to secure the remuneration of the database maker. All these reasons are directly relevant to the challenges that surveyors face in obtaining protection for their geospatial databases because data contained within the databases have been produced through significant investment. Furthermore, until the enactment of the *sui generis* right, there was very limited protection against third parties which may extract or reutilise data from geospatial databases.

The main requirement to grant protection under Article 7(1) is the 'qualitative and/or quantitative substantial investment in either the obtaining, verification or presentation' of the contents of a database. This investment could be either financial, material (acquisition of equipment), or human (time, effort, or energy).[62] The term 'substantial' is yet to be interpreted by the CJEU, and because it could be interpreted strictly or broadly, it has been inconsistently applied at the national level.[63] However, some scholars have noted that, generally, national courts have granted protection even for relatively low-level investments.[64] The terms 'qualitative' and 'quantitative' were defined in the case of *Fixtures Marketing Ltd v AB Svenska Spel*[65] as follows: '[t]he quantitative assessment refers to quantifiable resources and the qualitative assessment to efforts which cannot be quantified, such as intellectual effort or energy, according to the 7th, 39th and 40th recitals'.[66] The term 'obtaining' has been defined by the CJEU to include only the collection of data and not the creation of the same.[67] Therefore, the *sui generis* right will be attached to databases only if there has been a substantial investment in gathering the created data. In other words, if the database content is created as a by-product of the main activity, then it will rarely be protected by the *sui generis* right.[68] National courts in France,[69] Germany,[70] and Spain[71] have adopted the distinction between collection and obtaining data, holding on numerous occasions that substantial investment in data creation will not result in the *sui generis* right. The term 'verification' was defined in *Fixtures Marketing Ltd v AB Svenska Spel*[72] as 'ensuring the reliability of the information contained in the database, monitoring the accuracy of the materials collected when the database was created and during its operation'.[73] Thus, checking, correcting, and updating content would be sufficient to prove substantial investment in verification. The term 'presentation' was defined by the CJEU as:

> the resources used for the purpose of giving the database its function of processing information, that is to say, those used for the systematic or methodical arrangement of the materials contained in that database and the organisation of their individual accessibility.[74]

Therefore, not only the structuring or organisation of the data, but also how the contents are made accessible to users by means of the creation of an index or thesaurus would also fall within the definition of 'presentation'.[75]

The application of this right in the context of spatial databases would mean that if the investment is made in creating the data within the spatial databases, such data would not be protected because there would not be an investment in *obtaining* the contents of the database. This requirement significantly reduces the applicability of the *sui generis* right in the context of spatial databases. Given the significant investment made in relation to spatial databases involved with the creation of accurate data for a given land parcel – whether it is the dimensions, ownership details, or rights attached to that land parcel – it is doubtful whether such an investment would qualify as an investment in 'obtaining' the data. Thus, surveyors will have to seek protection within the *verification* or *presentation* aspects – such as checking, correcting, and updating content that has been created – to claim the *sui generis* right for such spatial data.

Regarding ownership of the *sui generis* right, Recital 41 provides that the database maker is 'the person who takes the initiative and the risk of investing'. Therefore, claiming ownership of the database will have to be the person – whether an individual or legal entity – who or which made the substantial investment. There are no references as to the ownership by employees, so it may be possible to adopt the employers' rights as discussed in relation to Article 4 of the DD. The DD does not address the issue of ownership by employees, commissioners, or joint owners as to the *sui generis* right; therefore, it will be decided based on the national laws of Member States.

The rights granted under the *sui generis* right are twofold: the database owner is protected from the 'extraction'[76] and/or 're-utilisation'[77] of the whole or a substantial part of the database. While these rights are similar to the reproduction and communication to the public in copyright law, they differ in some respects. The term 'extraction' has been defined to include both the removal and copying of content, such as 'copying, e.g. writing down by hand, typing on a computer or any machine, scanning a paper database, as well as downloading, printing or any other reproduction in whatever (permanent or temporary) form'.[78] For a transfer to be permanent, the data must be stored permanently in a medium other than the database for more than a limited period after extraction.[79] Merely consulting the database will not be considered an extraction, as long as the consultation is related to non-electronic databases. For electronic databases, a consultation will always involve a temporary reproduction.[80] In relation to spatial databases, this means that any removal or copying of a whole or substantial part of the database would result in an infringement of the *sui generis* right. With the digitalisation of spatial databases, this right will become automatically applicable to all electronic databases where the spatial data is kept. This is because the onscreen display of the contents of a spatial database necessitates the temporary transfer of all or a substantial part of those contents to another medium to be used for such consultation.[81]

Re-utilisation is also considered as a broad concept encompassing communications made via online, analogue, wire or wireless, and direct or indirect methods.[82] It has been held in the case of *Innoweb BV v Wegener ICT Media BV, Wegener Mediaventions BV*[83] that activities of meta-search engines would be an infringement of the *sui generis* right, in which all the hits to an inquiry are presented in one place using scraping websites. This is primarily because these search engines obtain data from the websites rather than directing the users to the websites.

The *sui generis* right under Article 7(1) could be transferred, assigned or granted under contractual licence, and is applicable irrespective of whether a database or its contents are protected under copyright or by other rights (Article 7(4)). Contrary to copyright law, it is possible for a public establishment to lend a database that is protected under the *sui generis* right. According to Article 7(1), the *sui generis* right is infringed if a whole or substantial part of the database contents (evaluated qualitatively and/or quantitatively) are extracted and/or reutilised. Furthermore, Article 7(5) provides that even a repeated and systematic extraction and/or reutilisation of insubstantial parts could be an infringement if such acts are in conflict with the normal exploitation of that database or if they unreasonably prejudice the legitimate interests of the database maker. In the context of infringement, the terms 'substantial part', 'insubstantial part', 'quantitative', and 'qualitative' have been discussed in the case of *British Horseracing Board, The v William Hill Organization*.[84] It was noted in this case that:

> the assessment, in qualitative terms, of whether the part at issue is substantial, must, like the assessment in quantitative terms, refer to the investment

> in the creation of the database and the prejudice caused to that investment by the act of extracting or re-utilising that part.[85]

The expression 'substantial part, evaluated quantitatively' of the contents of a database was defined to mean the 'volume of data extracted from the database and/or re-utilised, and must be assessed in relation to the volume of the contents of the whole of that database'.[86]

Further guidance was provided in the case of *Apis-Hristovich EOOD v Lakorda AD*,[87] in which a legal database consisting of several sub-databases (modules) was at issue. In deciding on the substantiality issue, the CJEU held that as long as each module was an independent database with substantial investment, any determination about substantiality would be assessed in comparison to the sub-database and not the whole database.[88] If data is taken from multiple modules, however, substantiality would be assessed based on the whole database. The term 'substantial part, evaluated qualitatively' was defined to:

> refer to the scale of the investment in the obtaining, verification or presentation of the contents of the subject of the act of extraction and/or re-utilisation, regardless of whether that subject represents a quantitatively substantial part of the general contents of the protected database.[89]

There are important considerations in these judicial statements. First, when determining the qualitative and quantitative terms of whether a part is substantial, the question will be determined based on whether the database maker has made significant investments in that particular part. Second, the Court definitions recognise that quantitative evaluation will be based on the percentage of data extracted compared to the whole database. Finally, the qualitative evaluation recognises that in terms of obtaining, verifying, or presenting the contents, a quantitatively negligible part may represent a significant human, technical, or financial investment.[90] While there has been no reference to a particular percentage that constitutes substantiality under the decisions of the CJEU, decisions of the national courts indicate that it could range from a 'majority'[91] to even 20%.[92]

Article 8 of the DD provides for lawful users' rights and obligations regarding the *sui generis* right. A 'lawful user' includes anyone who acquires access to a database as a result of a contract, public lending, gift, sale, resale, licence, inheritance, or rental contract.[93] In the case of *UsedSoft v Oracle International*,[94] the Court held that buying a program downloaded online from the software manufacturer's website, even under a so-called licence agreement, was a sale – and thus, the person acquiring it from this first owner via resale was a lawful acquirer.[95]

Exceptions to the *sui generis* right are provided in Article 9 of the DD. They include private reproduction for non-electronic databases, teaching and research, public security, or an administrative or judicial procedure. Since the enactment of the Directive on copyright in the digital single market, an additional exception has been added in relation to general text and data mining.[96]

Article 10 of the DD provides for the term of protection for the *sui generis* right, which lasts 15 years. If a database is made available to the public in that 15-year period, then the 15 years run from 1 January following the date of the first act of making the database publicly available. However, Article 10(3) provides that if a database maker makes a substantial change to the database – whether by way of accumulating successive additions, deletions, or alterations which would result in the database being considered to be a substantial new investment – then that database would be qualified for a new term of 15 years. It has been argued that dynamic databases (namely, databases that are continually being updated, such as electronic databases available online) could be protected perpetually due to Article 10(3).[97] Furthermore, this protection would be available to not only the updated elements but the whole database.[98]

Article 11 of the DD highlights that the *sui generis* right's protection is limited to EU nationals or habitual residents, as well as to firms established under the laws of a Member State and with their registered office, administration, or principal place of business located within the EU. It is possible for nationals of non-EU countries to benefit from the *sui generis* right on the basis of reciprocity. If a foreign company wishes to obtain the *sui generis* right, it can do so by conducting business in the EU using a subsidiary company or co-producer with an individual. The remedies are provided as per the Enforcement Directive,[99] through which all infringement of IP rights is addressed.

The DD has been reviewed twice since its adaptation; both the 2005 and 2018 evaluations were critical of the economic impact of the *sui generis* right on database production.[100] The need for reform was highlighted in view of the data economy's technical developments. Thus, it is important to consider the impact of the European data economy on the application of the *sui generis* right, as well as applicable copyright principles. The next section will investigate these aspects under the European data strategy, the proposed Data Governance Act/Data Act, and the General Data Protection Regulation (GDPR).

4.7 European data strategy, the proposed Data Governance Act/Data Act, and the GDPR

The EU's data governance initiatives are essential for understanding when discussing the *sui generis* right and application of copyright in general. The digitalisation of the cadastre and increased use of geospatial data necessitate understanding data protection, security, and privacy measures in the EU, and how such measures interact with copyright and *sui generis* right of databases in the EU.

The EU data strategy has been in development for a long time.[101] In its most recent iteration, in February 2020, the European Commission published 'A European Strategy for Data' (European data strategy) to create a single data market and ensure Europe's global competitiveness and data sovereignty.[102] The common European data spaces were expected to facilitate more data being available for the economy and society, providing sufficient control for those who generate data.[103]

In March 2021, the European Commission announced Europe's Digital Decade, which aims to create a digitally empowered Europe by 2030.[104] As part of these initiatives, the European Commission introduced two main data protection measures: the Data Governance Act[105] and the Data Act.[106]

The Data Governance Act seeks to 'increase trust in data sharing, strengthen mechanisms to increase data availability and overcome technical obstacles to the reuse of data'[107] and to establish measures for the reuse of data (not subject to open data initiatives) held by public bodies, a notification and supervisory framework for the provision of data intermediation services, a framework for the voluntary registration of entities that collect and process data made available for altruistic purposes, and a framework for establishing a European Data Innovation Board.[108] One category of data held by public bodies that has been made subject to the new rules under the Data Governance Act is the data protected by the IP rights of third parties.[109] The Data Governance Act also provides for the setup and development of common European data spaces involving private and public stakeholders. The Data Governance Act will be applicable from September 2023.

The European Commission initially proposed the Data Act in February 2022. This is the second legislative initiative under the EU's Data Strategy (the first being the Data Governance Act). The Data Act aims to facilitate data access, including specific provisions addressing the Internet of Things (IoT) and cloud service providers. The Data Act aims to make more data available for use by ensuring that whenever a customer buys connected products like a smart car, they have access to the data those products harvest. The customer would thus be able to share the data generated by the vehicle with third parties (e.g., an insurance company). This initiative enhances the data portability right to the customer, so that they can copy and transfer data easily across different services.[110] The Data Act also invalidates any unfair contractual terms on data access and use that are unilaterally imposed on micro, small, and medium-sized enterprises, thereby enabling fair and balanced business-to-business data sharing agreements. The Data Act proposal introduces the obligation to make private sector data available to public bodies and EU institutions, agencies, or bodies, upon request, in situations of exceptional need. The proposed rules aim to facilitate switching between cloud and edge services. The Data Act also proposes measures to prevent the unlawful transfer of or access to non-personal data by non-EU/European Economic Area governments. On 14 March 2023, the European Parliament approved the Data Act by an overwhelming majority.[111] On 24 March 2023, the Council of the EU agreed on its own position, and the final version of the legislation is now being drafted.

Given these principles, there are several important considerations for surveyors regarding spatial data and spatial products. The application of the *sui generis* right has been limited by initiatives under the European data strategy. Article 5(7) of the Data Governance Act provides that data reuse shall only be allowed in compliance with IP rights. In relation to public bodies, the *sui generis* right provided under the DD must not be exercised to prevent data reuse or restrict reuse beyond the limits set by the Data Governance Act. One of the proposal's main objectives is to increase legal certainty around sharing data obtained using products or related services. This specifically relates to applying the DD in the context of databases containing data from the IoT. According to draft Article 35 of the Data Act, the *sui generis* right provided by the DD does not apply to databases containing data obtained from or generated by a product or related service. Put differently, if the *sui generis* right conflicts with the legal principles of the Data Act, then the data strategy would prevail over the right granted under the DD. Thus, if spatial databases are created with data obtained through the IoT, such databases will not be able to use the *sui generis* right to protect the data, even though such data has been collected with significant investment and effort.

The European data strategy is built upon the general privacy and data security framework by the General Data Protection Regulation (EU) 2016/679 (GDPR). The GDPR sets out the legal framework for protecting natural persons concerning the processing of personal data and the free movement of such data in the EU. The GDPR was implemented on 25 May 2018, replacing the Data Protection Directive 95/46/EC. Considered the strictest law on data protection globally, the GDPR protects the privacy and personal data of EU citizens by giving them greater control over their personal data.[112] Thus, any organisation collecting data related to people in the EU would be subject to the principles of the GDPR. The GDPR applies to data 'processing'[113] by 'controllers'[114] and 'processors'[115] of personal data. The term personal data has been defined in the GDPR to include:

> any information relating to an identified or identifiable natural person ('data subject'); an identifiable natural person is one who can be identified, directly or indirectly, in particular by reference to an identifier such as a name, an identification number, location data, an online identifier or to one or more factors specific to the physical, physiological, genetic, mental, economic, cultural or social identity of that natural person.[116]

Pseudonymous data could also fall under the definition if it is relatively easy to identify. When processing personal data, the GDPR identifies seven key principles that controllers and processors must consider. These are lawfulness, fairness, and transparency; purpose limitation; data minimisation; accuracy; storage limitation; integrity and confidentiality (security); and accountability (Article 5). Article 6 provides instances in which it is legal to process personal data. Collecting, storing, and selling personal data are prohibited under Article 6, unless done within the situations set out in the Article. These include processing data with unambiguous consent; entering into a contract with the data subject, due to legal obligations; protecting the vital interests of the data subject or natural person, for the public interest; or having a legitimate interest in processing personal data. Failure to comply with the principles of GDPR could result in substantial fines. According to Article 83(5)(a), any infringements of the basic principles for processing personal data are subject to administrative fines of up to €20 million, or in the case of an undertaking, up to 4% of the total worldwide annual turnover of the preceding financial year, whichever is higher. The rights of the data subjects[117] (persons whose data is processed) are provided in Chapter III of the GDPR. These include the following rights: to be informed, of access, to rectification, to erasure, to restrict processing, to data portability, to object, and relating to automated decision-making and profiling.

As the European Commission states, the Data Governance Act creates processes and structures to promote data sharing by companies, individuals, and the public sector (focusing on the reuse of public sector data, and rules for data intermediaries or data altruism). The Data Act regulates access to and use of data, clarifying who can create value from data and under what conditions. While the GDPR relates to personal data only, the Data Act proposal covers both personal and non-personal data. Thus, the proposed Data Act complements the principles of the GDPR without prejudice.[118]

The European Strategy for Data (European data strategy) has made a significant impact on geospatial data usage in the EU. As noted by EuroGeographics (the peak body representing the national mapping, cadastre, and land registry authorities of Europe),[119] geospatial data underpins and is ubiquitous across all data spaces[120] set out in the strategy. According to the World Geospatial Industry Council, the 'power of location, technologies that collect, analyse, visualise, store, and distribute geolocation and other types of geospatial information are being used more often in government, industry, academia and by citizens'.[121] The increase in the quality and scope of data collected due to technology requires special attention to data protection and privacy laws because location information is increasingly important when identifying individuals and making decisions about their movements, activities and associations, and relationships.

The first issue to be considered in this context is whether geospatial data could be regarded as personal data, thereby making it subject to the requirements of the GDPR. Because geospatial data systems do not always relate back to or provide the possibility of identifying individuals, such information generally falls outside the definition of 'personal data' described under the GDPR. However, if the information attributed to the geospatial data allows individuals to be identified, then the GDPR principles would apply to the geospatial information systems. 'Location data' is specifically described in the GDPR as an indicator or example of a possible identifier through which an individual can be identified. Thus, there is a possibility that geospatial data and the geospatial products which surveyors create may fall within the ambit of the protection granted by the GDPR. This position is explained in the following example as illustrated in the report of the World Geospatial Industry Council:

> A geographical map of a country for instance would not qualify as personal data in and of itself. However, when the map is used in conjunction with GPS data to show the real-time movement of individuals, the geospatial information should be considered personal data.[122]

The types of geodata that may be relevant to the work carried out by surveyors include addresses, building information, cadastral data, land registry data, satellite images, images from oblique angles, and aerial images.[123] In these cases, the data subjects would include people who live at the address/building or real estate owners, people who are registered in the cadastre as owners, and people who are shown in the images or the owners of such buildings.[124] To determine whether any of the mentioned data could qualify as personal data, one must ascertain whether the data 'relates' to the mentioned data subjects. Therefore, when a surveyor uses geospatial data that require the processing of personal data, they will qualify as data controllers or data processors. Because personal data can be only processed for legitimate purposes, surveyors in this context will have to specify a clear goal for the processing and determine its legitimacy.[125]

Another aspect that surveyors must consider is the interaction between the EU's open data initiatives and the requirements of the GDPR. The open data initiatives of the EU advocate for maximum access to data held by public bodies. In the context of geospatial data made available by public bodies, these datasets may well include personal data connected to or linked with other datasets, thereby making it possible for them to be used as identifiers of natural persons. In this instance, while the primary responsibility in complying with the GDPR will be with national authorities, the surveyors who receive these datasets must exercise extreme diligence about how they are linked and utilised.

Furthermore, surveyors will have to rethink the processes and lifecycles around data collection and management.[126] With digitalisation initiatives underway across Europe as to spatial data, Esri's GIS platform technology is used by many of Europe's NMCAs.[127] In Lithuania, for instance, Esri's GIS platform technology has enabled integrated cadastral systems which surveyors can use to not only engage in electronic submissions but also to upload new cadastral (parcel) surveys in different formats to compare them with registered parcels to ensure that parcel boundaries are correct.[128] Lithuania has also allowed private surveyors to upload data.[129] In these circumstances, private surveyors may be considered data processors. They may be required to follow the GDPR's requirements when processing this kind of information if personal data is included in the process.

There is an important interaction among the European data strategy, the copyright initiatives relating to Article 17 of the Directive on Copyright in the Digital Single Market, and the principles of the GDPR. Article 17 provides that content hosting providers try their best to prevent the upload or reupload of copyright-protected works, which can only be achieved with upload filters. Upload filters work when the context is ascertained. This is achieved by obtaining the information surrounding the upload, including the personal data of the person uploading the content. The issue here is whether this activity is permitted under the GDPR. It is possible that platforms would be considered as controllers for the purposes of the GDPR. They would thus be subject to the rules provided in Article 6(1) for processing personal data.[130]

The EU principles regarding data security and privacy are primarily territorial in nature. However, given the possibility of application of these data initiatives or any entity engaging with EU citizens, or the application due to reciprocity in non-EU countries, there is an increasing need for non-EU surveyors to be knowledgeable about the EU's data protection initiatives, because these have the potential to become global norms,[131] as with the GDPR.[132]

4.8 Copyright of survey plans and data

This section will discuss the primary elements of EU copyright law concerning geospatial products. Given the previous detailed discussion of the copyright of data and databases, this section will focus on the protection of geospatial products under general copyright principles. For such purpose, references will be made to the Berne Convention and several EU legislations, including the Information Society Directive (InfoSoc Directive),[133] SD,[134] Term Directive,[135] and Digital Single Market Directive (DSMD).[136]

Copyright protection in the EU has been based primarily on the condition that the work be authored by someone fulfilling the originality requirement. In addition, Member States require such work to be fixed and fall into some identified category to satisfy the subject matter requirement. Some Member States also require additional requirements to be satisfied in relation to applied arts, whether by establishing an aesthetic effect or artistic value.[137] Primarily, these requirements are redefined by the CJEU decisions. The case *Infopaq International A/S v Danske Dagblades Forening*[138] and subsequent cases have provided much-needed clarity to the copyright elements. While some have identified this approach as 'harmonisation by stealth',[139] it has shed light on fundamental aspects of EU copyright law. Following the recent decisions of the CJEU, however, there is now:

> an EU-wide approach to all the foundational requirements of copyright protection. In other words: an EU approach to 'work', 'originality', 'fixation', 'categorisation' and, clearly and despite that, no referral has yet reached the CJEU specifically on this issue, 'authorship' (and joint authorship).[140]

The following section will discuss the legislation and case law concerning fundamental elements of copyright in the EU.

The Advocate General[141] summarised the basic principles of copyright as applicable in the EU in *Cofemel – Sociedade de Vestuário SA v G-Star Raw CV*[142] as follows:

> The concept of a work being 'its author's own intellectual creation' is the main component of the definition of a work. That definition was subsequently developed in the case-law of the Court, which explained that an intellectual creation is an author's own if it reflects the author's personality. That is the case if the author was able to express their creative abilities in the production of the work by making free and creative choices. However, where the expression of the components of the subject matter at issue is dictated by their technical function, the criterion of originality is not met, since the different methods of implementing an idea are so limited that the idea and the expression become indissociable. Such a situation does not permit the author to express their creativity in an original manner and achieve a result which is an intellectual creation of their own. Only the author's own intellectual creation, as defined above, has the status of work eligible for copyright protection.

> Elements such as the intellectual work and the skill of the author cannot, as such, justify the protection of the subject matter at issue by copyright, if such work and skill do not express any originality. Lastly, the subject matter protected by copyright must be identifiable with sufficient precision and objectivity.[143]

Based on this decision, there are two main aspects of copyright protection: 'First, that concept entails that there exists an original subject matter, in the sense of being the author's own intellectual creation. Second, classification as a work is reserved for the elements that are the expression of such creation.'[144] While the EU principles provide minimal opportunities for the iteration of copyright elements, as discussed under the Australian and U.S. case studies, the following sections will separate the components and analyse them in the context of spatial products and data.

4.9 Subject matter

The European principles of copyright are centred around the notion of an authorial work that justifies copyright's existence and the scope of its protections.[145] Article 1 of the Berne Convention[146] recognises that the signatories must protect authors' rights in their literary and artistic works. Neither the Convention nor EU legislation provide for a definition of the term 'work'. Some scholars have argued that 'work' should be identified as 'bounded expressive objects that have a certain unity and stability of expressive form'.[147] Identifiability has been recognised as another attribute of a work whereby 'the shape, substance and contours of the work are clear and consistent, and that the distinctiveness and particularity of the work are objectively known'.[148] Article 2 of the Berne Convention, however, clarifies that the expression 'literary and artistic works' includes 'every production in the literary, scientific and artistic domain, whatever may be the mode or form of its expression'. It contains a comprehensive but non-exhaustive list of examples of what may fall within this definition, including, among others, 'illustrations, maps, plans, sketches and three-dimensional works relative to geography, topography, architecture or science'.[149] Thus, works under this definition include any artefactual objects of expressive or informational significance.[150] Furthermore, as per Article 2(3), translations, adaptations, arrangements of music, and other alterations of a literary or artistic work are protected as original works. The collections of literary or artistic works are protected under Article 2(5), as long as the selection and arrangement of the collection's contents constitute intellectual creations.

These principles pose no challenge in identifying paper-based or digital spatial products, including survey plans, as they fall within the ambit of this definition. Therefore, they could be considered as 'literary and artistic works' for copyright, as long as such work can be proved to be the author's own intellectual creation.

It is crucial to identify the distinction made in the EU compared to the Australian and U.S. traditions regarding recognising the closed subject matter categorisation for copyright protection. The open-ended subject matter categorisation, as indicated in the Berne Convention and InfoSoc Directive, has been upheld in the case of *Infopaq International A/S v Danske Dagblades Forening*,[151] where it was found that 'copyright . . . is liable to apply only in relation to a subject-matter which is original in the sense that it is its author's own intellectual creation'.[152] Since *Cofemel – Sociedade de Vestuário SA v G-Star Raw CV*, an exhaustive list of protectable subject matter (such as provided in the national legislation of the United Kingdom [UK]) would be incompatible with EU copyright principles.[153] Unlike in Australia and the USA, copyright would thus not be subject to different requirements, depending on the category to which such an object belongs.[154]

In relation to computer programs, Article 1 of the SD recognises computer programs, including the preparatory design materials, as literary works. However, the Directive does not define what a computer program is. The preparatory documents give some guidance, explaining that a computer program 'encompass[es] the expression in any form, language, notation or code of a set of instructions, the purpose of which is to cause a computer or information processing device to execute a particular task or function'.[155] Therefore, while the source code, object code, and preparatory design materials are protected as computer programs, the user manuals, other user documents, interfaces, graphic user interfaces, algorithms, functionality, data files' format and programming languages, and video games would not be considered computer programs under the Directive.[156] Article 1(3) sets out that originality is the only criterion to determine the eligibility for protection as a computer program, and the standard is set as 'the author's own intellectual creation'. In assessing the originality of computer programs, it has been noted that even though there are many algorithms and sub-routines used to design a computer program, it would be sufficient to reflect the author's own intellectual creation if the programmer arranges all these elements with creativity, skill, and inventiveness.

These principles are essential concerning the distinction between digital maps, as an output of a computer program, and the computer program itself as a distinct subject matter. The SD provides specific protection to computer software designed to create spatial products. While the source code and object code could be protected under the SD, the computer program and graphic user interfaces could be protected under the InfoSoc Directive. The case *Bezpečnostní softwarová asociace – Svaz softwarové ochrany v Ministerstvo kultury*,[157] in determining an issue regarding graphic user interfaces, held that even though graphic user interfaces could not be considered to be computer programs, they could still be protected under the InfoSoc Directive 'as a work, [to] be protected by copyright if it is its author's own intellectual creation'.[158] This identification has led some scholars to argue that the 'CJEU appeared to identify "work" with "original", rather than with the prior requirement that a work is "a production in the literary, scientific and artistic domain" according to Article 2(1) Berne Convention'.[159] In relation to video games, the case of *Nintendo Co Ltd and Others v PC Box Srl and 9Net Srl*[160] held that video games are not to be just considered to be computer programs but rather as complex multimedia works expressing conceptually autonomous narrative and graphic creations.[161] Thus, the distributive approach (protecting different elements of the video game separately) adopted by some Member States when protecting video games should be changed to reflect the protection of the whole creation under copyright principles.[162] This has led commentators to wonder, should 'one separate the complex work in question into its single components, or instead adopt a holistic approach?'[163] Thus, it would be possible to protect a spatial product – that is, the screen display of a computer program under the InfoSoc Directive – but also to protect spatial products as a whole rather than breaking them down into individual components for copyright protection.

4.10 Material form

The Berne Convention and the SD both recognise that ideas and information are not considered works projected under copyright principles.[164] In situations when a work's ideational or informational and expressive properties are indistinguishable because there is only one or a small number of ways in which such an idea or information could be expressed, the CJEU has denied copyright protection based on a lack of originality rather than the absence of work in such instances.[165] The European principles rely on objective perceptibility, thereby denying copyright protection for the taste of food[166] or the aesthetic effect of clothing.[167]

Under European law, there is no requirement for form; thus, copyright protection is not conditional upon having unified and stable expressive properties.[168] The Berne Convention in Article 2(2) recognises the rights of individual countries to introduce requirements on a material's form. The fixation in the EU serves an evidentiary function as opposed to being a material condition for granting copyright protection.[169] The case of *Levola Hengelo BV v Smilde Foods BV Deutschland* identified that, for there to be a 'work' as referred to in Directive 2001/29, the subject matter protected by copyright must be expressed in a manner that makes it identifiable with sufficient precision and objectivity, even though that expression is not necessarily in permanent form.[170]

Setting requirements for fixation appears to have been taken away from the Member States' realm and made an EU-mandated requirement. Since the decision of *Cofemel – Sociedade de Vestuário SA v G-Star Raw CV*, which accepted and applied this principle, there is little possibility for Member States to exercise their discretion in the EU.[171] For spatial products to satisfy the material form requirement under EU law, therefore, all that is necessary is that the product can be identifiable with sufficient precision and objectivity. Furthermore, there is no requirement that the expression should be in a permanent form.[172] Therefore, copyright protection would be available regardless of whether the spatial products are static or dynamic in nature. Survey plans, boundary demarcations, building designs, and historical datasets and blueprints all could be protected as spatial products with static nature. Given the judicial recognition of non-permanent expressions, even dynamic spatial products like constantly updating maps could be considered as satisfying the expression requirement under copyright law.

4.11 Originality

The EU's approach to originality in the legislation has been to define it in relation to specific works.[173] As previously discussed, the CJEU case law has harmonised these different reiterations of originality and has expressed a single explanation of the originality requirement as constituting 'an author's own intellectual creation'.[174] This term has been further elaborated in the case law to include the 'expression of creativity in an original manner',[175] use of 'creative freedom',[176] making 'free and creative choices',[177] and 'stamping the work with a personal touch'.[178] To satisfy the creativity element, it is not sufficient for a work to require labour and skill.[179] It will also not be satisfied when the creation of a work is dictated by 'technical considerations, rules or constraints which leave no room for creative freedom'.[180]

EU Member States have made numerous reiterations of the originality requirement based on the legal system's common law and civil law origins.[181] The early cases that applied these principles concerning maps resulted in different outcomes for different cases. The Austrian Supreme Court in 1992 noted that a bare representation of geographic facts using common symbols would not satisfy the originality requirement.[182] In French courts, the colour combinations and fonts of the names of the maps in a travel guide were considered the result of the author's personality and merited copyright protection.[183] In a later case, the making of walking trails was considered an intellectual creation, the French Supreme Court holding that originality is derived from the 'mise en oeuvre of geographic, cultural and human criteria that reflect the author's personality'.[184] The Belgian Court of Appeals of Antwerp made an important determination on the originality requirement of maps concerning street plans, holding that the accuracy with which a city is depicted would not prevent a finding of originality because the presentation, elaboration, or layout could indicate the required level of originality in a street plan.[185] Courts in both the Netherlands and Germany have agreed that the generalisation involved in the map-making process would reflect originality, because 'generalisation demands great accuracy and an excellent "feel" for geography on the part of the cartographer'.[186]

The *Infopaq International A/S v Danske Dagblades Forening*[187] case has provided valuable guidance on the originality requirement as applicable in the modern context. This case was a matter between Infopaq International A/S ('Infopaq') and Danske Dagblades Forening ('DDF') regarding the acts of reproduction of newspaper articles using an automated process consisting of the scanning, conversion into digital files, and electronic processing of those files. The issue was raised under the InfoSoc Directive, regarding the infringement of the right of reproduction for authorial works under Article 2(a), not the notion of originality. In deciding this issue, the Court decided that the 11-word excerpts produced by using the original articles could be protected as part of the original article. The implication of this decision was that even short excerpts could be protected as an author's intellectual creation. The 'choice, sequence and combination of . . . words' were considered as an expression of the author's creativity.[188] Thus, only individual words would not be capable of satisfying the originality requirement, given that the creation of such words 'lack the act of combination constitutive of a literary author's intellectual creation'.[189] This broader conception of originality would ensure copyright protection for any selection and arrangement of literary or artistic expressive elements.[190] This position has been accepted in the case of *SAS Institute Inc. v World Programming Ltd*,[191] in which the Court held that 'the keywords, syntax, commands and combinations of commands, options, defaults and iterations consist of words, figures or mathematical concepts which, considered in isolation, are not, as such, an intellectual creation of the author of the computer program'.[192] The Court thus considered the user manual, which 'through the choice, sequence and combination of those words, figures or mathematical concepts that the author may express his creativity in an original manner and achieve a result,'[193] to be the intellectual creation of the author.

Works whose expressive form is determined exclusively by their nature, purpose, or other factors external to the author are considered incapable of satisfying the originality threshold under EU law.[194] Falling within this category are 'databases and graphic user interfaces whose expressive properties are dictated by technical constraints'.[195] The case of *Football Dataco Ltd v Yahoo! UK Ltd*[196] confirmed this view, holding that technical considerations, rules, and constraints would make it impossible to claim the creative freedom required to establish the originality requirement in copyright.

Following the previous decisions of the Court, the case of *Cofemel – Sociedade de Vestuário SA v G-Star Raw CV*[197] emphasised the need for uniformity in the EU. The case involved two clothing companies: G-Star and Cofemel. G-Star alleged that the designs of T-shirts and jeans were works under copyright law and, therefore, Cofemel copying those designs was a violation of its copyright. Cofemel argued that clothing items are not works and, therefore, could not be protected by copyright law. The Court affirmed the previous decisions, concluding that, to be considered a work, all that is required are 'that [the] concept entails an original subject matter, in the sense of being the author's own intellectual creation . . . [and] classification as a work is reserved to the elements that are the expression of such creation'.[198] The Court decision expressly recognised that, if a national law were to require some sort of 'aesthetic' value for a design to be eligible for copyright protection, this would contradict the requirement of objectivity as mandated under EU law.[199]

An important comment about the European principles on originality is that these principles lead to even trivial works being recognised as original, thereby granting copyright protection to the same. As one commentator states, 'a sequence of human movements enacted on a stage, and a pile of bricks exhibited in an art gallery, will plainly be original works; while the same sequence enacted on a football field, and pile of bricks on a construction site, will equally plainly not'.[200] The former's non-formalistic properties is considered as rendering copyright protection, including 'the intention or expectation of the persons who produced them, and the view of society regarding their nature'.[201]

In the context of spatial products, such an identification would be beneficial, given that it would provide a higher level of protection. Whether it is paper-based or digital maps, as long as the creators can demonstrate that there have been free and personal choices regarding the production of the products that reflect the author's personality, then such works would be considered protected under copyright law. While the technical functions, rules, and restraints involved in the spatial product creation process may adversely affect any finding of originality in spatial products, it must be noted that the courts have been willing to consider the choice, sequence, and combination of elements that – in isolation – may not satisfy the originality requirement.

4.12 Authorship

One aspect that is not defined in the EU legislation is authorship. The Berne Convention is also silent regarding authorship. The issue of authorship is thus dealt with at the national level. However, some directives provide guidance on authorship in relation to specific works. The Software and Database directives, for example, define who may be regarded as an author of a software or database. Article 2(1) of the SD provides that the author of a computer program shall be the natural person or group of natural persons who have created the program or, where the legislation of the Member State permits, the legal person designated as the rights holder by that legislation. Article 4(1) of the Database Directive contains similar provisions. While the InfoSoc Directive does not have a similar reference, the case law decided under the Directive indicates that the authorship is meant to be a human act.[202]

In the EU, authorship is linked directly with the concept of originality. References to terms such as 'author's own intellectual creation', 'personal touch', and 'free and creative choices' in cases like *Cofemel – Sociedade de Vestuário SA v G-Star Raw* and *Funke Medien NRW GmbH v Bundesrepublik Deutschland*[203] indicate that they are intended for human authors rather than machines.[204] In *Eva-Maria Painer v Standard Verlags GmbH and Others*, while referring to Article 6 of the Term Directive, Advocate General Trstenjak upheld that 'only human creations are therefore protected, which can also include those for which the person employs a technical aid, such as a camera'.[205] Therefore, human agency has been identified as a requirement under copyright authorship in the EU. EU law regarding co-authorship is not yet harmonised. Each Member State has the discretion to determine the principles applicable to co-authorship.[206]

The ability of machines to produce works with expressive properties has challenged the requirement for a human act for copyright protection.[207] In view of recent developments in artificial intelligence (AI) systems, it has been recommended that authorship as a human creative practice needs to be expanded to include AI and other transformative technologies.[208] The corroborative process in using AI and other transformative technologies, as well as how the inclusion of AI and other transformative technologies may affect the concept of authorship, are important aspects that should be discussed in the EU context.

Consequently, the authorship of survey products and data is vested with the human creator of such works. When maps are created in digital form, however, the attribution of authorship will not be straightforward. Digital maps can be either AI-generated or AI-assisted products. If a digital map is an AI-assisted output, then authorship will be determined based on who has exercised 'creative freedom' concerning such products. To determine the authorship of AI-generated works, one must consider whether the work is 'caused by free and creative choices made by humans, or whether the operation of an AI system in one way or another breaks the causal link between those choices and the output'.[209] Because the technology related to AI is developing at a rapid rate, it would be prudent to identify relevant factors considering the authorship aspect in copyright, rather than attempting to find general answers that are applicable in all situations. Using the principles of tort law about causation, Rognstad provides one formulation of such requirements as whether the 'free and creative choices of humans have *caused* the work to the extent that those choices 'are reflected' in the expression of the work'.[210] The decision of *Eva-Maria Painer v Standard Verlags GmbH and Others* recognised three phases of the creative process: preparation, execution, and finalisation.[211] The preparation and finalisation parts have been considered as difficult to be performed by an AI, while AI can easily carry out the execution.[212]

In the context of machine learning (ML), several stages are involved, including 'problem definition, data collection, data cleaning, summary statistics review, model (algorithm) selection, model training, and feature selection'.[213] Creating digital maps may very well mean that the person who designed the algorithm may not be the person who collected and used data to train it. To determine the authorship in maps, the various creative choices involved in the ML process, as well as the extent to which such choices are reflected in the final output, should be considered. In this regard, an important challenge is the features of ML that make it impossible to predict the system's outcomes. The lack of foreseeability, indeterminacy, and randomness involved in the ML process may affect the causal link between the creative choices made by humans and how they are reflected in the final product. Using the example of the 'painting dripping technique' adopted by artist Jackson Pollock, Rognstad argues that in the same way that Pollock could not control every detail of his work when he flung paint at the canvas, it would be possible for copyright protection to arise for AI-generated work as long as the author has a general conception of the work before it is expressed.[214] Therefore, while there is no doubt about human authorship in digital maps, what remains to be determined is what is protected in the work.[215]

In the context of AI-assisted maps, as long as it is possible to prove a causal link between the creative choices made by human actors and the reflection of such choices in the final product (i.e., the digital map), the human authors would be able to claim the authorship for such creations. When the 'black box' features of ML are involved in the process, however, it would not be possible to determine why the AI made certain decisions, thereby creating doubt about the output and process. It may result in works whereby the creative choices made by human actors may not be reflected entirely in the digital map. There could be limitations on the scope of the protection where only those parts of the digital map that could be attributed to free and creative choices would result in authorship of the surveyor involved. What follows from such a formulation of authorship is a situation in which there will be no copyright protection if no free and creative choices of surveyors are reflected in the expression. Thus, surveyors will have to expect situations in which digital maps may contain both protected and unprotected elements. Joint/co-authorship as a concept has been recognised in EU Member States whereby a collaboration between two or more authors may provide rights as joint authors. With joint authorship, it would be possible for two or more surveyors to generate a digital map, as long as they collaborate to create an expression that jointly represents their free and creative choices.

When an issue of this nature presents to the CJEU, the inclination is to uphold the *droit d'auteur* tradition (author's rights) of the EU *aquis*.[216] However, the question remains whether AI can be treated as another tool, given the mediation and attenuation that AI plays between the author and work. The suggested possibilities for authorship for AI-generated work include introducing special neighbouring rights to protect authorless AI-generated work against misappropriation.[217] The EU's policy decisions indicate that AI is indeed a priority in its technological initiatives,[218] and the Commission made a proposal in 2021 for an Artificial Intelligence Act (AI Act).[219]

4.13 Ownership

Authorship is generally considered as the basis for ownership in the EU. The author of a work is regarded as the owner unless proven otherwise. As previously discussed concerning originality, the first inquiry is whether 'the work is of a type that affords scope for the exercise of free and creative choices (formative freedom) in its production'.[220] Second, the consideration must be 'whether the person claiming authorship of the work has exploited that scope sufficiently to produce a work that is their own intellectual creation in the sense of reflecting their personality'.[221] Thus, the owner of a work is the person who has exploited their free and creative choices sufficiently to produce the work. The EU legislation makes some reference to the 'work made for hire' doctrine. Article 2(3) of the SD recognises the rights of an employer to exercise all economic rights concerning a computer program created by an employee in the execution of their duties or following the employer's instructions.

Surveyors who produce spatial products and data can be considered as the owners of the same under EU copyright law. In the EU, how the cadastre is managed will determine the ownership of the spatial products and data. In relation to EU Member States where there are no licensed cadastral surveyors, such as in, Spain, and Sweden, cadastral work is carried out by the employees in service of an NMCA (e.g., Sweden)), or is contracted individually by public authorities (e.g., Spain).[222] In these contexts, the copyright ownership will not be vested in the individual surveyors who do the work.

An important aspect to consider in the context of AI-generated works is the ownership of spatial products. The traditional notions of ownership in copyright have been used to identify five entities that may claim ownership for AI-generated works: the AI system itself, the AI programmer, the AI user, the AI owner, and the public domain.[223] Because of the lack of personhood in AI systems, recognising the AI system as the owner is not a viable option in the current context. While the idea of AI-generated work being opened to the public has earned some support, the main issue would be the resulting lack of incentive to invest financially and intellectually in the development of AI systems. The owner of the AI (i.e., the company or person who invests in the creation of AI) has the ownership of the AI-generated work and reflects the work-for-hire concept in copyright, whereas the employers are granted the economic rights in work produced by employees within the course of their employment.[224] One development in the UK regarding computer-generated work has been the recognition of ownership in the 'person by whom the arrangements necessary for the creation of the work are undertaken'.[225] This provision has been used to recognise the work generated by a computer without a human author.[226] The copyright duration is shorter for computer-generated works (50 years) and no moral rights[227] are attributed.[228] With the clarification provided by recent decisions of the CJEU, originality is only vested in works created as a result of free and creative choices. In this context, it would be impossible to have copyright on works without human authors.[229] Out of the five options, the preferred method in the EU appears to be the ownership of the programmer and user. However, the difficulty of establishing the causal link between the output and input of the programmers and users to the AI-generated work is the main argument against granting sole recognition to programmers and users as to the right of ownership for AI-generated works. Due to the difficulties in recognising one entity as the owner of an AI-generated work, hybrid options have been suggested. One such option is the idea of an AI legal entity, embodying the AI system, its programmer, the user and the company under the umbrella of a legal entity such as an artificial personality.[230]

4.14 Copyright protection and AI-generated survey products in the EU

When discussing the copyright of AI-generated works, the EU's policy on AI and emerging technologies should be considered. As noted in the policy initiative *Shaping Europe's Digital Future*: 'the EU's approach to artificial intelligence centres on excellence and trust, aiming to boost research and industrial capacity while ensuring safety and fundamental rights.'[231] The European AI strategy includes several policy initiatives in which the Commission has presented the European approach to AI, a coordinated plan on AI, and the proposed AI Act.[232] The interrelationship between copyright and AI was discussed in detail in the 2018 study 'Trends and Developments in Artificial Intelligence: Challenges to the Intellectual Property Rights Framework'.[233] In view of these developments, the EU Parliament passed a resolution in 2020 highlighting the importance of IP rights for developing AI technologies.[234] A recent initiative on copyright and AI was the publication of the report *Study on Copyright and New Technologies: Copyright Data Management and Artificial Intelligence*.[235] The copyright principles discussed so far raise several issues concerning AI applications in the context of survey products. These could be divided into input and output issues.[236] Input issues include using copyright-protected content for AI training and generation purposes, and the human actors' contribution to the input process. In terms of output issues, one major issue is the copyrightability of AI-assisted content (creations produced autonomously by AI with varying degrees of human intervention, whereby the AI is used as a tool by human authors). The concept, subject matter, originality, expression, authorship and ownership of the work warrants particular discussion in relation to AI-assisted and AI-generated works (creations produced autonomously by AI with little or no human intervention).

Concerning the copyrightability of AI-assisted and AI-generated works, the first issue is whether such work would fall within the term 'literary and artistic works'. As discussed, the main aspects are those of expression and originality. With expression, the distinction between ideas and expression is important in the context of using copyright-protected works as input for an AI system. Digital transcription occurs when the content (metadata) is used to facilitate supervised ML. The transcription process would make it impossible for human senses to perceive such content. However, suppose the content used as input is protected by copyright. In that case, obtaining the permission of the content creators before using it for the ML process is necessary.[237] If surveyors plan to use any spatial data in the ML process, therefore, they should inquire about the copyright attached to such input data. This may include copyright, related rights, and *sui generis* rights for databases and datasets.

AI-generated work without human intervention will not be protected by copyright principles in the current context.[238] For instance, weather and news reports generated fully by automation have been held to be outside of copyright protection.[239] In such circumstances, it should be considered how such works may be protected by using other legal measures, whether by contract or related rights. The related and *sui generis* rights would be relevant for both the developers and users of AI systems and the producers of AI outputs. As long as AI-generated works only imitate the 'style' of a given work 'without necessarily including any discernible protected elements',[240] then it would not be possible for the surveyors to rely on copyright to prohibit the making and commercialising of AI-generated works.

AI-assisted work can demonstrate sufficient originality as long as the human authors exercise free and creative input and output choices. One example from the creative and cultural industry is the album *Hello World!*, in which the human authors not only selected the work to be part of the dataset used to train the model, but also made changes to the final output by choosing, modifying the final output, and adding further elements into the music proposed by the AI. This situation is easily considered as similar to a situation in which a photographer uses a camera to take a photo. In the context of survey products, considerations have to be made about the selection of the datasets used as input and the level of modification and changes made as to the final output. If the surveyors' contribution to the final output is merely curating various AI-generated products, however, such action may not meet the required originality threshold.

Article 5 of the Enforcement Directive[241] provides owners of copyright or related rights with the benefit of the presumption of authorship or ownership to enforce their rights. The producers and users of AI may use such a presumption to claim authorship in an AI-generated work. This would be more prominent when it would be impossible to distinguish whether a work has been created with human assistance due to a lack of information regarding the creation process. The issue of false authorship could result in limiting works that should be made available in the public domain. Because it is nearly impossible to provide that the human author is not, in fact, the author of the work, this will result in granting protection to works that do not qualify within the copyright regime. Given these legal uncertainties, the European Parliament has made important observations about the future of AI in Europe,[242] recommending that the following factors should be considered when determining the AI implication for IP rights, including copyright: the degree of human intervention, the autonomy of the AI, the importance of the role and the origin of the data and copyright-protected material used, and the possible involvement of other relevant factors.[243] In Europe, there has been little support for developing a *sui generis* right for AI-generated works.[244]

4.15 Neighbouring rights/related rights in photographs and satellite and UAV imagery

Photographs are considered as literary and artistic works under Article 2(1) of the Berne Convention. Therefore, the same requirements for originality apply to photographs. Photographs must be original in the sense that they are the author's own intellectual creations. In *Eva-Maria Painer v Standard VerlagsGmbH and Others*, for instance, the CJEU provided the following observations. As regards a portrait photograph, the photographer can make free and creative choices in several ways and at various points in its production. In the preparation phase, the photographer can choose the background, the subject's pose, and the lighting. When taking a portrait photograph, he can choose the framing, the angle of view, and the atmosphere created. Finally, when selecting the snapshot, the photographer may choose from a variety of developing techniques the one he wishes to adopt or, where appropriate, use computer software.[245]

Therefore, if it can be demonstrated that the satellite and UAV imagery are products of the independent choices made by surveyors, it is possible to grant copyright protection to satellite and UAV imagery. The issue is that the opportunities for surveyors to exercise such choices are limited, however, given the automated nature of the process. This position was illustrated by the French Court of Appeal, which held that geographical maps directly based on unprotected satellite photographs could qualify for copyright protection. The decision identified that copyright protection for the final product must be granted because it was a 'result of personalised implementation of a complex technology by a process of transformation and improvement of choices, in particular colours, contrasts and luminosity'.[246]

Member States have recognised this difficulty with photographs, where it is not always possible to exercise the level of originality even when there has been significant effort and investment in the process.[247] For example, Germany and Spain protect non-original photographs under related rights. These rights 'reward economic or entrepreneurial expenditure rather than human creativity'.[248] In Germany, photographs that do not satisfy the originality requirement are still protected subject to a reduced period of protection (50 years instead of 70 years of protection for copyright). Similar provisions are found in Italy, where 'images of persons, or aspects, elements or events of natural or social life, obtained by photographic or analogous processes, including reproductions of works of figurative art and stills of cinematographic film' are considered for protection for 20 years. Spain provides similar protection for 25 years.[249] These legal provisions are important in the context of less creative satellite imagery and in AI-generated works, whereas similar rights may protect weaker human creativity.[250]

4.16 Copyright infringements and exceptions and limitations to copyright

The EU principles of copyright do not reference the idea of Crown copyright. While some Member States with legal systems based on common law have adopted this concept within their jurisdictions, the European approach favours free and complete access to public sector information. The open data initiatives discussed in detail in Section 4.20 highlight the importance placed on free access to public sector information and how Member States are expected to further EU principles regarding transparency, accessibility, and reuse of information. There is a preference towards limiting the rights of government copyright ownership in EU Member States for official works, including legislations, judicial decisions, and administrative texts.[251]

4.17 Fair use defences in the EU

The fair use defence, as understood in the Australian and U.S. contexts, does not exist in the EU copyright regime.[252] The civil law basis of the EU has contributed mainly to the lack of recognition of open-ended limitations to copyright.[253] Thus, the European approach to defences has been to introduce an exhaustive list of specific exceptions and limitations.[254] Some scholars argue, however, that the increased use of fundamental rights in copyright disputes has the effect of the 'fair use' limitation being wielded in EU copyright law, especially the weighting of interests and use of the proportionality test in relation to fundamental rights.[255] The EU principles regarding exceptions and copyright limitations are mainly found in Article 5 of the InfoSoc Directive. The general principles of exceptions and limitations are provided under mandatory and optional categories. Therefore, the harmonisation in this regard is not complete. Article 5(1) provides for the mandatory limitation for transient or incidental copies. This exempts any:

> transmissions between networks, servers or routers of internet service providers where multiple copies are made in order to facilitate the transmission process, and which are not stored or are stored for a limited amount of time and only in the process of such transmission, are exempted altogether. The same applies to copies that are made in the process of conducting a lawful action, such as, for example, the making of copies in the RAM memory of a computer.[256]

Article 5(2) contains five optional exceptions and limitations regarding reproduction right.[257] Article 5(3) provides for 15 optional exceptions and limitations regarding both the right to reproduce and the right to communicate or make available to the public.[258] The DD[259] and SD[260] also provide exceptions for the specific rights introduced, respectively. An important aspect of the exceptions and limitations in the EU copyright law was introduced by Articles 3–6 of the DSMD.[261] These provide for limitations on text and data mining (TDM), digital and cross-border teaching activities, and the preservation of cultural heritage, thereby amending the InfoSoc and Database directives.

TDM exceptions are directed towards addressing issues encountered in the digital environment and ensuring that the European copyright framework can address new technological developments. The data-driven economy requires that Big Data should be analysed to obtain insights and knowledge. TDM provides this capability by processing, extracting, and analysing an infinite number of digital data. From a copyright perspective, however, this may be an issue because this interferes with the copyright owners' rights as to copyright. For example, the datasets used to train AI systems may contain datasets/data protected under copyright, related rights, or *sui generis* rights. The TDM activities may involve the reproduction of copyright-protected content, the extraction of a substantial part of the database, or the reproduction and adaptation of a computer program.[262] Dealing with these exercises on a case-by-case basis, when the consent of the rights holders is required, will negatively affect the use of various mechanisms to analyse and create new knowledge. The TDM exception under the DSMD aims to address this issue by relieving the developers and users of AI systems in prescribed situations.[263]

Article 2 of the DSMD defines TDM as 'any automated analytical technique aimed at analysing text and data in digital form in order to generate information which includes but is not limited to patterns, trends and correlations'. While the main focus of TDM is the right of reproduction, it also includes rights of translation, adaptation, arrangement, and any other alterations. TDM activities may be carried out against a work, performance, fixation, or database protected under copyright.

Article 3 of the DSMD contains a mandatory TDM exception for scientific research carried out by research organisations and cultural heritage institutions. Therefore, the TDM exception can be exercised against the right of reproduction in whole or part of works. The TDM exception specifically applies to cultural or public institutions that provide services in the interest of society on a not-for-profit basis.[264] Public–private partnerships may result in private actors also being protected by this exception. The purpose for which the TDM exception can be used is limited to scientific research, including both natural and human sciences. To use the TDM exception, institutions must have legal access to the resources to be mined. To ensure that the rights holders of copyright are not unfairly disadvantaged, the Directive prescribes some requirements as to storage and security measures.

Article 4 of the DSMD contains a more general TDM exception applicable to anyone with lawful access to the resources being mined. The protection under Article 4 applies to anyone and is not subject to any limitations regarding profit motives or purpose. However, Article 4 applies on condition that the rights holders have not expressly reserved the use of works and other subject matter in an appropriate manner, such as machine readable means in the case of content made publicly available online. Therefore, a rights holder can use licensing or other contractual means to determine the nature by which the TDM exception may be exercised, or opt out of the Article 4 TDM exception altogether.

The TDM exception in the EU copyright regime provides a good example of protecting copyright holders' rights while promoting innovation and technological developments. Surveyors who are the copyright holders of datasets will have the opportunity to determine access to their datasets, and the level of TDM permitted. When surveyors need to carry out TDM activities, they will need to ensure that the required permission is obtained from the copyright and related rights holders of the datasets, and that proper care is taken as to the storage, making copies, and security of the data obtained.

4.18 Unfair competition as an alternative protection method for spatial products and data

The EU law concerning unfair competition is yet to be harmonised,[265] and Member States have adopted different unfair competition regimes based on their civil/common law traditions. Unfair competition has been used as a substitute in Europe when IP rights are absent or no longer applicable.[266] Unfair competition principles will be much more relevant in dealing with imitations in general or imitations of functional or aesthetic features not covered under copyright. While a detailed discussion of the applicable principles in the Member States is neither possible nor intended in this section, some basic principles are discussed related to the use of unfair competition principles as an alternative to copyright protection. The concept of protection against 'parasitic competition' and 'slavish imitation' or misappropriation often forms the basis of unfair competition law protection in EU Member States.[267] Some scholars have identified the enactment of the DD and introduction of a *sui generis* right for data as a legislative initiative driven by the principle of misappropriation.[268] Furthermore, the 2005 Unfair Commercial Practices Directive[269] and the Misleading and Comparative Advertising Directive[270] have led to a more approximated view of fairness in the EU.[271]

An important application of unfair competition principles in the absence of copyright can be found in the *Voodoo v Rollic Games* case.[272] The issue in this case involved a copyright infringement claim by Voodoo, a French video game developer, concerning a video game called *Woodturning 3D*, a hyper-casual game based on a single-game concept with very few game mechanics. Initially, *Woodturning 3D* was a global success, with 35.2 million installations within three months.[273] Voodoo claimed that a similar hyper-casual video game created by Rollic Games and Hero Games infringed its copyright in both the software conception and graphic representation. The Tribunal Judiciaire de Paris dismissed Voodoo's copyright infringement claims because the games did not reflect the author's personality in creating the gameplay and visual creation.[274] The Tribunal referred to the French law on unfair competition, however, and held that while a product that is not subject to any property rights could be freely reproduced, such reproduction should be done without giving rise to the likelihood of confusion about the origins of the product in the consumers' minds. When determining the likelihood for confusion, the Tribunal referred to several factors, including 'how slavish, systematic or reiterated the reproduction or imitation is, as well as of the duration of the use, originality and notoriety of the copied product . . . [and] parasitic behaviour'.[275] The Tribunal found that Rollic Games and Hero Games had violated unfair competition principles because their video game was a quasi-slavish copy of *Woodturning 3D*, confusing the mind of an average person regarding its origin.

This decision has addressed the issue of game cloning by using unfair competition principles. It provides a valuable avenue for the protection of spatial products that may be unable to be protected by copyright principles. In this case, a distinction has been made between copying a single game mechanic and copying the whole game. Thus, while spatial products could be protected from unlawful copying as a whole, the individual elements may not enjoy such protection. One way in which cloners may avoid applying unfair competition principles is by ensuring that consumers have limited possibility for confusion about the origin of the products by altering original elements and substituting elements with completely different ones.[276] In relation to spatial products replicating reality, it would not be possible to raise such an argument. To prove the likelihood of confusion, however, the imitated product would have to have been known to the consumers for some time. This may pose a challenge to the developers of spatial products that are new to the market, or to small-scale developers who are not widely known in the market.

4.19 Trade secrets as an alternative protection method for spatial products and data

The Trade Secrets Directive[277] (TSD) harmonises the protection of trade secrets across the EU. The Preamble to the TSD highlights businesses' investments in acquiring, developing and applying know-how and information, which forms the core of the knowledge economy. The TSD provides rules on the protection against the unlawful acquisition, use and disclosure of trade secrets. The term 'trade secret' is defined in Article 2 as information which meets all of the following requirements.

(a) It is secret in the sense that it is not, as a body or in the precise configuration and assembly of its components, generally known among or readily accessible to persons within the circles that normally deal with the kind of information in question.
(b) It has commercial value because it is secret.
(c) It has been subject to reasonable steps under the circumstances, by the person lawfully in control of the information, to keep it secret.

The TSD highlights the importance of secrecy. Article 3 of the Directive provides that the acquisition of trade secrets will be lawful if it is obtained by independent discovery or creation, reverse engineering, and/or the exercise of the right of workers or workers' representatives to information and consultation. Article 4 describes the unlawful acquisition, use, and disclosure of trade secrets as:

> unauthorised access to, appropriation of, or copying of any documents, objects, materials, substances or electronic files, lawfully under the control of the trade secret holder, containing the trade secret or from which the trade secret can be deduced and any other conduct which, under the circumstances, is considered contrary to honest commercial practices.

Furthermore, limitations on the use or disclosure of the trade secrets include that whenever such secrets are used or disclosed without the consent of the owner, such trade secrets have been acquired unlawfully, in breach of a confidentiality agreement or contractual obligations (Article 4[3]). Article 4(4) of the TSD bans the use of secret information that another person has unlawfully acquired. Article 4(5) extends the protection against the unlawful use of trade secrets to the production, offering, or placement of infringing goods on the market or the importation, export, or storage of infringing goods for those purposes. Exceptions to the right granted under Article 4 are provided in Article 5, which permits the acquisition, use, or disclosure of the trade secret concerning exercising the right to freedom of expression and information as set out in the EU Charter or for whistleblowing purposes.

With the limited protection granted by copyright for ideas, facts, and information, the TSD provides a valuable alternative to protect spatial data and products as long as secrecy, commercial value, and reasonable steps for protection are satisfied. To be protected under TSD, spatial products and data are not required to be kept in absolute secrecy. As long as there is relative secrecy, this would be sufficient to satisfy the first requirement. Thus, surveyors must be mindful that including data gathered through connected devices or drawn from public sources would unlikely be considered as falling within the definition of the 'secrecy' element.[278] Because the commercial value is assessed based on numerous considerations – including technical, business, financial, or the ability to compete – to obtain protection under the TSD, surveyors are expected to demonstrate that the unlawful acquisition, use, and disclosure has provided an undue advantage to the other party. The raw (or unprocessed) spatial data gathered predominantly by machines will be less likely to be protected under the TSD because it would be difficult to establish the commercial value of such data. However, when such data is subject to analytical processing, and becomes inferred or derived data, it is possible to claim commercial value if there is a market for such data and such data is subject to secrecy, thereby making it valuable.[279] To satisfy the third element, surveyors may consider what reasonable steps can be taken to protect and maintain secrecy. While the nature of the steps would depend on several considerations (including particular circumstances, cost, nature of the information, etc.), surveyors can adopt simple measures – such as non-disclosure agreements, non-disclosure obligations as terms of licence agreements, physical security measures, labelling practices, restrictions to employee and ex-employee access to information, or to a digital material's use of technological protection measures – to control access to spatial data and products.[280]

4.20 Open data initiatives in the EU

In the EU, open data initiatives focus on generating value for the economy and society by reusing the information primarily generated and produced by the public sector. The EU public sector is considered to be highly data-intensive and expected to create a direct economic value of €194 billion in 2030.[281] The public sector information includes – but is not limited to – geographical information, statistics, weather data, data from publicly funded research projects and digitised books from libraries.[282] The first EU-level initiative was implemented by the Public Sector Information Directive in 2003,[283] replaced in 2019 by the Directive on the Reuse of Public Sector Information (Open Data Directive).[284] The public sector information covered in the Open Data Directive is quite broad, and includes spatial and cadastral data in any format, including print, digital, or electronic media.[285] The executive, legislative, judicial, and administrative agencies at federal, national, and local government levels are subject to the information-sharing obligations of the Open Data Directive. This includes sectorial institutions such as registrars and cadastres.[286]

The Open Data Directive introduced the concept of high-value datasets which have important benefits to society when reused. The Open Data Directive requires high-value datasets to be subject to a separate set of rules that facilitate the reuse purpose by making those available for free in machine-readable formats and for bulk download. Geospatial data are the first thematic scope of high-value datasets identified in the annex to the Directive.[287] The Open Data Directive is focused on the reuse of data for both commercial and non-commercial purposes, fostering innovation, creativity, and maximum benefit to the economy and society. Copyright protection in the EU applies to original works, whether public sector information or not. Thus, most information created by public sector bodies would be subject to copyright protection. However, raw geographical data will not be subject to such protection. Most Member States have national legislation that exempts public sector information from copyright protection, making it available for easy sharing. The information created by employees or third parties on behalf of public sector bodies is subject to reuse obligations. Given the absence of direction regarding ownership rights in the Berne Convention or EU legislation, employment contracts, governmental contracts, and licence arrangements provide the main avenues for exercising rights related to public sector information. As per Article 1 of the Open Data Initiative, the obligations for reuse are not applicable to the public sector information protected by copyright owned by third parties. In such situations, if public sector bodies wish to acquire such rights, the sharing and reuse can be made subject to any contractual arrangement between the parties. In relation to employees and third-party contractors, while the economic rights may be transferred to public sector bodies, the moral rights in a work may remain with the parties that created or produced the work. Even if the public sector information is not protected by copyright, it may be subject to other related rights, including database and *sui generis* rights. One important development in this regard is the Data Governance Act, which furthers the aims of the reuse of public sector information. The Data Governance Act establishes a mechanism for reusing certain categories of protected public sector data, including those subject to IP rights and third-party copyright protection. While the Data Governance Act does not create a right to reuse these types of data, it provides a set of harmonised basic conditions under which the reuse of such data may be allowed. Thus it is clear that the reuse of public sector information is possible and effective only when copyright and public sector information laws have an effective dialogue.[288] Merely accessing data is not the aim of the Open Data Directive; only a coordinated and systematic approach that integrates copyright protection can achieve the aims of reproducing, exploiting or further releasing the document obtained under public sector information law.[289]

4.21 EU experience with blockchain and smart contracts in land management

The EU blockchain strategy aims to become an innovator in blockchain and a home to significant platforms, applications, and companies.[290] In this regard, the EU Regulation 2022/858 on Distributed Ledger Technology Market Infrastructures[291] and proposed Data Act articles related to smart contracts provide the main legislative directions of the EU. The former sets out a pilot regime for regulating cryptoassets that qualify as financial instruments and lays down the distributive ledger technology market infrastructure requirements. The six-year pilot programme is expected to propose amendments to the EU legislation based on the findings.

The smart contract provisions in Article 2 of the Data Act define a smart contract as ‘a computer program stored in an electronic ledger system wherein the outcome of the execution of the program is recorded on the electronic ledger’. The Data Act contains provisions in Chapter VIII that specify the essential smart contract requirement. Article 30 specifies the five essential requirements of smart contracts: robustness, safe termination and interruption, data archiving and continuity, access control, and conformity assessment. The most significant parts of the EU strategy on blockchain and smart contracts in the present context include the pan-European public services blockchain and smart contracts and digital assets promoting legal certainty.[292]

Land registration and management has been one of the sectors in which EU Member States have adopted blockchain technology. Sweden, Poland, and Georgia[293] have taken steps to incorporate blockchain into their land registration systems. The Swedish experience is considered to be one of the most advanced, which has provided a blueprint for other European countries. The Sweden Mapping, Cadastre, and Land Registration Authority (*Lantmäteriet*) have implemented the integration of blockchain into land administration by partnering with the private blockchain network of the Swedish start-up ChromaWay, telecom company Telia, and consulting firm Kairos Future.[294] Blockchain integration has been implemented with the basic tenets of openness and transparency, highlighting the right to access public records.[295] The Swedish blockchain registry project is based on the already digitalised land registry. All real estate property in Sweden is registered through the computerised Real Property Register that facilitates and connects real estate transaction parties. The land registry is an integrated system whereby property-related information has been merged with the spatial information of the Swedish Cadastral and Land Registration Authority.[296] The previous IT infrastructure had limited access granted to members of the public, who could not access the verification records, but the Swedish blockchain registry has enabled the 'land registry to become a more central actor in the conveyance process as the transaction chain would take place in the "digital consensus space" of the application owned by the land registry'.[297] The electronic identification system embedded into the blockchain ensures that parties can conduct secure transactions with minimum interference by intermediaries. The pilot programme successfully carried out a real estate transaction, and it is expected when the pilot regime comes into effect in the EU.

The Republic of Georgia has also adopted blockchain technology. The post-socialist era resulted in land privatisation, which then led to the establishment of the land registration process. A digital database was created to store land titles, satellite photos, and cadastral codes.[298] The Republic of Georgia's pilot project with Bitfury in 2016 led to the development of the first national blockchain-based land titling initiative. This Georgian experience is the only one that has moved beyond its pilot phase.[299] Its land management system has been built by creating a blockchain-based time-stamping layer on top of the existing digital land registry system. The blockchain integration has enabled 'certificates to be time-stamped and hashed in the Bitcoin Blockchain, one of the largest and most secure public Blockchain application'.[300] Instead of lawyers using the database to obtain verification, an individual can use their mobile device to get verification delivered by the execution of a smart contract which is stored in the blockchain. The land registration system in the Republic of Georgia had been commended as one of the world's best in terms of ease of property registration, a process which generally takes about one day to complete a transaction.[301] After the introduction of blockchain technology, however, this transaction time has been reduced to just 10 minutes.[302] The next phase in this integration is to facilitate land sales and transfers. The proposal includes the possibility of the buyer accessing and using property information through the system and putting it up for sale, and the network nodes to verify the buyer's availability of the funds and seller's ownership/title.[303] Once the verification is completed, the contract will be executed through smart contracts.

The preceding discussion highlights the potential benefits of blockchain as a land management system. The blockchain function in this area is its ability to link two essential aspects of the land governance system: the land registry and the cadastre. The examples indicate how the blockchain has been used to achieve this integration. Surveyors and land surveying activities would be imperative in any land management system based on blockchain, because the surveyors are the ones who map the legal rights of ownership. One of the lessons highlighted as a non-negotiable factor in the system's success is the availability of high-quality data for land and ownership. The role of surveyors in this process would be vital. Given the recommendations made in the *Second Interim Report* of the Australian Senate Select Committee on Australia as a Technology and Financial Centre in 2021[304] on supporting a blockchain land registry initiative, the discussion of the EU experience is relevant for all stakeholders, including surveyors. The report also highlighted the need for legal certainty with the enforcement of smart contracts.[305] Recommendation 14 in the report highlights the importance of emerging and existing international standards in the blockchain and smart contracts space; the European experience in land registry systems will be significant in this process. Surveyors in Australia will have to be informed about the role of surveyors in this process as providers of high-quality data and auditors of existing data.

4.22 Technological protection measures (TPMs)

The InfoSoc Directive, in Article 6, provides harmonised legal protection against circumventing TPMs designed to protect the holders of copyright, related rights, or *sui genesis* rights. Article 6 is drafted to ensure a balance between the need for protection against circumvention and the unnecessary burden on technological advancements and innovations. The Article 6 provisions are expressly excluded from being applied to computer programs. Article 7(1)(c) of the SD provides for TPM protection in the context of computer programs, while Article 6 is a more general application aimed to prohibit the circumvention of any effective technological devices used by the holders of copyright or related rights to protect their works. It covers a wide range of preparatory activities, including the manufacture, importation, distribution, sale, rental, advertisement for sale or rental, or possession for commercial purposes of such devices. The terms 'technological measures' and 'effective' are defined in Article 6(3).[306] These definitions are broad enough to include both software and hardware, which are either independent or part of another entity.[307]

In the case of *Nintendo Co. Ltd e.a. v PC Box Srl and 9Net Srl*,[308] the CJEU recognised that with video games, not only the game itself but also any portable equipment or consoles intended to access the game are covered under the Article 6 definition of effective TPMs.[309] Furthermore, the Court guided national courts when deciding to balance the interests of third parties and the protection of copyright holders.[310] One important aspect of the EU's approach is the requirement of intention or gross negligence to be considered as infringing TPMs. Regarding Internet intermediaries, website blocking orders can be obtained to prevent access to websites that advertise or sell devices aimed at circumventing TPMs.[311] A recent decision at the national level confirms the application of these principles, in which the copyright holder's right to seek an injunction against Internet intermediaries has been upheld to prevent and block access to websites dealing with TPM-circumventing devices.[312] In *Nintendo Co Ltd v Sky UK Ltd & Ors*,[313] five large internet service providers (ISPs) – Sky, EE, Virgin, BT (formerly British Telecom), and TalkTalk – were required to block access to four websites advertising and selling devices that allow the circumvention of Nintendo Switch games console TPMs. Nintendo had been successful in other EU countries, including Spain, where websites that offered pirated games for the Nintendo console had been blocked.[314]

Article 7 of the InfoSoc Directive deals with rights management information (RMI) and implements international obligations into EU law. This Article aims to protect how content is identified and managed.[315] Similar to Article 6, the protection under Article 7 extends to copyright, related rights and the *sui generis* database right. Article 7(2) defines RMI as:

> any information provided by rights holders, which identifies the work or other subject matter, the author or any other right holder, or information about the terms and conditions of use of the work or other subject matter as well as any numbers or codes that represent such information.

Article 7(1) protects RMIs by prohibiting acts that either remove or alter any RMIs, or that distribute, import for distribution, broadcast, communicate, or make available to the public works or protected subject matter from which RMI information has been removed or altered without authority. TPMs are valuable protection tools for surveyors when considering additional protection for their survey products. Because copyright holders do not need to implement TPMs, surveyors must proactively introduce and maintain TPMs into their products.

4.23 Conclusion

The EU law on copyright is a good illustration of how the principles of civil law and common law traditions have been merged in the efforts of harmonisation. While EU copyright principles are yet to achieve complete harmonisation, a substantial part of it is harmonised across Europe, primarily due to the efforts of the CJEU. While a group of academics have made significant efforts towards complete harmonisation of EU copyright law in the form of a 'Copyright Code',[316] the likelihood of such harmonisation is unlikely.[317] Therefore, while the EU principles provide a broad outline of the copyright principles in the EU, the Member States have considerable discretion in determining the specific nature of how these principles are applied.

The European approach to copyright provides a different perspective on the protection granted to intellectual creations. The CJEU's recent efforts have resulted in a general principle of copyrightability being formulated based on the idea of authors' rights in the civil law tradition. The distinction between the author's right and copyright in civil law and common law has played a significant role in reaching a compromise to formulate principles that can be applied in both the UK and Germany. The best example in this regard is the originality aspect, in which the 'author's intellectual creation' has found a 'middle way between the British "skill and labour" test and the German requirement of a certain level of creativity (Gestaltungshöhe)'.[318]

The European agenda for the digital and data economy – and the initiatives adopted regarding data management and protection, AI, and personal data protection – have resulted in legislative and policy initiatives that are also instructive to other jurisdictions. The EU's approach to copyright and the data economy has been to achieve a balance that will promote and encourage innovation and growth while protecting the rights holders of copyright. With the harmonisation efforts witnessed in the last decade, however, the data strategy seems to be taking over copyright principles in terms of priority. For instance, the report *Shaping Europe's Digital Future* lacks any reference to copyright.[319] The European data strategy also lacks reference to either copyright or IP at any point in the document.[320] Therefore,

> at least for the next period of Commission policy-making, actions in the field of copyright are likely to be an afterthought, rather than the main focus, of a more normatively-informed, value-based approach to social and economic regulation in digital spaces.[321]

This study discusses the DD of the EU and its application in the context of spatial data and products. The database right and *sui generis* right to protect the contents of a database provide valuable guidance on the management of data and databases in other jurisdictions. Caution must be exercised in adapting European measures, however, given the need for integrating the same in the context of data initiatives. The Data Act and the Data Governance Act have enacted specific exemptions to the DD. Other jurisdictions that are interested in a similar approach to the DD would benefit from considering the integration of data initiatives in the context of databases and database contents.

The European preference towards an open-ended subject matter categorisation is an important distinction to the common law approach. While these preferences are the result of social, economic, historical, and political factors, the flexibility that it has offered to accommodate the ever-changing nature of works must be noted, especially in the context of the digital environment. The absence of subject matter–related restrictions in Europe has resulted in a more agile system which can accommodate new developments and afford a higher level of protection to a wider category of works.

The European emphasis on authors' rights necessarily recognises the importance of human acts. So far, the European Commission and European Parliament have not indicated any policy preference towards recognising authorship for AI systems. This study has found, however, that the increased use of AI-assisted and AI-generated works has led the EU to recognise the need to reassess authorship rules and the concept of ownership in light of technological developments.

The interrelation between the EU's open data initiatives and how it has affected copyright protection in the EU provides valuable guidance on the reuse of public sector information in other jurisdictions. The European approach is based on strong foundations, whereby the infrastructure necessary for effectively sharing and reusing data was implemented with a significant investment towards education and training. The value placed on the EU public sector's transparency and accountability has provided the value framework to make open data initiatives a success. Therefore, when implementing open data initiatives in common law jurisdictions, it is essential to reconcile with concepts such as Crown copyright, which promotes the state's power of public sector information.

Europe's lessons in using blockchain and smart contracts in land management are encouraging for other jurisdictions. The availability of digital land management systems in the EU has made it possible to integrate these technologies into existing ones, thereby increasing the system's efficiency and reliability. Having high-quality data is vital when implementing any system of this nature. Furthermore, the experiences of EU countries highlight the importance of consultation and communication with all stakeholders involved in the process.

The EU principles of copyright – and how such principles interact with other policy initiatives – provide valuable insights and potential policy solutions for other jurisdictions. However, caution must be exercised with not only the legal origins but also the political considerations at the centre of the EU principles.

Notes

1 Directive on the harmonisation of certain aspects of copyright and related rights in the information society ('InfoSoc Directive'), 22 May 2001; Directive on rental right and lending right and on certain rights related to copyright in the field of IP ('Rental and Lending Directive'), 12 December 2006; Directive on the resale right for the benefit of the author of an original work of art ('Resale Right Directive'), 27 September 2001; Directive on the coordination of certain rules concerning copyright and rights related to copyright applicable to satellite broadcasting and cable retransmission ('Satellite and Cable Directive'), 27 September 1993; Directive on the legal protection of computer programs ('Software Directive'), 23 April 2009; Directive on the enforcement of intellectual property right ('IPRED'), 29 April 2004; Directive on the legal protection of databases ('Database Directive'), 11 March 1996; Directive on the term of protection of copyright and certain related rights amending the previous 2006 Directive ('Term Directive'), 27 September 2011; Directive on certain permitted uses of orphan works ('Orphan Works Directive'), 25 October 2012; Directive on collective management of copyright and related rights and multi-territorial licensing of rights in musical works for online use in the internal market ('CRM Directive'), 26 February 2014; Directive on certain permitted uses of certain works and other subject matter protected by copyright and related rights for the benefit of persons who are blind, visually impaired or otherwise print-disabled (Directive implementing the Marrakech Treaty in the EU), 13 September 2017; Regulation on the cross-border exchange between the Union and third countries of accessible format copies of certain works and other subject matter protected by copyright and related rights for the benefit of persons who are blind, visually impaired or otherwise print-disabled (Regulation implementing the Marrakech Treaty in the EU), 13 September 2017; Regulation on cross-border portability of online content services in the internal market (''Portability Regulation'), 14 June 2017; Directive on copyright and related rights in the Digital Single Market '(DSM Directive'), 17 April 2019; Directive on the exercise of copyright and related rights applicable to certain online transmissions of broadcasting organisations and retransmissions of television and radio programmes ('Satellite and Cable II'), 17 April 2019.

2 The areas such as moral rights, performance and adaptation rights and author's contracts are not yet harmonised in the EU.

3 T. Dreier & P. B. Hugenholtz, *Concise European Copyright Law* (Kluwer Law International B.V., The Netherlands, 2016).

4 Ibid.

5 These include mainly the TRIPS Agreement, Berne Convention (1886), WIPO Copyright Treaty (1996), Rome Convention (1961), the Geneva Convention (1971), WIPO Performances and Phonograms Treaty (1996), Beijing Treaty on Audiovisual Performances (2012), and the Marrakesh Treaty to Facilitate Access to Published Works for Persons Who are Blind, Visually Impaired or Otherwise Print Disabled (2013).

6 Eleonora Rosati, '30 years of EU copyright law'. In Eleonora Rosati (ed.), *The Routledge Handbook of EU Copyright Law* (Taylor & Francis Group, 2023) xi, xii at <http://ebookcentral.proquest.com/lib/monash/detail.action?docID=6514334>.

7 EuroGeographics, 'The European council of geodetic surveyors and geometer Europas' *European Requirements for Cadastral Surveyor Activities* (2007) 23, 3 at <www.clge.eu/wp content/uploads/2008/04/european_requirements_for_cadastral_surveyor_activity.pdf>.

8 Ibid., 4. The distinction must be made in this regard as to the differences in the historical origin of the cadastre in Europe and the common law countries. The development of cadastre as a fiscal or judicial measure provides the main distinction between these two approaches. A further development in this regard is the multi-purpose cadastre, where additional information is added to either the fiscal or judicial cadastre. I. P. Williamson, 'Cadastres and land information systems in common law jurisdictions' (1985) 28 (217) *Survey Review* 114–117.

9 Ibid., 6.

10 Ibid.

11 Ibid., 11.

12 Ibid., 13. Therefore, the focus is on the sanctions rather than the financial compensation for losses suffered by the clients. There are four types of sanctions that could be identified: a notice, a fine, a suspension of the license (certificate), and a termination of the license. It must be noted that the level of sanctions is closely linked to the conditions of the licences issued to the surveyors.

13 Ibid., 14.

14 The European Council of Geodetic Surveyors, European Requirements for Cadastral Surveyor Activities_Revision of 2018 (2018) 67, 86 at <www.clge.eu/wp-content/uploads/2019/04/cadastral_surveyor_requirement_rev2018.pdf>.

15 European Commission, 'INSPIRE directive' *INSPIRE Knowledge Base* (5 May 2023) at <https://inspire.ec.europa.eu/inspire-directive/2>.

16 Ibid.

17 A. Zwirowicz-Rutkowska, 'Evaluating spatial data infrastructure as a data source for land surveying' (2016) 142 (4) *Journal of Surveying Engineering* at <https://ascelibrary.org/doi/10.1061/%28ASCE%29SU.1943-5428.0000185>. It has been noted that

> surveyors use mainly view services to display, navigate, zoom in/out, pan, or overlay viewable spatial data sets and to display legend information. . . . WMS [web map service] is commonly accessible via Geoportal 2 without limits or fees. Other services, such as WFS [web feature service], are limited to the public and require a fee. Access to spatial data through download services is possible after placing an order with the geodetic and cartographic central service center and paying a fee.

18 EuroGeographics, 'About us', <https://eurogeographics.org/about-us/>. EuroGeographics is an independent international not-for-profit organisation representing around 90% of Europe's National Mapping, Cadastral and Land Registration Authorities.

19 European Land Registry Association, 'Home' at <www.elra.eu/>. European Land Registry Association represents 30 official land registry organisations from 25 European countries. The Association's primary purpose is to support the development and understanding of the role of land registration in real property and capital markets in Europe.

20 Permanent Committee on Cadastre in the European Union, 'About us' at <www.eurocadastre.org/aboutus.html>. The membership consists of the representatives of the institutions responsible for cadastre in the 27 Member States of the European Union and promotes the full awareness of the activities developed by the European Union and the Member States related to Cadastre and, by means of this information, to develop strategies and propose common initiatives with the aim of achieving greater coordination among the different European cadastral systems and their users.

21 The European Council of Geodetic Surveyors, *European Requirements for Cadastral Surveyor Activities_Revision of 2018* (2018) 67, 86 at <www.clge.eu/wp-content/uploads/2019/04/cadastral_surveyor_requirement_rev2018.pdf>. This is a permanent

forum for European geodetic surveyors and represents and promotes the interests of the geodetic surveying profession in the private and the public sectors in Europe.

22 EuroGeographics, 'Status and adopted innovations over the last decade in cadastre and land administration in Europe' 20 at <https://eurogeographics.org/wp-content/uploads/2021/04/210512-SummaryReport-PCCQuestionnaire.pdf>.

23 Ibid., 21.

24 Ibid., 28.

25 Ibid., 23.

26 M. Davison, 'Database protection: Lessons from Europe, congress, and WIPO law, technology and the arts symposium: The WIPO copyright treaties: 10 years later' (2006) 57 (4) *Case Western Reserve Law Review* 829–831.

27 Ibid.

28 EuroGeographics, 'EuroGeographics briefing paper evaluation of the database directive 96/9/EC' at <https://eurogeographics.org/wp-content/uploads/2018/04/2017-EG-Briefing-Paper-Evaluation-of-the-Database-Directive-969EC.pdf>.

29 Ibid., 2.

30 Katleen Janssen and Jos Dumortier, 'The protection of maps and spatial databases in Europe and the United States by copyright and the Sui Generis Right' (2006) 24(2) *UIC John Marshall Journal of Information Technology & Privacy Law* 195–212.

31 Estelle Derclaye, 'The database directive'. In Irini Stamatoudi & Paul Torremans (eds), *EU Copyright Law* (Edward Elgar Publishing, 2021) 216–217 at <www.elgaronline.com/edcollchap/book/9781786437808/book-part-9781786437808-19.xml>.

32 *Fixtures Marketing Ltd v Organismos Prognostikon Agonon Podosfairou* (OPAP) (Court of Justice of the European Union, Case C-444/02, ECLI:EU:C:2004:697, 9 November 2004) [20, 30].

33 *Fixtures Marketing Ltd v Organismos Prognostikon Agonon Podosfairou* (OPAP) (Court of Justice of the European Union, Case C-444/02, ECLI:EU:C:2004:697, 9 November 2004) [29, 32].

34 *Football Dataco Ltd and Others v Yahoo! UK Ltd and Others* (Court of Justice of the European Union, Case C-604/10, EU:C:2012:115, 1 March 2012) [26].

35 Estelle Derclaye, 'The database directive'. In Irini Stamatoudi & Paul Torremans (eds), *EU Copyright Law* (Edward Elgar Publishing, 2021) 216, 218 at <www.elgaronline.com/edcollchap/book/9781786437808/book-part-9781786437808-19.xml>.

36 *Freistaat Bayern v Verlag Esterbauer GmbH* (Court of Justice of the European Union, Case C-490/14, ECLI:EU:C:2015:735, 29 October 2015).

37 *Freistaat Bayern v Verlag Esterbauer GmbH* (Court of Justice of the European Union, Case C-490/14, ECLI:EU:C:2015:735, 29 October 2015) [9].

38 *Freistaat Bayern v Verlag Esterbauer GmbH* (Court of Justice of the European Union, Case C-490/14, ECLI:EU:C:2015:735, 29 October 2015) [15].

39 *Freistaat Bayern v Verlag Esterbauer GmbH* (Court of Justice of the European Union, Case C-490/14, ECLI:EU:C:2015:735, 29 October 2015) [21].

40 *Freistaat Bayern v Verlag Esterbauer GmbH* (Court of Justice of the European Union, Case C-490/14, ECLI:EU:C:2015:735, 29 October 2015) [23].

41 *Freistaat Bayern v Verlag Esterbauer GmbH* (Court of Justice of the European Union, Case C-490/14, ECLI:EU:C:2015:735, 29 October 2015) [27].

42 Ibid.

43 Including planning travel between two points; preparing a bicycle trip; or searching for the name and location of a road, town, river, lake, or mountain, or the width of watercourses or the height of relief on the landscape. *Freistaat Bayern v Verlag Esterbauer GmbH* (Court of Justice of the European Union, Case C-490/14, ECLI:EU:C:2015:735, 29 October 2015) [25].

44 *Freistaat Bayern v Verlag Esterbauer GmbH* (Court of Justice of the European Union, Case C-490/14, ECLI:EU:C:2015:735, 29 October 2015) [28].

45 Estelle Derclaye, 'The database directive'. In Irini Stamatoudi & Paul Torremans (eds), *EU Copyright Law* (Edward Elgar Publishing, 2021) 216, 220 at <www.elgaronline.com/edcollchap/book/9781786437808/book-part-9781786437808-19.xml>.

46 Directive 2009/24/EC of the European Parliament and of the Council of 23 April 2009 on the legal protection of computer programs.

47 Article refers to not only computer programs but also rental rights, lending rights, and certain rights related to copyright in the field of IP and the term of protection of copyright and certain related rights.

48 *Football Dataco Ltd and Others v Yahoo! UK Ltd and Others* (Court of Justice of the European Union, C-604/10, EU:C:2012:115, 1 March 2012) [38].

49 Ibid.

50 Ibid.

51 Ibid., [39].

52 Ibid., [41, 42].

53 Katleen Janssen & Jos Dumortier, 'The protection of maps and spatial databases in Europe and the United States by copyright and the Sui Generis right' (2006) 24 (2) *UIC John Marshall Journal of Information Technology & Privacy Law* 195, 212.

54 Ibid.

55 Ibid.

56 These rights include: (a) temporary or permanent reproduction by any means and in any form, in whole or in part; (b) translation, adaptation, arrangement, and any other alteration; or (c) any form of distribution to the public of the database or of copies thereof; the first sale in the Community of a copy of the database by the rights holder or with his consent shall exhaust the right to control resale of that copy within the Community; (d) any communication, display, or performance to the public; or (e) any reproduction, distribution, communication, display, or performance to the public of the results of the acts referred to in (b).

57 Article 6(2) provides that Member States shall have the option of providing for limitations on the rights set out in Article 5 in the following cases: (a) in the case of reproduction for private purposes of a non-electronic database; (b) when there is use for the sole purpose of illustration for teaching or scientific research, as long as the source is indicated and to the extent justified by the non-commercial purpose to be achieved; (c) when there is use for the purposes of public security or for the purposes of an administrative or judicial procedure; or (d) where other exceptions to copyright which are traditionally authorised under national law are involved, without prejudice to points (a), (b) and (c).

58 Estelle Derclaye, 'The database directive'. In Irini Stamatoudi & Paul Torremans (eds), *EU Copyright Law* (Edward Elgar Publishing, 2021) 216, 228 at <www.elgaronline.com/edcollchap/book/9781786437808/book-part-9781786437808-19.xml>.

59 Article 7(1).

60 Estelle Derclaye, 'The database directive'. In Irini Stamatoudi & Paul Torremans (eds), *EU Copyright Law* (Edward Elgar Publishing, 2021) 216, 231 at <www.elgaronline.com/edcollchap/book/9781786437808/book-part-9781786437808-19.xml>.

61 Ibid.

62 Ibid.

63 Katleen Janssen & Jos Dumortier, 'The protection of maps and spatial databases in Europe and the United States by copyright and the Sui Generis right' (2006) 24 *UIC John Marshall Journal of Information Technology & Privacy Law* 195, 220.

64 Ibid.

65 *Fixtures Marketing Ltd v AB Svenska Spel* (Court of Justice of the European Union, Case C-338/02, ECLI:EU:C:2004:696, 9 November 2004) [28]; *Fixtures Marketing Ltd v Organismos Prognostikon Agonon Podosfairou* (OPAP) (Court of Justice of the European Union, Case C-444/02, ECLI:EU:C:2004:697, 9 November 2004) [43]; *Fixtures Marketing Ltd v Oy Veikkaus AB* (Court of Justice of the European Union, Case Case C-46/02, ECLI:EU:C:2004:694, 9 November 2004) [38].

66 *Fixtures Marketing Ltd v AB Svenska Spel* (Court of Justice of the European Union, Case C-338/02, ECLI:EU:C:2004:696, 9 November 2004) [28]; *Fixtures Marketing Ltd v Organismos Prognostikon Agonon Podosfairou* (OPAP) (Court of Justice of the European Union, Case C-444/02, ECLI:EU:C:2004:697, 9 November 2004) [43].

67 *Fixtures Marketing Ltd v AB Svenska Spel* (Court of Justice of the European Union, Case C-338/02, ECLI:EU:C:2004:696, 9 November 2004) [24]; *The British Horseracing Board Ltd and Others v William Hill Organization Ltd.* (Court of Justice of the European Union, Case C-203/02, ECLI:EU:C:2004:695, 9 November 2004) [31]; *Fixtures Marketing Ltd v Oy Veikkaus AB* (Court of Justice of the European Union, Case C-46/02, ECLI:EU:C:2004:694, 9 November 2004) [34]; *Fixtures Marketing Ltd v AB Svenska Spel* (Court of Justice of the European Union, Case C-338/02, ECLI:EU:C:2004:696, 9 November 2004) [40].

68 Estelle Derclaye, 'The database directive'. In Irini Stamatoudi & Paul Torremans (eds), *EU Copyright Law* (Edward Elgar Publishing, 2021) 216, 233 at <www.elgaronline.com/edcollchap/book/9781786437808/book-part-9781786437808-19.xml>.

69 *Précom, Ouest France Multimedia v Direct Annonces, Court of Cassation* (Cass.), 1st civ., 5 March 2009.

70 *Bundesgerichtshof (Market Surveys) (I ZR 1/02)* (2005) GRUR 940 (Germany) reported in Case Comment, Germany: *Copyright Act*, secs. 17(2), 87a(1), 87(1) and (2) – 'Market Surveys' [2006] IIC 489.

71 *Ryanair v Atrapalo* Case STS 572/2012, 9 October 2012.

72 *Fixtures Marketing Ltd v AB Svenska Spel* (Court of Justice of the European Union, Case C-338/02, ECLI:EU:C:2004:696, 9 November 2004) [27].

73 Ibid.

74 Ibid.

75 Estelle Derclaye, 'The database directive'. In Irini Stamatoudi & Paul Torremans (eds), *EU Copyright Law* (Edward Elgar Publishing, 2021) 216, 234 at <www.elgaronline.com/edcollchap/book/9781786437808/book-part-9781786437808-19.xml>.

76 Defined in Article 7(1) as 'the permanent or temporary transfer of all or a substantial part of the contents of a database to another medium by any means or in any form'.

77 Defined in Article 7(1) as 'any form of making available to the public all or a substantial part of the contents of a database by the distribution of copies, by renting, by online or other forms of transmission. The first sale of a copy of a database within the Community by the right holder or with his consent shall exhaust the right to control resale of that copy within the Community'.

78 Estelle Derclaye, 'The database directive'. In Irini Stamatoudi & Paul Torremans (eds), *EU Copyright Law* (Edward Elgar Publishing, 2021) 216, 235 at <www.elgaronline.com/edcollchap/book/9781786437808/book-part-9781786437808-19.xml>.

79 *The British Horseracing Board Ltd and Others v William Hill Organization Ltd.* (Court of Justice of the European Union, Case C-203/02, ECLI:EU:C:2004:695, 9 November 2004) [27].

80 *Directmedia Publishing v Albert-Ludwigs-Universität Freiburg* (Court of Justice of the European Union, C-304/07, ECLI:EU:C:2008:552,9 October 2008) [53].

81 Ibid.

82 *The British Horseracing Board Ltd and Others v William Hill Organization Ltd.* (Court of Justice of the European Union, Case C-203/02, ECLI:EU:C:2004:695, 9 November 2004) [67].

83 *Innoweb BV v. Wegener ICT Media BV, Wegener Mediaventions BV* (Court of Justice of the European Union, Case C-202/12, ECLI:EU:C:2013:850, 19 December 2013).

84 *The British Horseracing Board Ltd and Others v William Hill Organization Ltd.* (Court of Justice of the European Union, Case C-203/02, ECLI:EU:C:2004:695, 9 November 2004) [69].

85 Ibid.

86 *The British Horseracing Board Ltd and Others v William Hill Organization Ltd.* (Court of Justice of the European Union, Case C-203/02, ECLI:EU:C:2004:695, 9 November 2004) [70].
87 *Apis-Hristovich EOOD v Lakorda AD* (Court of Justice of the European Union, Case C-545/07, ECLI:EU:C:2009:132, 5 March 2009).
88 *Apis-Hristovich EOOD v Lakorda AD* (Court of Justice of the European Union, Case C-545/07, ECLI:EU:C:2009:132, 5 March 2009) [73].
89 *The British Horseracing Board Ltd and Others v William Hill Organization Ltd.* (Court of Justice of the European Union, Case C-203/02, ECLI:EU:C:2004:695, 9 November 2004) [71].
90 Ibid.
91 *Wegener v Hunter Select, CA Leeuwarden*, 27 November 2002, at <www.rechtspraak.nl> (50 out of 90 elements constituted a substantial part of the database).
92 *Credinfor v Artprice.com, CA Paris*, 18 June 2003, Jurisdata, n. 223155 (the extraction of information containing the name, first name, and dates of birth and death of more than 36,000 artists is a quantitatively substantial extraction of the contents of a database related to the market of works of art containing information on 184,000 artists).
93 Estelle Derclaye, 'The database directive'. In Irini Stamatoudi & Paul Torremans (eds), *EU Copyright Law* (Edward Elgar Publishing, 2021) 216, 241 at <www.elgaronline.com/edcollchap/book/9781786437808/book-part-9781786437808-19.xml>.
94 *UsedSoft v Oracle International* (Court of Justice of the European Union, Case C-128/11, ECLI:EU:C:2012:407,3 July 2012).
95 *UsedSoft v Oracle International* (Court of Justice of the European Union, Case C-128/11, ECLI:EU:C:2012:407, 3 July 2012) [78–80].
96 Estelle Derclaye, 'The database directive'. In Irini Stamatoudi & Paul Torremans (eds), *EU Copyright Law* (Edward Elgar Publishing, 2021) 216, 244 at <www.elgaronline.com/edcollchap/book/9781786437808/book-part-9781786437808-19.xml>.
97 Ibid., 246.
98 Estelle Derclaye, 'The database directive'. In Irini Stamatoudi & Paul Torremans (eds), *EU Copyright Law* (Edward Elgar Publishing, 2021) 216, 246 at <www.elgaronline.com/edcollchap/book/9781786437808/book-part-9781786437808-19.xml>: S. Smith, 'Legal protection of factual compilations and databases in England: How will the database directive change the law in this area?' (1997) *Intellectual Property Quarterly* 450; J. Reichman and P. Samuelson, 'Intellectual property rights in data?' (1997) *Vanderbilt Law Review* 50, 90.
99 Directive. 2004/48 EC of the European Parliament and of the Council of 29 APRIL 2004 on the enforcement of IP rights, OJ L 157/45, 30.4.2004.
100 European Commission. Directorate General for Communications Networks, Content and Technology et al., *Study to Support an Impact Assessment for the Review of the Database Directive: Final Report* (Publications Office, 2022) at <https://data.europa.eu/doi/10.2759/647387>.
101 T. Streinz, 'The evolution of European data law'. In P. Craig & G. de Búrca (eds), *The Evolution of EU Law* (Oxford University Press, Oxford, 2021) at <https://doi.org/10.1093/oso/9780192846556.003.0029>.
102 'A European strategy for data | Shaping Europe's digital future' *European Commission* (16 May 2023) at <https://digital-strategy.ec.europa.eu/en/policies/strategy-data>; G. Carvalho & E. Kazim, 'Themes in data strategy: Thematic analysis of "a European strategy for data" ' (EC) (2022) 2 (1) *AI and Ethics* 53.
103 European Commission, 'A European strategy for data' at <https://eur-lex.europa.eu/legal-content/EN/TXT/PDF/?uri=CELEX:52020DC0066>.
104 European Commission, 'Europe's digital decade: Digital targets for 2030' at <https://commission.europa.eu/strategy-and-policy/priorities-2019-2024/europe-fit-digital-age/europes-digital-decade-digital-targets-2030_en>.
105 Regulation (EU) 2022/868 of the European Parliament and of the Council of 30 May 2022 on European data governance and amending Regulation (EU) 2018/1724.

106 Proposal for a Regulation of the European Parliament and the Council on Harmonised Rules on Fair Access to and Use of Data (Data Act) COM/2022/68 final.
107 European Commission, 'European data governance Act | Shaping Europe's digital future' (16 May 2023) at <https://digital-strategy.ec.europa.eu/en/policies/data-governance-act>.
108 Article 1 of the *Data Governance Act*.
109 Article 3(1)(c) of the *Data Governance Act*.
110 Cyber Risk GmbH, 'The European data' at <www.eu-data-act.com/>.
111 Council of the European Union, 'Data act: Member states agree common position on fair access to and use of data' (n.d.) at <www.consilium.europa.eu/en/press/press-releases/2023/03/24/data-act-member-states-agree-common-position-on-fair-access-to-and-use-of-data/>.
112 Ben Wolford, 'What is GDPR, the EU's new data protection law?' *GDPR.eu* (7 November 2018) at <https://gdpr.eu/what-is-gdpr/>.
113 Article 4 of the GDPR defines data 'processing' as:

> any operation or set of operations which is performed on personal data or on sets of personal data, whether or not by automated means, such as collection, recording, organisation, structuring, storage, adaptation or alteration, retrieval, consultation, use, disclosure by transmission, dissemination or otherwise making available, alignment or combination, restriction, erasure or destruction.

114 Article 4 of the GDPR defines a controller as:

> the natural or legal person, public authority, agency or other body which, alone or jointly with others, determines the purposes and means of the processing of personal data; where the purposes and means of such processing are determined by Union or Member State law, the controller or the specific criteria for its nomination may be provided for by Union or Member State law.

115 Article 4 of the GDPR defines a processor as 'a natural or legal person, public authority, agency or other body which processes personal data on behalf of the controller'.
116 Article 4 GDPR.
117 Article 4 of the GDPR refers to a data subject as an identified or identifiable natural person to whom the personal data relates. Chapter 3 of the GDPR provides for the rights of such data subjects.
118 Explanatory Memorandum of the Proposal for a Regulation of the European Parliament and of the Council on harmonised rules on fair access to and use of data (Data Act) COM/2022/68 final.
119 M. Cory, 'EuroGeographics information paper communication from the commission on a European strategy for data' *EuroGeographics* (n.d.) at <https://eurogeographics.org/wp-content/uploads/2020/05/EG-response-on-ES4D-FINAL.pdf>.
120 The nine identified data spaces are industrial, green deal, mobility, health, financial, energy, agriculture, public administrations, and skills. Simon Scerri et al., 'Common European data spaces: Challenges and opportunities'. In Edward Curry, Simon Scerri & Tuomo Tuikka (eds), *Data Spaces: Design, Deployment and Future Directions* (Springer International Publishing, 2022) 337 at <https://doi.org/10.1007/978-3-030-98636-0_16>.
121 World Geospatial Industry Council, 'Geospatial information and privacy: Policy perspectives and imperatives for the geospatial industry' at <https://wgicouncil.org/wp-content/uploads/2020/03/Geospatial-Informaion-and-Privacy-report-Final.pdf>.
122 Ibid., 9.
123 GDPR Working Group, 'Nordic GDPR working group report' 6 at <https://norden.lmi.is/wp-content/uploads/2019/08/Nordic-GDPR-working-group-Report.pdf>.
124 Ibid.
125 World Geospatial Industry Council, 'Geospatial information and privacy: Policy perspectives and imperatives for the geospatial industry' at <https://wgicouncil.

org/wp-content/uploads/2020/03/Geospatial-Informaion-and-Privacy-report-Final.pdf> 23.

126 N. Conway, 'Why geospatial needs to listen to GDPR' (2019) *GiS Professional* 79, 32.

127 'European Cadastres and National Mapping Agencies | ArcNews Online' at <www.esri.com/news/arcnews/spring11articles/european-cadastres-and-national-mapping-agencies.html>.

128 Ibid.

129 Ibid.

130 Felipe Romero Moreno, '"Upload filters" and Human Rights: Implementing Article 17 of the directive on copyright in the digital single market' (2020) 34 (2) *International Review of Law, Computers & Technology* 153.

131 Pascal D. König, 'Fortress Europe 4.0? An analysis of EU data governance through the lens of the resource regime concept' (2022) 8 (4) *European Policy Analysis* 484.

132 G. Carvalho & E. Kazim, 'Themes in data strategy: Thematic analysis of "a European strategy for data"' (EC) (2022) 2 (1) *AI and Ethics* 53.

133 Directive 2001/29/EC of the European Parliament and of the Council of 22nd May 2001 on the harmonisation of certain aspects of copyright and related rights in the information society OJ L 167/10, 22.6.2001.

134 Directive 91/250/EEC of the European Parliament and of the Council of 14th May 1991 on the legal protection of computer programs, OJ L 122/42, 17.5.1991.

135 Directive 2011/77/EU of the European Parliament and of the Council of 27 September 2011 amending Directive 2006/116/EC on the term of protection of copyright and certain related rights OJ L 265, 11.10.201.

136 The Council Directive (EU) 2019/790 of the European Parliament and of the Council of 17 April 2019 on copyright and related rights in the Digital Single Market and amending Directives 96/9/EC and 2001/29/EC PE/51/2019/REV/1, OJ L 130, 17.5.2019.

137 Eleonora Rosati, 'Copyright at the CJEU: Back to the start (of copyright protection)'. In Eleonora Rosati (ed.), *Developments and Directions in Intellectual Property Law. 20 Years of the IPKat* (Oxford University Press, Oxford, 2023).

138 *Infopaq International A/S v. Danske Dagblades Forening* (Court of Justice of the European Union, Case C-5/08, ECLI:EU:C:2009:465, 16 July 2009).

139 Eleonora Rosati, 'Copyright at the CJEU: Back to the start (of copyright protection)'. In Eleonora Rosati (ed.), *Developments and Directions in Intellectual Property Law. 20 Years of the IPKat* (Oxford University Press, Oxford, 2023) at 11.

140 Ibid., 8.

141 *Cofemel – Sociedade de Vestuário SA v G-Star Raw CV* (Opinion of Advocate General Szpunar, Case C-683/17), ECLI:EU:C:2019:363, delivered on 2 May 2019).

142 *Cofemel – Sociedade de Vestuário SA v G-Star Raw CV* (Court of Justice of the European Union, Case C-683/17, ECLI:EU:C:2019:721, 12 September 2019).

143 *Cofemel – Sociedade de Vestuário SA v G-Star Raw CV* (Opinion of Advocate General Szpunar, Case C683/17), ECLI:EU:C:2019:363, delivered on 2 May 2019) [23].

144 Ibid.

145 Justine Pila, 'The authorial works protectable by copyright'. In Eleonora Rosati (ed.), *The Routledge Handbook of EU Copyright Law* (Taylor & Francis Group, 2023) 64 at <http://ebookcentral.proquest.com/lib/monash/detail.action?docID=6514334>.

146 Berne Convention for the Protection of Literary and Artistic Works 1886, as amended. (Berne Convention).

147 Justine Pila, 'The authorial works protectable by copyright'. In Eleonora Rosati (ed.), *The Routledge Handbook of EU Copyright Law* (Taylor & Francis Group, 2023) 64 at <http://ebookcentral.proquest.com/lib/monash/detail.action?docID=6514334> at 66.

148 Jani McCutcheon, 'The concept of the copyright work under EU law: More than a matter of taste' (No 3428844, SSRN, 30 July 2019) 11 at <https://papers.ssrn.com/sol3/papers.cfm?abstract_id=3428844>.

149 The full list includes:

> books, pamphlets and other writings; lectures, addresses, sermons and other works of the same nature; dramatic or dramatic musical works; choreographic works and entertainments in dumb show; musical compositions with or without words; cinematographic works to which are assimilated works expressed by a process analogous to cinematography; works of drawing, painting, architecture, sculpture, engraving and lithography; photographic works to which are assimilated works expressed by a process analogous to photography; works of applied art; illustrations, maps, plans, sketches and three-dimensional works relative to geography, topography, architecture or science.

150 Justine Pila, 'The authorial works protectable by copyright'. In Eleonora Rosati (ed.), *The Routledge Handbook of EU Copyright Law* (Taylor & Francis Group, 2023) 64 at <http://ebookcentral.proquest.com/lib/monash/detail.action?docID=6514334> at 65.

151 *Infopaq International A/S v. Danske Dagblades Forening* (Court of Justice of the European Union, Case C-5/08, ECLI:EU:C:2009:465, 16 July 2009).

152 Ibid., [37].

153 Eleonora Rosati, 'CJEU rules that copyright protection for designs only requires sufficient originality' (2019) 14 (12) *Journal of Intellectual Property Law & Practice* 931.

154 Marianne Levin, 'Chapter 5: The cofemel revolution – originality, equality and neutrality'. In Eleonora Rosati (ed.), *The Routledge Handbook of EU Copyright Law* (Taylor & Francis Group, 2023) 82, 95 at <http://ebookcentral.proquest.com/lib/monash/detail.action?docID=6514334>.

155 Marie-Christine Janssens, 'The software directive'. In Irini Stamatoudi & Paul Torremans (eds), *EU Copyright Law* (Edward Elgar Publishing, 2021) 75, 79 at <www.elgaronline.com/edcollchap/book/9781786437808/book-part-9781786437808-15.xml>.

156 Ibid., 81–84.

157 *Bezpecˇnostní Ahcnostní softwarová asociace – Svaz softwarové ochrany v Ministerstvo kultury* (Court of Justice of the European Union, Case C-393/09, ECR I-13971, 22 December 2010).

158 Ibid., [46].

159 Eleonora Rosati, 'Closed subject-matter systems are no longer compatible with EU copyright' (SSRN Scholarly Paper No 2468104, 18 July 2014) 5 at <https://papers.ssrn.com/abstract=2468104>.

160 *Nintendo Co. Ltd e.a. v PC Box Srl and 9Net Srl* (Court of Justice of the European Union, Case C-355/12, ECR I-0000; EU:C:2014:25, 23 January 2014) [23]. The Court held that video games:

> constitute complex matter comprising not only a computer program but also graphic and sound elements, which, although encrypted in computer language, have a unique creative value which cannot be reduced to that encryption. In so far as the parts of a videogame . . . are part of its originality, they are protected, together with the entire work, by copyright in the context of the system established by Directive 2001/29.

161 Eleonora Rosati, 'Closed subject-matter systems are no longer compatible with EU copyright' (SSRN Scholarly Paper No 2468104, 18 July 2014) 5 at <https://papers.ssrn.com/abstract=2468104> at 6.

162 Ibid.

163 Ibid., 10.

164 Justine Pila, 'The authorial works protectable by copyright'. In Eleonora Rosati (ed.), *The Routledge Handbook of EU Copyright Law* (Taylor & Francis Group, 2023) 64 at <http://ebookcentral.proquest.com/lib/monash/detail.action?docID=6514334> at 68.

165 *Funke Medien NRW GmbH v. Bundesrepublik Deutschland* (Court of Justice of the European Union, Case C–469/17, ECLI:EU:C:2019:623, 29 July 2019) [24].

166 *Levola Hengelo BV v. Smilde Foods BV Deutschland* (Court of Justice of the European Union, Case C– 310/17, ECLI:EU:C:2018:899,13 November 2018).
167 *Cofemel – Sociedade de Vestuário SA v G-Star Raw CV* (Opinion of Advocate General Szpunar, Case C-683/17), ECLI:EU:C:2019:363, delivered on 2 May 2019).
168 Justine Pila, 'The authorial works protectable by copyright'. In Eleonora Rosati (ed.), *The Routledge Handbook of EU Copyright Law* (Taylor & Francis Group, 2023) 64 at <http://ebookcentral.proquest.com/lib/monash/detail.action?docID=6514334> at 66.
169 Ibid.
170 *Levola Hengelo BV v. Smilde Foods BV Deutschland* (Court of Justice of the European Union, Case C310/17, ECLI:EU:C:2018:899,13 November 2018) [40].
171 Eleonora Rosati, 'CJEU rules that copyright protection for designs only requires sufficient originality' (2019) 14 (12) *Journal of Intellectual Property Law & Practice* 931.
172 Marianne Levin, 'Chapter 5: The cofemel revolution – Originality, equality and neutrality'. In Eleonora Rosati (ed.), *The Routledge Handbook of EU Copyright Law* (Taylor & Francis Group, 2023) 82, 95 at <http://ebookcentral.proquest.com/lib/monash/detail.action?docID=6514334> at 93.
173 For computer programs, see Article 1(3) of the SD; for photographs, see Article 6 of Term Directive; and for databases, see Article 3(1) of the Database Directive.
174 *Infopaq International A/S v. Danske Dagblades Forening* (Court of Justice of the European Union, Case C5/08, ECLI:EU:C:2009:465, 16 July 2009) [35].
175 *Bezpecˇnostní Ahcnostní softwarová asociace – Svaz softwarové ochrany v Ministerstvo kultury* (Court of Justice of the European Union, Case C-393/09, ECR I-13971, 22 December 2010).
176 *Football Association Premier League Ltd and Others v QC Leisure and Others* and *Karen Murphy v Media Protection Services Ltd* (Court of Justice of the European Union, C-403/08 and C-429/08, ECLI:EU:C:2011:63, 4 October 201).
177 *Eva-Maria Painer v Standard VerlagsGmbH and Others* (Court of Justice of the European Union, C-145/10, EU:C:2011:798, 7 March 2013).
178 Ibid.
179 *Football Dataco Ltd and Others v Yahoo! UK Ltd and Others* (Court of Justice of the European Union, C-604/10, EU:C:2012:115, 1 March 2012) [35].
180 Ibid., [39].
181 R. C. Valles, 'The requirement of originality'. In E. Derclaye (ed.), *Research Handbook on the Future of EU Copyright* (Edward Elgar Publishing Limited), 102–106 at <http://ebookcentral.proquest.com/lib/monash/detail.action?docID=420703>. 'France ('oeuvres de l'esprit ': works of the mind, article L 122-1, Intellectual Property Code 1992), the Netherlands ('ieder voortbrengsel op het gebied van letterkunde, wetenschap of kunst ': any creation in the literary, scientific or artistic areas, art. 10, *Copyright Act 1912*), Germany ('persönliche geistige Schöpfungen': personal intellectual creations, ss. 1 and 2 Copyright and Related Rights Act 1965), Italy ('opere dell ingegno di carattere creativo ': works of the mind having a creative character, art. 1, *Copyright Act 1941*) or Portugal ('criações intelectuais do domínio literário, científico e artístico': intellectual creations in the literary, scientific or artistic areas, art. 2 Code of Author's Right 1985).'
182 Katleen Janssen & Jos Dumortier, 'The protection of maps and spatial databases in Europe and the United States by copyright and the Sui Generis right' (2006) 24 *UIC John Marshall Journal of Information Technology & Privacy Law* 195, 201.
183 Ibid., 202.
184 Ibid.
185 Ibid.
186 Ibid., 203.
187 *Infopaq International A/S v. Danske Dagblades Forening* (Court of Justice of the European Union, Case C-5/08, ECLI:EU:C:2009:465, 16 July 2009).
188 Ibid., [45].
189 Ibid., [46].

190 Justine Pila, 'The authorial works protectable by copyright'. In Eleonora Rosati (ed.), *The Routledge Handbook of EU Copyright Law* (Taylor & Francis Group, 2023) 64 at <http://ebookcentral.proquest.com/lib/monash/detail.action?docID=6514334>.
191 *SAS Institute Inc. v. World Programming Ltd Case* (Court of Justice of the European Union, C-406/10 ECLI:EU:C:2012:259, 2 May 2012) [65]–[67].
192 Ibid., [66].
193 Ibid., [67].
194 Justine Pila, 'The authorial works protectable by copyright'. In Eleonora Rosati (ed.), *The Routledge Handbook of EU Copyright Law* (Taylor & Francis Group, 2023) 64 at <http://ebookcentral.proquest.com/lib/monash/detail.action?docID=6514334> at 73.
195 Ibid.
196 *Football Dataco Ltd and Others v Yahoo! UK Ltd and Others* (Court of Justice of the European Union, C-604/10, EU:C:2012:115, 1 March 2012) [38]–[39]. 'As regards the setting up of a database, that criterion of originality is satisfied when, through the selection or arrangement of the data which it contains, its author expresses his creative ability in an original manner by making free and creative choices' (see, by analogy, Infopaq International, paragraph 45; Bezpečnostní softwarová asociace, paragraph 50; and Painer, paragraph 89) and thus stamps his 'personal touch' (Painer, paragraph 92). By contrast, that criterion is not satisfied when the setting up of the database is 'dictated by technical considerations, rules or constraints which leave no room for creative freedom'.
197 *Cofemel – Sociedade de Vestuário SA v G-Star Raw CV* (Opinion of Advocate General Szpunar, Case C-683/17), ECLI:EU:C:2019:363, delivered on 2 May 2019).
198 Ibid., [29].
199 Eleonora Rosati, 'CJEU rules that copyright protection for designs only requires sufficient originality' (2019) 14 (12) *Journal of Intellectual Property Law & Practice* 931.
200 Ibid., 76.
201 Ibid.
202 Ole-Andreas Rognstad, 'Creations caused by humans (or Robots)? artificial intelligence and causation requirements for copyright protection in EU law'. In Taina Pihlajarinne & Alén-Savikko (eds), *Artificial Intelligence and the Media* (Edward Elgar Publishing, 2022) 172, 174 at <www.elgaronline.com/display/edcoll/9781839109966/9781839109966.00015.xml>.
203 *Funke Medien NRW GmbH v Bundesrepublik Deutschland* (Court of Justice of the European Union, Case C-469/17, ECLI:EU:C:2019:623, 29 July 2019): *Cofemel – Sociedade de Vestuário SA v G-Star Raw CV* (Court of Justice of the European Union, Opinion C-683/17, ECLI:EU:C:2019:721, 12 September 2019).
204 Y. Xiao, 'Decoding authorship: Is there really no place for an algorithmic author under copyright law?' (2023) 54 (1) *IIC – International Review of Intellectual Property and Competition Law* 5.
205 *Eva-Maria Painer v Standard VerlagsGmbH and Others* (Court of Justice of the European Union, Opinion C-145/10, ECLI:EU:C:2011:239, 12 April 2011).
206 Giulia Priora, 'Copyright law and the promotion of scientific networks: Some reflections on the rules on co-authorship in the EU' (2019) 9 (2) *Queen Mary Journal of Intellectual Property* 217.
207 Justine Pila, 'The authorial works protectable by copyright'. In Eleonora Rosati (ed.), *The Routledge Handbook of EU Copyright Law* (Taylor & Francis Group, 2023) 79 at <http://ebookcentral.proquest.com/lib/monash/detail.action?docID=6514334>.
208 Ibid., 79–80.
209 Ole-Andreas Rognstad, 'Creations caused by humans (or Robots)? Artificial intelligence and causation requirements for copyright protection in EU law'. In Taina Pihlajarinne & Alén-Savikko (eds), *Artificial Intelligence and the Media* (Edward Elgar Publishing, 2022) 172, 178 at <www.elgaronline.com/display/edcoll/9781839109966/9781839109966.00015.xml>.
210 Ibid., 182.

211 *Eva-Maria Painer v Standard VerlagsGmbH and Others* (Court of Justice of the European Union, C-145/10, EU:C:2011:798, 7 March 2013).
212 Y. Xiao, 'Decoding authorship: Is there really no place for an algorithmic author under copyright law?' (2023) 54 (1) *IIC – International Review of Intellectual Property and Competition Law* 5.
213 Ole-Andreas Rognstad, 'Creations caused by humans (or Robots)? Artificial intelligence and causation requirements for copyright protection in EU law'. In *Artificial Intelligence and the Media* (Edward Elgar Publishing, 2022) 172, 174 at <www.elgaronline.com/display/edcoll/9781839109966/9781839109966.00015.xml>.
214 Ibid., 187.
215 Ibid., 190.
216 Ibid., 212
217 P. Bernt Hugenholtz & João Pedro Quintais, 'Copyright and artificial creation: Does EU copyright law protect AI-assisted output?' (2021) 52 (9) *IIC – International Review of Intellectual Property and Competition Law* 1190, 1191.
218 European Commission, 'A European approach to artificial intelligence | Shaping Europe's sigital suture' (31 May 2023) at <https://digital-strategy.ec.europa.eu/en/policies/european-approach-artificial-intelligence>.
219 Proposal for a Regulation of the European Parliament and of the Council Laying down harmonised rules on Artificial Intelligence (Artificial Intelligence Act) and amending certain Union Legislative Acts COM/2021/206 final (hereafter AI Act proposal).
220 Justine Pila, 'The authorial works protectable by copyright'. In Eleonora Rosati (ed.), *The Routledge Handbook of EU Copyright Law* (Taylor & Francis Group, 2023) 79 at <http://ebookcentral.proquest.com/lib/monash/detail.action?docID=6514334> at 71.
221 Ibid.
222 EuroGeographics, 'The European council of geodetic surveyors and geometer Europas' (2007) *European Requirements for Cadastral Surveyor Activities* 23, 4 at <www.clge.eu/wp-content/uploads/2008/04/european_requirements_for_cadastral_surveyor_activity.pdf>.
223 Atif Aziz, 'Artificial intelligence produced original work: A new approach to copyright protection and ownership' (2023) 2 (2) *European Journal of Artificial Intelligence and Machine Learning* 9, 12.
224 Ibid., 212.
225 *Copyright, Designs and Patents Act, 1988,* C 48, § 9(3) (UK).
226 Atif Aziz, 'Artificial intelligence produced original work: A new approach to copyright protection and ownership' (2023) 2 (2) *European Journal of Artificial Intelligence and Machine Learning* 9, 12.
227 Moral rights, according to the Berne Convention for the Protection of Literary and Artistic Works, are:

> Independently of the author's economic rights, and even after the transfer of the said rights, the author shall have the right to claim authorship of the work and to object to any distortion, mutilation or other modification of, or other derogatory action in relation to, the said work, which would be prejudicial to his honor or reputation.

228 Section 12(1), 81 and 89 of the Copyright, Designs and Patents Act, 1988.
229 Crowell & Moring et al., 'Study on copyright and new technologies: copyright data management and artificial intelligence' (Publications Office of the European Union, 2022) at <https://data.europa.eu/doi/10.2759/570559>.
230 Atif Aziz, 'Artificial intelligence produced original work: A new approach to copyright protection and ownership' (2023) 2(2) *European Journal of Artificial Intelligence and Machine Learning* 9, 12 ('Artificial Intelligence Produced Original Work') at 12.
231 European Commission, 'A European approach to artificial intelligence | Shaping Europe's digital future' (31 May 2023) at <https://digital-strategy.ec.europa.eu/en/policies/european-approach-artificial-intelligence>.

Proposal for a Regulation of the European Parliament and of the Council Laying down harmonised rules on Artificial Intelligence (Artificial Intelligence Act) and amending certain Union Legislative Acts COM/2021/206 final (hereafter AI Act proposal).

232 Ibid.

233 Content and Technology (European Commission) Directorate-General for Communications Networks et al., *Trends and Developments in Artificial Intelligence: Challenges to the Intellectual Property Rights Framework: Final Report* (No KK-02-20-789-EN-C, Publications Office of the European Union, 2020) at <https://data.europa.eu/doi/10.2759/458120>.

234 European Parliament resolution of 20 October 2020 on intellectual property rights for the development of artificial intelligence technologies, 2020/2015(INI).

235 Crowell & Moring et al., 'Study on copyright and new technologies: Copyright data management and artificial intelligence' (Publications Office of the European Union, 2022) at <https://data.europa.eu/doi/10.2759/570559>.

236 Ibid., 20.

237 Ibid., 151.

238 European Parliament resolution of 20 October 2020 on IP rights for the development of artificial intelligence technologies, 2020/2015(INI).[16].

239 Content and Technology (European Commission) Directorate-General for Communications Networks et al., *Trends and Developments in Artificial Intelligence: Challenges to the Intellectual Property Rights Framework: Final Report* (No KK-02-20-89-EN-C, Publications Office of the European Union, 2020) at <https://data.europa.eu/doi/10.2759/458120>.

240 Crowell & Moring et al., 'Study on copyright and new technologies: copyright data management and artificial intelligence' (Publications Office of the European Union, 2022) at https://data.europa.eu/doi/10.2759/570559.

241 European Parliament and the Council, Directive 2004/48/EC of 29 April 2004 on the enforcement of IP rights, Art. 5, (O.J. L 157, 30.04.2004).

242 European Parliament resolution of 20 October 2020 on IP rights for the development of artificial intelligence technologies, 2020/2015(INI).[10].

243 Ibid.

244 Crowell & Moring et al., 'Study on copyright and new technologies: Copyright data management and artificial intelligence' (Publications Office of the European Union, 2022) 21 at <https://data.europa.eu/doi/10.2759/570559>.

245 *Eva-Maria Painer v Standard VerlagsGmbH and Others* (Court of Justice of the European Union, C-145/10, EU:C:2011:798, 7 March 2013) [87–94].

246 P. Bernt Hugenholtz & João Pedro Quintais, 'Copyright and artificial creation: Does EU copyright law protect AI-assisted output?' (2021) 52 (9) *IIC – International Review of Intellectual Property and Competition Law* 1190, 1191.

247 Crowell & Moring et al., 'Study on copyright and new technologies: Copyright data management and artificial intelligence' (Publications Office of the European Union, 2022) 154 at <https://data.europa.eu/doi/10.2759/570559>.

248 Ibid., 149.

249 Ibid., 164.

250 Ibid., 150.

251 German Law on Copyright and Neighboring Rights, Art. 5(1) & 5(2) and the Netherlands *Copyright Act 1912*, Art. 11 & Art.15b.

252 I. Stamatoudi & P. Torremans, 'The digital single market directive'. In I. Stamatoudi & P. Torremans (eds), *EU Copyright Law* (Edward Elgar Publishing, 2021) 651–655 at <www.elgaronline.com/edcollchap/book/9781786437808/book-part-9781786437808-27.xml>.

253 Christophe Geiger, '"Fair use" through fundamental rights in Europe: When freedom of artistic expression allows creative appropriations and opens up statutory copyright limitations'. In Haochen Sun, Ng-Loy Wee Loon & Shyamkrishna Balganesh

(eds), *The Cambridge Handbook of Copyright Limitations and Exceptions* (Cambridge University Press, 2021) 174, 174 at <www.cambridge.org/core/books/cambridge-handbook-of-copyright-limitations-and-exceptions/fair-use-through-fundamental-rights-in-europe-when-freedom-of-artistic-expression-allows-creative-appropriations-and-opens-up-statutory-copyright-limitations/3826C8E04A6964923854752C136435B4>.

254 Christophe Geiger et al., 'The information society directive'. In Irini Stamatoudi & Paul Torremans (eds), *EU Copyright Law* (Edward Elgar Publishing, 2021) 279, 314 at <www.elgaronline.com/edcollchap/book/9781786437808/book-part-9781786437808-21.xml>.

255 Christophe Geiger, '"Fair use" through fundamental rights in Europe: When freedom of artistic expression allows creative appropriations and opens up statutory copyright limitations'. In Haochen Sun, Ng-Loy Wee Loon & Shyamkrishna Balganesh (eds), *The Cambridge Handbook of Copyright Limitations and Exceptions* (Cambridge University Press, 2021) 174, 174 at <www.cambridge.org/core/books/cambridge-handbook-of-copyright-limitations-and-exceptions/fair-use-through-fundamental-rights-in-europe-when-freedom-of-artistic-expression-allows-creative-appropriations-and-opens-up-statutory-copyright-limitations/3826C8E04A6964923854752C136435B4>.

256 I. Stamatoudi & P. Torremans, 'The digital single market directive'. In I. Stamatoudi & P. Torremans (eds), *EU Copyright Law* (Edward Elgar Publishing, 2021) 651–659 at <www.elgaronline.com/edcollchap/book/9781786437808/book-part-9781786437808-27.xml>.

257 Christophe Geiger, '"Fair use" through fundamental rights in Europe: When freedom of artistic expression allows creative appropriations and opens up statutory copyright limitations'. In Haochen Sun, Ng-Loy Wee Loon & Shyamkrishna Balganesh (eds), *The Cambridge Handbook of Copyright Limitations and Exceptions* (Cambridge University Press, 2021) 174, 315 at <www.cambridge.org/core/books/cambridge-handbook-of-copyright-limitations-and-exceptions/fair-use-through-fundamental-rights-in-europe-when-freedom-of-artistic-expression-allows-creative-appropriations-and-opens-up-statutory-copyright-limitations/3826C8E04A6964923854752C136435B4>; These include reprographic copying, private copying, non-profit copying by public libraries, educational establishments or museums, ephemeral copying by broadcasters, and reproductions of broadcasts made by social institutions.

258 Ibid. Article 5(3) contains:

> use for teaching and scientific purposes, uses for people with disabilities, use for reporting current events, quotations, uses for public security, use of political speeches, use during religious celebrations, use of works of architecture, incidental inclusion of a work or other subject-matter, use for advertising public exhibitions, use for caricature, parody or pastiche, use related to the demonstration or repair of equipment, use for the reconstruction of buildings, use for research or private study, and use in other cases of minor importance.

259 The DD has adopted an optional approach to the limitations related to private copy, illustration for teaching and research, and use for the purposes of public security, administrative or judicial procedure (Article 6). The Member States are given the discretion to expand the limitations based on principles from general copyright law. In relation to the *sui generis* right, is subject to three optional exceptions, in favour of private extraction in the case of non-electronic databases; extraction for teaching and research; and extraction for the purposes of public securities, administrative, or judicial procedures (Article 9).

260 The SD provides for mandatory limitations in the context of authorising decompilation for interoperability purposes (Article 6), study and testing to determine ideas

and principles underlying elements of the program (Article 5.3), and the making of a backup copy (Article 5.2). It also provides for optional limitation for uses necessary for running the software by a lawful acquirer (Article 3.1).

261 Directive (EU) 2019/790 of the European Parliament and of the Council of 17 April 2019 on copyright and related rights in the Digital Single Market and amending Directives 96/9/EC and 2001/29/EC (Text with EEA relevance.) PE/51/2019/REV/1 OJ L 130, 17.5.2019, pp. 92–125.

262 Crowell & Moring et al., 'Study on copyright and new technologies: Copyright data management and artificial intelligence' (Publications Office of the European Union, 2022) 192 at <https://data.europa.eu/doi/10.2759/570559>.

263 Ibid.

264 Ibid., 193.

265 The only provision relevant to transnational application were the Articles 10bis and 10ter of the Paris Convention (PC). Gustavo Ghidini & Giovanni Cavani, 'The relationship between the unfair competition regime and IP law'. In Ansgar Ohly et al. (eds), *Transition and Coherence in Intellectual Property Law: Essays in Honour of Annette Kur* (Cambridge University Press, 2021) 467, 468 at <www.cambridge.org/core/books/transition-and-coherence-in-intellectual-property-law/relationship-between-the-unfair-competition-regime-and-ip-law/58A997EDF87AAC009792110E33FD35B4>.

266 Ibid., 469.

267 Ansgar Ohly, 'The freedom of imitation and its limits – a European perspective' (2010) 41 (5) *International Review of Intellectual Property and Competition Law* 506, 508.

268 Debra B. Rosler, 'The European union's proposed directive for the legal protection of databases: A new threat to the free flow of information' (1995) 10 (1) *High Technology Law Journal* 105, 130.

269 Directive 2005/29/EC of the European Parliament and of the Council of 11 May 2005 concerning unfair business-to-consumer commercial practices in the internal market and amending Council Directive 84/450/EEC, Directives 97/7/EC, 98/27/EC and 2002/65/EC of the European Parliament and of the Council and Regulation (EC) No 2006/2004 of the European Parliament and of the Council ('Unfair Commercial Practices Directive') (Text with EEA relevance) OJ L 149, 11.6.2005, p. 22–39.

270 Directive 2006/114/EC of the European Parliament and of the Council of 12 December 2006 concerning misleading and comparative advertising (codified version) (Text with EEA relevance) OJ L 376, 27.12.2006, p. 21–27.

271 Ansgar Ohly, 'The freedom of imitation and its limits – a European perspective' (2010) 41 (5) *International Review of Intellectual Property and Competition Law* 506, 512.

272 *Voodoo v Rollic Games and Hero Games* (Tribunal Judiciaire De Paris, 4 September 2020) (January 4, 2021).

273 Emanuele Fava, 'Hyper-casual simulation video games may not be original enough to enjoy copyright protection but game cloning could still be prevented by relying on unfair competition: voodoo v rollic games and hero games | Westlaw UK' (2021) 43 (6) *European Intellectual Property Review* 402, 403.

274 Ibid.

275 Ibid.

276 Ibid., 407.

277 Directive (EU) 2016/943 of the European Parliament and of the Council of 8 June 2016 on the protection of undisclosed know-how and business information (trade secrets) against their unlawful acquisition, use and disclosure (Text with EEA relevance) OJ L 157, 15.6.2016, p. 1–18.

278 Tanya Aplin et al., 'The role of EU trade secrets law in the data economy: An empirical analysis' (2023) *IIC – International Review of Intellectual Property and Competition Law* 4.1.1 at <https://doi.org/10.1007/s40319-023-01325-8>.

279 Ibid., 4.1.2.
280 Ibid., 4.1.3.
281 European Commission, 'Open data | Shaping Europe's digital future' (15 February 2023) at <https://digital-strategy.ec.europa.eu/en/policies/open-data>.
282 Ibid.
283 Directive 2003/98/EC of the European Parliament and of the Council of 17 November 2003 on the re-use of public sector information OJ L 345, 31.12.2003.
284 Directive (EU) 2019/1024 of the European Parliament and of the Council of 20 June 2019 on open data and the re-use of public sector information (recast) PE/28/2019/REV/1.
285 Cristiana Sappa, 'Access and re-use of public sector information in a copyright perspective'. In Irini Stamatoudi & Paul Torremans (eds), *EU Copyright Law* (Edward Elgar Publishing, 2021) 762, 770 at <www.elgaronline.com/edcollchap/book/9781786437808/book-part-9781786437808-28.xml>. Public sector information includes documents and datasets, encompassing works of any nature such as geographical, meteorological, spatial, cadastral data, statistics, metadata, administrative documents, records, compilations, databases on corporate information and financial data, and any other information and contents.
286 Ibid.
287 'European legislation on open data | Shaping Europe's digital future' *European Commission* (15 February 2023) at <https://digital-strategy.ec.europa.eu/en/policies/legislation-open-data>.
288 Cristiana Sappa, 'Access and re-use of public sector information in a copyright perspective'. In Irini Stamatoudi & Paul Torremans (eds), *EU Copyright Law* (Edward Elgar Publishing, 2021) 762, 780 at <www.elgaronline.com/edcollchap/book/9781786437808/book-part-9781786437808-28.xml>.
289 Ibid.
290 'Blockchain strategy | Shaping Europe's digital future' *European Commission* (21 March 2023) at <https://digital-strategy.ec.europa.eu/en/policies/blockchain-strategy>.
291 Regulation (EU) 2022/858 of the European Parliament and of the Council of 30 May 2022 on a pilot regime for market infrastructures based on distributed ledger technology, and amending Regulations (EU) No 600/2014 and (EU) No 909/2014 and Directive 2014/65/EU (Text with EEA relevance).
292 European Commission, 'Blockchain strategy | Shaping Europe's digital future' (21 March 2023) at <https://digital-strategy.ec.europa.eu/en/policies/blockchain-strategy>.
293 Georgia is not an EU Member State (it is a candidate for membership) but it is the first to convert its land register to blockchain?
294 Daivi Rodima-Taylor, 'Digitalizing land administration: The geographies and temporalities of infrastructural promise' (2021) 122 *Geoforum* 140, 147.
295 Ibid.
296 Ibid., 148.
297 Ibid., 147.
298 Ibid., 146.
299 Ibid.
300 Qiuyun Shang & Allison Price, 'A blockchain-based land titling project in the republic of georgia: Rebuilding public trust and lessons for future Pilot projects' (2019) 12 (3–4) *Innovations: Technology, Governance, Globalization* 72, 76.
301 World Bank Group, *Doing Business 2016: Measuring Regulatory Quality and Efficiency* (World Bank, Washington, DC, 2016) 1, 203 at <https://openknowledge.worldbank.org/handle/10986/22771> ('*Doing Business 2016*').
302 Qiuyun Shang & Allison Price, 'A blockchain-based land titling project in the republic of georgia: Rebuilding public trust and lessons for future Pilot projects' (2019) 12 (3–4) *Innovations: Technology, Governance, Globalization* 72, 76.

303 Ibid., 77.

304 Commonwealth of Australia, *Second Interim Report of the Senate Select Committee on Australia as a Technology and Financial Centre* (text, The Senate, 28 April 2021) 1 at <www.aph.gov.au/Parliamentary_Business/Committees/Senate/Financial_Technology_and_Regulatory_Technology/FinancialRegulatoryTech/Second_Interim_Report>.

305 Ibid., 86–87.

306 Article 6(3) defines the expression 'technological measures' to mean any technology, device or component that, in the normal course of its operation, is designed to prevent or restrict acts, in respect of works or other subject matter, which are not authorised by the rights holder of any copyright or any right related to copyright as provided for by law or the *sui generis* right. The term 'effective' is defined in the same provision to mean situations in which the use of a protected work or other subject matter is controlled by the rights holders through application of an access control or protection process, such as encryption, scrambling, or other transformation of the work or other subject matter or a copy control mechanism, which achieves the protection objective.

307 Christophe Geiger et al., 'The information society directive'. In Irini Stamatoudi & Paul Torremans (eds), *EU Copyright Law* (Edward Elgar Publishing, 2021) 279, 355 at <www.elgaronline.com/edcollchap/book/9781786437808/book-part-9781786437808-21.xml>.

308 *Nintendo Co. Ltd e.a. v PC Box Srl and 9Net Srl* (Court of Justice of the European Union, Case C-355/12, ECR I-0000; EU:C:2014:25, 23 January 2014) [37].

309 The following have been identified as the three main TPMs by M.M Walter in M. Walter (ed.), *Europäisches Urheberrecht: Kommentar* (Springer, Vienna, 2001) 1068 cited in Christophe Geiger et al., 'The information society directive'. In Irini Stamatoudi & Paul Torremans (eds), *EU Copyright Law* (Edward Elgar Publishing, 2021) at <www.elgaronline.com/edcollchap/book/9781786437808/book-part-9781786437808-21.xml> at 355.: (a) those that protect access to and use of copyright works (e.g. encryption technologies, digital containers, passwords, serial numbers and copy-control devices such as CGMS and SCMS); (b) those that protect the integrity and authenticity of copyright works and devices (e.g. hash functions, digital signatures and challenge response controls); and (c) those that prevent a third party from tampering with security features (e.g. smart cards, code obfuscation, trusted computing technology and other tamper-resistant hardware and software). Even region coding systems found in commercial DVDs may also be considered anti-circumvention devices.

310 *Nintendo Co. Ltd e.a. v PC Box Srl and 9Net Srl* (Court of Justice of the European Union, Case C-355/12, ECR I-0000; EU:C:2014:25, 23 January 2014) [38]:It is for the national court to determine whether other measures or measures which are not installed in consoles could cause less interference with the activities of third parties or limitations to those activities, while still providing comparable protection of the rightsholder's rights. Accordingly, it is relevant to take account, inter alia, of the relative costs of different types of technological measures, of technological and practical aspects of their implementation, and of a comparison of the effectiveness of those different types of technological measures as regards the protection of the rightsholder's rights, that effectiveness however not having to be absolute. That court must also examine the purpose of devices, products or components, which are capable of circumventing those technological measures. In that regard, the evidence of use which third parties actually make of them will, in the light of the circumstances at issue, be particularly relevant. The national court may, in particular, examine how often those devices, products or components are in fact used in disregard of copyright and how often they are used for purposes which do not infringe copyright.

311 *UPC Telekabel Wien GmbH v Constantin Film Verleih GmbH and Wega Filmproduktionsgesellschaft mbH* (Court of Justice of the European Union, Case C-314/12, ECLI:EU:C:2014:192, 27 March 2014).

312 Eleonora Rosati, 'Circumventing technological protection measures and website blocking orders: An EU perspective' *MediaWrites* (27 November 2020) at <https://mediawrites.law/circumventing-technological-protection-measures-and-website-blocking-orders-an-eu-perspective/>.

313 *Nintendo Co Ltd v Sky UK Ltd & Ors* [2019] EWHC 2376 (Ch).

314 Chris Watson, 'Nintendo wins two court cases against piracy of nintendo switch in Spain' *FREEGAME TIPS* (19 January 2021) at <https://freegametips.com/nintendo-wins-two-court-cases-against-piracy-of-nintendo-switch-in-spain>.

315 Christophe Geiger et al., 'The information society directive'. In Irini Stamatoudi & Paul Torremans (eds), *EU Copyright Law* (Edward Elgar Publishing, 2021) 279, 361 at <www.elgaronline.com/edcollchap/book/9781786437808/book-part-9781786437808-21.xml>.

316 European Commission, 'A single market for intellectual property rights: – Boosting creativity and innovation to provide economic growth, high quality jobs and first-class products and services in Europe' (2011) *COM* 287, 11.

317 Benjamin Farrand, 'From a digital agenda for Europe', to a 'digital single market', to a 'Europe fit for the digital age', a decade of European union copyright policy in the shadow of crises'. In Irini Stamatoudi & Paul Torremans (eds), *EU Copyright Law* (Edward Elgar Publishing, 2021) 967, 982 at <www.elgaronline.com/edcollchap/book/9781786437808/book-part-9781786437808-34.xml>.

318 Agnès Lucas-Schloetter, 'Is there a concept of European'. In *Copyright Law? History, Evolution, Polices and Politics and Acquis Communautaire* (Edward Elgar Publishing, 2021) 10 at <www.elgaronline.com/display/book/9781786437808/book-part-9781786437808-10.xml>.

319 Benjamin Farrand, 'From a digital agenda for Europe', to a 'digital single market', to a 'Europe fit for the digital age', a decade of European union copyright policy in the shadow of crises'. In Irini Stamatoudi & Paul Torremans (eds), *EU Copyright Law* (Edward Elgar Publishing, 2021) 967, 982 at <www.elgaronline.com/edcollchap/book/9781786437808/book-part-9781786437808-34.xml>.

320 Ibid., 983.

321 Ibid., 985.

References

Act on Copyright and Related Rights (Copyright Act, as amended up to Act of September 1, 2017) (Germany).

Agreement on Trade-Related Aspects of Intellectual Property Rights (1869 U.N.T.S. 299).

Apis-Hristovich EOOD v Lakorda AD (Court of Justice of the European Union, Case C-545/07, ECLI:EU:C:2009:132, 5 March 2009).

Aplin, T., *et al*., 2023. The role of EU trade secrets law in the data economy: An empirical analysis. *IIC – International Review of Intellectual Property and Competition Law*, 56, 826–858. Available from: <https://doi.org/10.1007/s40319-023-01325-8>.

Aziz, A., 2023. Artificial intelligence produced original work: A new approach to copyright protection and ownership. *European Journal of Artificial Intelligence and Machine Learning*, 2 (2), 9.

Beijing Treaty on Audiovisual Performances (2012, U.N.T.S. 3376).

Berne Convention for the Protection of Literary and Artistic Works (1886, U.N.T.S. 828).

Bezpecˇnostní Ahcnostní softwarová asociace – Svaz softwarové ochrany v Ministerstvo kultury (Court of Justice of the European Union, Case C-393/09, ECR I-13971, 22 December 2010).

Bundesgerichtshof (Market Surveys) (I ZR 1/02) (2005) GRUR 940 (Germany).

Carvalho, G. and Kazim, E., 2022. Themes in data strategy: Thematic analysis of "A European Strategy for Data" (EC). *AI and Ethics*, 2 (1), 53.

Cofemel – Sociedade de Vestuário SA v G-Star Raw CV (Court of Justice of the European Union, Case C-683/17, ECLI:EU:C:2019:721, 12 September 2019).

Cofemel – Sociedade de Vestuário SA v G-Star Raw CV (Opinion of Advocate General Szpunar, Case C-683/17), ECLI:EU:C:2019:363, delivered on 2 May 2019).

Commonwealth of Australia, Second Interim Report of the Senate Select Committee on Australia as a Technology and Financial Centre (text, The Senate, 28 April 2021) 1. Available from: <www.aph.gov.au/Parliamentary_Business/Committees/Senate/Financial_Technology_and_Regulatory_Technology/FinancialRegulatoryTech/Second_Interim_Report>.

Convention for the Protection of Producers of Phonograms against Unauthorized Duplication of their Phonograms (1971, U.N.T.S. 866).

Conway, N., 2019. Why geospatial needs to listen to GDPR. *GiS Professional*, 79, 32.

Copyright, Designs and Patents Act, 1988, C 48, § 9(3) (UK).

Cory, M., n.d. EuroGeographics information paper communication from the commission on a European strategy for data. *EuroGeographics*. Available from: <https://eurogeographics.org/wp-content/uploads/2020/05/EG-response-on-ES4D-FINAL.pdf>.

Council of the European Union, n.d. Data act: Member states agree common position on fair access to and use of data. Available from: <www.consilium.europa.eu/en/press/press-releases/2023/03/24/data-act-member-states-agree-common-position-on-fair-access-to-and-use-of-data/>.

Credinfor v Artprice.com, CA Paris, 18 June 2003, Jurisdata, n. 223155.

Crowell and Moring *et al*., 2022. Study on copyright and new technologies: Copyright data management and artificial intelligence. Publications Office of the European Union. Available from: <https://data.europa.eu/doi/10.2759/570559>.

Cyber Risk GmbH, n.d. The European Data Act. Available from: https://www.eu-data-act.com/.

Davison, M., 2006. Database protection: Lessons from Europe, Congress, and WIPO law, technology and the arts symposium: The WIPO copyright treaties: 10 Years later. *Case Western Reserve Law Review,* 57 (4), 829–845.

Derclaye, E., 2021. The database directive. *In*: I. Stamatoudi and P. Torremans eds. *EU copyright law*. Edward Elgar Publishing, 216. Available from: <www.elgaronline.com/edcollchap/book/9781786437808/book-part-9781786437808-19.xml>.

Dillman, D.A., Smyth, J.D., and Christian, L.M. 2014. *Internet, phone, mail, and mixed mode surveys: The tailored design method,* 4th ed. Hoboken, NJ: John Wiley & Sons Inc.

Directorate-General for Communications Networks, Content and Technology (European Commission) *et al*., Trends and Developments in Artificial Intelligence: Challenges to the Intellectual Property Rights Framework: Final Report (No KK-02-20-789-EN-C, Publications Office of the European Union, 2020). Available from: <https://data.europa.eu/doi/10.2759/458120>.

Directive concerning misleading and comparative advertising (Codified version), 12 December 2006.

Directive concerning unfair business-to-consumer commercial practices in the internal market and amending council directive 84/450/EEC, Directives 97/7/EC, 98/27/EC and 2002/65/EC of the European Parliament and of the Council and Regulation (EC) No 2006/2004 of the European Parliament and of the Council (Unfair Commercial Practices Directive), 11 May 2005.

Directive establishing an infrastructure for spatial information in the European community (INSPIRE Directive), 14 March 2007.

Directive on certain permitted uses of certain works and other subject matter protected by copyright and related rights for the benefit of persons who are blind, visually impaired or otherwise print-disabled (Directive implementing the Marrakech Treaty in the EU), 13 September 2017.

Directive on certain permitted uses of orphan works ('Orphan Works Directive'), 25 October 2012.

Directive on collective management of copyright and related rights and multi-territorial licensing of rights in musical works for online use in the internal market ('CRM Directive'), 26 February 2014.

Directive on copyright and related rights in the digital single market ('DSM Directive'), 17 April 2019.

Directive on open data and the re-use of public sector information, 20 June 2019.

Directive on rental right and lending right and on certain rights related to copyright in the field of intellectual property ('Rental and Lending Directive'), 12 December 2006.

Directive on services in the internal market ('Service Directive'), 12 December 2006.

Directive on the coordination of certain rules concerning copyright and rights related to copyright applicable to satellite broadcasting and cable retransmission ('Satellite and Cable Directive'), 27 September 1993.

Directive on the enforcement of intellectual property right ('IPRED'), 29 April 2004.

Directive on the exercise of copyright and related rights applicable to certain online transmissions of broadcasting organisations and retransmissions of television and radio programmes ('Satellite and Cable II'), 17 April 2019.

Directive on the harmonisation of certain aspects of copyright and related rights in the information society ('InfoSoc Directive'), 22 May 2001.

Directive on the legal protection of computer programs ('Software Directive'), 23 April 2009.

Directive on the legal protection of databases ('Database Directive'), 11 March 1996.

Directive on the protection of undisclosed know-how and business information (trade secrets) against their unlawful acquisition, use, and disclosure, 8 June 2016.

Directive on the recognition of professional qualifications ('Free Movement of Professionals'), 7 September 2005.

Directive on the resale right for the benefit of the author of an original work of art ('Resale Right Directive'), 27 September 2001.

Directive on the term of protection of copyright and certain related rights amending the previous 2006 directive ('Term Directive'), 27 September 2011.

Directmedia Publishing v Albert-Ludwigs-Universität Freiburg (Court of Justice of the European Union, C-304/07, ECLI:EU:C:2008:552, 9 October 2008).

Directorate-General for Communications Networks, Content and Technology (European Commission) *et al.*, Trends and developments in artificial intelligence: Challenges to the intellectual property rights framework: Final report (No KK-02-20-789-EN-C, Publications Office of the European Union, 2020). Available from: <https://data.europa.eu/doi/10.2759/458120>.

Dreier, T. and Hugenholtz, P.B., 2016. *Concise European copyright law*. Alphen aan den Rijn, The Netherlands: Kluwer Law International B.V.

Esri, n.d. European cadastres and national mapping agencies. *ArcNews Online*. Available from: <www.esri.com/news/arcnews/spring11articles/european-cadastres-and-national-mapping-agencies.html>.

EuroGeographics, n.d.-a. About us. Available from: <https://eurogeographics.org/about-us/>.

EuroGeographics, n.d.-b. EuroGeographics briefing paper evaluation of the database directive 96/9/EC. Available from: <https://eurogeographics.org/wp-content/uploads/2018/04/2017-EG-Briefing-Paper-Evaluation-of-the-Database-Directive-969EC.pdf>.

EuroGeographics, n.d.-c. Status and adopted innovations over the last decade in cadastre and land administration in Europe. Available from: <https://eurogeographics.org/wp-content/uploads/2021/04/210512-SummaryReport-PCC-Questionnaire.pdf>.

EuroGeographics, The European Council of Geodetic Surveyors and AZIZ Europas, 2007. European requirements for cadastral surveyor activities, 23. Available from: <www.clge.eu/wp-content/uploads/2008/04/european_requirements_for_cadastral_surveyor_activity.pdf>.

European Commission, 2011. A single market for intellectual property rights: – Boosting creativity and innovation to provide economic growth, high quality jobs and first-class products and services in Europe. *COM,* 287, 11.

European Commission, 2023a. A European approach to artificial intelligence. *Shaping Europe's Digital Future*, 31 May 2023. Available from: <https://digital-strategy.ec.europa.eu/en/policies/european-approach-artificial-intelligence>.

European Commission, 2023b. A European strategy for data. *Shaping Europe's Digital Future*, 16 May 2023. Available from: <https://digital-strategy.ec.europa.eu/en/policies/strategy-data>.

European Commission, 2023c. Blockchain strategy. *Shaping Europe's Digital Future*, 21 March 2023. Available from: <https://digital-strategy.ec.europa.eu/en/policies/blockchain-strategy>.

European Commission, 2023d. Data act. *Shaping Europe's Digital Future*, 16 May 2023. Available from: <https://digital-strategy.ec.europa.eu/en/policies/data-act>.

European Commission, 2023e. European data governance act. *Shaping Europe's Digital Future*, 16 May 2023. Available from: <https://digital-strategy.ec.europa.eu/en/policies/data-governance-act>.

European Commission, 2023f. European legislation on open data. *Shaping Europe's Digital Future*, 15 February 2023. Available from: <https://digital-strategy.ec.europa.eu/en/policies/legislation-open-data>.

European Commission, 2023g. INSPIRE directive. *INSPIRE Knowledge Base*, 5 May 2023. Available from: <https://inspire.ec.europa.eu/inspire-directive/2>.

European Commission, 2023h. Open data. *Shaping Europe's Dzigital Future*, 15 February 2023. Available from: <https://digital-strategy.ec.europa.eu/en/policies/open-data>.

European Commission, n.d.-a. A European strategy for data. Avilable from: <https://eur-lex.europa.eu/legal-content/EN/TXT/PDF/?uri=CELEX:52020DC0066>.

European Commission, n.d.-b. Europe's digital decade: Digital targets for 2030. Available from: <https://commission.europa.eu/strategy-and-policy/priorities-2019-2024/europe-fit-digital-age/europes-digital-decade-digital-targets-2030_en>

European Commission, n.d.-c. Proposal for a regulation of the European Parliament and of the council laying down harmonised rules on artificial intelligence (Artificial Intelligence Act) and Amending Certain Union Legislative Acts COM/2021/206 final'. Available from: <https://eur-lex.europa.eu/legal-content/EN/TXT/?uri=celex%3A52021PC0206>.

European Commission. Explanatory memorandum of the proposal for a regulation of the European Parliament and of the Council on harmonised rules on fair access to and use of data (Data Act) COM/2022/68 final. Available from: <https://eur-lex.europa.eu/legal-content/EN/TXT/?uri=COM%3A2022%3A68%3AFIN>.

European Commission, Directorate General for Communications Networks, Content and Technology, Maier, N., *et al*, 2022. *Study to support an impact assessment for the review of the database directive: Final report*. Publications Office. Available from: <https://data.europa.eu/doi/10.2759/647387>.

European Land Registry Association, 'Home'. Available from: <www.elra.eu/>.

European Parliament, 'European Parliament resolution of 20 October 2020 on intellectual property rights for the development of artificial intelligence technologies, 2020/2015(INI)'. Available from: <www.europarl.europa.eu/doceo/document/TA-9-2020-0277_EN.html>.

Eva-Maria Painer v Standard VerlagsGmbH and Others (Court of Justice of the European Union, C-145/10, EU:C:2011:798, 7 March 2013).

Farrand, B., 2021. From a "Digital agenda for Europe", to a "Digital single market", to a "Europe fit for the digital age", a decade of European union copyright policy in the shadow of crises. *In*: I. Stamatoudi and P. Torremans eds. *EU Copyright Law*. Edward Elgar Publishing, 967. Available from: <www.elgaronline.com/edcollchap/book/9781786437808/book-part-9781786437808-34.xml>.

Fava, E., 2021. Hyper-casual simulation video games may not be original enough to enjoy copyright protection but game cloning could still be prevented by relying on unfair competition: Voodoo v Rollic games and hero games. *European Intellectual Property Review*, 43 (6), 402.

Fixtures Marketing Ltd v AB Svenska Spel (Court of Justice of the European Union, Case C-338/02, ECLI:EU:C:2004:696, 9 November 2004).

Fixtures Marketing Ltd v Organismos Prognostikon Agonon Podosfairou (OPAP) (Court of Justice of the European Union, Case C-444/02, ECLI:EU:C:2004:697, 9 November 2004).

Fixtures Marketing Ltd v Oy Veikkaus AB (Court of Justice of the European Union, Case Case C-46/02, ECLI:EU:C:2004:694, 9 November 2004).

Football Association Premier League Ltd and Others v QC Leisure and Others and Karen Murphy v Media Protection Services Ltd (Court of Justice of the European Union, C-403/08 and C-429/08, ECLI:EU:C:2011:63, 4 October 201).

Football Dataco Ltd and Others v Yahoo! UK Ltd and Others (Court of Justice of the European Union, Case C-604/10, EU:C:2012:115, 1 March 2012).

Freistaat Bayern v Verlag Esterbauer GmbH (Court of Justice of the European Union, Case C-490/14, ECLI:EU:C:2015:735, 29 October 2015).

Funke Medien NRW GmbH v. Bundesrepublik Deutschland (Court of Justice of the European Union, Case C–469/17, ECLI:EU:C:2019:623, 29 July 2019)

GDPR Working Group, 2019. Nordic GDPR working group report. Available from: <https://norden.lmi.is/wp-content/uploads/2019/08/Nordic-GDPR-working-group-Report.pdf>.

Geiger, C., 2021. Fair use through fundamental rights in Europe: When freedom of artistic expression allows creative appropriations and opens up statutory copyright limitations. *In:* H. Sun, N.-G. Wee Loon, and S. Balganesh eds. *The Cambridge handbook of copyright limitations and exceptions*. Cambridge University Press. Available from: <www.cambridge.org/core/books/cambridge-handbook-of-copyright-limitations-and-exceptions/fair-use-through-fundamental-rights-in-europe-when-freedom-of-artistic-expression-allows-creative-appropriations-and-opens-up-statutory-copyright-limitations/3826C8E04A6964923854752C136435B4>.

Geiger, C., *et al*, 2021. The information society directive. *In*: I. Stamatoudi and P. Torremans eds. *EU copyright law*. Edward Elgar Publishing, 279. Available from: <www.elgaronline.com/edcollchap/book/9781786437808/book-part-9781786437808-21.xml>.

Ghidini, G. and Cavani, G., 2021. The relationship between the unfair competition regime and IP Law. *In:* A. Ohly *et al.* eds. *Transition and coherence in intellectual property law: Essays in honour of Annette Kur*. Cambridge University Press, 467. Available from: <www.cambridge.org/core/books/transition-and-coherence-in-intellectual-property-law/relationship-between-the-unfair-competition-regime-and-ip-law/58A997EDF87AAC009792110E33FD35B4>.

Hugenholtz, P.B. and Quintais, J.P., 2021. Copyright and artificial creation: Does EU copyright law protect AI-assisted output?. *IIC – International Review of Intellectual Property and Competition Law*, 52 (9), 1190.

Infopaq International A/S v. Danske Dagblades Forening (Court of Justice of the European Union, Case C-5/08, ECLI:EU:C:2009:465, 16 July 2009).

Innoweb BV v. Wegener ICT Media BV, Wegener Mediaventions BV (Court of Justice of the European Union, Case C-202/12, ECLI:EU:C:2013:850, 19 December 2013).

International Convention for the Protection of Performers, Producers of Phonograms and Broadcasting Organisations (1961, U.N.T.S. 496).

Janssen, K. and Dumortier, J., 2006. The protection of maps and spatial databases in europe and the United States by copyright and the Sui Generis Right. *UIC John Marshall Journal of Information Technology and Privacy Law,* 24 (2), 195.

Janssens, M., 2021. The software directive. *In*: I. Stamatoudi and P. Torremans eds. *EU copyright law*. Edward Elgar Publishing, 75. Available from: <www.elgaronline.com/edcollchap/book/9781786437808/book-part-9781786437808-15.xml>.

König, P.D., 2022. Fortress Europe 4.0? An analysis of EU data governance through the lens of the resource regime concept. *European Policy Analysis*, 8 (4), 484.

Levin, M., 2023. Chapter 5: The cofemel revolution – Originality, equality and neutrality. *In*: E. Rosati ed. *The Routledge handbook of EU copyright law*. Taylor & Francis Group, 82. Available from: <http://ebookcentral.proquest.com/lib/monash/detail.action?docID=6514334>.

Levola Hengelo BV v. Smilde Foods BV Deutschland (Court of Justice of the European Union, Case C– 310/17, ECLI:EU:C:2018:899, 13 November 2018).

Lucas-Schloetter, A., 2021. *Is there a concept of european copyright law? history, evolution, policies and politics and the acquis communautaire*. Edward Elgar Publishing. Available from: <www.elgaronline.com/display/book/9781786437808/book-part-9781786437808-10.xml>.

Marrakesh treaty to facilitate access to published works for persons who are blind, visually impaired or otherwise print disabled (2013, WIPO Lex No. TRT/MARRAKESH/001).

McCutcheon, J., 2019. *The concept of the copyright work under EU Law: More than a matter of taste* (No 3428844, SSRN, 30 July 2019). Available from: <https://papers.ssrn.com/sol3/papers.cfm?abstract_id=3428844>.

Moreno, F.R., 2020. Upload filters and human rights: Implementing article 17 of the directive on copyright in the digital single market. *International Review of Law, Computers & Technology*, 34 (2), 153.

Nintendo Co. Ltd e.a. v PC Box Srl and 9Net Srl (Court of Justice of the European Union, Case C-355/12, ECR I-0000; EU:C:2014:25, 23 January 2014).

Nintendo Co Ltd v Sky UK Ltd & Ors [2019] EWHC 2376 (Ch).

Ohly, A., 2010. The freedom of imitation and its limits – A European perspective. *International Review of Intellectual Property and Competition Law*, 41 (5), 506.

Permanent Committee on Cadastre in the European Union, 'About Us'. Available from: <www.eurocadastre.org/aboutus.html>.

Pila, J., The authorial works protectable by copyright. *In*: E. Rosati ed. *The Routledge handbook of EU copyright law*. Taylor & Francis Group. Available from: <http://ebookcentral.proquest.com/lib/monash/detail.action?docID=6514334>.

Précom, Ouest France Multimedia v Direct Annonces, Court of Cassation (Cass.), 1st civ., 5 March 2009.

Priora, G., 2019. Copyright law and the promotion of scientific networks: Some reflections on the rules on co-authorship in the EU. *Queen Mary Journal of Intellectual Property*, 9 (2), 217.

Regulation on a pilot regime for market infrastructures based on distributed ledger technology, and amending regulations, 30 May 2022.

Regulation on the cross-border exchange between the union and third countries of accessible format copies of certain works and other subject matter protected by copyright and related rights for the benefit of persons who are blind, visually impaired or otherwise print-disabled ('Regulation implementing the Marrakech Treaty in the EU'), 13 September 2017.

Regulation on cross-border portability of online content services in the internal market ('Portability Regulation'), 14 June 2017.

Regulation on European data governance and amending regulation, 30 May 2022.

Regulation on the protection of natural persons with regard to the processing of personal data and on the free movement of such data, and repealing directive 95/46/EC ('General Data Protection Regulation'), 27 April 2016.

Reichman, J. and Samuelson, P., 1997. Intellectual property rights in data? *Vanderbilt Law Review*, 50.

Rodima-Taylor, D., 2021. Digitalizing land administration: The geographies and temporalities of infrastructural promise. *Geoforum*, 122, 140.

Rognstad, O., 2022. Creations caused by humans (or Robots)? Artificial intelligence and causation requirements for copyright protection in EU law. *In*: T. Pihlajarinne and Alén-Savikko eds. *Artificial intelligence and the media*. Edward Elgar Publishing, 172. Available from: <www.elgaronline.com/display/edcoll/9781839109966/9781839109966.00015.xml>.

Rosati, E., 2014. *Closed subject-matter systems are no longer compatible with EU copyright* (SSRN Scholarly Paper No 2468104, 18 July 2014). Available from: <https://papers.ssrn.com/abstract=2468104>.

Rosati, E., 2019. CJEU rules that copyright protection for designs only requires sufficient originality. *Journal of Intellectual Property Law & Practice*, 14 (12), 931.

Rosati, E., 2020. Circumventing technological protection measures and website blocking orders: An EU perspective. *MediaWrites*, 27 November 2020. Available from: <https://mediawrites.law/circumventing-technological-protection-measures-and-website-blocking-orders-an-eu-perspective/>.

Rosati, E., 2023a. 30 Years of EU copyright law. *In*: *The Routledge handbook of EU copyright law*. Taylor & Francis Group. Available from: <http://ebookcentral.proquest.com/lib/monash/detail.action?docID=6514334>.

Rosati, E., 2023b. Copyright at the CJEU: Back to the start (of copyright protection). *In:* E. Rosati ed. *Developments and directions in intellectual property law. 20 years of the IPKat*. Oxford: Oxford University Press.

Rosler, D.B., 1995. The European Union's proposed directive for the legal protection of databases: A new threat to the free flow of information. *High Technology Law Journal*, 10 (1), 105.

Ryanair v Atrapalo Case STS 572/2012, 9 October 2012.

Sappa, C., 2021. Access and re-use of public sector information in a copyright perspective. *In*: I. Stamatoudi and P. Torremans eds. *EU copyright law*. Edward Elgar Publishing, 762. Available from: <www.elgaronline.com/edcollchap/book/9781786437808/book-part-9781786437808-28.xml>.

SAS Institute Inc. v. World Programming Ltd Case (Court of Justice of the European Union, C-406/10 ECLI:EU:C:2012:259, 2 May 2012).

Scerri, S., *et al*., 2022. Common European data spaces: Challenges and opportunities. *In*: E. Edward Curry, S. Scerri and T. Tuikka eds. *Data spaces: Design, deployment and future directions*. Springer International Publishing. Available from: <https://doi.org/10.1007/978-3-030-98636-0_16>.

Shang, Q. and Price, A., 2019. A blockchain-based land titling project in the Republic of Georgia: Rebuilding public trust and lessons for future pilot projects. *Innovations: Technology, Governance, Globalization*, 12 (3–4), 72.

Smith, S., 1997. Legal protection of factual compilations and databases in England: How will the database directive change the law in this area? *Intellectual Property Quarterly*, 450.

Stamatoudi, I. and Torremans, P., 2021. The digital single market directive. *In*: I. Stamatoudi and P. Torremans eds. *EU copyright law*. Edward Elgar Publishing, 651. Available from: <www.elgaronline.com/edcollchap/book/9781786437808/book-part-9781786437808-27.xml>.

Streinz, T., 2021. The evolution of European data law. *In*: P. Craig and G. de Búrca eds. *The evolution of EU law*. Oxford University Press. Available from: <https://doi.org/10.1093/oso/9780192846556.003.0029>.

The British Horseracing Board Ltd and Others v William Hill Organization Ltd. (Court of Justice of the European Union, Case C-203/02, ECLI:EU:C:2004:695, 9 November 2004).

The Dutch Copyright Act (Auteurswet) 1912.

The European Council of Geodetic Surveyors, European Requirements for Cadastral Surveyor activities_Revision of 2018 (2018) 86. Available from: <www.clge.eu/wp-content/uploads/2019/04/cadastral_surveyor_requirement_rev2018.pdf>.

UPC Telekabel Wien GmbH v Constantin Film Verleih GmbH and Wega Filmproduktionsgesellschaft mbH (Court of Justice of the European Union, Case C-314/12, ECLI:EU:C:2014:192, 27 March 2014).

UsedSoft v Oracle International (Court of Justice of the European Union, Case C-128/11, ECLI:EU:C:2012:407, 3 July 2012).

Valles, R.C., 2009. The requirement of originality. *In:* E. Derclaye ed. *Research handbook on the future of EU copyright*. Edward Elgar Publishing Limited, 102. Available from: <http://ebookcentral.proquest.com/lib/monash/detail.action?docID=420703>.

Voodoo v Rollic Games and Hero Games (Tribunal Judiciaire De Paris, 4. September 2020) (4 January 2021).

Watson, C., 2021. Nintendo wins two court cases against piracy of Nintendo switch in Spain. *FREEGAME TIPS*, 19 January 2021. Available from: <https://freegametips.com/nintendo-wins-two-court-cases-against-piracy-of-nintendo-switch-in-spain>.

Wegener v Hunter Select, CA Leeuwarden, 27 November 2002. Available from: <www.rechtspraak.nl>.

Williamson, I.P., 1985. Cadastres and land information systems in common law jurisdictions. *Survey Review*, 28 (217)114.

WIPO Copyright Treaty (WCT) (1996, U.N.T.S. 2186).

WIPO Performances and Phonograms Treaty (1996, U.N.T.S. 2186).

Wolford, B., 2018. What is GDPR, the EU's new data protection law?. *GDPR.eu*, 7 November 2018. Available from: <https://gdpr.eu/what-is-gdpr/>.

World Bank Group, 2016. *Doing business 2016: Measuring regulatory quality and efficiency*. Washington, DC: World Bank, 1. Available from: <https://openknowledge.worldbank.org/handle/10986/22771>.

World Geospatial Industry Council, n.d. Geospatial information and privacy: Policy perspectives and imperatives for the geospatial industry. Available from: <https://wgicouncil.org/wp-content/uploads/2020/03/Geospatial-Informaion-and-Privacy-report-Final.pdf>.

Xiao, Y., 2023. Decoding authorship: Is there really no place for an algorithmic author under copyright law? *IIC – International Review of Intellectual Property and Competition Law*, 54 (1), 5.

Zwirowicz-Rutkowska, A., 2016. Evaluating spatial data infrastructure as a data source for land surveying. *Journal of Surveying Engineering*, 142 (4). Available from: <https://ascelibrary.org/doi/10.1061/%28ASCE%29SU.1943-5428.0000185>.

5 Conclusion

5.1 Introduction

From building the pyramids in ancient Egypt to modern-day land management and administration, surveyors have been essential to civilisation for thousands of years. Although the role of surveyors has evolved over the years, surveyors and the products they generate function as providers of vital information around which society is primarily organised. Their intellectual efforts and creative skills in this process need protection, and copyright is one of the primary methods by which protection can be granted. In view of the technological advancements and – most significantly – the incipient adoption of artificial intelligence (AI) in the surveying industry, this book critically examines the copyright protection granted to spatial products and data in Australia, the United States of America (USA), and the European Union (EU) by analysing the relevant legislation, case law, and policies. The analysis of how copyright law is applied to spatial products and data in these three jurisdictions indicates that while the copyright regime has the ability to offer protection to spatial products and data, emerging technologies make it difficult for such protection to take effect in practice. This chapter summarises and synthesises the findings of this book, offering recommendations to provide much-needed clarity on some of the grey areas concerning the copyright protection of spatial products and data.

5.2 Summary of the findings: consistencies and divergences

Historically, the three jurisdictions under study have considered traditional maps as 'artistic', 'pictorial, graphic, and sculptural', and/or 'literary' work which have obtained protection under copyright law as a **subject matter**. However, the increased use of digital maps – especially those that are dynamic in nature – has questioned this straightforward application of copyright principles. In Australia, whether a digital map constitutes an artistic or literary work is a complex legal issue which varies depending on the specific facts and circumstances of each case, such as the level of creativity involved in its creation, the purpose for which it was created, features of the map, and the extent to which it is original.[1] In the USA, even if a map is considered to fall within the category of 'pictorial, graphic, and

DOI: 10.4324/9781003479383-5

sculptural works,' some elements in the map would not receive copyright protection. The protection for survey plans in the USA has also been considered under the category of 'compilations'.[2] In the EU, the open-ended subject matter categorisation allows spatial products, including digital maps, to be protected as literary and artistic works under EU copyright principles.[3]

What constitutes **material form** in cadastral survey plans is an important consideration in all three jurisdictions. In Australia, the material form requirement of copyright law could be satisfied by the work being drawn on paper, saved as a digital file, or photographed. Digital maps pose a challenge, however, given their dynamic nature. In Australia, digital maps and spatial data in dynamic form are considered as lasting for too short a time to be truly perceived. Because of their short span, the courts might fail to find a fixation on digital maps and spatial data with dynamic form because they would not meet the storage requirement to be considered as material form. This book recognises that spatial databases can include fixed datasets. These usually represent historical data and could be thus considered as being fixed in a sufficiently permanent medium to satisfy the storage criteria for material form. Chapter 2 reveals the difficulty that might arise with dynamic maps such as Google Maps that are subject to constant change, thereby challenging the ability to recognise material form, particularly with works that are constantly updated.[4] In the USA, spatial products expressed using paper or digital files satisfy the fixation requirement under U.S. copyright law.[5] Chapter 3 notes that dynamic digital maps could be considered as fixed as long as the display is for a non-transitory duration. In the EU, this requirement could be satisfied if the spatial products are identifiable with sufficient precision and objectivity. Given the absence of permanency as a requirement, copyright protection would be available in the EU, regardless of whether spatial products are static or dynamic.[6]

The **originality** requirement in all three jurisdictions has been subject to significant changes with the expansion of possible authors from human to AI. In Australia, design plans, subdivision plans, reports, letters, opinions, and field notes would be protected by copyright law if they are an author's original creation. Originality would accrue if the author of the work in question has employed nominal skill, labour, and intellectual effort in creating the work, regardless of whether it could be considered a 'compilation'. Australia has not accepted the industrious collection test, which states that copyright could subsist in a factual compilation on the basis of the labour undertaken or expense incurred.

With issues raised regarding the originality of the AI-created spatial products and maps, two important aspects are required to be discussed: the originality that could be attributed to the AI and the impact of the same on the originality that is required to be proven by the surveyors involved in the work. The first aspect was discussed in detail under the element of authorship. The decision of *Acohs Pty Ltd v Ucorp Pty Ltd*[7] indicated a general trend towards the lack of recognition granted to human actors for creating materials generated by automated processes. Since an AI fails to fall within the purview of 'human author', its inability to claim originality would create a vacuum in which the spatial products generated by automated processes may not have sufficient originality to satisfy copyright requirements. In terms of spatial products that surveyors create by selection and arrangement, the selector needs the ability to control the work's output and determine the nature of the final product to claim originality in such work. Concerning spatial workflows, this means that copyright would exist in the arrangement of the instructions (spatial workflow) itself, but not necessarily its output. The spatial workflow could be thus protected as a computer program. Third parties would be liable for copyright infringement if they consciously copied the code or instructions. The ability to control the output is one of the important aspects when determining the originality of satellite or uncrewed aerial vehicle (UAV) photography, even those subject to a high level of automation. The surveyor's ability to set the parameters at the time of making the photographs, by way of pre-shoot choices and rendition requirements, along with their post-production creative choices and ability to determine the outcome, mean that they could claim originality in such situations.[8] In the USA, the decision of *Feist Publications, Inc. v Rural Telephone Service Co.* (*Feist*) has greatly influenced the originality requirement.[9] Under current U.S. copyright principles, the originality requirement could be satisfied by the establishment of independent creation and creativity. The originality of maps as compilations would thus be satisfied only if the selection, coordination, and arrangement of the facts being depicted show a minimum degree of creativity.[10] In the EU, the concept of originality indicates the compromise the civil law and common law systems reached regarding the threshold of originality for copyright protection. The EU's copyright principles are premised on the principle of the author's own intellectual creation. The originality requirement identifies free and creative choices, as well as the need for a personal touch, as fundamental aspects of the application of the originality principle to spatial products and data.[11]

The **authorship** of spatial products and data has been subject to significant challenges in recent years due to the increased use of AI in generating and using spatial data. Australia only attributes copyright to works created by a human author. The Australian legislation contains no specific provisions addressing the effect of using computerised or digital technologies when creating materials that fall within the scope of protected works and other subject matter protected under the copyright regime.[12] In the USA, a human act is required to satisfy the authorship requirement. Recent U.S. Copyright Office decisions indicate that copyright authorship will not be granted to autonomous AI-generated works.[13] The EU's emphasis on authors' rights also recognises the importance of human acts. So far, the EU's approach has been to grant authorship to human actors only. The increased use of AI-assisted and AI-generated works, however, has led the EU to recognise the need to reassess authorship rules in light of technological developments.[14]

The use of AI when generating spatial products has resulted in copyright **ownership** issues; the definition of copyright may have to be expanded to include non-human authors as copyright owners. In Australia, copyright ownership of spatial data and products produced by the surveyor would be with the surveyors, and the state does not have an implied licence. While the state has a statutory defence against the infringement of this right against surveyors, which it uses for public service, such use could not be done without proper remuneration.[15] Chapter 3 notes that copyright ownership in the USA resides with the author of the work, and in the absence of the Crown copyright concept, surveyors could protect the copyright in their spatial products, even if copies are placed in public files.[16] Regarding copyright infringement in the USA, government use has not been recognised as a statutory defence. This book has noted how authorship and ownership are closely related in the EU, and that copyright principles assume that the author of a work has the copyright ownership.[17] The EU recognises the state infringement of copyright and specific defences regarding such infringements.

This book discusses the concept of the '**fair dealings defence**' primarily in relation to Australia. In Australia, 'fair use' (research or study) and 'fair dealing' (criticism, review, parody, satire, or reporting news) provide for a wide range of instances in which this defence could be claimed. Chapter 2 discusses the application of this principle regarding surveyors, specifically in the context of data and text mining. Currently, such aspects in Australia would be addressed largely by way of licensing and data sharing agreements.[18] In the USA, when copyright holders attempt to exert control outside the rightful scope of copyright and engage in anti-competitive conduct, the Court has been willing to accept fair use. The fair use defence would thus permit any person to use survey plans and spatial data, as long as such use is within the four factors identified in the U.S. statutory provisions.[19] Chapter 4 notes that the fair use defence, as understood in the Australian and U.S. contexts, does not exist in the EU copyright regime. Instead, the European approach has been to introduce an exhaustive list of specific exceptions and limitations.[20]

The regulatory developments in Australia, the USA, and the EU regarding **open data** sharing have significant implications for the copyright of spatial data. Thus far, the Australian data protection strategies have focused on data owned by the Australian governments (both state and federal). However, the relationship between the government's data strategy and privately owned data is yet to be defined. It remains unclear how the government would gain access to privately owned data. Given that the current exceptions under Australian law would not be extended to data or text mining, this book noted that a more comprehensive framework for the availability of geospatial data under open data–sharing schemes would need to be developed.[21] U.S. federal government initiatives towards open data sharing have resulted in creating one-stop platforms for obtaining geospatial data owned by the federal government without any restrictions. While this free access is available for federal government–owned data, however, access to copyright protected data on the platform is only made available subject to restrictions.[22] Chapter 4 discusses the Open Data Directive in the EU, which covers public sector information including spatial and cadastral data in any format, such as print, digital, or electronic media.[23] The European data strategy, Data Governance Act/Data Act (General Data Protection Regulation, or GDPR), and the interaction between these measures and copyright principles highlight that geospatial data could be regarded as personal data in certain circumstances. Chapter 4 also discusses the interaction between open data initiatives and the GDPR's requirements, and the challenge of the possible contradiction between the principles of the GDPR and Article 17 of the Directive on Copyright in the Digital Single Market.[24]

This book discusses the use of **blockchain and decentralised ledgers** regarding spatial data and products, identifying that they could provide advantages and disadvantages to the protection of spatial products and data.[25] Furthermore, it recognises the interaction between **technological protection measures** (TPMs) and copyright, and how these may offer an alternative means of protection for spatial products and data.[26]

This book investigates unfair competition law provisions and trade secrets law to explore alternative protection measures for spatial products and data. Regarding trade secret law in Australia, it would be possible to seek protection under the confidential information regime. However, the government's mandatory disclosure requirement for spatial data would affect the element of secrecy – and thereby the ability to seek protection under trade secrets provisions.[27] In the USA, alternative means of protection have been subject to the principles of pre-emption, in which any state law dealing with works that fall within the subject matter of copyright and equivalent rights would be pre-empted.[28] Because the EU is yet to harmonise the law relating to unfair competition, Chapter 4 notes that alternative methods to protect spatial products and data can only be adopted in some EU countries.[29]

In the context of **raw spatial data and databases** containing the same, while the raw spatial data would not be considered as subject matter for copyright purposes, the databases containing raw spatial data could be considered as copyrightable subject matter in certain circumstances. Chapter 2 and Chapter 3 note that Australia and the USA do not have *sui generis* protection for spatial database contents.[30] Database protection has thus been sought broadly through contract law and licensing regimes. A *sui generis* protection provides an opportunity to overcome many of the difficulties discussed in this book regarding technological developments. The experience and evaluation of the *sui generis* right's application in the EU, however, has indicated that while it may provide the data with some additional protection than what is already provided under copyright, the new data initiatives have been a significant challenge. The *sui generis* right in the EU has been subject to severe limitations in view of the emerging data protection laws.[31]

The comparative exercise carried out in this book indicates that, while traditional maps have been protected under the copyright regime, new technological developments have challenged the status quo and clarity is needed regarding the protection of spatial data through judicial pronouncements and legislative interventions. Therefore, the next section will look into possible policy recommendations that may be implemented to address some of the challenges identified in this book.

5.3 Protection of spatial products and data: a way forward

5.3.1 Liberalise the definition of 'originality' to include original compilations, arrangements, and creative selection of spatial data

To address the limitations currently experienced as to the element of 'originality', the definition of 'originality' should be liberalised to include original compilations, arrangements, and creative selection of spatial data. Surveyors' original compilations, arrangements, and creative selection of spatial data require a high level of expertise to meet the accuracy/precision requirements for their specific tasks. Even with the status quo on the technological advancement of data collection equipment (e.g., robotic total stations, LiDAR [light detection and ranging technology], and drones), the surveyor's judgement and expertise are crucial, necessitating that originality should apply to these circumstances.

5.3.2 Adopt sui generis *protection for spatial data*

With the increasing use and popularity of digital spatial models (e.g., digital maps and digital twins), the need for surveyors to collect spatial data is soaring. Spatial products involve substantial investments of time, expertise, and financial resources to generate outputs of material value. *Sui generis* protection would grant the surveyors of spatial products exclusive rights, allowing them to control the extraction, use, and commercial exploitation of their spatial data/databases.

5.3.3 Mandatory metadata standards that require spatial data sources should be properly attributed and identified

The relevant organisations must coordinate a comprehensive framework to introduce mandatory metadata standards, which require spatial data sources to be properly attributed and identified. This would ensure that the original creators of spatial data are acknowledged and would facilitate the data's traceability and compliance with copyright requirements.

5.3.4 Explore alternative means of protection for spatial products and data

At present, surveyors largely rely on copyright to protect their products. Unfair competition law can be a valuable tool in protecting spatial data against unfair practices and unlawful use by third parties. This can include the unlawful acquisition, copying, or exploitation of valuable data assets, such as survey databases, trade secrets, or proprietary algorithms. It can also address the unauthorised 'scraping' or extraction of data from survey work. Having dual arguments for why it is unconscionable for other players to profit from the work of data creators strengthens surveyors' positions. Furthermore, TPMs – such as encryption or access control mechanisms – can help to prevent unauthorised access, copying, or alteration of spatial data, enhancing the protection of surveyors' rights.

5.4 Concluding remarks

The findings presented in this book have significant implications for surveyors and other professionals who are interested in creating spatial data. The high level of skill and experience required to create spatial data, as well as the time and effort invested, require that spatial products is provided with adequate protection, given its significance in the broader socioeconomic context.

While the uncertainties created by new technological developments are going to be commonplace, these uncertainties will have a significant impact on how data is created, verified, and used. They will have a significant impact as surveyors and other professionals look forward to other protection mechanisms, including contract law, to protect their rights regarding spatial data. With countries' aspiring visions for the digital economy, the value of spatial data necessitates replacing the present scattered regulatory approach with a more coherent and futuristic regulatory governance mechanism. Going forward, it is important to ensure that copyright elements are expanded to include new technological developments and that spatial data and products fall within copyright protection.

Notes

1 See: Chapter 2, Section 2.1.
2 See: Chapter 3, Section 3.2.
3 See: Chapter 4, Section 4.8.
4 See: Chapter 2, Section 2.3.
5 See: Chapter 3, Section 3.4.
6 See: Chapter 4, Section 4.9.
7 (2021) 201 FCR 173.
8 See: Chapter 2, Section 2.4.
9 499 U.S. 340 (1991).
10 See: Chapter 3, Section 3.5.
11 See: Chapter 4, Section 4.10.
12 See: Chapter 2, Section 2.4.
13 See: Chapter 3, Section 3.6.
14 See: Chapter 4, Section 4.11.
15 See: Chapter 2, Section 2.5.
16 See: Chapter 3, Section 3.7.
17 See: Chapter 4, Section 4.12.
18 See: Chapter 2, Section 2.8.
19 See: Chapter 3, Section 3.10.
20 See: Chapter 4, Section 4.16.
21 See: Chapter 2, Section 2.7.
22 See: Chapter 3, Section 3.9.
23 See: Chapter 4, Section 4.19.
24 Ibid.
25 See: Chapter 2, Section 2.11, Chapter 3, Section 3.13, and Chapter 4, Section 4.20.
26 See: Chapter 2, Section 2.12, Chapter 3, Section 3.14, and Chapter 4, Section 4.21.
27 See: Chapter 2, Sections 2.9–2.10, Chapter 3, Sections 3.11–3.12, and Chapter 4, Sections 4.17–4.18.

28 See: Chapter 3, Sections 3.11–3.12.
29 See: Chapter 4, Sections 4.17–4.18.
30 See: Chapter 2, Section 2.13, and Chapter 3, Section 3.15.
31 See: Chapter 4, Section 4.5.

References

1–800 Contacts, Inc. v. WhenU.com, Inc. 414 F.3d 400 (2d Cir. 2005).

Aborujilah, A., Yatim, M.N.B.M., and Al-Othmani, A., 2021. Blockchain-based adoption framework for authentic land registry system in Malaysia. *TELKOMNIKA (Telecommunication Computing Electronics and Control)*, 19 (6), 2038.

Achos Pty Ltd v. R.A. Bashford Pty Ltd, 1997, 37 I.P.R. 542, 562.

Acohs Pty Ltd v Ucorp Pty Ltd.

Act on Copyright and Related Rights (Copyright Act, as amended up to Act of September 1, 2017) (Germany).

Advanced Computer Services of Michigan, Inc. v. MAI Systems Corp., 845 F. Supp. 356, 364 (E.D. Va. 1994).

Agreement on Trade-Related Aspects of Intellectual Property Rights (1869 U.N.T.S. 299).

Ahmed, A. and Mihaela, C., 2017. Advancements in GIS map copyright protection schemes – A critical review. *Multimedia Tools and Applications,* 76, 12205–12231.

Aitken, Hazen, Hoffman, Miller, P. C. v. Empire Const. Co., 542 F. Supp. 252, 254 (D. Neb. 1982).

Alexander, I. and Jankowska, M., 2018. Rights in geospatial information: A shifting legal terrain. *Melbourne University Law Review*, 3 (41), 957.

Alexander, I. and Jankowska, M., 2018. Rights in geospatial information: A shifting legal terrain. *Melbourne University Law Review*, 3 (41), 957–973.

Alfred Bell & Co. v. Catalda Fine Arts, Inc. 191 F.2d 99 (2d Cir. 1951).

Ameyaw, P.D. and de Vries, W.T., 2020. Transparency of land administration and the role of blockchain technology, A four-dimensional framework analysis from the Ghanaian land perspective. *Land*, 9 (12), 491.

Amsterdam v. Triangle Publication, Inc. 93 F. Supp. 79 (E.D. Pa. 1950), aff'd, 189 F.2d 104 (3d Cir. 1951).

An Act for Preventing the Frequent Abuses in Printing Seditious Treasonable and Unlicensed Books and Pamphlets and for Regulating of Printing and Printing Presses 1622 (Licensing of the Press Act 1662) (UK).

An Act for the Encouragement of Learning, by Securing Copies of Maps, Charts, and Books, to the Authors and Proprietors of Such Copies, during the Times Therein Mentioned 1790 (Copyright Act 1790) (USA).

An Act for the Encouragement of Learning, by Vesting the Copies of Printed Books in the Authors or Purchasers of such Copies, during the Times Therein Mentioned 1710 (Statute of Anne 1710) (UK).

An Act to Amend and Consolidate the Acts Respecting Copyright 1909 (USA).

Anderson, S., 2018. The missing link between blockchain and copyright: How companies are using new technology to misinform creators and violate Federal Law. *North Carolina Journal of Law & Technology*, 19 (4), 1.

Andrews v. Guenther Publishing Co., 60 F.2d 555 (S.D.N.Y. 1932).

Ansah, B.O., *et al.*, 2023. A systematic review of the institutional success factors for blockchain-based land administration. *Land Use Policy,* 125, 106473.

Apis-Hristovich EOOD v Lakorda AD (Court of Justice of the European Union, Case C-545/07, ECLI:EU:C:2009:132, 5 March 2009).

Aplin, T., *et al.*, 2023. The role of EU trade secrets law in the data economy: An empirical analysis. *IIC – International Review of Intellectual Property and Competition Law*. Available from: <https://doi.org/10.1007/s40319-023-01325-8>.

Apple Computer, Inc. v. Franklin Computer Corp., 1240 (3d Cir. 1983).

Arizona Business Law Deskbook, Thomson West, 2022–2023 ed., Vol 9, § 15:16.

Artificial intelligence in surveying, n.d. *The Constructor*. Available from: <https://theconstructor.org/artificial-intelligence/artificial-intelligence-surveying/555010/>.2

Arts+Law, n.d. Copyright. Available from: <www.artslaw.com.au/information-sheet/copyright/>.

Atazadeh, B., *et al*., 2021. 3D cadastre in Australian and New Zealand jurisdictions: Similarities and differences. Available from: <www.gdmc.nl/3DCadastres/workshop2021/programme/j_3D_CAD_2021_paper_14.pdf>.

Attorney-General's Department, 2023. Submission P61, 11 November.

Australia – US Free Trade Agreement, Australian Treaty Series [2005] ATS 1.

Australian Bureau of Statistics, 2014/2021. https://www.abs.gov.au/statistics/detailed-methodology-information.

Australian Bureau of Statistics, 2023a. *Total value of dwellings*, viewed 31 October 2023. Available from: <www.abs.gov.au/statistics/economy/price-indexes-and-inflation/total-value-dwellings/latest-release>.

Australian Bureau of Statistics, 2023b. *Lending indicators*, viewed 31 October 2023. Available from: <www.abs.gov.au/statistics/economy/finance/lending-indicators/latest-release>.

Australian Bureau of Statistics, 2023c. *Australian national accounts: National income, expenditure and product*, viewed 31 October 2023. Available from: <www.abs.gov.au/statistics/economy/national-accounts/australian-national-accounts-national-income-expenditure-and-product/latest-release>.

Australian Competition and Consumer Act 2010 (Cth).

Australian Competition and Consumer Commission, 2019. Digital platforms inquiry final report. Available from: <www.accc.gov.au/about-us/publications/digital-platforms-inquiry-final-report>.

Australian Copyright Act 1968 (Cth).

Australian Copyright Council, n.d. *Photograph and copyright*. Available from: https://www.copyright.org.au/browse/book/Frances-Coyne-Photographers-&-Copyright-9781920778439

Australian Government, n.d.-a. Australian data strategy: The Australian government's whole-of-economy vision for data. Available from: <www.finance.gov.au/sites/default/files/2022-10/australian-data-strategy.pdf>.

Australian Government, n.d.-b. Cost Recovery Guidelines (RMG 304): Data availability and use. Available from: <www.crcsi.com.au/assets/Resources/ANZLIC-Economic-Study-Stage-1-Report.pdf> at 49.

Australian Law Reform Commission, 2012. Data and text mining, 16 August. Available from: <www.alrc.gov.au/publication/copyright-and-the-digital-economy-ip-42/data-and-text-mining/>.

Australian Law Reform Commission, 2013a. Copyright and the digital economy, 30 November. Available from: <www.alrc.gov.au/wp-content/uploads/2019/08/final_report_alrc_122_2nd_december_2013_.pdf>.

Australian Law Reform Commission, 2013b. Text and data mining, 4 June. Available from: <www.alrc.gov.au/publication/copyright-and-the-digital-economy-dp-79/8-non- consumptive-use/text-and-data-mining/>.

Australian Law Reform Commission, 2013c. What is fair use, 2 December. Available from: <www.alrc.gov.au/publication/copyright-and-the-digital-economy-alrc-report-122/4-the-case-for-fair-use/what-is-fair-use-2/>.

Australian Law Reform Commission, n.d. Genetic databases. Available from: <www.alrc.gov.au/publication/genes-and-ingenuity-gene-patenting-and-human-health-alrc-report-99/28-copyright-and-databases/genetic-databases/#_ftn43>.

Australian Medic-Care Comp*any Ltd v Hamilton Pharmaceutical Pty Limited* (ACN 008 204 635) [2009] FCA 1220 (30 October 2009).

Autodesk Inc v Dyason (AutoCAD case) [1992] HCA 2; (1992) 173 CLR 330 (12 February 1992).

A.V. ex rel. Vanderhye v. iParadigms, LLC, 562 F.3d 630, 642, 90 U.S.P.Q.2d 1513 (4th Cir. 2009).

Aziz, A., 2023. Artificial intelligence produced original work: A new approach to copyright protection and ownership. *European Journal of Artificial Intelligence and Machine Learning*, 2 (2), 9.

Bachiega Jr, J., Holanda, M., and Araujo, A.P.F., 2021. A proposal to minimize the cost of processing big geospatial data in public cloud providers. *Transactions in GIS*, 25 (3). Available from: <https://doi.org/10.1111/tgis.12754>.

Barclays Capital, Inc. v. Theflyonthewall.com, Inc. 650 F.3d 876 (2d Cir. 2011).

Beijing Treaty on Audiovisual Performances (2012, U.N.T.S. 3376).

Bella, L.L., 2017. *Drones and entertainment*. Rosen Publishing.

Berne Convention for the Protection of Literary and Artistic Works (1886, U.N.T.S. 828).

Bessero, G., 2016. Copyright case law: A map is a database. *International Hydrographic Review*, 37–38.

Best Medium Publishing Co. v. National Insider, Inc. 385 F.2d 384 (7th Cir. 1967).

Bezpecˇnostní Ahcnostní softwarová asociace – Svaz softwarové ochrany v Ministerstvo kultury (Court of Justice of the European Union, Case C-393/09, ECR I-13971, 22 December 2010).

Bird and Bird, n.d. Trade secrets: An overview and update on the protection of trade secrets in Australia. Available from: <www.twobirds.com/-/media/pdfs/in-focus/trade-secrets/trade-secrets-points-to-note-article-series – australia – september-2020.pdf>.

Bleistein v. Donaldson Lithographing Co. 188 U.S. 239 (1903).

Bodó, B., Gervais, D., and Quintais, J.P., 2018. Blockchain and smart contracts: The missing link in copyright licensing? *International Journal of Law and Information Technology*, 26 (4), 311–336.

Bogden, M.A., 2011. Fixing fixation: The RAM copy doctrine. *Arizona State Law Journal*, 43 (1), 181.

Boland-Devito, J., 2006. Yo ho and a bottle of rum – The DMCA takes on movie pirates. *Currents: International Trade Law Journal*, 15, 70-73.

Bracha, O., 2016. United States copyright, 1672–1909. *In*: I. Alexander and H. Tomás Gómez-Arostegui eds. *Research handbook on the history of copyright law*. Edward Elgar Publishing, 335–343.

Brandriss, I.L., 1995. Writing in frost on a window pane: E-mail and chatting on RAM and copyright fixation part I. *Journal of the Copyright Society of the U.S.A*., 43 (3), 237.

Britannica, n.d. Compilation. Available from: <www.britannica.com/science/map/Map-projections>.

Brown, E., 2014. Fixed perspectives: The evolving contours of the fixation requirement in copyright law. *Washington Journal of Law, Technology &* Arts, 10 (1), 17.

Bundesgerichtshof (Market Surveys) (I ZR 1/02) (2005) GRUR 940 (Germany).

Burge v Swarbrick [2007] HCA 17; (2007) 234 ALR 204; 81 ALJR 950 (26 April 2007).

Burrow – Giles Lithographic Co v Sarony, 111 US 53 (1884) (US).

Burshtyn, P., 1998. Illuminating the law of copyright: Holographic data storage takes intellectual property to a new dimension. *Fordham Intellectual Property, Media and Entertainment Law Journal*, 9 (1), 384.

C.S. Hammond & Co. v. International College Globe, Inc. 210 F. Supp. 206 (S.D.N.Y. 1962).

Cadastral Survey Requirements, n.d. Available from: <www.resources.qld.gov.au/?a=109113:policy_registry/cadastral-survey-requirements.pdf&ver=7.10>.

Cadastre 2034, n.d.-b. *Cadastral reform and innovation for Australia – A national strategy*. Available from: <www.icsm.gov.au/sites/default/files/Cadastre2034_0.pdf>.

Campaigntrack Pty Ltd v Real Estate Tool Box Pty Ltd [2021] FCA 809.

Campbell v. Acuff-Rose Music, Inc. 510 U.S. 569, 577, 579,114 S. Ct. 1164, 1170, 127 L. Ed. 2d 500, 22 Media L. Rep. (BNA) 1353, 29 U.S.P.Q.2d 1961 (1994).

Carpenter, M. and Hetcher, S., 2013. Function over form: Bringing the fixation requirement into the modern era. *Fordham Law Review*, 82 (5), 2221-2252.

Carter v. Hawaii Transp. Co., 201 F. Supp. 301 (D. Haw. 1961).

Cartoon Network LP v. CSC Holdings, Inc. 536 F.3d 121 (2d Cir. 2008).

Carvalho, G. and Kazim, E., 2022. Themes in data strategy: Thematic analysis of "A European Strategy for Data" (EC). *AI and Ethics*, 2 (1), 53.

Casastre 2034, n.d.-a. *A vision for cadastre 2034*. Available from: <www.icsm.gov.au/sites/default/files/Cadastre2034_0.pdf>.

CCC Info. Servs., Inc. v. Maclean Hunter Mkt. Reps., Inc. 44 F.3d 61 (2d Cir. 1994).

Chamberlain Group, Inc. v. Skylink Tech., Inc. 292 F. Supp. 2d 1040, 1040 (N.D. Ill. 2003).

Chamberlin v. Bekins Van & Storage Co., 23 F.2d 541 (S.D. Cal. 1928).

Chen, Y. and Yang, M., 2005. Legal issues on public access to remote sensing data in Taiwan. *In*: *Proceedings of 2005 IEEE international geoscience and remote sensing symposium, 2005. IGARSS '05*.

Chicago B. & Q. R.R. v. City of Chicago, 166 U.S. 226, 227 (1897).

Cho, G., 1995. Legal dilemmas in geographic information: Property, ownership and patents. *Journal of Law, Information and Science*, 6 (2), 193.

Coco v A N Clark (Engineers) Ltd [1969] RPC 41.

Code, A., 2021. *Static maps vs interactive maps: When to use them*. Available from: <www.line-45.com/post/static-maps-vs-interactive-maps-when-use-them>.

Cofemel – Sociedade de Vestuário SA v G-Star Raw CV (Court of Justice of the European Union, Case C-683/17, ECLI:EU:C:2019:721, 12 September 2019).

Cofemel – Sociedade de Vestuário SA v G-Star Raw CV (Opinion of Advocate General Szpunar, Case C-683/17), ECLI:EU:C:2019:363, delivered on 2 May 2019).

Commonwealth of Australia, Data and the Digital Economy, 2021. Available from: <https://digitaleconomy.pmc.gov.au/sites/default/files/2022-03/factsheet-data-and-digital-economy-0322–2.pdf>.

Commonwealth of Australia, Second Interim Report of the Senate Select Committee on Australia as a Technology and Financial Centre (text, The Senate, 28 April 2021) 1. Available from: <www.aph.gov.au/Parliamentary_Business/Committees/Senate/Financial_Technology_and_Regulatory_Technology/FinancialRegulatoryTech/Second_Interim_Report>.

Commonwealth v John Fairfax & Sons Ltd (1980) 147 CLR 39.

Community for Creative Non-Violence v. Reid, 490 U.S. 730, 739–740, 109 S. Ct. 2166, 2172–2173 (1989).

Competition and Consumer Act 2010 (Cth).

Competition Policy and Intellectual Property Rights 1997, OECD at 73.

Computer Assocs. Int'l, Inc. v. Atlai, Inc. 982 F.2d 693, 703 (2d Cir. 1992).

Convention for the Protection of Producers of Phonograms against Unauthorized Duplication of their Phonograms (1971, U.N.T.S. 866).

Conveyancing Act 1919 (NSW).

Conway, N., 2019. Why geospatial needs to listen to GDPR. *GiS Professional*, 79, 32.

Copyright Agency Limited v State of New South Wales [2008] HCA 35.

Copyright Amendment (Digital Agenda) Act 2000 (Cth).

Copyright Office Regulations C.F.R. § 202.9 (1959).

Copyright Review Board, 2022. Second request for reconsideration for refusal to register a recent entrance to paradise (Correspondence ID 1–3ZPC6C3; SR # 1–7100387071) (Case Determination. Copyright Review Board. Available from: <www.copyright.gov/rulings-filings/review-board/docs/a- recent-entrance-to-paradise.pdf>.

Copyright, Designs and Patents Act, 1988, C 48, § 9(3) (UK).

Corby v Allen & Unwin Pty Limited [2013] FCA 370 (24 April 2013).

Corporations Act 2001 (Cth).

Cory, M., n.d. EuroGeographics information paper communication from the commission on a European strategy for data. *EuroGeographics*. Available from: <https://eurogeographics.org/wp-content/uploads/2020/05/EG-response-on-ES4D-FINAL.pdf>.

CoStar Group, Inc. v. LoopNet, Inc (CoStar) 373 F.3d 544 (4th Cir. 2004).

Council of the European Union, n.d. Data act: Member states agree common position on fair access to and use of data. Available from: <www.consilium.europa.eu/en/press/press-releases/2023/03/24/data-act-member-states-agree-common-position-on-fair-access-to-and-use-of-data/>.

Credinfor v Artprice.com, CA Paris, 18 June 2003, Jurisdata, n. 223155.

Crocker v. General Drafting Co., 50 F. Supp. 634 (S.D.N.Y. 1943).

Cronin, C., 2016. Symposium: Possession is 99% of the law: 3D printing, public domain cultural artefacts and copyright. *Minnesota Journal of Law, Science & Technology*, 17 (2), 709.

Cross, J.T., 2000. Suing the states for copyright infringement. *Brandeis Law Journal*, 39 (2), 337.

Crowell and Moring *et al*., 2022. Study on copyright and new technologies: Copyright data management and artificial intelligence. Publications Office of the European Union. Available from: <https://data.europa.eu/doi/10.2759/570559>.

Cutts, T., 2019. Smart contracts and consumers. *Western Virginia Law Review,* 122 (2), 389.

Cyber Risk GmbH, n.d. *The European Data Act*. Available from: <www.eu-data-act.com/>.

Daho, B., 2020. Crypto-spatial: An open standards smart contracts library for building geospatially enabled decentralized applications on the Ethereum blockchain. *International Archives of the Photogrammetry, Remote Sensing and Spatial Information Sciences*, 421–426.

Dasgupta, A., n.d. Geospatial technology enabling workflows. Available from: <www.geospatialworld.net/article/geospatial-technology-enabling-workflows/>.

Data Policy Statements, Data.gov. Available from: <www.data.gov/data-policy/>.

Data.Gov. Data.gov, 27 July 2021. Available from: <www.data.gov/>.Davidson, S., de Filippi, P., and Potts, J., 2018. Blockchains and the economic institutions of capitalism. *Journal of Institutional Economics*, 14 (4), 639.

Davies Collison Save, n.d. High court of Australia rules on chipping of game consoles. Available from: <https://dcc.com/news-and-insights/high-court-%20of-australia-rules-on-chipping-of-game-consoles/>.

Davison, M., 1998. Sui generis or too generous: Legislative protection of databases, its implications for Australia and some suggestions for reform. *UNSW Law Journal*, 21 (3) 729-730.

Davison, M., 2006. Database protection: Lessons from Europe, Congress, and WIPO law, technology and the arts symposium: The WIPO copyright treaties: 10 Years later. *Case Western Reserve Law Review,* 57 (4), 829–845.

Davison, M., 2020. Databases and copyright protection. *In:* T. Aplin ed. *Research handbook on intellectual property and digital technologies*. Edward Elgar Publishing Limited, 75. Available from: <http://ebookcentral.proquest.com/lib/monash/detail.action?docID=6029047>.

Defend Trade Secrets Act 2016 (Public Law No. 114–153).

Del Madera Props. v. Rhodes & Gardner, Inc. 820 F.2d 973, 976 (9th Cir.1987).

Deloitte, 'Open by default: Revisiting open data in government'. Available from: <https://www2.deloitte.com/content/dam/Deloitte/au/Documents/public-sector/deloitte-au-ps-revisiting-open-data-government-300120.pdf>.

Derclaye, E., 2021. The database directive. *In:* I. Stamatoudi and P. Torremans eds. *EU copyright law*. Edward Elgar Publishing, 216. Available from: <www.elgaronline.com/edcollchap/book/9781786437808/book-part-9781786437808-19.xml>.

Desktop Marketing Systems Pty Ltd v Telstra Corporation [2002] FCAFC 112.

Desktop Marketing Systems Pty Ltd v Telstra Corporation Ltd (2002) 192 ALR 433.

Dickenson, J., Morgan, A., and Clark, B., 2017. Creative machines: Ownership of copyright in content created by artificial intelligence applications. *European Intellectual Property Review*, 39 (8), 458, 459.

Digital at Arup, 2019. Blockchain and the built environment. *ARUP*, 2019. Available from: <www.arup.com/en/perspectives/publications/research/section/blockchain-and-the-built-environment>.

Digital Land Surveys, 'Copyright and the digital economy: Submission in respect of question 34'. Available from: <www.alrc.gov.au/wp-content/uploads/2019/08/27.__org__digitallandsurveys.pdf>.

Digital Millennium Copyright Act 1998 (Public Law No. 105–304, 112 Stat. 2860 (1998).

Dillman, D.A., Smyth, J.D., and Christian, L.M. 2014. *Internet, phone, mail, and mixed mode surveys: The tailored design method,* 4th ed. Hoboken, NJ: John Wiley & Sons Inc.

Directive 96/9/EC of the European Parliament and of the Council of 11 March 1996. Available from: <https://eur-lex.europa.eu/legal-content/EN/TXT/PDF/?uri=CELEX:31996L0009&from=EN>.

Directive concerning misleading and comparative advertising (codified version), 12 December 2006.

Directive concerning unfair business-to-consumer commercial practices in the internal market and amending Council Directive 84/450/EEC, Directives 97/7/EC, 98/27/EC and 2002/65/EC of the European Parliament and of the Council and Regulation (EC) No 2006/2004 of the European Parliament and of the Council ('Unfair Commercial Practices Directive'), 11 May 2005.

Directive establishing an Infrastructure for Spatial Information in the European Community ('INSPIRE Directive'), 14 March 2007.

Directive on certain permitted uses of certain works and other subject matter protected by copyright and related rights for the benefit of persons who are blind, visually impaired or otherwise print-disabled (Directive implementing the Marrakech Treaty in the EU), 13 September 2017.

Directive on certain permitted uses of orphan works ('Orphan Works Directive'), 25 October 2012.

Directive on collective management of copyright and related rights and multi-territorial licensing of rights in musical works for online use in the internal market ('CRM Directive'), 26 February 2014.

Directive on copyright and related rights in the Digital Single Market ('DSM Directive'), 17 April 2019.

Directive on open data and the re-use of public sector information, 20 June 2019.

Directive on rental right and lending right and on certain rights related to copyright in the field of intellectual property ('Rental and Lending Directive'), 12 December 2006.

Directive on services in the internal market ('Service Directive'), 12 December 2006.

Directive on the coordination of certain rules concerning copyright and rights related to copyright applicable to satellite broadcasting and cable retransmission ('Satellite and Cable Directive'), 27 September 1993.

Directive on the enforcement of intellectual property right ('IPRED'), 29 April 2004.

Directive on the exercise of copyright and related rights applicable to certain online transmissions of broadcasting organisations and retransmissions of television and radio programmes ('Satellite and Cable II'), 17 April 2019.

Directive on the harmonisation of certain aspects of copyright and related rights in the information society ('InfoSoc Directive'), 22 May 2001.

Directive on the legal protection of computer programs ('Software Directive'), 23 April 2009.

Directive on the legal protection of databases ('Database Directive'), 11 March 1996.

Directive on the protection of undisclosed know-how and business information (trade secrets) against their unlawful acquisition, use, and disclosure, 8 June 2016.

Directive on the recognition of professional qualifications ('Free Movement of Professionals'), 7 September 2005.

Directive on the resale right for the benefit of the author of an original work of art ('Resale Right Directive'), 27 September 2001.

Directive on the term of protection of copyright and certain related rights amending the previous 2006 Directive ('Term Directive'), 27 September 2011.

Directmedia Publishing v Albert-Ludwigs-Universität Freiburg (Court of Justice of the European Union, C-304/07, ECLI:EU:C:2008:552,9 October 2008).

Directorate-General for Communications Networks, Content and Technology (European Commission) et al, Trends and Developments in Artificial Intelligence: Challenges to the Intellectual Property Rights Framework : Final Report (No KK-02–20–789-EN-C, Publications Office of the European Union, 2020). Available from: <https://data.europa.eu/doi/10.2759/458120>.

Dorotheou, E., 2015. Reap the benefits and avoid the legal uncertainty: Who owns the creations of artificial intelligence?. *Computer and Telecommunications Law Review*, 21 (4), 85, 91.

Dreier, T. and Hugenholtz, P.B., 2016. *Concise European copyright law*. Kluwer Law International B.V.

EIFY Systems Pty Ltd v 3D Safety Services Pty Ltd [2017] NSWSC 1310 (EIFY v 3D).

Esri, European cadastres and national mapping agencies. *ArcNews Online*. Available from: <www.esri.com/news/arcnews/spring11articles/european-cadastres-and-national-mapping-agencies.html>.

EuroGeographics, 'EuroGeographics briefing paper evaluation of the database directive 96/9/EC'. Available from: <https://eurogeographics.org/wp-content/uploads/2018/04/2017-EG-Briefing-Paper-Evaluation-of-the-Database-Directive-969EC.pdf>.

EuroGeographics, 'Status and adopted innovations over the last decade in cadastre and land administration in Europe'. Available from: <https://eurogeographics.org/wp-content/uploads/2021/04/210512-SummaryReport-PCC-Questionnaire.pdf>.

EuroGeographics, About us. Available from: <https://eurogeographics.org/about-us/>.

EuroGeographics, The European Council of Geodetic Surveyors and AZIZ Europas, European Requirements for Cadastral Surveyor Activities, 2007, 23. Available from: <www.clge.eu/wp-content/uploads/2008/04/european_requirements_for_cadastral_surveyor_activity.pdf>.

European Commission, 'A European strategy for data'. Available from: <https://eur-lex.europa.eu/legal-content/EN/TXT/PDF/?uri=CELEX:52020DC0066>.

European Commission, 'Explanatory memorandum of the proposal for a regulation of the European parliament and of the council on harmonised rules on fair access to and use of data (Data Act) COM/2022/68 final'. Available from: <https://eur-lex.europa.eu/legal-content/EN/TXT/?uri=COM%3A2022%3A68%3AFIN>.

European Commission, 'Proposal for a regulation of the European parliament and of the council laying down harmonised rules on artificial intelligence (Artificial Intelligence Act) and amending certain Union Legislative Acts COM/2021/206 final'. Available from: <https://eur-lex.europa.eu/legal-content/EN/TXT/?uri=celex%3A52021PC0206>.

European Commission, 2011. A single market for intellectual property rights: – Boosting creativity and innovation to provide economic growth, high quality jobs and first-class products and services in Europe. *COM*, 287, 11.

European Commission, 2023. A European approach to artificial intelligence. *Shaping Europe's Digital Future*, 31 May 2023. Available from: <https://digital-strategy.ec.europa.eu/en/policies/european-approach-artificial-intelligence>

European Commission, 2023. A European strategy for data. *Shaping Europe's Digital Future*, 16 May 2023. Available from: <https://digital-strategy.ec.europa.eu/en/policies/strategy-data>.

European Commission, 2023. Blockchain strategy. *Shaping Europe's Digital Future*, 21 March 2023. Available from: <https://digital-strategy.ec.europa.eu/en/policies/blockchain-strategy>.

European Commission, 2023. Data act. *Shaping Europe's Digital Future*, 16 May 2023. Available from: <https://digital-strategy.ec.europa.eu/en/policies/data-act>.

European Commission, 2023. European data governance act. *Shaping Europe's Digital Future*, 16 May 2023. Available from: <https://digital-strategy.ec.europa.eu/en/policies/data-governance-act>.

European Commission, 2023. European legislation on open data. *Shaping Europe's Digital Future*, 15 February 2023. Available from: <https://digital-strategy.ec.europa.eu/en/policies/legislation-open-data>.

European Commission, 2023a. INSPIRE directive. INSPIRE knowledge base, 5 May 2023. Available from: <https://inspire.ec.europa.eu/inspire-directive/2>.

European Commission, 2023b. Open data. *Shaping Europe's Digital Future*, 15 February 2023. Available from: <https://digital-strategy.ec.europa.eu/en/policies/open-data>.

European Commission, Europe's digital decade: Digital targets for 2030. Available from: <https://commission.europa.eu/strategy-and-policy/priorities-2019-2024/europe-fit-digital-age/europes-digital-decade-digital-targets-2030_en>

European Commission. Directorate General for Communications Networks, Content and Technology, et al., 2022. *Study to support an impact assessment for the review of the database directive: Final report*. Publications Office. Available from: <https://data.europa.eu/doi/10.2759/647387>.

European Land Registry Association, 'Home'. Available from: <www.elra.eu/>.

European Parliament, 'European Parliament resolution of 20 October 2020 on intellectual property rights for the development of artificial intelligence technologies, 2020/2015(INI)'. Available from: <www.europarl.europa.eu/doceo/document/TA-9-2020-0277_EN.html>.

Eva-Maria Painer v Standard VerlagsGmbH and Others (Court of Justice of the European Union, C-145/10, EU:C:2011:798, 7 March 2013).

Fabian, S., 2020. Blockchain and intellectual property rights comments. *Intellectual Property and Technology Law Journal*, 25 (2), 147, 157.

Falwell v. Penthouse International, Ltd., 521 F. Supp. 1204 (W.D. Va 1981).

Farr, E.H., 1989. Copyrightability of computer-generated works. *Rutgers Computer & Technical Law Journal*, 15, 63–74.

Farrand, B., 2021. From a "digital agenda for Europe", to a "digital single market", to a "Europe fit for the digital age", a decade of European union copyright policy. In the shadow of crises. *In:* I. Stamatoudi and P. Torremans eds. *EU copyright law*. Edward Elgar Publishing, 967. Available from: <www.elgaronline.com/edcollchap/book/9781786437808/book-part-9781786437808-34.xml>.

Fava, E., 2021. Hyper-casual simulation video games may not be original enough to enjoy copyright Protection but game cloning could still be prevented by relying on unfair competition: Voodoo v Rollic Games and Hero Games. *European Intellectual Property Review*, 43 (6), 402.

Federal GeoAgraphic Data Committee (FGDC), 'About | GeoPlatform.Gov'. Available from: <www.geoplatform.gov>.

Federal Procedure, L.Ed. 2023. Thomson Reuters, Lawyers Cooperative Publishing.

Feist Publications, Inc. v. Rural Telephone Service Company, Inc. 113 L.Ed.2d 358, 111 S. Ct. 1282 (1991), 499 U.S. 340 (1991).

Fenning, K, 'Origin of the Patent and Copyright Clause of the Constitution' (1928) 17(2) *Georgetown Law Journal* 109.

Fieldfisher, The CJEU confirms a topographic map is a database, 2015. Available from: <www.fieldfisher.com/en/services/intellectual- property/intellectual-property-blog/the-cjeu-confirms-a-topographic-map-is-a-database>.

Finck, M. and Moscon, V., 2019. Copyright law on blockchains: Between new forms of rights administration and digital rights management 2.0. *International Review of Intellectual Property and Competition Law*, 50, 77–108.

Firoozye v. Earthlink Network 153 F.Supp.2d 1115, 1124 (N.D.Cal.2001).

Fitzgerald, A. and Seidenspinner, T., 2013. Copyright and computer-generated materials – Is it time to reboot the discussion about authorship? *Victoria University Law and Justice Journal*, 3 (1), 37, 42.

Fitzgerald, A., 2011. Crown copyright. Available from: <https://ses.library.usyd.edu.au/bitstream/handle/2123/7326/FitzgeraldA_9781920899714_TEXT.pdf?sequence=1&isAllowed=y>.

Fitzgerald, A., Pappalardo, K., and Austin, A., 2008. *Understanding the legal implications of data sharing, access and reuse in the Australian research landscape*. Sydney: Sydney University Press.

Fitzgerald, B. and Bartlett, C., 2002. Database protection under Australian copyright law: Desktop marketing systems Pvt Ltd v Telstra Corporation. *FCAFC*, 112. Available from: <http://138.25.65.110/au/journals/SCULawRw/2003/8.pdf>

Fitzgerald, B., *et al.*, 2008. *Copyright law, digital content and the internet in the Asia-Pacific*. Sydney: Sydney University Press, 260–261.

Fixtures Marketing Ltd v AB Svenska Spel (Court of Justice of the European Union, Case C-338/02, ECLI:EU:C:2004:696, 9 November 2004).

Fixtures Marketing Ltd v Organismos Prognostikon Agonon Podosfairou (OPAP) (Court of Justice of the European Union, Case C-444/02, ECLI:EU:C:2004:697, 9 November 2004).

Fixtures Marketing Ltd v Oy Veikkaus AB (Court of Justice of the European Union, Case Case C-46/02, ECLI:EU:C:2004:694, 9 November 2004).

Fleming, G., *et al.*, n.d. *Weather on the internet and other new technologies*. World Meteorological Organisation. Available from: <https://library.wmo.int/doc_num.php?explnum_id=9193>.

Football Association Premier League Ltd and Others v QC Leisure and Others and Karen Murphy v Media Protection Services Ltd (Court of Justice of the European Union, C-403/08 and C-429/08, ECLI:EU:C:2011:63, 4 October 201).

Football Dataco Ltd and Others v Yahoo! UK Ltd and Others (Court of Justice of the European Union, Case C-604/10, EU:C:2012:115, 1 March 2012).

Foundations for Evidence-Based Policymaking Act 2018 (Public Law No.115–435).

Fractional Villas, Inc. v. Tahoe Clubhouse, No. 08CV1396-IEG-POR, 2009 U.S. Dist. LEXIS 39522, at 5, 2009 WL 1298532, at 2 (S.D. Cal. May 8, 2009).

Freistaat Bayern v Verlag Esterbauer GmbH (Court of Justice of the European Union, Case C-490/14, ECLI:EU:C:2015:735, 29 October 2015).

Funke Medien NRW GmbH v. Bundesrepublik Deutschland (Court of Justice of the European Union, Case C–469/17, ECLI:EU:C:2019:623, 29 July 2019)

Gandi, A. and Olsen, M., 2021. AI, invention and authorship expanding intellectual property rights to non-human outputs. *INTLB*, 23 (7), 119.

GDPR Working Group, 'Nordic GDPR working group report'. Available from: <https://norden.lmi.is/wp-content/uploads/2019/08/Nordic-GDPR-working-group-Report.pdf>.

Geiger, C., 2021. Fair use through fundamental rights in Europe: When freedom of artistic expression allows creative appropriations and opens up statutory copyright limitations. *In*: S. Haochen, W.L. Ng-Loy, and B. Shyamkrishna eds. *The Cambridge handbook of copyright limitations and exceptions*. Cambridge: Cambridge University Press. Available from: <www.cambridge.org/core/books/cambridge-handbook-of-copyright-limitations-and-exceptions/fair-use-through-fundamental-rights-in-europe-when-freedom-of-artistic-expression-allows-creative-appropriations-and-opens-up-statutory-copyright-limitations/3826C8E04A6964923854752C136435B4>.

Geiger, C., *et al.*, 2021. The information society directive. *In*: I. Stamatoudi and P. Torremans eds. *EU copyright law*. Edward Elgar Publishing, 279. Available from: <www.elgaronline.com/edcollchap/book/9781786437808/book-part-9781786437808-21.xml>.

General Drafting Co. v. Andrews, 37 F.2d 54 (2d Cir. 1930).

Geophysical Service Inc. v. TGS-NOPEC, 784 Fed.Appx. 253, 2019 WL 4410259, at 2 (5th Cir. Sept. 13, 2019).

Georgakopoulos, D. and Hornick, M., 1995. An overview of workflow management: From process modelling to workflow automation infrastructure. *Distributed and Parallel Databases*, 3, 119–153.

Georgia et al v. Public.Resource.Org 140 S. Ct. 1498 (2020).

Ghidini, G. and Cavani, G., 2021. The relationship between the unfair competition regime and IP law. *In:* A. Ohly *et al.* eds. *Transition and coherence in intellectual property law: Essays in honour of Annette Kur*. Cambridge University Press, 467. Available from: <www.cambridge.org/core/books/transition-and-coherence-in-intellectual-property-law/relationship-between-the-unfair-competition-regime-and-ip-law/58A997EDF87AAC009792110E33FD35B4>.

GIS for Cadastre Management, n.d. Available from: <www.esri.com/content/dam/esrisites/sitecore archive/Files/Pdfs/library/brochures/pdfs/gis-for-cad-mgmt.pdf>.

Golan v. Holder 565 U.S. 302, 323–25 (2012).

Golder, T. and Ladd, S., 2021. 'Copyright in software – The latest word from the federal court. Available from: <www.allens.com.au/insights-news/insights/2021/09/copyright-in-software-the-latest-word-from-the-federal-court/>.

Gomes, V.C.F., Queiroz, G.T., and Ferreira, K.R., 2020. An overview of platforms for big earth observation data management and analysis. Available from: <www.mdpi.com/2072–4292/12/8/1253>.

Google LLC v. Oracle Am., Inc. 141 S.Ct. 1183.

Gosnell, S., 2023. Database protection down under: Would a 'Sweaty' Australia be better off with a Northerly change?. *University of New South Wales Law Journal*, 639.

Graglia, J.M. and Mellon, C., 2018. Blockchain and property in 2018: At the end of the beginning. *Innovations: Technology, Governance, Globalization*, 12 (1–2), 90.

Grant Matthews v ACP Publishing Pty Ltd (includes corrigendum dated 18 December 1998) [1998] FCA 1122 (10 September 1998).

Guadamuz, A., 2017. Artificial intelligence and copyright. *WIPO Magazine*. Available from: <www.wipo.int/wipo_magazine/en/2017/05/article_0003.html>.

Harper & Row Publishers, Inc. v. Nation Enterprises et al. 471 U.S. 539, 558 (1985).

Hayden v. Chalfant Press, Inc. 281 F.2d 543 (9th Cir. 1960).

Healthcare Advocates, Inc. v. Harding, Earley, Follmer & Frailey, 49 7 F. SUPP. 2D 62 7 (E.D. PA. 2007).

Hilty, R.M., Hoffmann, J., and Scheuerer, S., 2021. Intellectual property justification for artificial intelligence. *Artificial Intelligence and Intellectual Property*, 50–72.

Hoaward, D. and McAdamis, E.M., 2006. Available from: <https://airandspacelaw.olemiss.edu/pdfs/jsl-32-2.pdf> at 257.

Honig, A., 'Copyright Protection of Databases under Australian Law – Nine Network Australia Pty Ltd v IceTV Pty Ltd' [2007] FCA 1172. Available from: <http://classic.austlii.edu.au/au/journals/ANZCompuLawJl/2007/13.pdf>.

House of Representatives Standing Committee on Legal and Constitutional Affairs, *Advisory Report on the Copyright Amendment (Digital Agenda) Bill 1999*, November 1999.

House of Representatives Standing Committee on Legal and Constitutional Affairs, '*Review of technological protection measures exceptions*,' February 2006 Canberra, The Parliament of the Commonwealth of Australia, ISBN 0 642 78764 6.

House of Representatives, *Copyright Law Revision* (H.R. Rep. No. 1476, 94th Cong., 2d Sess. 58 (1976).

Hubanov, S., 2006. The multifaceted nature and problematic status of fixation in U.S. Copyright law comment. *Intellectual Property Law Bulletin*, 11 (1), 111–113.

Hubbertz, A., 1990. Crown copyright and privatization of government information in Canada, with comparisons to the United States experience. *Government Publications Review*, 17 (2), 159.

Hugenholtz, P.B. and Quintais, J.P., 2021. Copyright and artificial creation: Does EU copyright law protect AI-assisted output?. *IIC – International Review of Intellectual Property and Competition Law*, 52 (9), 1190.

Hughes, J., 2020. Restating copyright law's originality requirement. *Columbia Journal of Law & the Arts*, 44 (3), 383–390.

HWL Ebsworth Lawyers, 'Copyright in Computer Programs', 2018. Avaialble from: <https://hwlebsworth.com.au/copyright-in-computer-programs/>.

Ian Cubitts Classic Home Improvements Pty Ltd v Granny Flat Projects [2015] FCCA 2630 (30 September 2015).

Ice Tv Pty Ltd v Nine Network Australia Pty Ltd (2009) 239 CLR 458.

IceTV Pty Limited v Nine Network Australia Pty Limited [2009] HCA 14.

In re Jackson, 972 F.3d 25, 44–45 (2d Cir. 2020).

Infopaq International A/S v. Danske Dagblades Forening (Court of Justice of the European Union, Case C-5/08, ECLI:EU:C:2009:465, 16 July 2009).

Innoweb BV v. Wegener ICT Media BV, Wegener Mediaventions BV (Court of Justice of the European Union, Case C-202/12, ECLI:EU:C:2013:850, 19 December 2013).

International Convention for the Protection of Performers, Producers of Phonograms and Broadcasting Organisations (1961, U.N.T.S. 496).

International News Service Inc. v Associated Press 248 U.S 215 (1918).

Janssen, K. and Dumortier, J., 2006. The protection of maps and spatial databases in Europe and the United States by copyright and the Sui Generis Right. *UIC John Marshall Journal of Information Technology & Privacy Law*, 24 (2), 195.

Janssens, M., 2021. The software directive. *In*: Irini Stamatoudi and Paul Torremans, eds. *EU Copyright Law*. Edward Elgar Publishing, 75 at <www.elgaronline.com/edcollchap/book/9781786437808/book-part-9781786437808-15.xml>.

Javaid, M., *et al*., 2022. A review of blockchain technology applications for financial services. *BenchCouncil Transactions on Benchmarks, Standards and Evaluations*, 2 (3), 100073.

Jeweler's Circular Pub. Co. v. Keystone Pub. Co. 281 F. 83 (2d Cir. 1922).

John G. Danielson, Inc. v. Winchester-Conant Props., Inc. 186 F. Supp. 2d 1, 16 & n.2 (D. Mass. 2002).

Johnson, J., 2013. *Copyright and online technologies*. Australian Copyright Council, 27.

Joyce, C. and Ochoa, T.T., 2016. Reach out and touch someone: Reflections on the 25th anniversary of Feist Publications, Inc. v. Rural Telephone Service Co. Authorship in America (and beyond): Institute for intellectual property & information law symposium: Historical essay. *Houston Law Review*, 54 (2), 257, 268.

JR Consulting & Drafting Pty Ltd v Cummings (2016) 329 ALR 625, 672 [264].

Junnila, A.S.S. and Vimpari, J., 2022. Blockchain's grand promise for the real estate sector: A systematic review' *Applied Sciences*, 12 (23), 11940.

Kabushiki Kaisha Sony Computer Entertainment v Stevens (2003) 200 ALR 96.

Kabushiki Kaisha Sony Computer Entertainment v Stevens [2003] FCAFC 157 (30 July 2003).

Kampakis, S., 2022. Auditing tokenomics: A case study and lessons from auditing a stablecoin project. *The JBBA*, 5 (2), 1–7.

Karjala, D.S., 1991. Copyright and misappropriation copyright symposium part II – Copyright protection for computer databases, CD-ROMs and factual compilations. *The University of Dayton Law Review*, 17 (3), 885–886.

Karjala, D.S., 1994. Copyright in electronic maps symposium. *Jurimetrics Journal*, 35 (4), 395.

Karjala, D.S., 1995. Copyright in electronic maps. *Jurimetrics*, 35 (4), 395–415.

Key Maps, Inc. v. Pruitt 470 F. Supp. 33 (S.D. Tex. 1978).

König, P.D., 2022. Fortress Europe 4.0? An analysis of EU data governance through the lens of the resource regime concept. *European Policy Analysis*, 8 (4), 484.

Koronczok, M., 2019. The new chain of title: How blockchain will affect land title research, recordation, and insurance. *Texas A&M Journal of Property Law*, 5 (3), 401.

Kraak, M.-J. and Ormeling, F., 2010. *Cartography: Visualization of spatial data*. London: Pearson Education Limited, 147.

Kwall, R.R., 1998. Governmental use of copyright property: The Sovereign's prerogative. *Texas Law Review*, 67 (4), 685–692.

Kwon, P., 2013. Spatial data process using Python script and visual programming language in ArcGIS. *Computer Technology and Application*, 4, 275–283.

Lahore, J., 1996. *Copyright and designs: Looseleaf service*. Sydney: Butterworths, 1996, 10,065, 10,115.

Lane, A.M., and Platz, C., 2021. The other side of the ledger: Blockchain makes a new entry in the historical record of copyright law and technology. *European Intellectual Property Review*, 43 (2), 83–97.

Leaffer, M., 2006. Database protection in the United States is alive and well: Comments on davison law, technology and the arts symposium: The WIPO copyright treaties: 10 years later. *Case Western Reserve Law Review*, 57 (4), 855.

Lee, M.S., 2023. *Entertainment and intellectual property law*. Thomson Reuters, LegalWorks.

Lee, S., Lee, J., and Lee, Y., 2023. Dissecting the terra-LUNA crash: Evidence from the spillover effect and information flow. *Finance Research Letters*, 53.

Lehman, B.A., 1995. Intellectual property and the national information infrastructure -The report of the working group on intellectual property rights, September 1995, 26. Available from: <www.eff.org/files/filenode/DMCA/ntia_dmca_white_paper.pdf>.

Levi, S.D. and Lipton, A.B., 2018. An introduction to smart contracts and their potential and inherent limitations. Available from: <https://corpgov.law.harvard.edu/2018/05/26/an-introduction-to-smart-contracts-and-their-%20potential-and-inherent-limitations/>.

Levin, M., 2023. Chapter 5: The cofemel revolution – Originality, equality and neutrality. *In*: *The Routledge Handbook of EU Copyright Law*, ed. Eleonora Rosati. Taylor & Francis Group, 82. Available from: <http://ebookcentral.proquest.com/lib/monash/detail.action?docID=6514334>.

Levola Hengelo BV v. Smilde Foods BV Deutschland (Court of Justice of the European Union, Case C– 310/17, ECLI:EU:C:2018:899, 13 November 2018).

Lloyd, A., 2010. Inherently transitory transistors: Legal, factual, and policy issues with "Ram fixation. *In: Copyright*. Michigan State University College of Law, 2010, 4. Available from: <www.law.msu.edu/king/2009-2010/Lloyd.pdf>.

Longhorn, R.A., Henson-Apollonio, V., and White, J.W., 2002. Legal issues in the use of geospatial data and tools for agriculture and natural resource management. International Maize and Wheat Improvement Center (CIMMYT), Mexico. Available from: <https://repository.cimmyt.org/bitstream/handle/10883/905/447972.pdf?sequence=4&isAllowed=y >.

López, C., 2002. Watermarking of digital geospatial datasets: A review of technical, legal and copyright issues. *International Journal of Geographical Information Science*, 16 (6), 589–607.

Lucas-Schloetter, A., Is there a concept of European copyright law? *In: History, Evolution, Policies and Politics and The Acquis Communautaire*. Edward Elgar Publishing, 2021. Available from: <www.elgaronline.com/display/book/9781786437808/book-part-9781786437808-10.xml>.

Luna-Reyes, L.F., *et al*., 2019. The US open data initiative: The road ahead. *Information Polity: The International Journal of Government & Democracy in the Information Age*, 24 (2), 163.

Mackay, J. and McLachlan, J., 1992. Are computer screen displays capable of attracting copyright protection? *AIPJ*, 3, 203–207.

MAI Systems Corp. v. Peak Computer, Inc. 991 F.2d 511 (9th Cir. 1993).

Mann, P. and Denoncourt, J., 2009. Copyright issues on the protection of architectural works and designs. *In: 25th Annual Conference of Association of Researchers in Construction*

Management (ARCOM), September 2009. Available from: <https://centaur.reading.ac.uk/4621/1/Mann-Denoncourt.pdf at 708>.

Mannion v Coors Brewing, 377 F Supp 2d 444 (SDNY, 2005) (US).

Maptitude Australia Mapping Software, n.d. Available from: <www.caliper.com/maptitude/gis-software/gis-software-australia.htm>.

Markunas, J.D., 2019.Blockchain for surveyors. *Land Journal* 10.

Marrakesh Treaty to Facilitate Access to Published Works for Persons Who Are Blind, Visually Impaired or Otherwise Print Disabled (2013, WIPO Lex No. TRT/MARRAKESH/001).

Martin, D. and Rob, K., 2001. *Mapping cyberspace*. London: Routledge.

Martinelli, M. and de Souza Machado-Hess, E., 2014. Static and dynamic maps, developed from analytical or synthesis reasoning. *In*: *School geographic atlas: The methodological feasibility*. Available from: <https://seer.ufu.br/index.php/revistabrasileiracartografia/article/view/44746/23760>.

Marvel Geospatial. Available from: <www.marvelgeospatial.com/how-are-drones-replacing-other-surveying-techniques/>.

Mason v. Montgomery Data, Inc. (Mason) 967 F.2d 135 (5th Cir. 1992).

Mathews Conveyer Co. v. Palmer-Bee Co., 135 F.2d 73, 85 (6th Cir. 1943).

Matthew Bender & Co. v. West Pub. Co. 158 F.3d 693 (2d Cir. 1998).

McCutcheon, J., 2013. The vanishing author in computer-generated works. *Melbourne University Law Review*, 36, 915.

McCutcheon, J., 2019. 'The concept of the copyright work under EU law: More than a matter of taste' (No 3428844, SSRN, 30 July 2019). Available from: <https://papers.ssrn.com/sol3/papers.cfm?abstract_id=3428844>.

McCutcheon, J., 2021. Point and shoot: Originality, authorship, and the identification of the copyright work in modern photography. *Sydney Law Review*, 43 (2), 163–179.

McMillan, J., 2013. *Open Public Sector Information – from Principles to Practice*. Office of the Australian Information Commissioner.

McNally, R. and Co. v. Fleet Management Sys., Inc. 634 F. Supp. 604 (N.D. Ill. 1986).

Mehta, R., 2021. Artificial intelligence translating geospatial data into knowledge. Available from: <www.spatialsource.com.au/artificial-intelligence-translating- geospatial-data-into-knowledge/>.

Michel, A., AI-generated creations: Challenging the traditional concept of copyright, a research into the question of works that are created by an artificial intelligence program have copyright protection in the Netherlands and the European Union. Available from: <http://arno.uvt.nl/show.cgi?fid=148002>.

Midtbø, T. and Larsen, E., n.d. Map animations versus static maps – When is one of them better? Available from: <http://ishm.elte.hu/cet/madrid-2005/midtbo.pdf> at 1.

Missouri Pac. Ry. v. Nebraska, 164 U.S. 403, 417 (1896).

Moellering, H., *et al.*, n.d. Analytical cartography: UCGIS emerging research themes in GIScience. Available from: <http://dusk.geo.orst.edu/ucgis/web/emerging/ac.pdf>.

Moreno, F.R., 2020. Upload filters and human rights: Implementing Article 17 of the directive on copyright in the digital single market. *International Review of Law, Computers & Technology*, 34 (2), 153.

Mulder, A.E., Wiersma, M.G., and van Loenen, B., 2020. Status of national open spatial data infrastructures: A comparison across continents. *International Journal of Spatial Data Infrastructures Research*, 15, 68.

Müller, H. and Seifert, M., Blockchain, a feasible technology for land administration?. Available from: <www.fig.net/resources/proceedings/fig_proceedings/fig2019/papers/ts01i/TS01I_seifert_mueller_10110.pdf>.

Nahan, N.Y., 2015. The duty of confidence revisited: The protection of confidential information. *University of Western Australia Law Review*, 39 (2), 270–293.

New Era Publications Intern., ApS v. Carol Pub. Group, 904 F.2d 152, 157, 17 Media L. Rep. (BNA) 1913, 14 U.S.P.Q.2d 2030 (2d Cir. 1990).

New Zealand Copyright Act 1994.

New Zealand Layout Designs Act 1994.

Nicholson, D.R., 2009. Digital rights management and access to information: A developing country's perspective. *Library and Information Science Research Electronic Journal*, 19 (1), 1–17.

Nimmer, M.B. and Nimmer, D., 2023. *Nimmer on Copyright* (Matthew Bender, Rev. Ed.).

Nintendo Co Ltd v Sky UK Ltd & Ors [2019] EWHC 2376 (Ch).

Nintendo Co. Ltd e.a. v PC Box Srl and 9Net Srl (Court of Justice of the European Union, Case C-355/12, ECR I-0000; EU:C:2014:25, 23 January 2014).

Nordhaus, W.D., 1969. *Invention, Growth, and Welfare: A Theoretical Treatment of Technological Change*. Cambridge: MIT Press.

NSW Government, 2019. Digital survey plans review. Available from: <www.registrargeneral.nsw.gov.au/__data/assets/pdf_file/0010/603595/Grosvenor-Digital-Survey-Plans-Review-Final-Report.pdf>.

NSW Government, 2020. Digital survey plans now available to industry. Available from: <www.spatial.nsw.gov.au/news/digital_survey_plans_now_available_to_industry>.

NSW Government, 2020. Digital survey plans now available to industry. Available from: <www.spatial.nsw.gov.au/news/digital_survey_plans_now_available_to_industry>.

NSW Government, 2021. Discussion paper – Transitioning from paper to digital survey plans. Available from: <www.registrargeneral.nsw.gov.au/__data/assets/pdf_file/0007/1005865/Discussion-paper_Transitioning-from-paper-to-digital-survey-plans.pdf>.

'Open Government', *Data.gov*. Available from: <www.data.gov/open-gov/>.

O'Reilly Stevens Lawyers, Avoid a hard landing for bundled software. Available from: <https://oreillystevens.com/2022/08/01/avoid-a-hard-landing-for-bundled-software/>.

Ohly, A., The freedom of imitation and its limits – a European perspective. *International Review of Intellectual Property and Competition Law*, 41 (5), 506.

Ooms, K., n.d. Maps, how do users see them? An in-depth investigation of the map users' cognitive processes. Available from: <http://cartogis.ugent.be/kooms/PhD/PhD_kooms.pdf> at 4.

Painer v Standard VerlagsGmbH (Court of Justice of the European Union, C-145/10, ECLI:EU:C:2011:798, 1 December 2011) (EU).

Paris Convention for the Protection of Industrial Property, 10bis (2).

Party, W.F., 2023. *Party on Copyright*. Thomson West.

Pech, S., 2020. Copyright unchained: How blockchain technology can change the administration and distribution of copyright protected works. *Northwestern Journal of Technology and Intellectual Property*, 18 (1), 1.

Peiro, N.N. and Garcia, E.J.M., 2017. Blockchain and land registration systems. *European Property Law Journal (EPLJ)*, 6 (3), 296.

Permanent Committee on Cadastre in the European Union, 'About us'. Available from: <www.eurocadastre.org/aboutus.html>.

Perris v. Hexamer 99 U.S. 674 (1879).

Peterson, P., 2019. Problems blockchain doesn't solve. *Illinois Bar Review*, 107 (2), 36.

Photographic Illustrators Corp. v. Orgill, Inc. 953 F.3d 56 (1st Cir. 2020).

Pila, J., 2008. Works of artistic craftsmanship in the high court of Australia: The exception as paradigm copyright work. *Federal Law Review*, 36 (3), 363.

Pila, J., 2023. The authorial works protectable by copyright. In *The Routledge Handbook of EU Copyright Law*, ed. Eleonora Rosati. Taylor & Francis Group, 2023. Available from: <http://ebookcentral.proquest.com/lib/monash/detail.action?docID=6514334>.

Pokemon Company International, Inc. v Redbubble Ltd [2017] FCA 1541 (19 December 2017).

Porter, A., 1996. Data access corporation v Powerflex Services Pvt Ltd. *ANZCompuLawJl*. Available from: <http://classic.austlii.edu.au/au/journals/ANZCompuLawJl/1996/32.html>.

Précom, Ouest France Multimedia v Direct Annonces, Court of Cassation (Cass.), 1st civ., 5 March 2009.

Preston de Guise, 2020. *Data Protection: Ensuring Data Availability*. Aurebach Publishers.

PricewaterhouseCoopers, 2016. Understanding the costs and benefits of introducing a 'fair use' exception' (February 2016), Executive Summary. Available from: <www.screenrights.org/wp-content/uploads/2017/10/PwC_Fair_Dealing_CBA_Final.pdf> ('*PwC – 'fair use' exception*').

Priora, G., 2019. Copyright law and the promotion of scientific networks: Some reflections on the rules on co-authorship in the EU. *Queen Mary Journal of Intellectual Property*, 9 (2), 217.

ProCD, Incorporated v. Matthew Zeidenberg and Silken Mountain Web Services, Inc. 86 F.3D 1447 (7TH CIR. 1996).

Productivity Commission, 'Data Availability and Use' (Productivity Commission Inquiry Report No 82, 31 March 2017).

Productivity Commission, *Productivity commission review of cost recovery: Comment on draft report*. Available from: www.pc.gov.au/inquiries/completed/cost-recovery/submissions/australian_surveying_and_land_information_group/subdr131.pdf>.

Q.ai, 2022. What really happened to LUNA Crypto?. *Forbes Magazine*, 20 September 2022. Available from: <www.forbes.com/sites/qai/2022/09/20/what-really-happened-to-luna-crypto/>.

QLD, 2021. Submitting survey plans under the Survey and Mapping Infrastructure Act 2003. Available from: <www.resources.qld.gov.au/?a=109113:policy_registry/submitting-survey-plans-under-smia.pdf&ver=1.00>.

Queensland Government, n.d.-a. Glossary of mapping and surveying terms. Availabe from: <www.business.qld.gov.au/running-business/support-assistance/mapping-data-imagery/maps/mapping-glossary>.

Queensland Government, n.d.-b. Survey plans. Available from: <www.business.qld.gov.au/industries/building-property-development/surveying/survey-plans>.

Rajbhandari, R., 2021. License to sublicense: The legal possibility of impliedly sublicensing a copyrighted work annual survey of federal En Banc and other significant cases: Comments. *Boston College Law Review E. Supp*. II., 62, 425.

Real Networks, Inc. v. Streambox, Inc. No. 2:99CV02070, 2000 U.S. Dist. WL 127311 (W.D. Wash. Jan. 18, 2000).

Regulation on a Pilot Regime for Market Infrastructures Based on Distributed Ledger Technology, and Amending Regulations, 30 May 2022.

Regulation on Cross-Border Portability of Online Content Services in the Internal Market (Portability Regulation), 14 June 2017.

Regulation on European Data Governance and Amending Regulation, 30 May 2022.

Regulation on the Cross-Border Exchange between the Union and Third Countries of Accessible Format Copies of Certain Works and Other Subject Matter Protected by Copyright and Related Rights for the Benefit of Persons Who are Blind, Visually Impaired or Otherwise Print-Disabled (Regulation implementing the Marrakech Treaty in the EU), 13 September 2017.

Regulation on the Protection of Natural Persons with Regard to the Processing of Personal Data and on the Free Movement of Such Data, and Repealing Directive 95/46/EC (General Data Protection Regulation), 27 April 2016.

Reichman, J.H. and Samuelson, P., 1997. Intellectual property rights in data. *Vanderbilt Law Review*, 50 (1), 49.

Reinicke v. Creative Empire, LLC, 2016 WL 5845734 (9th Cir. Oct. 6, 2016).

Restatement (Second) of Agency (1958).

Rice, M.T., *Intellectual property control for maps and geographic data*. Ph.D., University of California, Santa Barbara. Avilable from: <www.proquest.com/docview/305003538/abstract/4B513DD2D2AA45DCPQ/1>.

Richter, H., 2021. Copyright protection of government-related material before the courts of the United States and Canada: Considerations for future reforms. *IIC-International Review of Intellectual Property and Competition Law*, 52, 6–33.

Robinson, E.A., 2009. Digital rights management, fair use, and privacy: Problems for copyright enforcement through technology. Available from: <https://soar.usa.edu/cgi/viewcontent.cgi?article=1012&context=other>.

Rockford Map Pub., Inc. v. Directory Serv. Co., of Colo., 768 F.2d 145 (7th Cir. 1985).

Rodima-Taylor, D., 2021. Digitalizing land administration: The geographies and temporalities of infrastructural promise. *Geoforum*, 122, 140.

Rognstad, O., 2022. Creations caused by humans (or Robots)? Artificial intelligence and causation requirements for copyright protection in EU law. In *Artificial Intelligence and the Media*, eds. Taina Pihlajarinne and Alén-Savikko. Edward Elgar Publishing, 172. Available from: <www.elgaronline.com/display/edcoll/9781839109966/9781839109966.00015.xml>.

Rosati, E., 2014. Closed subject-matter systems are no longer compatible with EU copyright (SSRN Scholarly Paper No 2468104, 18 July 2014). Available from: <https://papers.ssrn.com/abstract=2468104>.

Rosati, E., 2019. CJEU rules that copyright protection for designs only requires sufficient originality. *Journal of Intellectual Property Law & Practice*, 14 (12), 931.

Rosati, E., 2020. Circumventing technological protection measures and website blocking orders: An EU perspective. *MediaWrites*, 27 November 2020. Available from: <https://mediawrites.law/circumventing-technological-protection-measures-and-website-blocking-orders-an-eu-perspective/>.

Rosati, E., 2023a. 30 years of EU copyright law. *In*: *The Routledge handbook of EU copyright law*. Taylor & Francis Group. <http://ebookcentral.proquest.com/lib/monash/detail.action?docID=6514334>.

Rosati, E., 2023b. Copyright at the CJEU: Back to the start (of copyright protection). *In*: *Developments and Directions in Intellectual Property Law. 20 Years of The IPK*, ed. Eleonora Rosati. Oxford University Press.

Rosler, D.B., 1995. The European union's proposed directive for the legal protection of databases: A new threat to the free flow of information. *High Technology Law Journal*, 10 (1), 105.

Ryanair v Atrapalo Case STS 572/2012, 9 October 2012.

Saltman Engineering Co Ltd v Campbell Engineering Co Ltd (1948) 65 RPC 203.

Sands & McDougall Pty Ltd v Robinson (1917) 23 CLR 49.

Sappa, C., 2021. Access and re-use of public sector information in a copyright perspective. *In*: *EU Copyright Law*, eds. Irini Stamatoudi and Paul Torremans. Edward Elgar Publishing, 762. Available from: <www.elgaronline.com/edcollchap/book/9781786437808/book-part-9781786437808-28.xml>.

SAS Institute Inc. v. World Programming Ltd Case (Court of Justice of the European Union, C-406/10 ECLI:EU:C:2012:259, 2 May 2012).

Savelyev, A., 2018. Copyright in the blockchain Era: Promises and challenges. *Computer Law & Security Review*, 34 (3), 550–561.

Scassa, T., 2003. Originality and utilitarian works: The uneasy relationship between copyright law and unfair competition. *University of Ottawa Law & Technology Journal*, 1, 51.

Scerri, S., *et al.*, 2022. Common European data spaces: Challenges and opportunities. *In*: *Data Spaces: Design, Deployment and Future Directions*, eds. Edward Curry, Simon Scerri and Tuomo Tuikka. Springer International Publishing. Available from: <https://doi.org/10.1007/978-3-030-98636-0_16>.

Schneider, M., 1998. The European union database directive. *The Berkeley Technology Law Journal*, 13, 551.

Seafolly Pty Limited v Fewstone Pty Ltd [2014] FCA 321 (1 April 2014).

Senftleben, M., Status report on the protection against unfair competition in WIPO member states. Available from: <www.wipo.int/export/sites/www/sct/en/meetings/pdf/wipo-strad-inf-8-prov.pdf>.

Shang, Q. and Price, A., 2019. A blockchain-based land titling project in the republic of georgia: Rebuilding public trust and lessons for future pilot projects. *Innovations: Technology, Governance, Globalization*, 12 (3–4), 72.

Sieman, J.S., 2007. Using the implied license to inject common sense into digital copyright. *The North Carolina Law Review*, 85, 885.

Simplexgrinnell LP v. Integrated Systems & Power, Inc. 2009 WL 857504 (S.D.N.Y. 31 March, 2009).

Smith, S., 1997. Legal protection of factual compilations and databases in England: How will the database directive change the law in this area? *Intellectual Property Quarterly*, 450.

Sorjama, T., 2016. I, Author – Authorship and copyright in the age of artificial intelligence'. Avilable from: <https://helda.helsinki.fi/bitstream/handle/10138/166456/sorjamaa.pdf?sequence=3&isAllowed=y26> 47.

Spatial Industries Business Association, 2012. Submission to ALRC inquiry – Copyright and the digital economy. Available from: <www.alrc.gov.au/wp content/uploads/2019/08/116._org_siba.pdf>.

Spatial Information Systems, 2008. The value of spatial information: The impact of modern spatial information technologies on the Australian economy. Available from: <www.crcsi.com.au/assets/Resources/7d60411d-0ab9-45be-8d48-ef8dab5abd4a.pdf>.

Spatial Source, 2018. The mysterious art of cadastral land surveying. Available from: <www.spatialsource.com.au/the-mysterious-art-of-cadastral-land-surveying/.

Stamatoudi, I. and Torremans, P., 2021. The digital single market directive. *In: EU Copyright Law*, eds. I. Stamatoudi and P. Torremans. Edward Elgar Publishing, 651. Available from: <www.elgaronline.com/edcollchap/book/9781786437808/book-part-9781786437808-27.xml>.

StatusCard Australia Pty Ltd v. Rotondo & Anor [2008] QSC 181 (19 August 2008).

Stevens v Kabushiki Kaisha Sony Computer Entertainment [2005] HCA 58.

Stewart v. Abend, 495 U.S. 207, 237, 110 S. Ct. 1750, 109 L. Ed. 2d 184, 14 U.S.P.Q.2d 1614 (1990).

Streinz, T., 2021. The evolution of European data law. *In*: *The evolution of EU law*, eds. P. Craig and G. de Búrca. Oxford University Press. Available from: <https://doi.org/10.1093/oso/9780192846556.003.0029>.

Strong, W.S., 2014. *The copyright book*: *A practical guide* (6th ed.). MIT Press. Available from: <http://ebookcentral.proquest.com/lib/monash/detail.action?docID=3339814>

Submitting Survey Plans under the Survey and Mapping Infrastructure Act' (2003). Available from: <www.resources.qld.gov.au/?a=109113:policy_registry/submitting-survey-plans-under-smia.pdf&ver=1.00>.

Surveyors Board Queensland, n.d. Cadastral surveyor. Available from: <http://sbq.com.au/about-surveyors/cadastral-surveyor/>.

Surveys & Mining Ltd v Morrison [1969] Qd R 470.

Swope, M.J., 1995. Recent developments in patent law: Implied license – An emerging threat to contributory infringement protection. *Temple Law Review*, 68, 287–305.

Tandy Corp v. Personal Microcomputers, Inc. 524 F. Supp. 171 (N.D. Cal. 1981).

Telstra Corp Ltd v Phone Directories Co Pty Ltd.

Thales Australia Limited v Madritsch KG & Anor [2022] QCA 205 (21 October 2022).

The British Horseracing Board Ltd and Others v William Hill Organization Ltd. (Court of Justice of the European Union, Case C-203/02, ECLI:EU:C:2004:695, 9 November 2004).

The Dutch Copyright Act (Auteurswet) 1912.

The European Council of Geodetic Surveyors, 'European Requirements for Cadastral Surveyor activities_Revision of 2018' (2018) 86. Avilable from: <www.clge.eu/wp-content/uploads/2019/04/cadastral_surveyor_requirement_rev2018.pdf>.

The Surveying and Spatial Sciences Institute (SSSI), n.d. Available from: <https://sssi.org.au/>.

Ticketmaster v. Tickets.com, Inc. No. CV 99–7654 HLH (BQRx), 2000 U.S. Dist. LEXIS 4553.

Tobler, W., 1976. Analytical cartography. *The American Cartographer*, 3 (1), 21–31.Tresise, A., Goldenfein, J., and Hunter, D., 2018. What blockchain can and can't do for copyright. *Australian Intellectual Property Journal*, 28, 144.

Types of land surveys & what they are used for, n.d. *ADC*. Available from: <www.adcqld.com.au/5-types-of-land-surveys-what-they-are-used-for/>.*U.S.C Title 17- Copyright.*

Ubaldi, B., 'Open government data: Towards empirical analysis of open government data initiatives. (OECD Working Papers on Public Governance No 22, 27 May 2013) 6. Available from: <www.oecd- ilibrary.org/governance/open-government-data_5k46bj4f03s7-en>.

Uniform Trade Secrets Act 1979 (U.T.S.A.) (Uniform Law Commission).

United States Constitution (1789).

United States Copyright Office, 'Zarya of the Dawn' (Registration # VAu001480196) (Case Determination No 1–5GB561K, United States Copyright Office, 21 February 2023) at <www.copyright.gov/docs/zarya-of-the-dawn.pdf>.

United States Copyright Office, 2021. 'Compendium of U.S. Copyright Office Practices' (3rd ed.), 102. Available from: <www.copyright.gov/comp3/>.

United States v. Hamilton, 583 F.2d 448, 451 (9th Cir. 1978).

UPC Telekabel Wien GmbH v Constantin Film Verleih GmbH and Wega Filmproduktionsgesellschaft mbH (Court of Justice of the European Union, Case C-314/12, ECLI:EU:C:2014:192, 27 March 2014).

U.S.C Title 43 -Public Lands.

US Free Trade Agreement Implementation Act 2004 (Cth).

UsedSoft v Oracle International (Court of Justice of the European Union, Case C-128/11, ECLI:EU:C:2012:407, 3 July 2012).

Valles, R.C., 2009. The requirement of originality. *In*: *Research handbook on the future of EU copyright*, ed. E. Derclaye. Edward Elgar Publishing Limited, 102. Available from <http://ebookcentral.proquest.com/lib/monash/detail.action?docID=420703>.

Vekstein, J.E., 2011. A hot mess: How hot-news misappropriation bypassed copyright law in barclays v. theflyonthewall.Com and gave originators a property right in facts note. *Catholic University Law Review,* 61 (1), 297-298.

Verrocchi v Direct Chemist Outlet Pty Ltd [2015] FCA 234 (17 March 2015).

Victor Lalli Enterprises, Inc. v. Big Red Apple, Inc. 936 F.2d. 671 (2d Cir. 1991).

Victoria State Government, 'Elevation data'. Available from: <www.land.vic.gov.au/maps-and-spatial/imagery/elevation-data>.

Victorian Cadastral Surveys, 2021. *Practice directives* (2nd ed.), 5. Available from: <www.spatialsource.com.au/the-mysterious-art-of-cadastral-land-surveying/>.

Von Gunten, A., 2015. *Intellectual property is common property: Arguments for the abolition of private intellectual property rights*. Zürich: Buch & Netz.

Voodoo v Rollic Games and Hero Games (Tribunal Judiciaire De Paris, 4. September 2020) (January 4, 2021).

Vučković, R.M., Kanceljak, I., and Jurić, M., Is it time for new data governance. *In: 2021 44th International Convention on Information, Communication and Electronic Technology (MIPRO)*.

Wang, B., 2016. Blockchain and the law. *Internet Law Bulletin*, 19 (1), 250–254.

Watson, C., 2021. Nintendo wins two court cases against piracy of Nintendo Switch in Spain. *FREEGAME TIPS*, 19 January 2021. Available from: <https://freegametips.com/nintendo-wins-two-court-cases-against-piracy-of-nintendo-switch-in-spain>.

Wegener v Hunter Select, CA Leeuwarden, 27 November 2002. Available from: <www.rechtspraak.nl>.

Weller & Anor v Smith [2016] FCCA 2822 (4 November 2016).

Wells Fargo & Co. v. WhenU.Com, Inc. 293 F. Supp. 2d 734, 771 (E.D. Mich. 2003).

Werbach, K. and Cornell, N., 2017. Contracts Ex Machina. *Duke Law Journal*, 67, 313.

What is geospatial data?, n.d. Availabe from: <www.ibm.com/au-en/topics/geospatial-data>.

White-Smith Publishing Co. v. Apollo Co. 209 U.S. 1, 28 S. Ct. 319, 52 L. Ed. 655 (1908).

Wille, D.G, Jewell, D., and Ratliff, P., 2001. Protection and enforcement of new intellectual property symposium – Exploring emerging issues: New intellectual property, information technology, and security in borderless commerce. *Texas Wesleyan Law Review*, 8 (3), 467.

Williams Electronics, 685 F.2d at 874; Atari Games Corp. v. Oman, 888 F.2d 878, 884n.6 (D.C. Cir. 1989).

Williams, S., 2023. Edge contracts. *University of Pennsylvania Journal of Business Law*, 25 (3), 839.

Williamson, I.P., 1985. Cadastres and land information systems in common law jurisdictions. *Survey Review*, 28 (217), 114.

Willms, J., 2016. Is blockchain-powered copyright protection possible? *Bitcoin Magazine*, 9 August. WIPO Copyright Treaty (WCT) (1996, U.N.T.S. 2186).

WIPO Performances and Phonograms Treaty (1996, U.N.T.S. 2186).

Wolf, D.B., 1991. Is there any copyright protection for maps after feist part I. *Journal of the Copyright Society of the U.S.A.*, 39 (3), 224-226.

Wolford, B., 2018. What is GDPR, the EU's new data protection law?. *GDPR.eu*, 7 November 2018. Available from: <https://gdpr.eu/what-is-gdpr/>.

World Bank Group, 2016. *Doing business 2016: Measuring regulatory quality and efficiency*. Washington, DC: World Bank, 1. Available from: <https://openknowledge.worldbank.org/handle/10986/22771>.

World Bank, 'Starting an open data initiative | Data' (13 May 2021). Available from: <https://opendatatoolkit.worldbank.org/en/data/opendatatoolkit/starting>.

World Geospatial Industry Council, 'Geospatial information and privacy: Policy perspectives and imperatives for the geospatial industry'. Available from: <https://wgicouncil.org/wp-content/uploads/2020/03/Geospatial-Informaion-and-Privacy-report-Final.pdf>.

World Intellectual Property Organization, Agreement on Trade-Related Aspects of Intellectual Property Rights. Available from: <https://www.wipo.int/wipolex/en/treaties/details/231>

World Intellectual Property Organization, Copyright treaty. Available from: https://www.wipo.int/treaties/en/ip/wct/.

World Intellectual Property Organization, n.d. Berne convention for the protection of literary and artistic works. Available from: <www.wipo.int/treaties/en/ip/berne/trtdocs-woOO1.html>

World Intellectual Property Organization, Performance and phonogram treaty.

Xiao, Y., 2023. Decoding authorship: Is there really no place for an algorithmic author under copyright law? *IIC – International Review of Intellectual Property and Competition Law*, 54 (1), 5.

Yang, L., *et al*., 2022. Google earth engine and artificial intelligence (AI): A comprehensive review. *Remote Sensing,* 14, 3253.

Yiu, M., *et al*., 2010. Enabling search services on outsourced private spatial data. *The International Journal on Very Large Databases*, 19, 363.

Your Europe, 'Data protection'. Available from: <https://europa.eu/youreurope/business/running-business/intellectual- property/database-protection/index_en.htm>.

Yout, LLC v. Recording Indus. Ass'n of Am., Inc. No. 3:20-CV-1602 (SRU), 2022 WL 4599203, at 6 (D. Conn. Sept. 30, 2022).

Zdena Dobesova, 'Visual programming language in geographic information systems'. Available from: <www.researchgate.net/profile/ZdenaDobesova/publication/236586776_V_isual_programming_for_novice_programmers_in_geoinformatics/links/0deec52c812d2b90f3000000/V-isual-programming-for-novice-programmers-in-geoinformatics.pdf>.

Zeitz, B., 2004. How high is up: Interstitial Dilemmas in nonexclusive copyright licensing cases in the Ninth Circuit. *The UCLA Entertainment Law Review*, 11, 429.

Zhao, P., *et al*., 2022. Towards geospatial blockchain: A review of research on blockchain technology applied to geospatial data. *AGILE: GIScience Series*, 3, 71. Available from: <https://agile-giss.copernicus.org/articles/3/71/2022/agile-giss-3-71-2022.pdf>.

Zimu, W., 2021. Blockchain technology: Opportunities and challenges in copyright industry. *In: 18th International Computer Conference on Wavelet Active Media Technology and Information Processing (ICCWAMTIP)*.

Zope-Chaudhari, S. and Venkatachalam, P., 2013. Conceptual framework for geospatial data security. *International Journal of Database Management Systems*, 5 (5), 29–35.

Zwirowicz-Rutkowska, A., 2016. Evaluating spatial data infrastructure as a data source for land surveying. *Journal of Surveying Engineering*, 142 (4). Available from: <https://ascelibrary.org/doi/10.1061/%28ASCE%29SU.1943-5428.0000185>.

Index

Made in the USA
Las Vegas, NV
19 September 2026

104c9f8d-1dee-4ea6-94b4-32cfa2bf0bcaR01